ASSESSMENT FOR READING INSTRUCTION

Selected Works by the Authors

Developing Reading Comprehension:
Effective Instruction for All Students in PreK–2
Katherine A. Dougherty Stahl and Georgia Earnest García

Developing Word Recognition
Latisha Hayes and Kevin Flanigan

How to Plan Differentiated Reading Instruction, Second Edition:
Resources for Grades K–3
Sharon Walpole and Michael C. McKenna

Reading Assessment in an RTI Framework
Katherine A. Dougherty Stahl and Michael C. McKenna

Assessment for Reading Instruction

FOURTH EDITION

Katherine A. Dougherty Stahl
Kevin Flanigan
Michael C. McKenna

THE GUILFORD PRESS
New York   London

Library of Congress Cataloging-in-Publication Data is available from the publisher.

ISBN 978-1-4625-4157-7 (paperback) — ISBN 978-1-4625-4158-4 (hardcover)

In memory of Michael C. McKenna

About the Authors

Katherine A. Dougherty Stahl, EdD, is Clinical Professor of Reading at New York University, where she serves as Director of the Literacy Program and teaches graduate courses. In addition to teaching in public elementary school classrooms for over 25 years, Dr. Stahl has extensive experience working with struggling readers in clinical settings. Her research focuses on reading acquisition, struggling readers, and comprehension. She is coauthor of *Developing Reading Comprehension: Effective Instruction for All Students in PreK–2* and *Reading Assessment in an RTI Framework.* Dr. Stahl is a recipient of the Jeanne Chall Visiting Researcher Award from Harvard University and the Teaching Excellence Award from the Steinhardt School of Culture, Education, and Human Development at New York University.

Kevin Flanigan, PhD, is Professor in the Literacy Department at West Chester University of Pennsylvania (WCU). He works in the WCU Reading Center along with master's students to assess and teach children who struggle to read and write. A former middle-grades classroom teacher and reading specialist/coach, Dr. Flanigan researches and writes about developmental word knowledge and struggling readers. He is coauthor of several books, including *Developing Word Recognition* and *Words Their Way, Second Edition: Vocabulary for Middle and Secondary Students*x.

Michael C. McKenna, PhD, was Thomas G. Jewell Professor of Reading in the Curry School of Education at the University of Virginia until his death in 2016. He authored, coauthored, or edited more than 20 books, including *How to Plan Differentiated Reading Instruction, Second Edition: Resources for Grades K–3* and *Organizing the Early Literacy Classroom,* as well as over 100 articles, chapters, and technical reports on a range of literacy topics. Dr. McKenna also served as Series Editor, with Sharon Walpole, of *The Essential Library of PreK–2 Literacy.* He was a corecipient of the Edward B. Fry Book Award from the Literacy Research Association and the Award for Outstanding Academic Books from the American Library Association, and was a member of the Reading Hall of Fame.

Preface

Much has changed in literacy and the world since Michael McKenna and Steven Stahl published the first edition of *Assessment for Reading Instruction* in 2003. However, the cognitive model of reading that they refined while sitting in Mike's sunroom has withstood the test of time. It still serves as the centerpiece for implementing diagnostic assessment and intervention in this newest edition of the book.

The loss of Mike McKenna as our first author is undoubtedly the most significant change. However, we know that as you read this edition, you will continue to hear Mike's wisdom and his clever sense of humor in the text that he created throughout the first three editions. With loss, too, comes rebirth. This edition is clearly imprinted with Kevin Flanigan's experience and knowledge associated with the intermediate grades and middle school. It seems a fitting tribute to Mike, whose experiential home was with older students, that we are finally able to give specific attention to the needs of these students.

THE MIDDLE GRADES (GRADES 4–8)

Too often, we assume that students in the middle grades have the fundamental literacy skill set required for capably reading novels and texts that they need to be successful in the content areas. When hurdles in learning are encountered, it can be complicated to determine where things went off track and what needs to be done to alter the trajectory. In this edition, we have devoted an entire chapter (Chapter 11) to the procedures and tools needed to apply the diagnostic process with students in the middle grades. Not only do we address diagnostic tools that work well with older students, but we face head-on the unique challenges encountered in middle school settings.

Each chapter that addresses the reading constructs (word recognition, fluency, vocabulary, and comprehension) also has been revised to provide specific diagnostic and instructional recommendations for the middle grades. Finally, we have included in the Appendix a new middle-grades case study (Case Study 1: Moe), which utilizes an entirely new abbreviated format that works well for the demands of middle school contexts.

ABBREVIATED CASE STUDY

When the third edition of *Assessment for Reading Instruction* was published, many schools were working to comply with the federal regulations surrounding response to intervention (RTI) or a multi-tiered system of supports (MTSS). We consciously framed that edition to dovetail with *Reading Assessment in an RTI Framework* (Stahl & McKenna, 2013) as a way to support schools and teachers who were in the process of designing an RTI/MTSS framework. Today that diagnostic and intervention process has been implemented in most elementary schools and is becoming more prevalent in middle schools. Managing data, grouping students, and tracking their progress are challenges associated with RTI/MTSS. The new abbreviated case study that profiles a middle school student illustrates a simple, concise means of synthesizing a student's test results for the purpose of identifying specific needs, documenting appropriate interventions, and grouping students with similar needs together. Unlike the more elaborate case studies, which provide the detailed precision needed for students in special education, tutoring settings, and other clinical contexts, the new abbreviated case study format is well suited for RTI/MTSS planning and documentation in both elementary and middle schools.

INFORMATION ON COMPUTER-BASED COMPREHENSION TESTS

Advances in technology are quickly changing the face of instruction and assessment. Among the advances in literacy assessment that hold the most promise are the development and increasing utilization of computer-based comprehension tests, particularly adaptive assessments. We address how schools might take advantage of what computer-based tests offer and why schools should consider using them. However, we also recognize the limits of computer-based assessments, and we explain how to balance these tests with the other assessments found in this book in an effective, efficient manner. We also recognize that these tests do require a financial investment that calls for schools to be critical consumers in selecting a computer-based assessment. To support schools that are comparing the tests that are currently on the market, we have provided a Computer-Adaptive Test (CAT) Comparison Worksheet to help readers select the "just-right" test to meet their school's needs.

INFORMAL READING INVENTORIES

Technology can accomplish what teachers can't in collecting and reporting general screening information about large groups of students quickly. However, as we have suggested earlier, there is still no substitute for an informal reading inventory (IRI) in seeking diagnostic information about students who struggle to achieve grade-level performance. In this edition, we have considerably revised Chapter 3, on IRIs. These tests are particularly useful with students in the intermediate grades, or with older students functioning at intermediate grade levels who are encountering challenges with fluency and/or comprehension. The revision of this chapter provides more in-depth information on how to interpret ambiguous results and those scores that tend to look gray, rather than providing black-and-white diagnostic portrayals of students. Specific instructions for utilizing flash word list scores, fluency data, and retelling to arrive at a more accurate diagnostic profile make transparent what expert teacher diagnosticians tend to do intuitively as needed.

COMPANION WEBSITE

In the third edition, we began making the forms that are available in our book easier for purchasers to print by posting them on a Guilford-hosted website. In this edition, the companion website (see the box at the end of the table of contents for details) has been expanded to include a full, large-print version of a form (the Elementary Reading Attitude Survey, or ERAS) that is described and appears in Chapter 10 but is less commonly used by classroom teachers. Our book is not a book that is intended to be read page by page from start to finish. Instead, as you read, you will flip from descriptions of test usage in the body of the chapter to the forms found at the end of each chapter. Many readers tell us that they prefer handling a print version of our book. Therefore, we wanted to keep the print version of the text relatively lightweight, manageable, and conservatively priced. By expanding the companion website, we are able to meet the varying needs of our wide range of readers more comprehensively.

ADDITIONAL CHANGES

We have described the book's significant changes in the sections above. We have incorporated some other changes as responses to our readers, to new directions in the literacy landscape, to our observations in schools, to current research, and to our desire to provide increased specificity for the middle grades. These changes include the following:

- Synthesis of the stage model in reading, writing, and spelling.
- New IRI summary form.
- New Concept of Word Scale for emergent readers.
- Major revisions in the Checklist for Concepts of Print.
- New edition of the Informal Decoding Inventory.
- New (2017) Hasbrouck and Tindal fluency norms.
- New task for assessing morphological knowledge of middle-grades readers, including a new list of high-utility Latin and Greek roots, and five key "root knowledge" terms all older students should know.
- New "focus question with vocabulary bank" assessment, specifically designed for older readers' application of academic language and easily adaptable to any content area.
- New comprehension retelling supports for teachers: standardized script for administering a retelling, form for scoring a narrative retelling, form for scoring an informational text retelling.
- Revised informal surveys of reading attitudes and preferences, to provide insights into ways that today's students view and use new forms of literacy.
- Content-area exit tickets for identifying reading motivation in middle school.

Contents

ONE

Introduction
to Reading Assessment

THREE STRUGGLING READERS: A PREFACE

Consider these three children:

Josh is a third grader reading approximately at the mid-first-grade level. He struggles to pronounce unfamiliar words, sometimes by making guesses from their first letter and sometimes by attempting to sound them out from left to right. He does, however, know a fair number of words by sight, and whenever he encounters one of them, he can pronounce it immediately.

Latrelle, a fourth grader reading at a second-grade level, has acquired a good store of words that she recognizes at sight, and she can successfully pronounce almost any familiar word she encounters while reading. Her pace is slow, however, and her oral reading is expressionless. She does not group words into meaningful phrases as she reads, and she tends to ignore punctuation.

Dom, a sixth grader, is a proficient oral reader who can read aloud just about anything he is given, but he often has problems comprehending new material. This difficulty is especially evident when he is asked to read informational texts in the content areas. He is a fair student when his teacher explains new content, but he has problems whenever he must learn it on his own from print.

These three children were each categorized as *Not Proficient* on their high-stakes state assessments. However, they each struggled with the test for different reasons, and they each need different instructional interventions. The children described above are composites of real cases and represent important profiles of reading difficulties that teachers must be prepared to identify and address. When students leave the primary grades with significant academic problems, they present grave challenges to their subsequent teachers. They struggle, regardless of the cause, until they either catch up or give up. Therefore, we would like to begin this book by considering where declining trajectories can lead. In an era when the demands of the Common Core State Standards (CCSS) require more of children than at any previous time in our history, it is important that we get it right. And assessment is the first step in addressing the most urgent needs of our developing readers.

MODELS OF READING ASSESSMENT

All reading assessment is based on a model. This model can be explicitly laid out, as we intend to do here, or haphazardly formulated. Without a model, a reading specialist has no way of making sense of the observations derived from a reading assessment battery. The model helps the reading specialist recognize patterns in the data, determine the course of instruction, identify a child's strengths, and identify which aspects of reading knowledge are creating reading problems for the child.

A model should provide a roadmap, a set of directions to help the reading specialist navigate the assessment procedure and provide guidelines for interpretation. Not every child needs to receive every assessment. An effective model helps you determine which measures may best inform you about each child's needs.

The Deficit Model

The term *diagnosis,* as you might suspect, has a medical origin. Its use is based on the assumption that reading difficulties are much like physiological disorders. This conventional view, the *deficit model* (sometimes called the *medical model*), assumes that the difficulty or deficiency resides within the student, and that the teacher, like a physician, must identify it and respond appropriately with instructional techniques designed to have a medicinal or therapeutic effect. This thinking has led, predictably, to terms such as *remediation* and *remedial reading.*

Very few in the field of reading still explicitly defend this model. There is little evidence that most children's reading problems are due to a single remediable cause. Even though research in the field of neuropsychology continues to identify possible neurological causes for reading problems (e.g., Conant, Liebenthal, Desai, & Binder, 2014), this work has not produced definitive results; nor does it show promise of "remediating" children with reading problems in the near future.

The Contextual Model

An alternative view of reading assessment does not deny that reading difficulties often reflect deficits within students, but it broadens the perspective to include two other possibilities. One is the notion that there may be a mismatch between the type of instruction provided and the manner in which a given child learns. The second possibility is that contextual factors beyond the scope of the school (e.g., a disadvantaged or emotionally troubled home life) may impair reading development. The *contextual model* suggests that reading difficulties can be traced to an interaction between the student, the methods or materials used with the student, and the broader context in which the student functions.

This model is quite different from a *learning style model*, which suggests that children have individual learning styles that can be diagnosed and matched to appropriate instruction (e.g., Carbo, Dunn, & Dunn, 1986). In the learning style model, children are classified as either visual or auditory learners and matched with either more holistic or more phonics-oriented instruction. This model has been tested repeatedly and has not been found to be valid (Stahl, 1999). In fact, cognitive scientists have shown conclusively that learning styles do not exist—despite our instinctive belief that they do (Riener & Willingham, 2010). The contextual model, in contrast, views individual students as well as instructional methods as more complex than the learning model concept, with students having individual needs that are or are not met by the instruction they receive. Student needs can be categorized as attitudinal, motivational, or cognitive, and instruction may or may not meet any of those needs.

Stage Models

Stages of Reading Development

The first of the stage models that can be used in analyzing the literacy development of children was formulated by Chall (1996), who characterized reading development as progressing through six stages as a child moves from emergent literacy, or the beginning period of becoming aware of print, to advanced literacy activity, such as that needed to assimilate material in a graduate course. An overview of Chall's model is presented in Table 1.1, in which we have adapted her terminology.

Growth of Reading, Writing, and Spelling by Stage

Although Chall's model provides an excellent blueprint for overall reading development, it was not developed specifically to align with reading assessments or identify reader strengths and areas of difficulty. For that purpose, we prefer using Bear, Invernizzi, Templeton, and Johnston's (2020) stage model of reading, writing, and spelling development, coupled with Ehri's (1998) stage model of word recognition growth. Bear et al.'s model describes how reading, writing, and spelling all develop in synchrony, with growth in one strand strengthening the overall "braid of literacy" (Bear et al., 2020).

Table 1.2 summarizes the key components of these two models, from left to right across the following five columns: (1) Bear et al.'s (2020) reading and spelling stages; (2) the approximate reading and grade level(s) typically associated with a stage; (3) the strategy readers at that stage use to decode, process, and store words; (4) the reading and writing characteristics typical of that stage; and (5) the instructional focus of word study (spelling, decoding, and vocabulary) at that stage.

Ehri's (1998) model describes the growth of children's knowledge of words as progressing through four qualitatively different phases. At first, children recognize words through distinctive visual features, such as the "tail" in *monkey* or the two "eyes" in

TABLE 1.1. Jeanne Chall's Model of the Stages of Reading Development

Stage	Name	What child is learning	Typical activities	Materials
Stage 0 Birth to grade 1	Emergent literacy	Functions of written language, alphabet, phonemic awareness	Story reading, "pseudoreading," alphabet activities, rhyming, nursery rhymes, invented spelling	Books (including predictable stories), letters, writing materials, *Sesame Street*
Stage 1 Beginning grade 1	Decoding	Letter–sound correspondences	Teacher-directed reading instruction, phonics instruction	Preprimers and primers, phonics materials, writing materials, trade books
Stage 2 End of grade 1 to end of grade 3	Confirmation and fluency	Automatic word recognition, use of context	Reading narratives, generally about known topics	Basal readers, trade books, workbooks
Stage 3 Grades 4 to 8	Learning the new (single viewpoint)	How to learn from text, vocabulary knowledge, strategies	Reading and studying content-area materials, use of encyclopedias, strategy instruction	Basal readers, novels, encyclopedias, textbooks in content areas
Stage 4 High school and early college	Multiple viewpoints	Reconciling different views	Critical reading, discourse synthesis, report writing	Texts containing multiple views, encyclopedias and other reference materials, magazines and journals, nonfiction books, etc.
Stage 5 Late college and graduate school	A worldview	Developing a well-rounded view of the world	Learning what not to read as well as what to read	Professional materials

look. Ehri has called this phase *visual cue reading*. In one study (Gough, Juel, & Griffith, 1992), a group of prereaders learned words presented on a series of flash cards, one of which had a thumbprint in the corner. When shown the cards again, this time with the thumbprint on a different card, they tended to misread the card with the thumbprint as the word in the first set, suggesting that they were attending to the thumbprint rather than to the letters.

As children learn more and more words, a purely visual system of identification, such as the one these children were using, becomes unwieldy. As children develop rudimentary phonemic awareness, they begin to use individual letters (usually the first, but sometimes the last) to identify words. Ehri calls this phase *phonemic cue reading* or *partial alphabetic coding*. To get to this phase, a child needs to have an "alphabetic insight": the realization that letters correspond to sounds in words. This insight requires both rudimentary phonological awareness and some letter–sound knowledge.

As children's written vocabulary increases, they need to further analyze words, examining more parts of an unfamiliar word to identify it. This ability leads to the *full alphabetic coding* phase, in which a child examines each letter in the word. This abil-

TABLE 1.2. The Development of Reading, Writing, and Spelling across Stages

Reading/ spelling stage (from Bear et al., 2020)	Reading levels	Reading strategy: How readers process and store words	Reading and writing characteristics and focus	Word-study focus (spelling, decoding, and vocabulary)
Emergent readers/ emergent writers	K	Prealphabetic phase (Ehri, 1998) "Reads" words by visual cues (*M* in *McDonald's*; the "tail" at the end of *monkey*)	Pretending to read Learning concepts of print Do *not* have concept of word in text	Alphabet knowledge (letter names, sounds, and formation) Beginning to build rudimentary phonological awareness (syllables, onsets, and rimes)
Beginning readers/ letter name spellers	First grade	Partial to full alphabetic phase (Ehri, 1998) Partial alphabetic decoding at beginning of stage (*H* in *hat*) Full alphabetic decoding by end of stage (letter-by-letter decoding: *H-A-T* for *hat*) allows sight words to "stick"	Text-bound reading Reading aloud or mumble reading Solid concept of word (can match spoken to written words) in reading and writing, as indicated by fingerpointing Word-by-word reading and writing Fingerpoint reading	Learning sight words Developing full alphabetic decoding by end of stage Word-study features: Beginning and ending consonants Short vowels Beginning and ending blends and digraphs
Transitional readers/ within word pattern spellers	Late first to late third grades	Consolidated alphabetic phase (Ehri, 1998) Processes words in letter "chunks" or patterns as single units (-*ake* in *cake*)	Approaching reading and writing fluency Beginning to read silently, with expression and in phrasal units Increased reading rates, nearing 100 WPM by end of stage	Word-study features: Common long-vowel patterns (c*a*k*e*, r*ai*n) *r*-Influenced vowels (c*are*, st*ore*) Less common vowel patterns (*eight*) Complex consonant patterns (ju*dge*, pat*ch*) Ambiguous vowels (br*ow*n, s*oi*l) Homographs and homophones (*bear* vs. *bare*)
Intermediate readers/ syllables and affixes spellers	Late third to sixth grades	Processes multisyllabic words by syllable (*autocracy* as *au-toc-ra-cy*) Processes and stores words by across-syllable patterns (VCCV, *hopping*, vs. VCV, *hoping*)	Solid reading fluency by end of stage Reading challenges stem increasingly from conceptual load, vocabulary, and background knowledge Increased focus on strategic reading, content-area learning, and writer's craft	Word-study features: Compound words (*pancake*) Inflectional endings and doubling (*hopping* vs. *hoping*) Open and closed syllables (VCCV, *button*, vs. VCV, *bacon*) High-frequency prefixes and suffixes with base words (*reuse*, *redo*)

(continued)

TABLE 1.2. *(continued)*

Reading/ spelling stage (from Bear et al., 2020)	Reading levels	Reading strategy: How readers process and store words	Reading and writing characteristics and focus	Word-study focus (spelling, decoding, and vocabulary)
Advanced readers/ derivational relations spellers	Sixth grade and up	Processes words by morphemes, including Greek and Latin affixes/roots (*autocracy* as *auto-cracy*)	Exploring and developing expertise in specific topics, genres, styles, texts, and academic vocabulary Learning discipline-specific reading/writing/ thinking approaches (e.g., reading like a historian)	Word-study features: Prefixes and suffixes (*inter-*, "between"—*intercontinental*) Consonant and vowel alternations (*sign/signal/ signature*) Greek and Latin word elements (*-crat/-cracy*, "rule" —*demo<u>cracy</u>*)

Note. Based on Bear, Invernizzi, Templeton, and Johnston (2020) and Ehri (1998).

ity may come as the result of receiving instruction in decoding, or some children can develop it on their own. This letter-by-letter decoding gives way, with practice, to *consolidated word recognition*—the phase in which a reader uses groups of letters, either as chunks or through analogies, to recognize words automatically, as proficient readers do (Chall, 1996; LaBerge & Samuels, 1974).

This development of word recognition occurs not in a vacuum, but in conjunction with growth in phonemic awareness and exposure to different types of text. Phonemic awareness is a part of *phonological awareness,* which "refers to a broad class of skills that involve attending to, thinking about, and intentionally manipulating the phonological aspects of spoken language" (Scarborough & Brady, 2002, p. 25). Phonemic awareness is the part of phonological awareness that processes phonemes rather than syllables or onsets and rimes. We (Stahl & McKenna, 2001; Stahl & Murray, 1998) suggest that phonological awareness develops first from an awareness of syllables, onsets, and rimes; it then progresses to an awareness of initial phonemes, final phonemes, and lastly vowels. Bear et al. (2020) have found a parallel process of development in spelling.

Although phonemic awareness is related to reading, especially the decoding aspects of reading, the relationship does not seem to be strictly causal. Instead, the relationship appears to be reciprocal, with simple phonemic awareness being necessary (although probably not sufficient) for children to develop rudimentary word-recognition skills. After that point, growth in word recognition seems to enable further analysis of spoken words, which in turn enables further ability to decode more complex words (Beach, 1992; Perfetti, Beck, Bell, & Hughes, 1987).

The Development of Spelling

Children's invented spelling provides a "window" into their developing knowledge of words, and thus is an incredibly rich source of diagnostic information, particularly when planning for word study instruction (Bear et al., 2020). In this section, we delve a bit deeper into the spelling strand of the literacy stages introduced above. As we have discussed, children pass through a set of stages with respect to how they invent spellings for words. Bear and his colleagues (2020) suggest a five-stage model, ranging from prealphabetic spellings to sophisticated knowledge of the morphemic structure of derived words (refer to Table 1.3).

Initially a child may spell a word by drawing a picture or scribbling something that looks like writing. As children learn that words need letters, they may use random letters to represent a word. This stage could be called *prealphabetic* or *prephonemic spelling.* At this point, the children themselves are the only ones who can read what they have written.

As children begin to think about sounds in words, their spelling may represent only one sound in a word—usually an initial sound, and occasionally a final sound. This stage is called *early letter name spelling* and correlates with the *beginning reading stage* in Table 1.3 and Ehri's *partial alphabetic phase.* Sometimes children represent a word with a single letter or pair of letters, but often they represent a word with the correct initial letter followed by some random letters. For example, one child in our reading clinic wrote *fish* with an initial *f* and continued by adding six more letters, stating that "words that begin with *f* have a lot of letters in them." As children analyze words further, they may use the names of letters to represent sounds. At this stage, children represent at least all of the consonants in a word, often not using vowels. For example, they might spell *girl* as GRL or *ten* as TN.

As children learn more about how words are spelled, they use vowels, and the words they write resemble the actual word, like DRAGUN for *dragon.* Children usually master short vowels first, then long-vowel patterns. This may reflect instruction, or it may reflect the simplicity of short-vowel codings. Bear and colleagues (2020) call the stage in which children are including vowels, although not always correctly, *letter name spelling,* which correlates with Ehri's *full alphabetic phase.* At this point, children realize that all words need vowels, although they still have not mastered the correct spelling of short vowels. When they can spell short vowels consistently, but are "using but confusing" long vowels (e.g., spelling *rain* as RANE), Bear and colleagues term their spelling *within word pattern spelling.* Table 1.3 summarizes these early stages of spelling development.

TABLE 1.3. Early Stages of Spelling Development

Spelling stage	Characteristics	Example
Prephonemic spelling	Child uses random letters, without regard to the sounds they may represent.	JNVW for *hat*
Early letter name spelling	Child begins this stage by representing only one sound in a word, usually the first, but eventually represents all consonant sounds.	Early: FDZWD for *fish* Late: GRL for *girl*
Letter name spelling	Child uses vowels but often does so incorrectly.	DRAGUN for *dragon*
Within word pattern spelling	Child can consistently spell words with short vowels but not words with long vowels.	HOT for *hot* METE for *meet*

(A caveat before we leave the topic of spelling: It is our experience that children's spelling difficulties often linger long after their reading problems have disappeared. We see college students who have a history of reading problems and who have compensated for, or have even overcome, these problems, but still experience great difficulty spelling.)

We use the developmental models described above to help us identify the overall stage of a child's reading, and thus, generally what he or she needs to work on to move forward at that stage. Rather than simply saying, "Chris is a fifth grader reading at the third-grade level," stage models provide us a much more useful and informative framework and language to describe Chris as "a transitional reader and a within word pattern speller. This means Chris can do the following . . . and Chris needs to work on . . . " However, not all readers in the transitional stage are the same. For example, some may need to concentrate more on developing their fluency, while others may struggle more with comprehension. Therefore, we feel the need to complement these stage models with a cognitive model, which provides a broader cognitive view of reading to guide more specific assessments and instruction within each stage.

Josh, Latrelle, and Dom Revisited

Let's return to the three struggling readers described at the beginning of this chapter. The developmental stage models can help us understand some of their needs. We suggest that before proceeding, you go back to the beginning of the chapter and try to place each of these children at the appropriate stage.

Josh seems to be a beginning reader in the early stages of acquiring alphabetic insight, in spite of his 3 years in school. In general, he seems to be a compensatory reader who uses his sight-word knowledge to compensate for his rudimentary decoding ability. We would want to know more about his specific abilities in decoding, and we might want to know more about his ability to comprehend. Latrelle would be classified as a reader in the nonautomatic, early transitional stage, because she can read accurately but extremely slowly and without expression. Dom is a word caller who does not comprehend what he is reading, in spite of quick and accurate word reading; comprehension rather than fluency is his major difficulty, as it is for many intermediate readers.

The stage model is useful for giving us a general idea about these children, but it does not necessarily tell us specifically which components of reading we need to prioritize at that stage. The cognitive model, discussed below, provides a more accurate roadmap for intervention.

A Cognitive Model

A fourth model suggests that reading consists of three separate components. Reading comprehension, the purpose of reading, depends on (1) automatic recognition of the words in the text, (2) comprehension of the language in the text, and (3) the ability to use the strategies needed to achieve one's purpose in reading the text. A child will have difficulties with comprehension if he or she has difficulty with any of these three components. If a child's word recognition is not automatic or sufficiently accurate, then comprehension will suffer. If the child does not understand the vocabulary, lacks appropriate background knowledge, or lacks knowledge of text structure or genre, comprehension will suffer. Children read different texts for different purposes. Sometimes these purposes are general, such as enjoyment or literal comprehension. But sometimes the purposes are specific, such as studying for a test or learning facts to include in a report. If a child can read a text but does not achieve the purpose of reading, then comprehension also will suffer.

This cognitive model, shown in Figure 1.1, is discussed in the sections that follow. We use this model systematically to ask ourselves questions such as "Does the child have a reading problem?" and, if so, "Does the child have difficulty with automatic word recognition?" The answers to these questions help us identify areas of strength and weakness in the child and provide guidance about instructional targets. We call this model *cognitive* simply because it includes only the cognitive, or "thinking," aspects of reading and not the affective dimensions. Using the model requires that *we* be cognitive as well! We must think systematically about these questions in order to reach justifiable inferences based on the answers.

The first question to ask is whether the child has a reading problem. Often teachers or reading specialists are told (by parents or other teachers) that a child has a reading problem, when in fact the child does not. Sometimes a child has behavioral–emotional issues that prohibit him or her from being able to demonstrate literacy skills consistently in a classroom setting. Sometimes a child does poorly on a standardized test, even when he or she is able to read grade-level material in the classroom without difficulty. Remember that a standardized test is one observation, covering 1 or 2 days. Sometimes children simply have a hard time with testing or have difficulties on the day of that test. Children who come to school without breakfast or after witnessing an argument, or with some other problem, may not do as well on a standardized test as they might have. As we note

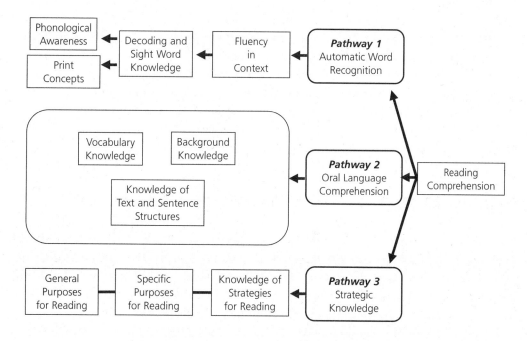

FIGURE 1.1. The cognitive model.

in the next chapter, such tests should not be the only source of information about a child's performance in reading (or math or any other subject, for that matter). Instead, multiple sources of information must be compiled before anyone can understand whether the child's reading performance is part of a consistent pattern. This compilation involves not only standardized test results, but also how the child reads the books used in the classroom, informal reading inventory (IRI) results, and other information.

To determine whether a child has a reading problem, keep in mind that the purpose of reading is comprehension. If a child can comprehend texts at a level appropriate for his or her grade, then it may not matter whether the child can demonstrate mastery of other reading skills. Often a child may do relatively poorly on a measure of phonics or decoding, but may still be able to comprehend acceptably. This discrepancy may reflect a problem with the assessment rather than a deficit in the child's skills. Observe the child closely to see whether he or she can use the skills in connected text, even though the child may have difficulties applying them in isolation or with stating a rule.

So Step 1 in the assessment process is to consider the reason a problem is suspected:

- If you have seen the child struggle with books in the classroom, then check the child's standardized test scores.
- If the child scored poorly on standardized tests, then closely observe the child in class.
- If further observation suggests that the child has difficulties both on standardized measures and in reading classroom texts, then give an IRI.

If a child has a significant problem with comprehension of age-appropriate texts, then you should further examine the child's reading. Following our model, ask the following questions about the child:

- Is the child able to read texts at his or her grade placement level, using automatic word recognition and adequate expression?
- Is the child able to comprehend the language of the text?
- Does the child have adequate knowledge of the purposes for reading?
- Does the child have strategies available to achieve those purposes?

These questions are explored in the remainder of this chapter.

COGNITIVE MODEL PATHWAY 1: AUTOMATIC WORD RECOGNITION

If a child struggles with word recognition, comprehension will inevitably suffer (LaBerge & Samuels, 1974). Word recognition needs to be automatic, so that the child does not have to devote conscious attention to the words in the text and can devote all of his or her cognitive effort to understanding what is read. When a child stumbles over words or sounds out many words, the child's understanding typically suffers.

To answer the first question about automatic word recognition (is the child able to read texts at his or her grade placement level, using automatic word recognition and adequate expression?), you must listen to the child read material intended for his or her grade level. This can be done by pulling the child aside and listening to him or her reading from a selected text, or it can be done through an IRI, as described in Chapter 3. If the child's reading is expressive and he or she can read at an instructional level appropriate to the grade placement, then you can reasonably conclude that the child's problem lies elsewhere. However, our clinical experience suggests that as many as 75% of the children we see have difficulties in this area. Sometimes the problems lie exclusively in this area; at other times the child will have difficulties with language comprehension and strategic knowledge as well. But word-recognition difficulties underlie the vast majority of reading problems, so we spend a lot of time assessing them to determine exactly where the process begins to deteriorate.

If a child is deemed to have difficulties in automatic word recognition, then the question that follows is this:

- Can the student read fluently in connected text?

Context

Some educators (e.g., Goodman, 1993) suggest that children use context as a means of predicting words in a passage. According to these theorists, readers use information from context to minimize the use of letter–sound information to recognize words. For example, for the sentence

The boy pulled the red _____.

a reader may predict the word *wagon* before recognizing the word. If the first letter is *w*, then the reader may move on, without sounding out the word or using other word-recognition skills. Other educators (e.g., Clay, 1993) suggest that children use three types of cues to recognize words—*graphophonemic, syntactic* (part-of-speech), and *semantic* (meaning) information—and that effective word recognition involves the use of these three cueing systems. In the example above, a reader would predict the word to be a noun, because nouns always follow the article *the* and adjectives such as *red*. The reader would predict *wagon*, since wagons are pulled, typically by young children, and they are often red. If, instead of a *w*, the initial letter were a *c*, the reader might mentally search for words that begin with *c* and satisfy those semantic (meaning) constraints, and might come up with *cart*. A substitution such as *wagging* would violate both syntactic and semantic constraints and might indicate that the child was paying more attention to sounding out the word than to the context.

This model is intuitively appealing, but research does not support it as a model of efficient reading behavior. Effective readers would recognize the word *wagon* more quickly and reliably than they would be able to predict the word through the use of syntactic and semantic information (Stanovich, 1991). Research using a number of different approaches has found that good readers do not predict words, but instead use their automatic word-recognition processes to propel reading (Adams, 1990, 1998; Rayner, Pollatsek, Ashby, & Clifton, 2012).

Although we do not feel that research supports the model proposed by Goodman (see Adams, 1998), we have found that good readers do use context in two principal ways. First, they use context to monitor their reading. A reader who produces *wagging* for *wagon* in the target sentence would realize that the word does not make sense and would go back and self-correct. Thus a good reader's miscues tend to make sense in context because of active monitoring, not predicting. This is particularly important in kindergarten and early first grade, when children are still in the partial cue-reading stage (Ehri, 1998) or the early letter name stage (Bear et al., 2020). Prior to instruction in a variety of vowel patterns, children's reading of natural connected text will call for them to use context until they know enough about how words work to engage in full alphabetic coding. However, in order to succeed with texts at a mid-first-grade reading level and beyond, students must be utilizing the alphabetic system (McGee, Kim, Nelson, & Fried, 2015).

Good readers also use context to rapidly select the intended meaning of multiple-meaning words. Consider this sentence:

The rancher hired a new hand.

The word *hand* has several meanings, but proficient readers have no trouble discerning the correct one. They do so *after* the word is located in memory, not before. That is to say, the good reader uses context not to predict the word, but to select the appropriate meaning once the word has been located.

Children who fail to acquire decoding skills in a normal developmental trajectory may continue to rely on context to help them identify words. As Stanovich (1980) puts it, they compensate for this deficit by using context to identify words. This relationship is illustrated in Figure 1.2: As decoding improves, reliance on context diminishes. When we evaluate children in our clinics, we find that usually 80% or more of their miscues are syntactically acceptable (i.e., are the same part of speech as the text word), and 70% or more are semantically acceptable (i.e., make sense in the context of the sentence, even if their meaning is not the same as the word in the text). When children do not use context effectively, either the text is extremely difficult for them and they make random guesses, or they are not focused on context.

When children do not view connected text as meaningful, they do not consider context. Sometimes, if children are taught to rely excessively on sounding out words (something that often occurs in radical phonics programs), then they may lose sight of the

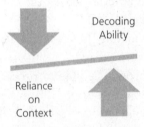

FIGURE 1.2. The relationship between context and word recognition.

importance of textual meaning, and reading becomes nothing more than a rote exercise. This extreme position is rare, but occasionally we do see children who have been taught to focus in this manner. These children also tend to be significantly better at calling words than at comprehending text. If the text is within a child's instructional level, and the child is not making contextually acceptable miscues, then the child's attention needs to be redirected to the meaning of the text, and he or she needs to be taught that texts are meaningful.

If a child is poor at using context, we would look at the child's interview data to see how he or she perceives reading, and we would evaluate the child's comprehension of texts read orally, to see whether he or she is focusing on comprehension during reading.

Fluency

Many children with reading problems can read accurately, but cannot read quickly enough to make sense of what they are reading. If reading is not fluent, then comprehension usually suffers. We learn about a child's degree of fluency through observation of oral reading. Sometimes this observation is done through an IRI, but it also can be done by observing the child read a trade book, by using benchmark texts for running records, or by using leveled passages as in the Dynamic Indicators of Basic Early Literacy Skills—Next (DIBELS Next), AIMSweb, or the Formative Assessment System for Teachers (FAST) assessment batteries. In Chapter 6, we include a rubric or scoring guide that can be used to decide whether reading is fluent. Generally, however, the criteria can be stated simply, as whether the child's reading sounds like language:

- Is the child's reading halting or smooth?
- Does the child stop to sound out words excessively?
- Does the child have to repeat phrases excessively or self-correct excessively?

If a child engages in halting reading, with excessive sounding out, repetition, or self-correction, then he or she may need work in fluency. If the child is not fluent or accurate at reading texts written at his or her grade placement level, then we need to ask two questions about the child's word recognition:

- Does the child have adequate sight-word knowledge?
- Does the child have adequate knowledge of decoding strategies?

Sight Words

The term *sight words* can be defined in two principal ways. Ehri (1998) uses *sight words* to refer to all the words that a child recognizes "at sight," or automatically. Under this definition, both common words, such as *the* and *what*, and uncommon words, such as *wolf* and *rescue*, might all be sight words for a given individual. It is important to distinguish sight words from high-frequency words—that is, the words that occur most often in print. Obviously, high-frequency words are likely to become sight words for a beginning reader. But for assessment purposes, we use the term *high-frequency words*. Adams

(1990) points out that the 105 words that occur most frequently account for about 50% of running text. This is just as true for adult text as it is for children's text. While a number of these high-frequency words are irregular (e.g., *of*), many others are at least partially or entirely regular (e.g., the digraph *th-* in *the, this,* and *that*), and thus can be studied with commonly occurring patterns. Either way, these words need to be learned completely so that they can be retrieved quickly and automatically.

There are several lists of the most frequently used words in English, notably the lists developed by Dolch (1936) and Fry (1980). As one might expect, there is considerable overlap among lists. In addition, the words on any of these lists are worth assessing and teaching. We include both lists in Chapter 5. We recommend using one of these two lists as opposed to creating your own.

In assessing children's knowledge of high-frequency words, it is important to note both speed and accuracy. Because so many textual words are sight words, slow recognition entails slow text reading in general. Sounding out a word such as *with*, even if the child arrived at the correct pronunciation, would still impair comprehension, as would a halting pronunciation after a long pause. Therefore, the assessor should note both the accuracy and speed of recognition. Each word on a list should be recognized in roughly half a second or less—that is, without hesitation.

In addition, one should observe children's recognition of high-frequency words in context. Since these words account for such a large percentage of the words in any text, an informal reading inventory also gives ample opportunity to observe children's skills at recognizing high-frequency words in context. Again, these are words that should be recognized *automatically*, without hesitation or sounding out.

Decoding

We are also interested in whether a child has the ability to decode unknown words. The ability to decode requires knowledge of the processes involved in decoding, as well as knowledge of specific letter–sound relationships. We need to assess both.

Assessing the Process of Decoding

As suggested by Ehri's (1998) model, the process of decoding involves three successive understandings: (1) acquisition of the alphabetic principle, (2) the ability to blend letter sounds into words, and (3) the ability to use both phonograms and analogies. Children's acquisition of the alphabetic principle—the principle that letters can be used to represent sounds—is revealed by their use of letters as cues for words in both word recognition and spelling. Spelling may be a better means of assessing children's knowledge of the alphabetic principle, since children may use the first letter as a visual rather than a phonemic cue.

Letter-by-letter decoding—the ability to blend letters together to make words—is the hallmark of Ehri's (1998) full alphabetic coding phase and Bear et al.'s (2020) letter name stage. Although this phase is fairly short-lived, it is critical: Children need to appreciate individual letter–sound correspondences in order to move toward automatic word recognition. This ability can be evaluated by measures that tap children's knowledge of individual letter sounds as well as their decoding of short-vowel words. Because short vowels are usually the first vowel types taught first in most phonics curricula, we use short vowels as the test of children's blending ability.

Ehri's last stage, *consolidation*, involves being able to use both phonograms, or chunks of letters (e.g., *ick*, *ill*, *and*), and analogies (e.g., decoding *strike* by comparing it with *like*). Proficient readers decode words using these strategies. Studies have found that children must be able to understand letter-by-letter decoding before they are able to benefit from analogy or phonogram instruction, but children need to use phonograms in order to read proficiently (e.g., Ehri & Robbins, 1992). Children are first able to use phonograms and analogies to decode monosyllabic words; later, they can use them to decode polysyllabic words.

Assessing the Content of Decoding

Even if a child has knowledge of a process such as letter-by-letter decoding, he or she still needs to learn certain phonics/spelling features. For letter-by-letter decoding, the phonics/spelling features would be these:

- Consonant sounds (<u>s</u>un, <u>f</u>an, <u>t</u>oy, <u>d</u>og)
- Consonant digraphs (<u>th</u>at, <u>th</u>in, <u>sh</u>eep, <u>ch</u>ick, <u>wh</u>o, <u>ph</u>one)
- Consonant blends (<u>bl</u>ue, <u>st</u>ar, <u>sl</u>eep, <u>dr</u>ink, <u>str</u>ipe)
- Short vowels in consonant–vowel–consonant (CVC) words (c<u>a</u>t, p<u>e</u>t, p<u>i</u>n, d<u>u</u>ck, l<u>o</u>g)
- Vowel digraphs (b<u>oa</u>t, gr<u>ee</u>n, w<u>ai</u>t, p<u>ea</u>)
- Rule of silent *e* (r<u>a</u>c<u>e</u>, h<u>o</u>s<u>e</u>, b<u>i</u>k<u>e</u>)
- Vowel diphthongs (j<u>oi</u>n, c<u>ow</u>, b<u>oy</u>, p<u>aw</u>)
- *r*-Controlled vowels (st<u>ar</u>, b<u>ir</u>d, w<u>or</u>ld, h<u>er</u>)
- *l*-Controlled *a* (b<u>all</u>, c<u>all</u>)
- Other variant vowels (c<u>au</u>ght, p<u>u</u>t)

This list does not mean that children need to learn rules. The "rules" often do not apply to enough words to render them clear-cut. For example, the rule "when two vowels go walking, the first one does the talking" works only about 45% of the time (Clymer, 1963). It works for *boat*, but not for *bread* or *join* or *does*. And the "rule" of silent *e* applies only about 60% of the time. It works in *home* but not in *come*, in *drove* but not in *dove* or *love*, in *save* but not in *have*. Instead, children need to know *patterns* to help them identify individual words. Rather than presenting a rule, present lists of words that adhere to the pattern, so that children can internalize the pattern and do not have to think about the rule. As Cunningham (2001) has observed, the brain is more comfortable recognizing patterns than applying rules.

As for phonograms, or rimes, there are hundreds in the English language. Wylie and Durrell (1970) found 286 phonograms in their examination of primary-grade texts, 272 of which are pronounced the same way in every word in which they appear, and they found 37 rimes that account for nearly 500 words. These rimes have been used as a basis for the Z-Test presented in Chapter 5. Clearly, these phonograms could be the start of a phonogram-based program, but they should be seen as only a start. One cannot teach all

272 phonograms, but one might expand beyond the initial set. If a child has difficulties in letter-by-letter decoding, then the next question we ask is this:

- What aspects of phonological awareness are under the child's control?

However, if an older reader is proficient in letter-by-letter decoding, but experiences difficulty decoding multisyllabic words, the difficulty is probably *not* with phonological awareness, but with an awareness of the structure of multisyllabic words. In this case, we recommend administering the Multisyllabic Words section of the Informal Decoding Inventory (see Chapter 5).

Phonological Awareness

Phonological awareness—or the awareness of the sounds that constitute spoken words—is a prerequisite for children to learn to decode. It is not uncommon for young children, kindergartners, and even some first graders to be unable to think of words as a collection of sounds and, for example, to be unable to provide the first sound of *dog* or *fish*. Stanovich (1986), among many, suggests that early difficulties in phonological awareness underlie later reading problems. Children who do not think of the first sound of *mouse* as /m/ will be unable to use the letter *m* to help recognize the word.

One child in our clinic, Heather, is a wonderful (and amusing) example of this problem. Heather was a first grader when we saw her, the daughter of a dentist and a stay-at-home mother, living in a small Midwestern town. Her mother reported that Heather had difficulties in learning phonics, although she had no problems reading easy preprimer text by memorizing the words. From discussions with her mother, we suspected that she had difficulties with phonological awareness. When asked to say *meat* without the /m/, Heather thought for a while, then said, "Chicken." Although nonplussed, we went on, asking her to say *coat* without the /k/. After some thought, she said, "Jacket."

Heather's difficulties came about because she tended to view words as semantic units, as we might, in order to understand them in speech and reading. We suspect that her answers were attempts to make the concepts themselves smaller by going from the broader categories of *meat* and *coat* to the category members *chicken* and *jacket*. However, to learn to use an alphabetic language, to reach that vital alphabetic insight, a child needs to recognize that words are both meaningful *and* collections of abstract sounds. Because Heather did not have that alphabetic insight, she could not move forward. She was easy to teach, figured out the relations between letters and sounds, and went on to be a good reader. But she did need initial help to make sense of word recognition.

For beginning readers, it is important to consider one last barrier to automatic word recognition. The following question is critical, regardless of the child's level of phonological awareness:

- About which concepts of print does the child have knowledge?

We want to identify the child's range of knowledge regarding basic print concepts, including the left-to-right directionality of English, the fact that spaces are word boundaries, and so forth. These concepts are fundamental to an appreciation of how print works, and they are the foundation for the development of decoding skills. Extremely important is a *concept of word in text* (COW-T), the pivotal insight that differentiates emergent from beginning readers (Bear et al., 2020; Morris, Bloodgood, Lomax, & Perney, 2003). COW-T is the ability to match spoken words to written words while reading a familiar text. For example, Andrew, a second grader who had repeated first grade, was still puzzled by the difference between a word and a letter, despite his experience of 2½ years in primary school. When asked to slide two cards together to show a word, he slid them together to reveal one letter. When asked to show two words, he showed two letters. When asked to show one *letter*, he was puzzled, thinking that he had already done that. This child would have been extremely confused during lessons that talk about the "first letter in the word _____." If his teachers had spotted his confusion and dealt with it early, it is likely that many of Andrew's subsequent problems would not have developed. We have provided several measures in this book that evaluate children's concept of what a word is.

We have placed print concepts and phonological awareness in separate boxes in our schematic in Figure 1.1. However, it is important to consider how they relate to each other. For example, as young readers are able to attend to the beginning sounds in words (rudimentary phonological awareness), they are better able to match spoken words accurately to written words while reading (COW-T). It is important to consider both and how they relate to each other.

We have now traced word recognition back to its roots—from automatic word recognition, to fluency in context, to knowledge of sight words and decoding, to phonological awareness and print concepts. This cognitive view complements the stage views of the developmental models described earlier. Once these views are put together, it is clear how a reader can fall behind, and how a teacher can target instruction to put the reader back on the road to proficiency.

COGNITIVE MODEL PATHWAY 2: LANGUAGE COMPREHENSION

Even if a reader is proficient in word calling, the child also must be able to comprehend what is read. We encounter children who are able to read fluently but cannot understand what they read. Sometimes this is just a matter of not attending to meaning. When children are given intensive phonics instruction without being asked to attend to meaning, they may not focus on the meaning. This situation is rare and easily fixed.

Most other children who have comprehension problems have difficulties understanding the language of the text, even if they can read the words. Although language comprehension involves a great number of elements, we find that the problems we see occur largely in three areas. Put as questions, we ask ourselves:

- Does the child have an adequate *vocabulary* for his or her age and grade?
- Does the child have the *background knowledge* necessary to understand the particular passage that he or she is reading?
- Is the child able to use common *text and sentence structures* to aid in comprehension?

Vocabulary

Children's knowledge of word meanings is the best predictor of their comprehension, both of passages containing those words and of passages in general (Stahl & Nagy, 2006). This factor may be predictive because knowledge of words enables children to comprehend passages, or because vocabulary knowledge is a measure of children's general knowledge or their general intelligence. Either way, children with reading problems tend to have problems with word meanings.

These problems also tend to worsen as children progress through school. Stanovich (1986) attributes this decline to what he calls *Matthew effects*—a term coined by the sociologist Robert Merton, in reference to a Biblical verse (Matthew 25:29) echoing the old adage that the "rich will get richer and the poor will get poorer." Stanovich used the term to refer to the widening gap between proficient and struggling readers (see Figure 1.3).

Stanovich (1986) has suggested that many of the problems struggling readers encounter are not due to underlying causes, but to these children's increasing lack of reading experience. In the case of vocabulary, children who have reading problems both read less text and read less challenging texts. Because they read increasingly less challenging material, they are exposed to fewer words of increasing difficulty. Because most words are learned from exposure in context, children with reading problems learn fewer words. Because they know fewer words, they are less able to read challenging texts and therefore encounter fewer difficult words—thus engaging in a downward cycle that exacerbates the differences between proficient and struggling readers.

Because vocabulary knowledge constitutes an important component of intelligence tests, we find that children with reading problems produce intelligence test scores that decline over time. This finding does not mean that they have less native intelligence, just that they have relatively smaller vocabularies than their peers. But the decline in

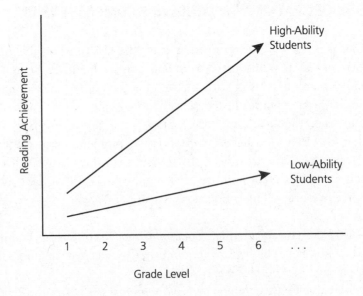

FIGURE 1.3. An example of the Matthew effect.

intelligence test scores can mean that these children lose a legal categorization, such as "learning disability," that may be determined by intelligence test scores.

Over the school years, children learn an impressive number of word meanings. Estimates are that children typically enter first grade knowing between 3,000 and 6,000 words, learn between 1,000 and 3,000 new words per year, and know as many as 45,000 words by the end of 12th grade (Nagy, 1988). This large number of words cannot be tested directly. Instead, tests are based on samples of words. We suggest a number of standardized tests that assess vocabulary, but we do not provide one in this book because of the difficulties in accurately sampling such a large number of words.

Background Knowledge

Much has been written about the contribution of background knowledge to children's reading comprehension (e.g., Anderson & Pearson, 1984). Because the purpose of this book is to talk about assessment, we limit our discussion of background knowledge to its effects on assessment.

Children obviously differ in the amount and depth of their background knowledge, and these differences affect their performance on reading tasks. Standardized measures deal with the issue of background knowledge by utilizing many short passages. If a child has strong knowledge of one topic and weak knowledge of another, the effects of background knowledge should average out over a number of passages.

On IRIs, each level can be assessed in a single passage. On the Qualitative Reading Inventory–5 (Leslie & Caldwell, 2011), selections at the fifth-grade level include passages on Martin Luther King, Jr., and Margaret Mead. Because knowledge of Dr. King is taught each year, whereas Margaret Mead is rarely taught prior to high school, the passage on Dr. King is more familiar to most students. Children may answer questions correctly on the basis of their prior knowledge, rather than what they have just read. Often children's retellings and answers to questions seem plainly based on previous knowledge rather than on what was read. Teachers need to be cautious in interpreting the scores from passages about familiar topics; students may have relied on prior knowledge in their responses to questions. In particular, some inferential questions may be less dependent on text comprehension and more dependent on a reader's background knowledge.

Some IRIs provide a pretest for prior knowledge; others do not. If possible, we recommend that teachers administer passages on familiar as well as unfamiliar topics to compare children's responses under both conditions; this is particularly important for older readers, who, as they move through middle and high school, are increasingly likely to encounter texts for which they have limited background knowledge across the content areas.

Sentence Structures

The texts that children encounter as they move through school contain progressively more complicated sentences. On average, sentences grow longer and are likely to contain multiple clauses and phrases. Because these academic language structures—some specific to disciplines and content areas—are seldom heard in conversation, children must learn them by reading widely across a variety of topics, genres, and content areas. Because there is no sequence that we can use to predict which grammatical structures are likely to be encountered at which grades, it is important for teachers to be aware of the occurrence of challenging syntax. Syntactic challenges make excellent targets for questioning and for think-alouds.

Because the length of a sentence and its complexity are highly correlated, examining the average sentence length of a text is a shortcut to appraising its grammatical complexity. This is the approach taken by most readability formulas, including Lexiles. We feel that by attempting to create a good match between a student's instructional reading level and the readability level of a text, a teacher can do much to ensure that the grammatical structures the student faces are appropriate.

Text Structures

We also see children in the clinic who differ in their knowledge of text structures. By *text structures*, we mean structural patterns in text that are common to particular genres. For example, one can identify the following elements for narratives:

- Setting and characters, including
  - Time
  - Place
  - Major characters
  - Minor characters
- Problem that major character encounters
- Goal that major character is trying to achieve
- Events
  - Event 1
  - Event 2
- Resolution

Research has found that children tend to include these elements in their recall of narratives (e.g., Yussen & Ozcan, 1996). A narrative also can be thought of as comprising chains of events, with one event causing the next. These causal chains form the plot of the narrative.

Other genres have different elements. Most expository genres are structured around main ideas and supporting information. Sometimes the main idea is a cause-and-effect relationship or the presentation of a problem and solution, whereas at other times the main idea is the topic around which the passage provides supporting and descriptive information. Text structure of informational text is important, because it often reflects the conceptual organization of the information being presented. An inability to recognize the organizational structure of a text could reflect a lack of understanding concerning how the ideas fit together conceptually, and/or difficulty remembering the ideas.

We find that children who have reading problems also have difficulties perceiving text structures. They could be having these difficulties because labored decoding renders them unable to integrate information into a coherent whole, or because they do not understand how to discern the overall structure of a text. Either way, such children can benefit from instruction on text structure.

We assess children's knowledge of text structure through free recall. As we discuss in Chapter 8, this recall involves having a child retell what he or she has read. Ordinarily we expect the recall to include most of the important information, be it important story elements (narrative text) or main idea information (expository text). We also ordinarily expect the recall to roughly mirror the order the information was presented in the text. Any significant divergence from either inclusion of important information or text order is a cause for concern. Some children recall information haphazardly, as if they were picking out random facts, suggesting poor recall and the need for work in this area.

A word of caution is in order. Some children, because of shyness or a lack of understanding of the task, simply do not recall text well, and their responses may lead a teacher to underestimate how well they have comprehended. Interpretation of poor recall should involve considering whether limited responses may have been the results of reticence or failure to grasp the task.

COGNITIVE MODEL PATHWAY 3: STRATEGIC KNOWLEDGE

Consider how you, as a proficient reader, are probably reading this text. Chances are that you are in a comfortable (but not too comfortable) place, perhaps one you typically reserve for studying. The lighting is good. As to the actual process of studying, there is considerable variation. Some people study with music; others need quiet. Some people use highlighters; others write in the margins, use note cards, or simply read quietly. Some people gain an overview by skimming the whole text; others read it carefully from start to finish. Whatever approach you are taking, chances are that it is the same approach you have taken to reading textbooks in the past. You have found a set of strategies that work for you while you are studying.

Contrast this set of strategies with those used for reading a recreational novel. You probably read the novel in a different place, possibly in bed or in a noisier environment. The contrast between the two activities shows how you, as a proficient reader, have different strategies for reading different types of texts for different purposes. Prior to reading, you decided what your purpose was and chose a set of strategies to help you achieve your purpose. The strategies are related to environment and learning set (e.g., place to work, quiet or noise) and to cognitive strategies for remembering (e.g., using a highlighter or note cards, reading end-of-chapter summaries first).

We find that children with reading problems often have difficulties assimilating different strategies and knowing which should be used for a given purpose. For example, Cameron is a sixth grader with severe reading difficulties. His primary problems involve his slow reading rate and his ponderous process of word recognition. When given the Textbook Interview (see Chapter 9) and asked how he would study a chapter for a test, he replied that he would read it straight through. Because of his labored focus on the individual words and consequent slow reading rate, we doubted that he would be able to finish it in a week or that he would remember much of what he had read. When we asked him, he confirmed that he rarely finished half of his weekly reading assignment. When asked what kind of grades he got, he replied, "D's and F's." Cameron was not successful at studying and did not know how to modify his behaviors so that he could succeed. There are techniques that can be used to help children who have reading problems study more effectively, even material they might have difficulty reading straight through (see Schumaker, Deshler, Alley, Warner, & Denton, 1982). We did teach him to use these techniques, which improved his grades somewhat.

The first question we ask is this:

- Does the child have a set of strategies that he or she can apply to achieve different purposes in reading?

This question is largely answered by interviews, self-assessments, reader think-alouds, and performance assessments (in which children are asked to apply a specific strategy for a specific purpose, like summarizing a text). We provide the Textbook Interview in Chapter 9 (see Form 9.3); with older children, we often spend a great deal of time talking about how they deal with content-area texts. Older children often have a great deal of insight into their difficulties, and we try to take advantage of that insight.

Not only do children with reading problems often not know specific strategies, but they also often do not understand general purposes for reading. In one study (Garner & Kraus, 1981), proficient readers were asked, "If I gave you something to read, how would you know you were reading it well?" They responded that they would know they were reading it well if they understood what they read, if they "got the big ideas," and so on. Struggling readers, on the other hand, often responded that they were reading well when "they said the words correctly" or when the teacher did not correct them. Worse yet, many struggling readers were unable to identify how they knew they were not reading a passage successfully. If readers do not know that the general purpose for reading is to get meaning from print, but instead view reading as a decoding act, they will experience difficulties.

To ascertain the child's understanding of the general purposes of reading, we need to ask a question such as this:

- What does the child view as the goal of reading in general?

As adults, we recognize that the general goal of reading is to comprehend text. Our specific goals inevitably affect how we comprehend, of course, but we clearly understand why we read. Many children, on the other hand, harbor vague ideas about the general goal of reading. Many believe that the goal is to say all of the words correctly or simply to arrive at the last word. They might not deny that understanding what they read is important, but in reality this goal is dwarfed by the lesser goal of word recognition. Rather than viewing word recognition as a means to an end, they view it as an end in itself. Instruction and programs that overemphasize decoding may exacerbate this perception, but it is common among struggling readers everywhere. It is therefore important for teachers to learn about children's views concerning reading, and to attempt to broaden their outlooks if need be.

PUTTING IT ALL TOGETHER

Listing all the assessment questions that we ask in this chapter, as organized by our three-pathway cognitive model, we arrive at the following:

- **Cognitive Pathway 1:** Is the child able to read texts at his or her grade placement level with automatic word recognition and adequate expression?
    - Is the child fluent in context?
    - Does the child have adequate sight-word knowledge?
    - Does the child have adequate knowledge of decoding strategies?
    - Does the child have adequate phonological awareness?
    - About which concepts of print does the child have knowledge?
- **Cognitive Pathway 2:** Is the child able to comprehend the language of the text?
    - Does the child have an adequate vocabulary for his or her age and grade?
    - Does the child have the background knowledge necessary to understand the particular passage that he or she is reading?
    - Is the child able to use common text and sentence structures to aid in comprehension?
- **Cognitive Pathway 3:** Does the child have adequate knowledge of the purposes for reading and possess strategies to achieve those purposes?
    - Does the child have a set of strategies that he or she can use to achieve different purposes in reading?
    - What does the child view as the goal of reading in general?

These questions can be used to guide us through the assessment process. By the time we finish a complete assessment of a child, we should have answered most or all of these questions. (Some of the questions may prove unnecessary once we begin. For example, a child with strong decoding skills can be assumed to have acquired adequate phonological awareness.)

Now let's return to our three cases at the beginning of this chapter. For Josh, we are concerned about his decoding ability. The first questions we would ask concern his ability to decode and his phonological awareness, because we suspect that difficulties in these areas underlie his difficulties in automatic word recognition and reading connected text. We also would want to know about his ability to use context to support fluent reading, his comprehension ability, and his listening comprehension. As for Latrelle, we suspect that her decoding skills are adequate, although we would still want to assess them. We are more concerned about her automaticity and her ability to use context. We also want to know about her comprehension, and since she is required increasingly to read different kinds of text in fourth grade, we would want to know about her knowledge of strategies. For Dom, we are not as concerned with his word recognition as we are with his comprehension and strategic knowledge.

Chapter 2 focuses on general issues in assessment. Chapter 3 introduces the IRI, which is the keystone of classroom reading assessment, because it is so important in answering many of the questions we have raised here. The remainder of the book deals with more fine-grained assessment in the particular areas we have discussed.

TWO

General Concepts of Assessment

There are many means of acquiring the information necessary to make appropriate instructional decisions for your students. Some of these methods involve conventional tests, whereas others involve less structured methods of gathering information. We look at tests first, and then consider the alternatives.

TYPES OF TESTS

It is useful to categorize tests along four dimensions. Most of the commercial and teacher-constructed tests currently available can be readily categorized according to these four dimensions:

- Group versus individual tests
- Formal versus informal tests
- Norm-referenced versus criterion-referenced tests
- Screening versus diagnostic tests

Group versus Individual Tests

Some tests are designed to be administered to a group of students, whereas others must be administered individually. The primary reason for individual administration is that a test requires oral responses from the child. In addition, individual administration allows adaptive testing, in which the student's performance to a given point is used to determine how to proceed with the test administration. Needless to say, individually administered tests tend to provide more dependable results than group assessments, because the teacher can command the student's mental engagement (to some extent) during the testing process. On the other hand, of course, group tests are far more efficient, even if their results are less dependable.

Formal versus Informal Tests

Tests differ with respect to how rigidly they are administered and interpreted. A formal test is one in which the directions for administration are clear-cut and allow little, if any, discretion on the teacher's part. Moreover, formal tests are scored in a carefully prescribed manner. A group standardized achievement test, such as those often mandated by state or local education agencies, is a good example of a formal test. An informal test, on the other hand, is one in which teacher discretion plays a major part. For example, the teacher may decide on the basis of the student's early responses to modify how the test is given. Moreover, the teacher may exercise wide latitude in determining how to interpret the results. An essay test is one example of an informal test, and so is an IRI, which we discuss in Chapter 3.

Norm-Referenced versus Criterion-Referenced Tests

There are two major ways of bringing meaning to test scores. One way is to compare one child's results with the results of other children. In other words, we can compare one child's performance with what might be normally expected of other children—hence the word *norm*. Norms such as percentile ranks, grade equivalents, stanines, normal curve equivalents, scale scores, and many others are commonplace in educational parlance. (We discuss norms in greater detail later in this chapter.)

A second way to interpret a child's performance is to compare his or her test score with a preestablished criterion or benchmark. A good example is the written portion of the state driver's examination. An examinee is permitted to miss a predetermined number of questions and still pass the exam. This criterion has nothing to do with how others performed on the same test. The comparison is between the individual driver and the criterion established by the Department of Motor Vehicles.

As a general rule, norm-referenced tests are useful in determining a child's overall developmental level with respect to those of others. Criterion-referenced tests are useful for mastery-level learning or competency-based assessment. A curriculum that consists of many specific skills to be learned is probably well served by a series of criterion-referenced tests (one per skill).

Screening versus Diagnostic Tests

Another useful way to categorize tests is by the use that is made of them. Two types are particularly important: *screening* and *diagnostic* tests. Screening tests attempt to provide a broadly defined estimate of a student's overall achievement level in a given area. These tests, which are brief and fairly general, are typically administered individually and are used to identify students who are not meeting grade-level reading benchmarks. These tests also identify areas where more fine-grained assessments should be administered for particular students. Above all, the results indicate the next step to be taken in reading assessment: the administration of diagnostic instruments. Group achievement tests such as the Stanford Achievement Test, the Iowa Tests of Basic Skills, and others can serve as screening tests, although their results are more often used as outcome measures for large groups of children.

Diagnostic tests, on the other hand, provide detailed information useful in planning instruction. These tests may involve multiple dimensions, possibly represented by subtests or by a variety of tasks a student is asked to perform. By the same token, a test designed to tell whether a student has mastered a particular objective is also an example of a diagnostic test because the result documents progress in terms specific enough to help in planning instruction.

INTERPRETING NORM-REFERENCED READING TESTS

Perhaps the most important part of giving a test is making sense of the scores. In the case of a norm-referenced test, interpretation is guided by comparing a student's raw score (i.e., the number of items correct) with the scores of other students. In other words, we are interested in what a "normal" score might be and to what extent the score for a particular student differs from it. To make such a comparison, the student's raw score is converted into another score, called a *norm*. Many types of norms are in common use today; some of the most frequently encountered are presented in Table 2.1.

Figure 2.1 illustrates how some of these norms are related to one another in terms of the normal (what else?) curve. Notice, for example, that the fifth stanine always contains 20% of the group used to norm the test and extends from the 40th through the 59th percentile ranks. Also note that the nine stanines are perfectly symmetrical, so that the first and ninth stanine always contain 4% of the population, the second and eighth always contain 7%, and so on.

The lower graph in Figure 2.1 illustrates how a population of students varies from its own mean (average) score. The Greek letter *sigma* (σ) is used to represent the stan-

TABLE 2.1. Common Norms and What They Mean

Norm	Definition
Percentile rank	Percentage of children the same age whose scores a given child's equals or exceeds. (This is an approximate definition, not the one used in computation.) Percentile ranks cannot be averaged.
Stanine	One of nine statistically comparable divisions of the population tested, with the fifth positioned in the middle of the normal curve and accounting for 20% of those tested. (Short for "standard nine.")
Grade-equivalent score	An estimate of the grade level corresponding to a given student's raw score—a highly dubious norm whose use is officially discouraged by the International Literacy Association.
Normal curve equivalent	The score resulting from partitioning the normal distribution into 99 statistically equivalent sections. NCEs can be averaged, unlike percentile ranks.
Scale score	A statistically converted score, usually computed to combine the results of different tests or to weight items differentially.
Quartile	One-quarter of the norming group, permitting a given child's score to be grossly categorized as falling in one of four sections.

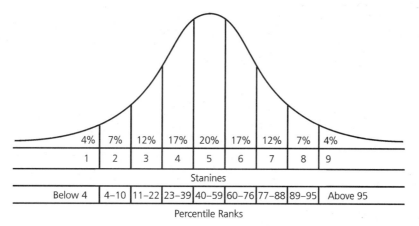

4%	7%	12%	17%	20%	17%	12%	7%	4%
1	2	3	4	5	6	7	8	9

Stanines

Below 4	4–10	11–22	23–39	40–59	60–76	77–88	89–95	Above 95

Percentile Ranks

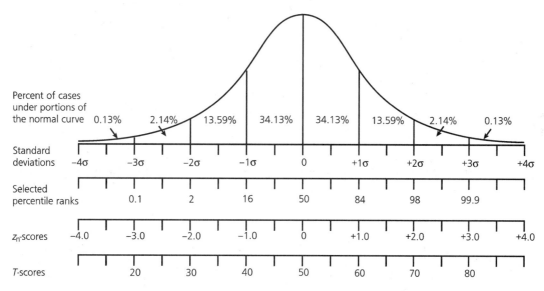

FIGURE 2.1. Common norms in relation to the normal distribution.

dard deviation of the group (i.e., the extent to which the scores made by group members tend to vary). You will observe that more than 68% of the population (about two-thirds) has scores that fall within one standard deviation of the group mean. The farther we get from this mean, the fewer individuals we find. For example, only 13.59% of those tested typically score more than one standard deviation above the mean, and far fewer than 1% score more than three standard deviations above it.

Not all tests produce these symmetrical, bell-shaped curves. Imagine a weekly spelling test of 20 words, on which all of the students in a gifted class score either 19 or 20. Results of this test will be skewed to the right, which should be of no concern to the teacher. The results of classroom tests of this nature are usually interpreted by comparing students not with one another, but against a criterion for mastery or a simple grading scale. Publishers of commercial norm-referenced tests, however, often go to great lengths to ensure that scores do tend to produce a normal distribution, such as those depicted in the diagrams. This goal is accomplished by field-testing potential test items and ultimately selecting only those that contribute to a normal distribution of scores.

Most teachers associate norm-referenced tests with the group achievement measures they may be required to administer and for which they are often held accountable. However, many norm-referenced tests are individually administered, such as those used by special educators to classify students. Another minor misconception about norm-referenced tests concerns the word *standardized*. This term is frequently used as a synonym for *norm-referenced*. In fact, however, a standardized test is any test for which the procedures for administration and scoring are rigorously prescribed. Even a criterion-referenced test (e.g., the written portion of the state driver's examination) can be thought of as standardized in this sense.

Standard Error of Measurement

How much confidence can we have that a student's score accurately reflects what the student knows or can do? In the best of all worlds, test scores would provide perfect indicators of student learning. But in the real world, both predictable and unpredictable factors influence scores in unpredictable ways. A typical class about to take a norm-referenced achievement test in reading may well contain individuals who skipped breakfast, argued that morning with their parents, are unmotivated to perform well, or failed to get a good night's sleep. It also may contain students who have been offered inducements by their parents to do well, or who enjoy the self-competition made possible by the norms. Such factors contribute to what is called *measurement error*, which reduces the reliance teachers can justifiably have on the test scores. All tests, even those constructed by teachers, suffer from measurement error. In the case of norm-referenced tests, however, it is possible to estimate just how large this error may be.

A simple equation may help us conceptualize the error factor. This equation depicts the relationship between a student's "true score" (i.e., the score the student should have received, based on the area being assessed) and the student's "actual score" (the score the student actually makes on the test).

$$\text{True score} = \text{Actual score} \pm \text{Error}$$

The true score can never be directly measured, only estimated. We hope that the actual score is reasonably close to the true score, but we can never be certain that this is the case. The standard error of measurement provides a way of estimating how far "off" the actual score may be. We can accomplish this estimate by creating a zone, or interval, around the actual score. First we add the standard error of measurement to the actual score to form the high point of the interval. Then we subtract the standard error from the actual score to find the low point. Because of the statistical properties of a test that has a normal distribution, we can conclude that there is roughly a 67% chance that the individual's true score falls somewhere within this interval. We call this region a *confidence interval,* because it permits us to make a statement with reasonable confidence about the true score. To say that there are roughly two chances in three that an individual's true score lies within one standard error of the actual score sounds appealing, but it also means that there is one chance in three that the true score is either above the interval or below it—with no way to tell which!

If you want to have more confidence in your conclusion, you simply construct a larger confidence interval by adding and subtracting twice the standard error from the actual score. The result is a 95% interval. In other words, we can be 95% certain that an individual's true score lies within two standard errors of the actual score. This seems very useful indeed—except that the 95% interval can be so large that the statement is virtually meaningless.

As an example, consider the diagram in Figure 2.2. In this case, a student has earned a raw score of 20 on a test that has a standard error of measurement of 2 raw score points. The 67% confidence interval is constructed by adding and subtracting 2 points from the raw score of 20, so that the interval extends from 18 to 22. The 95% interval is constructed by doubling the standard error before adding and subtracting, so that this interval extends from 16 to 24. When the end points of the interval (i.e., 16 and 24) are translated into norms such as percentile ranks, the range is disappointingly large.

One may well wonder, given the difficulties involved in attempting to estimate the true score, just why group achievement tests are given. Surely there is so much error involved that the results cannot be meaningfully interpreted. The response to this objection is that group achievement tests are not designed to assess individual students with a high level of accuracy. Rather, they are designed to assess groups and to answer educational questions about the achievement of groups. When large numbers of scores are averaged, the measurement error is diminished. A question such as "How well is the fifth grade doing in our school district?" is far better suited to group achievement testing than a question such as "How well is Johnny doing in reading?" Such tests provide us with only the most tentative measures of an individual student's learning, useful only for screening in the areas assessed.

Which Norms Are Best?

For the purpose of interpreting the results of group achievement testing, percentile ranks and stanines are perhaps the most useful norms for teachers. Percentile ranks give an indication of where an individual student's performance falls relative to other students the same age. Stanines do this as well, but because there are only nine possible stanine

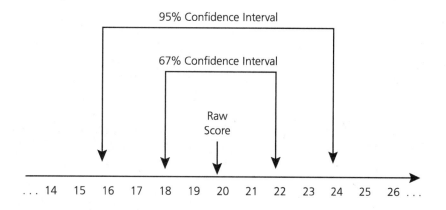

FIGURE 2.2. Examples of confidence intervals (standard error of measurement = 2).

scores, they are not as precise as percentile ranks. Why, then, report stanines at all? The reason is that stanines are statistically equivalent, allowing certain conclusions to be reached. It takes as much effort to move from the first to the second stanine as it does from the sixth to the seventh, for example. This is not true of percentile ranks, however, rendering stanines preferable for making pretest–posttest comparisons or for comparing the results of two subtests.

The Two-Stanine Rule

If the difference between the scores made by a student on two different subtests (or on pre- and postintervention administrations of the same test) is two stanines or greater, the difference is probably real. A difference of two stanines is typically sufficient to overcome measurement error. For example, if a child scores at the fourth stanine on a subtest of reading comprehension and at the sixth stanine on a subtest of vocabulary, it is reasonable to conclude that achievement in the area of reading comprehension is lower than achievement in vocabulary, compared with the norming group. On the other hand, if the stanine for one of these two areas is 3 and for the other area 4, we are statistically prevented from concluding that there is any real difference whatsoever.

A Limitation of Percentile Ranks

Some educators make the mistake of using percentile ranks to compute class or school averages. Doing so is not statistically appropriate, because percentile ranks are not on an equal-interval scale. That is to say, the "distance" between the 2nd and 3rd percentile ranks is not the same as the "distance" between the 32nd and 33rd percentile ranks. The closer a score is to the 50th percentile rank, the more volatile it becomes and the easier it is for the score to change from one administration to the next.

Because of this difficulty, statisticians rely on normal curve equivalents and scale scores (see Figure 2.1) in order to compute averages and other statistics. In fact, this is virtually the only use that norms of this kind have. They are hard to interpret in themselves. It is best to rely on percentile ranks and stanines to bring meaning to achievement test scores. The percentile rank of a class or some larger group can be ascertained, if desired, by first computing the average scale score or normal curve equivalent and *then* locating the percentile rank that corresponds to this average.

Which Norms Are Worst?

Without question, the worst norm typically reported on group achievement tests is the grade-equivalent score. This norm purports to indicate the grade level at which a student has performed on a particular subtest. A common way of interpreting a grade-equivalent score is by relating it to that of "average children" at a particular level. For example, if a seventh grader produces a grade-equivalent score of 2.6 on a subtest of reading comprehension, it is common for teachers to conclude that this student comprehends as well as the average second grader who is in the sixth month of school. This conclusion is very difficult to defend, however. For one thing, a test that is appropriate for middle schoolers is unlikely to have been given to second graders simply in order to establish norms. Indeed, many grade-equivalent scores are merely statistical projections that permit a student to be compared with students of other ages.

Another difficulty of grade-equivalent scores is that for most tests they have what are termed *floors* and *ceilings*. A floor is simply the lowest grade-equivalent score it is possible to make, because grade equivalents have not been projected below a certain level. For example, if the floor for a reading comprehension subtest is 2.0, then even a student who is a nonreader may be judged to be reading as well as the average beginning second grader (Silvaroli, 1977). Problems with floors are not as troublesome as they once were, but the potential for difficulties still exists.

A ceiling, on the other hand, is the highest grade-equivalent score a student can earn. It is rare for an achievement test to have a ceiling higher than 12th grade. Although ceilings could lead us to underestimate the achievement of advanced students, this possibility is not as troublesome as that of overestimating the achievement of struggling readers due to the effects of floors.

The International Literacy Association, in a 1980 Board of Directors position statement that is still in effect, officially condemned the use of grade-equivalent scores for all of these reasons. You may well ask: If such scores are so bad, why do test publishers compute them in the first place? The answer publishers often give is that educators demand grade-equivalent scores. The publishers are well aware of their limitations, of course, but contend that eliminating them would put them at a competitive disadvantage. Perhaps the solution to this dilemma lies in fostering better awareness in educators, policymakers, and other stakeholders who use test results. Until awareness is heightened, however, the best advice that can be offered to practitioners in the position of interpreting test results is simply to ignore grade-equivalent scores.

An important exception to the problematic nature of grade equivalents is the case of individually administered tests that have a large sequence of items progressing in difficulty. Special educators often use such tests. An example is the Peabody Picture Vocabulary Test—Fifth Edition (PPVT-5; Dunn, 2019), which has items ranging from very simple to very difficult. Because of this range and because easier items have actually been administered to younger students and the harder ones to older students, age and grade equivalents are much more meaningful.

Suggestions for "Reading" a Student Profile

The array of data contained in the score report for an individual student can be perplexing. The following suggestions are offered as a means of navigating this maze of data.

1. Ignore grade-equivalent scores. For all of the reasons we have discussed, such scores offer no usable information to teachers.
2. Consider the reading comprehension score as the best indicator of overall reading achievement.
3. In the case of low scores, note whether the number of items attempted is the same as the number possible, especially for subtests that are out of line with the general profile.

4. Be skeptical of specific skill results based on very few items. It is common for skill breakdowns to include results based on only a handful of items corresponding to a particular skill. The reliability of these embedded subtests is extremely low, and daily classwork constitutes a far better indicator of skill deficits. (See the sample contained in Figure 2.3.)

5. Use the national stanine to interpret achievement for each subtest. The percentile rank is more precise in some ways, but stanines can be more easily interpreted, as follows:

> Stanines 7–9 = Above average
> Stanine 6 = Borderline above average
> Stanine 5 = Average
> Stanine 4 = Borderline below average
> Stanines 1–3 = Below average

6. Use the two-stanine rule to compare subtest scores. Remember that if the difference is at least two stanines, there is a statistically good chance that a real difference exists. You cannot know precisely how large the difference is, however.

7. Use group achievement scores for broad-based screening purposes only. Be prepared to reinterpret results, using other evidence that may be more dependable. Such evidence might include classroom performance, results of individual assessments, and teacher observations.

8. Be on the lookout for students who do not take the testing seriously. It is unfortunately commonplace for some students to expend only minimal effort on taking achievement tests. The scores they produce are virtually worthless, and it is

Student: Joe Kelly
School: Kashinkerry Elementary
Grade: 03
Test Date: March

	Reading Subtests		
	Total Reading	Reading Vocabulary	Reading Comprehension
Number Possible	84	30	54
Raw Score	45	17	28
Scaled Score	590	582	595
National Percentile Rank	23–4	23–4	26–4
National Stanine	4	4	4
National NCE	34.4	34.4	34.4
Grade Equivalent	2.7	2.7	2.7

FIGURE 2.3. Sample reading profile from a fictitious nationally norm-referenced group achievement test. NCE, normal curve equivalent.

important to know who these students are. Otherwise, mistakes can be made when their achievement is being evaluated. Make a point of giving their names to next year's teachers if the results of the testing arrive too late in the year for you to make any use of them yourself.

The National Assessment of Educational Progress

The National Assessment of Educational Progress (NAEP) in reading is called "our nation's report card," since it is an assessment periodically given to students across the United States to assess growth in reading achievement over time. It has been administered since 1969, allowing policymakers to examine trends in achievement. The scores on the NAEP are reported on a scale from 0 to 500. These scores are developed separately for each subject area. All of the most up-to-date NAEP data can be found on *https:// nces.ed.gov/nationsreportcard*.

The NAEP does not report individual students' scores, and it does not report schoolwide scores for participating schools. Since 1990, scores have been reported for individual states, so that policymakers in states that participate (all states now do, but this has not always been the case) can compare the achievement of their students to that of students in other states and to the national averages.

If the test cannot be used for individual assessment, because the results are never reported that way, why discuss it here? We do so for two reasons. First, these results are widely reported in newspapers and other media, and it is important to understand what they are (and are not), so that teachers can respond intelligently. Second, the NAEP provides some benchmarks for judging children's performance, rather than only discussing how children scored in relation to a norming sample.

The NAEP reports scores in two ways. The first is the average scale score for the nation and for the states. A state's average can be compared with the nation's or with that of other states. For example, referring to the NAEP's reported reading scores on the website referenced above, we see that Maine's 2017 statewide average for grade 4 (221) was equal to the national average, whereas Virginia's was above average (228).

The second way in which results are reported are by benchmarks. The National Assessment Governing Board (2013) has divided performance into three levels: *Basic, Proficient,* and *Advanced.* These performance levels are translated into specific benchmarks for each grade.

Although these are listed as "benchmarks," they were designed as high standards for children to reach. The point of setting standards so high was that teachers would push their students toward these standards, rather than toward a more modest level of attainment. But children can fail to reach the Basic level for fourth grade, for example, and still demonstrate a literal understanding of what they read, understand a main idea from expository text, or follow a simple plot (Donahue, Voelkl, Campbell, & Mazzeo, 1999). These are all listed as below Basic skills at the 4th-grade level. At the 8th- and 12th-grade levels, below Basic implies an even higher level of skill. We need high standards to propel our students (and ourselves) to higher achievement, but we are concerned that statements such as "40% of our fourth graders are reading below the Basic level" can be misinterpreted.

Table 2.2 provides the definitions of all three benchmark levels for the 4th and 8th grades. Benchmark definitions for the 12th grade, and more information about the NAEP, can be found at *https://nces.ed.gov/nationsreportcard*. These definitions have been revised to reflect a better alignment with the Common Core State Standards (CCSS; National Governors Association Center for Best Practices and Council of Chief State School Officers [NGACBP & CCSSO], 2010). For example, there is careful attention to the distinction between informational and literary text, to the importance of an author's craft, and to texts that are argumentative in nature.

For policy planners, we suggest that a state's standing relative to the nation is less useful than the proportion of its students who read at each level. Figure 2.4 provides the distribution of 4th graders across these four levels for all 50 states. At the national level, note that 33% scored below the Basic level, 31% at the Basic level, 27% at the Proficient level, and 9% at the Advanced level.

Finally, the NAEP is a measure that is both standardized and formal, with aspects of a criterion-referenced measure. Item difficulties are calculated by comparing the numbers of children who got each item correct, creating a scale score. The test is formally administered according to a set of administration rules, but there also are criteria that were used to develop the test (the achievement-level definitions). Many state tests have been based on this model, being both formal and criterion-referenced.

RELIABILITY AND VALIDITY

Perhaps the most important statistical evaluators associated with tests are reliability and validity. These two related criteria are frequently confused. *Reliability* refers to the consistency of results—that is, the general dependability of a test. A test that produces similar results under similar conditions is said to be reliable. *Validity* refers to the degree to which a test measures what it purports to measure and what the examiner wishes to measure. Reliability is a prerequisite of validity, but validity is not needed for reliability. To put it another way, a valid test is always reliable, but a reliable test is not necessarily valid.

Consider an everyday analogy: McDonald's hamburgers. McDonald's hamburgers, we suggest, are reliable but not valid. If you walk into a McDonald's anywhere in the world, from Savannah to Hong Kong, you receive precisely the same product. Now that's reliability! But are these sandwiches what you really want when you think of a good hamburger? In our view, they are not. In other words, they are not valid examples of "true" hamburgers. To put it in testing terms, they have high reliability and low validity. The same can be true of a test. To use an extreme example, a math test may be highly reliable, but if used to assess reading ability, it would produce results that are clearly invalid.

Reliability is computed in various ways and is usually expressed as a decimal. The closer the reliability coefficient is to 1.00, the more reliable the test. Reliability coefficients of .90 or higher are considered extremely high and are hallmarks of reliable testing. Reliability is influenced by such factors as (1) the length of the test (the longer the test, the more reliable it is), (2) the clarity of directions, and (3) the objectivity of scoring.

Validity is a murkier concept and usually has no numerical translation. Rather, the producers of a commercial test simply make a case for its validity by presenting the evi-

TABLE 2.2. NAEP Performance-Level Definitions and Descriptions

---

Generic NAEP achievement levels and policy definitions

Basic

This level denotes partial mastery of prerequisite knowledge and skills that are fundamental for proficient work at each grade.

Proficient

This level represents solid academic performance for each grade assessed. Students reaching this level have demonstrated competency over challenging subject matter, including subject-matter knowledge, application of such knowledge to real-world situations, and analytical skills appropriate to the subject matter.

Advanced

This level signifies superior performance.

NAEP reading achievement levels at grade 4 and 8

Grade 4

Basic

Fourth-grade students performing at the Basic level should be able to locate relevant information, make simple inferences, and use their understanding of the text to identify details that support a given interpretation or conclusion. Students should be able to interpret the meaning of a word as it is used in the text.

When reading **literary** texts such as fiction, poetry, and literary nonfiction, fourth-grade students performing at the Basic level should be able to make simple inferences about characters, events, plot, and setting. They should be able to identify a problem in a story and relevant information that supports an interpretation of a text.

When reading **informational** texts such as articles and excerpts from books, fourth-grade students performing at the Basic level should be able to identify the main purpose and an explicitly stated main idea, as well as gather information from various parts of a text to provide supporting information.

Proficient

Fourth-grade students performing at the Proficient level should be able to integrate and interpret texts and apply their understanding of the text to draw conclusions and make evaluations.

When reading **literary** texts such as fiction, poetry, and literary nonfiction, fourth-grade students performing at the Proficient level should be able to identify implicit main ideas and recognize relevant information that supports them. Students should be able to judge elements of author's craft and provide some support for their judgment. They should be able to analyze character roles, actions, feelings, and motives.

When reading **informational** texts such as articles and excerpts from books, fourth-grade students performing at the Proficient level should be able to locate relevant information, integrate information across texts, and evaluate the way an author presents information. Student performance at this level should demonstrate an understanding of the purpose for text features and an ability to integrate information from headings, text boxes, graphics, and their captions. They should be able to explain a simple cause-and-effect relationship and draw conclusions.

Advanced

Fourth-grade students performing at the Advanced level should be able to make complex inferences and construct and support their inferential understanding of the text. Students should be able to apply their understanding of a text to make and support a judgment.

When reading **literary** texts such as fiction, poetry, and literary nonfiction, fourth-grade students performing at the Advanced level should be able to identify the theme in stories and poems and make complex inferences about characters' traits, feelings, motivations, and actions. They should be able to recognize characters' perspectives and evaluate character motivation. Students should be able to interpret characteristics of poems and evaluate aspects of text organization.

(continued)

TABLE 2.2. *(continued)*

When reading **informational** texts such as articles and excerpts from books, fourth-grade students performing at the Advanced level should be able to make complex inferences about main ideas and supporting ideas. They should be able to express a judgment about the text and about text features and support the judgment with evidence. They should be able to identify the most likely cause given an effect, explain an author's point of view, and compare ideas across two texts.

Grade 8

Basic

Eighth-grade students performing at the Basic level should be able to locate information; identify statements of main idea, theme, or author's purpose; and make simple inferences from texts. They should be able to interpret the meaning of a word as it is used in the text. Students performing at this level should also be able to state judgments and give some support about content and presentation of content.

When reading **literary** texts such as fiction, poetry, and literary nonfiction, eighth-grade students performing at the Basic level should recognize major themes and be able to identify, describe, and make simple inferences about setting and about character motivations, traits, and experiences. They should be able to state and provide some support for judgments about the way an author presents content and about character motivation.

When reading **informational** texts such as exposition and argumentation, eighth-grade students performing at the Basic level should be able to recognize inferences based on main ideas and supporting details. They should be able to locate and provide relevant facts to construct general statements about information from the text. Students should be able to provide some support for judgments about the way information is presented.

Proficient

Eighth-grade students performing at the Proficient level should be able to provide relevant information and summarize main ideas and themes. They should be able to make and support inferences about a text, connect parts of a text, and analyze text features. Students performing at this level should also be able to fully substantiate judgments about content and presentation of content.

When reading **literary** texts such as fiction, poetry, and literary nonfiction, eighth-grade students performing at the Proficient level should be able to make and support a connection between characters from two parts of a text.

They should be able to recognize character actions and infer and support character feelings. Students performing at this level should be able to provide and support judgments about character motivation across texts. They should be able to identify how figurative language is used.

When reading **informational** texts such as exposition and argumentation, eighth-grade students performing at the Proficient level should be able to locate and provide facts and relevant information that support a main idea or purpose, interpret causal relations, provide and support a judgment about the author's argument or stance, and recognize rhetorical devices.

Advanced

Eighth-grade students performing at the Advanced level should be able to make connections within and across texts and to explain causal relations. They should be able to evaluate and justify the strength of supporting evidence and the quality of an author's presentation. Students performing at the advanced level also should be able to manage the processing demands of analysis and evaluation by stating, explaining, and justifying.

When reading **literary** texts such as fiction, literary nonfiction, and poetry, eighth-grade students performing at the Advanced level should be able to explain the effects of narrative events. Within or across text, they should be able to make thematic connections and make inferences about character feelings, motivations, and experiences.

When reading **informational** texts such as exposition and argumentation, eighth-grade students performing at the Advanced level should be able to infer and explain a variety of connections that are intratextual (such as the relation between specific information and the main idea) or intertextual (such as the relation of ideas across expository and argument text). Within and across texts, students should be able to state and justify judgments about text features, choice of content, and the author's use of evidence and rhetorical devices.

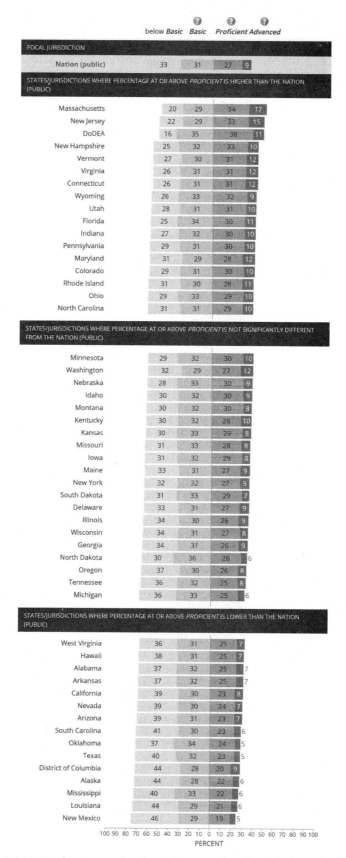

below *Basic* *Basic* *Proficient* *Advanced*

FOCAL JURISDICTION

	below Basic	Basic	Proficient	Advanced
Nation (public)	33	31	27	9

STATES/JURISDICTIONS WHERE PERCENTAGE AT OR ABOVE *PROFICIENT* IS HIGHER THAN THE NATION (PUBLIC)

	below Basic	Basic	Proficient	Advanced
Massachusetts	20	29	34	17
New Jersey	22	29	33	15
DoDEA	16	35	38	11
New Hampshire	25	32	33	10
Vermont	27	30	31	12
Virginia	26	31	31	12
Connecticut	26	31	31	12
Wyoming	26	33	32	9
Utah	28	31	31	10
Florida	25	34	30	11
Indiana	27	32	30	10
Pennsylvania	29	31	30	10
Maryland	31	29	28	12
Colorado	29	31	30	10
Rhode Island	31	30	28	11
Ohio	29	33	29	10
North Carolina	31	31	29	10

STATES/JURISDICTIONS WHERE PERCENTAGE AT OR ABOVE *PROFICIENT* IS NOT SIGNIFICANTLY DIFFERENT FROM THE NATION (PUBLIC)

	below Basic	Basic	Proficient	Advanced
Minnesota	29	32	30	10
Washington	32	29	27	12
Nebraska	28	33	30	9
Idaho	30	32	30	9
Montana	30	32	30	8
Kentucky	30	32	28	10
Kansas	30	33	29	8
Missouri	31	33	28	8
Iowa	31	32	29	8
Maine	33	31	27	9
New York	32	32	27	9
South Dakota	31	33	29	7
Delaware	33	31	27	9
Illinois	34	30	26	9
Wisconsin	34	31	27	8
Georgia	34	31	26	9
North Dakota	30	36	28	6
Oregon	37	30	26	8
Tennessee	36	32	25	8
Michigan	36	33	25	6

STATES/JURISDICTIONS WHERE PERCENTAGE AT OR ABOVE *PROFICIENT* IS LOWER THAN THE NATION (PUBLIC)

	below Basic	Basic	Proficient	Advanced
West Virginia	36	31	25	7
Hawaii	38	31	25	7
Alabama	37	32	25	7
Arkansas	37	32	25	7
California	39	30	23	8
Nevada	39	30	24	7
Arizona	39	31	23	7
South Carolina	41	30	23	6
Oklahoma	37	34	24	5
Texas	40	32	23	5
District of Columbia	44	28	20	9
Alaska	44	28	22	6
Mississippi	40	33	22	6
Louisiana	44	29	21	6
New Mexico	46	29	19	5

100 90 80 70 60 50 40 30 20 10 0 0 10 20 30 40 50 60 70 80 90 100
PERCENT

FIGURE 2.4. NAEP 2017 achievement-level results in reading for fourth-grade public school students by state/jurisdiction.

dence they have accumulated. It is up to consumers (i.e., teachers and administrators) to decide whether the test is truly valid for their purposes. Several types of validity are important; a quick overview may help clarify the general concept of validity.

Content Validity

A test that reflects the curriculum that is taught is said to possess *content validity*. The process of curriculum alignment, advocated by Fenwick English and others (English & Frase, 1999), is designed to ensure a good match between what is taught and what is tested, and is a popular means of improving content validity. Imagine a teacher who invests many hours in trying to foster critical reading comprehension ability, merely to find that students will be given only low-level questions on an achievement test. Such a test would have limited content validity for that teacher.

Construct Validity

Construct validity is how well a test measures what it was designed to measure. For example, the purpose of the DIBELS Next Retell Fluency subtest is to provide a measure of a child's reading comprehension after reading a passage (Good & Kaminski, 2011). This is done by counting the number of words (demonstrating the child's understanding of the story) that the child produces in 1 minute while retelling the just-read story. Many would argue that the number of words in a child's 1-minute retell of a partially read passage does not directly measure that child's comprehension of a text; therefore, this test would not have high construct validity.

Predictive Validity

Some tests are expressly designed to predict future performance or success. Results of the SAT and ACT, for instance, correlate well with the later college grade-point averages (GPAs) of the students who take them. College admissions officers use the results of these tests in the confidence that they do a good job of predicting success. That is to say, the tests possess good *predictive validity*.

In considering predictive validity, Paris (2005) theorizes that it may be important to distinguish among constrained and unconstrained skills. According to Paris, *constrained skills* are those skills that "develop from nonexistent to high or ceiling levels in childhood" (p. 187). Concepts about print, alphabetic knowledge, and phonics are highly constrained. Phonemic awareness and oral reading fluency are less constrained. However, comprehension and vocabulary are unconstrained, due to their scope, importance, and range of influence in domain and time span. They tend to develop over a lifetime. Simply put, some skills are mastered, whereas others continue to develop. This distinction can cause problems when the two types are both treated in the same way. As a result, we advise caution in using data analysis related to constrained skills to form developmental trajectories for more general reading proficiency (Paris, 2005; Riedel, 2007).

Concurrent Validity

If a new measure and an established measure are administered at about the same time to the same students, and if the two scores turn out to be highly correlated, this result can be regarded as evidence of validity for the new test. Because the two measures are administered at almost the same time, we call a strong relationship evidence of *concurrent validity*. When, for example, a convenient, easy-to-give measure such as the San Diego Quick Assessment (SDQA; see Chapter 8) is shown to provide reading-level estimates that are the same as or similar to those provided by more complex tests, evidence of concurrent validity is established.

Consequential Validity

Consequential validity addresses the consequences of test administration and score interpretation. Messick (1993) states that "the appraisal of the functional worth of the testing in pursuit of the intended ends should take into account all of the ends, both intended and unintended, that are advanced by the testing application, including not only individual and institutional effects but societal and systemic effects as well" (p. 85). Considering the consequences of the administration of a test, and interpreting test results as a validation of educational tests, are new and somewhat controversial ideas in psychometrics. What are the intended and unintended consequences of a particular assessment? Does the administration of a particular high-stakes test minimize the reading curriculum to skill-based instruction? Does the administration of a particular test yield instruction that supports a standards-based curriculum? Does the utilization of the assessment result in differentiated instruction that is targeted to each student's needs? These are a few questions that we might ask when considering the consequential validity of an assessment.

WHEN IS A TEST NOT A TEST?

Information useful in planning reading instruction does not always come in the form of test results. In fact, many teachers would argue that the most important information about students does not come from tests at all, but from other sources. These sources include written work, classroom observations, parent input, and portfolios.

Written Work

The products of written class assignments can provide important clues to a student's literacy development. Such products include compositions, journal entries, worksheets, e-mails, class notes, and many others. For younger children, written work samples may include scribbling and early writing, which yield potentially rich data about spelling development and phonological awareness.

Classroom Observations

As students engage in reading and writing activities during the school day, observant teachers often discern patterns useful in monitoring growth and identifying needs. Yetta Goodman has called this process *kidwatching* (e.g., Owocki & Goodman, 2002). In some cases, structured observations can be helpful, such as checklists of key behaviors. Unstructured observations are useful as well, especially for experienced teachers who know what they are looking for in terms of behavioral cues. In this case, a teacher notices a revealing pattern and either makes a mental note of it or (better yet) makes a brief anecdotal record for later reference.

Parent Input

Telephone conversations with parents, and remarks they make during face-to-face conferences, can provide insights into a child's behaviors. Documenting such input by making quick, dated notes for later reference can be useful. Occasionally, parent input also comes in written forms, such as notes, e-mails, or letters sent to the teacher or other educators.

Portfolios

A literacy portfolio is a collection of evidence that enables a teacher to document progress over time. The evidence might include the following:

- Samples of daily work
- Coded passages read orally by the student
- A chart of reading rate over time
- A record of reading interests and books read
- Journal entries (or anecdotal notes) by the teacher
- Journal entries by the student
- Test results

This list is far from exhaustive. Creative teachers can build portfolio contents that provide telling glimpses into the literacy growth and development of individual students. Following are guidelines and suggestions for getting started with portfolio projects.

1. All of the evidence should be dated, so that progress over time can be interpreted. Leafing through a portfolio, from start to finish, can provide a long-term perspective that would otherwise be hard to gain.
2. Unless a teacher is fairly selective about what is included in it, the portfolio can rapidly become cumbersome, difficult to store, and hard to use.
3. Roger Farr (1992) recommends keeping two portfolios for each student. One he terms the *working* portfolio, as described above. This is the portfolio used to monitor progress and guide instructional decision making. The other is the *show* portfolio, a dated collection of the student's best work. It is far smaller than the working portfolio and is used to signal progress during student conferences and

to discuss a student's strengths and needs during parent conferences. If you think that keeping two portfolios might be unmanageable, a compromise might consist of keeping only the working type and using sticky notes to identify specific entries prior to a conference so that they can be quickly located.

4. Consider passing portfolios along to next year's teachers. Logistics can be troublesome, but putting a well-maintained portfolio into the right hands can provide a wealth of information at the start of a new school year. Think how you might feel if you were on the receiving end of such a policy!

5. Use portfolios during postobservation conferences with an administrator or literacy coach. Their contents can enrich the discussion considerably and also document why you might have used certain instructional techniques with particular students. The observing administrator will not fail to be impressed, for portfolios are clearly one mark of a reflective teacher intent on using evidence of student performance to guide instructional planning.

SUMMARY

There are many different options available for assessment, and many different users of educational assessment. At the highest levels, policymakers in state and federal government might use information from the NAEP to judge the effectiveness of reading instruction in an entire state or the nation. These results can provide rough estimates of whether policies are improving achievement. Standardized norm- or criterion-referenced tests can provide a school superintendent with the same type of data on a smaller scale. These tests can tell the superintendent or the school board about the overall effectiveness of a curriculum in a district, or the performances of individual schools. Used correctly, standardized tests can provide important information about reading programs used in a district.

For an individual teacher, however, such measures usually do not provide much information above and beyond that available through informal measures and observations. Because of the standard error of measurement, scores on norm-referenced tests are rarely sufficiently accurate by themselves for individual interpretation. At best, they may be used to screen children. If a child does particularly poorly or particularly well, the teacher may want to retest the child with an IRI to confirm the score of the norm-referenced test. If the IRI produces divergent results, the teacher should at least question the results of the norm-referenced test. IRIs, running records, and other measures are closer to the child's curriculum and may be more relevant for individual diagnosis and planning instruction.

THREE

Informal Reading Inventories and Other Measures of Oral Reading

In reading assessment, we are always asking questions and using the results of our assessments to answer these questions. At the end of Chapter 1, we have asked a series of questions about children's reading skills. From our model, we are concerned globally about the child's abilities in the areas of automatic word recognition, language comprehension, and strategic knowledge. An expanded list of questions follows.

WHAT DO WE WANT TO LEARN FROM A READING ASSESSMENT?

Questions	Sources of information
Automatic word recognition	
Does the child read fluently and naturally?	Oral reading sample, observations
What level material should the child use for instruction?	Oral reading sample, level
Does the child use context to complement inadequate decoding skills?	Miscue analysis of oral reading
Does the child self-correct?	Miscue analysis of oral reading, observations
Does the child read words better in context or in isolation?	Oral reading sample, word lists, observations
With which spelling patterns is the child familiar?	Criterion-referenced decoding test, invented spellings, spelling inventory

Questions	Sources of information
Can the child decode words in isolation that he or she cannot decode in context? Or vice versa?	Comparison of decoding test with miscue analysis of oral reading
Does the child have an adequate level of phonemic awareness?	Phonological awareness inventory
What is the child's knowledge of basic print concepts?	Concepts about print tests, oral reading sample

Language comprehension

What level material can the child comprehend when reading silently?	Silent reading sample, informal reading inventory (IRI)
What level material can the child comprehend when reading orally?	Oral reading sample, IRI
Does the child comprehend better when reading orally than silently?	Comparison of oral and silent reading
Does the child comprehend what he or she can accurately read?	Oral reading sample, IRI
What types of questions give the child trouble?	Systematic examination of literal, inferential, etc., questions on IRI
Does the child understand material at his or her grade level when it is read aloud by the teacher?	Listening comprehension passage
Does the child have an adequate vocabulary for understanding?	Informal observations during discussions See Chapter 7
Does the child use text structure to aid in comprehension?	Retellings
Does the child have adequate background knowledge?	Background knowledge measures (varies with each story read)
What does the child do when he or she lacks background knowledge?	Analysis of IRI responses

Strategic control

Does the child use varied strategies flexibly during reading?	See Chapter 9
Does the child understand the purposes of reading?	See Chapters 9 and 10
How positive is the child's attitude toward reading?	See Chapter 10

A quick review of this table suggests that a great many of the questions we raise about children's reading can be answered through the sensitive use of an oral reading sample. Such a sample can come from an IRI or from running records. Many of the other questions can be answered through the use of other parts of the IRI—the silent reading and listening comprehension sections and the word list. For that reason, we consider the IRI to be the cornerstone of the reading assessment process. In addition to being a diagnostic assessment, an IRI can serve as a screening assessment, but it must be complemented by more targeted measures (Stahl & McKenna, 2013; Walpole & McKenna, 2006). Consequently, many of the other assessments in this book are used to confirm, elaborate, or explain the results garnered from an IRI. Relatively easy to administer (once a teacher has learned some simple notations), an IRI in the hands of a well-trained practitioner provides a great deal of information about a child's reading strengths and weaknesses. We believe that the results of a *traditional* IRI are needed to inform the instruction of any child with serious reading difficulties, particularly those children with identified reading disabilities. In this chapter, we also address the running record and the "benchmark kit" as other forms of reading assessments that are kin to the traditional IRI. In addition, teachers can use the analytic processes involved in interpreting an IRI in their everyday observations of children's reading. Therefore, familiarity with the IRI is a keystone for the teacher of reading.

What Is an IRI?

An IRI consists mainly of a sequence of graded passages, typically beginning at the preprimer level. Today most IRIs provide tables that align the grade-level passages with a refined primary text-level equivalency (e.g., Fountas & Pinnell, 2006) or a Lexile. Each passage is followed by comprehension questions and, occasionally, a retelling scoring guide. Most IRIs are also equipped with graded word lists for estimating where to begin in the passages and for assessing a child's ability to recognize words in isolation.

For each passage the child reads, the teacher judges whether the passage is on the child's independent, instructional, or frustration level. (We define these levels more precisely in a moment.) This judgment is based on accuracy of word recognition and success in answering the comprehension questions posed orally by the teacher. Fluency should also be considered in the determination of reading level. The teacher shows the child a copy of the passage and makes notations on a separate copy that includes the questions and scoring guides. Once the child completes a passage, the teacher must decide which, if any, of the remaining passages in a sequence should be given next. Following the IRI administration, the teacher must consider the child's performance on all of the passages read and then make an overall judgment as to the child's instructional reading level.

The summary form (Form 3.1, p. 75) is a generic table used to record, in an organized manner, some of the most important data produced by an IRI administration. Additionally, Case Study 1 in the Appendix (pp. 295–298) provides an example of a completed summary sheet with a brief analysis of the results. The summary tables found in commercial IRIs vary, of course.

Reading Levels

Traditionally, children were assigned a reading level by means of an IRI. These levels were based on those determined by Emmett Betts in the 1930s (see Betts, 1946). A passage of a particular readability level was judged to represent a child's independent, instructional, or frustration level, as defined below:

- *Independent level* is the highest level at which a child can read the material without assistance.
- *Instructional level* is the highest level at which a child could benefit from instructional support.
- *Frustration level* is any level at which a child is likely to be frustrated, even with instructional support.

How are these levels estimated by using an IRI? When the results of an IRI are quantified into percentages of questions answered correctly and percentages of words read accurately aloud, these two percentages can be used to estimate a child's reading levels. Conventionally, the independent level has been defined as the highest level at which a child can read with 99% accuracy and with at least 90% comprehension. The instructional level has been defined as the highest-level passage a child can read with 95–98% oral accuracy and with at least 75% comprehension. The frustration level has been defined as the lowest level at which the child can read with 90% or lower oral accuracy and with 50% comprehension or below. These criteria are presented in Table 3.1.

This classification has been used to the present day in many commercial IRIs (e.g., Johns, 2017; Leslie & Caldwell, 2016). There are problems with a strict application of such criteria, however. To begin with, comprehension assessment depends on the quality of the questions used. Some questions are more difficult; some are easier. A child's performance depends on the difficulty of the questions, and asking a different set of questions can lead to a different conclusion about whether a particular passage is on a child's independent, instructional, or frustration level (Peterson, Greenlaw, & Tierney, 1978). Therefore, when a teacher is selecting an IRI, it is wise to choose one that has been widely field-tested over time. It increases the likelihood that poor-quality questions have

TABLE 3.1. Criteria for Interpreting IRI Performance

Level	Flash word list recognition	Word recognition in context	Comprehension
Independent	90–100%	99–100%	90–100%
Instructional	75–89%	95–98%	75–89%
Gray area	50–74%	91–94%	51–74%
Frustration	Below 50%	90% or lower	50% or lower

Note. Flash word recognition criteria are from Betts's student Stauffer (Stauffer et al., 1978). Word recognition in context and comprehension criteria are from Betts (1946).

been eliminated through the process of ongoing psychometric validity and reliability checks conducted by the IRI developers.

Some researchers have questioned the oral accuracy levels. Clay (2013) and Fountas and Pinnell (2010) use a 90% accuracy level as the boundary for the instructional level through the end of first grade. This criterion makes sense, considering that the children are likely to receive supportive individualized or small-group instruction as they read simplistic picture books at this level.

It is also not clear whether the 95% cutoff for the instructional level should include self-corrections or how semantically acceptable miscues should be handled (e.g., substituting *crimson* for *scarlet*). Some IRIs recommend that semantically acceptable miscues be considered acceptable deviations from the text and not counted as errors. Others instruct users to count all miscues as errors. Some commercial IRIs, such as the Qualitative Reading Inventory–6 (Leslie & Caldwell, 2016), provide two ways of determining the instructional level: (1) counting all miscues and (2) counting only those that significantly change the meaning of the text.

It may strike you that Betts (1946) set a very high standard for oral accuracy, including high percentages and verbatim-only acceptability. Keep in mind that Betts based his notion of instructional levels on the instruction typical of the time. During that era, the directed reading activity (also developed by Betts) was the most commonly used instructional model. In this model, prior to reading, the teacher provides background information; preteaches key vocabulary; and provides a purpose or focus for reading. Children read segments of the text silently, stopping to discuss teacher-posed questions. Children reread the text that addresses the answer of the question orally. Following the reading of the whole selection, children answer a series of postreading questions. The directed reading activity provides relatively minimal instruction compared to more recent models.

In Fluency-Oriented Reading Instruction (FORI; Stahl & Heubach, 2005; see Chapter 6), the entire text is first read and discussed, followed by a number of repeated readings of the text. In this approach, children receive considerably more support in reading the text and thus should be able to benefit from reading more difficult text. Stahl and his colleagues found that children could benefit from reading text with only 85% accuracy—texts that would conventionally be considered to be at the frustration level—at the beginning of instruction. Like the accuracy criterion, this cutoff is also more consistent with the CCSS, because it results in the placement of children in more complex texts. Additionally, in order to close the achievement gap, it is essential for low-level readers to be exposed to texts above their instructional level in supportive settings.

Although determining an instructional level is diagnostically useful, we do not want to constrain a student's reading to texts at that level. In fact, research indicates that children can make accelerated progress when reading texts considerably above their instructional level (Brown, Mohr, Wilcox, & Barrett, 2018; O'Connor, Bell, Harty, & Larkin, 2002; Stahl & Heubach, 2005), This research demonstrates that supportive instruction using challenging texts in whole-class settings, student dyads, and intervention groups yields gains in achievement and motivation.

These findings do not imply that all children can read all texts. Consider Vygotsky's (1978) notion of the *zone of proximal development* (ZPD). Vygotsky suggested that children can do their most productive work within a particular zone. The bottom end of the zone (the easiest material) is the level at which children can work independently. The top end of the zone (the most difficult material) is the most challenging level, at which children can work successfully with extensive teacher support. Above that level, children cannot work productively with material even with teacher support. Our experience is that children can work with material that is relatively difficult, but still within the ZPD, if the teacher plans to provide extra support. Sometimes this support is provided through repeated readings or assisted readings of various kinds; at other times it can be provided through direct comprehension support, such as through reciprocal teaching. In short, across the day, a student should spend a significant amount of time reading texts at his or her estimated instructional level, but should also be exposed to so-called "stretch" texts (ones that they can read and comprehend with support).

This elasticity of readability and its relationship with instruction can be demonstrated through a discussion of the CCSS and the range of instructional contexts that are part of each classroom's literacy block. In order for students to achieve the CCSS, it is necessary for them to be exposed to challenging text that may be beyond their traditionally computed instructional reading levels of cold, unfamiliar text. Column 1 of Table 3.2 displays the CCSS text-level expectations, using the Lexile readability metric. Column

TABLE 3.2. Sample Text Levels for Classroom Reading Contexts

	Read-aloud	Shared reading	Guided reading
Kindergarten	Wide variety	Wide variety	A–D
Grade 1 CCSS 530L	G–M 190L–600L	F–K 100L–550L	D–J 190L–500L
Grade 2 CCSS 650L	L–P 500L–700L	K–N 475L–650L	J–M 425L–600L
Grade 3 CCSS 820L	O–S 700L–825L	N–Q 650L–800L	M–P 600L–750L
Grade 4 CCSS 940L	R–V 800L–950L	Q–T 775L–925L	P–S 750L–890L
Grade 5 CCSS 1010L	U–Y 935L–1020L	T–W 825L–1000L	S–V 800L–950L
Grade 6 CCSS 1070L	925L–1185L	V/W–Y 920L–1075L	
Grade 7 CCSS 1120L	925L–1185L	Y–Z 980L–1140L	
Grade 8 CCSS 1185L	>1000L	Y–Z 980L–1140L	

Note. Guided reading levels are based on Fountas and Pinnell's (2017) progress-monitoring grade-level recommendations. Lexiles are based on the College and Career Ready measures to guide reading.

4 presents the text-level expectations, based on the Fountas and Pinnell (2017) progress-monitoring trajectory and Lexile estimates for meeting College and Career Ready expectations. The level in column 4 is the level at which a child would be held accountable for successfully reading, understanding, and using the text with a bit of instructional support. However, this doesn't mean that the more challenging texts being required by the CCSS are bound to be frustrating for the students. It does mean that more instruction is required as the texts become more complex. Columns 2 and 3 provide some rough estimates of the level of support that might be required for the more difficult texts. The most difficult texts, or texts at the top of the students' ZPD, should be conducted as interactive teacher read-alouds. Texts that are challenging but within the students' ZPD would be included in shared reading, which would also involve supportive text reading (e.g., teacher-led, repeated, close reading; extensive discussion; and follow-up writing activities). These are not rigid, clearly defined boundaries! They should only be used as a reminder that teachers need to be cognizant of the estimated readability of texts and be deliberate in incorporating stretch texts in the curriculum for all students with instructional adjustments as needed.

We do not have precise guidelines for determining a ZPD for each child in an intervention or clinical setting. Our rough-and-ready guess is that if you are using intensive teaching techniques in a one-to-one or small-group intervention setting, you might try starting slightly above a child's instructional level, as measured by a conventional IRI. This is a guess, but it has worked well in our clinic. In both intervention and classroom settings, you need to monitor what the children are doing and make sure that the children are successful with, but somewhat challenged by, the level of material you are using.

GUIDELINES FOR ADMINISTERING AN IRI

There is no single best way to give an IRI. Much depends on what you want to know. The IRI is like a toolkit that can be used for a variety of purposes; not all of it may be appropriate on a given occasion, and the ways you use it will vary. It is imperative for you to familiarize yourself with your IRI manual. Although there are similarities across all IRIs, there are individual nuances in each. Additionally, passage differences, minor differences in administration and scoring procedures, test norms that may be included, and other unique attributes make it important to study the IRI that you have chosen.

This does not mean that there is no consensus about useful approaches to giving IRIs, however. If your goal is to estimate a child's instructional reading level and, in the process, gather data about how the child decodes words, then the following general steps may be helpful. But remember that as a teacher, you are empowered to "veto" any of these steps if the specific circumstances appear to warrant it.

Overall Strategy for Giving the IRI

1. *Estimate the child's independent reading level.* One way of doing this is by examining any available evidence you may have, such as classroom performance, results of a previous IRI, and so on. Another way is to give the graded word lists

of the IRI and to consider the highest word list on which no words are missed to be a tentative estimate of the independent reading level.

2. *Administer the passage corresponding to your estimate of the independent level.* Have the student read this passage orally while you code miscues. Then assess comprehension by asking the reader to provide a retelling and ask the comprehension questions. At this point, you must judge whether the passage is at the independent reading level by considering both the word-recognition accuracy (number of oral reading errors) and the child's comprehension performance (number of questions missed).

3. *Decide which passage to administer next.* If the initial passage is above the child's independent reading level, you must proceed to simpler passages until the independent level is reached. If the initial passage is judged to be at the student's independent reading level, you should proceed to more difficult passages until frustration is reached or appears to be imminent. In any case, each time you complete a passage, you must decide which passage to give next or whether to discontinue the IRI.

Strategy for Administering the Word Lists

Both word recognition in isolation and word recognition in context are important information sources. In a traditional IRI, the isolated word list is used to determine the starting point for administering the passages. However, it also provides a clean measure of a student's automatic word recognition, free of reliance on context. Most assessments define *automatic recognition* as correct pronunciation within 1 second. The best way to do this test is to make a timed PowerPoint slide presentation. Put a single word on each slide, with the timing mechanism set for a 1-second display (use what your manual suggests). This also guarantees consistency of administration between multiple test administrators.

1. Begin the word lists at the beginning for young students and approximately 2 years below the grade level of older students. Older students may also be given all lists if they lack confidence or are likely to be performing at lower levels.

2. Administer the timed slide show of a single graded word list, checking off the words that the child identifies automatically on a scoresheet with one column for timed responses and another column for untimed responses. Be sure to record the incorrect responses.

3. At the end of the timed administration of a single list, revisit each word that the child skipped or got wrong. Provide approximately 3 seconds for the "untimed" identification. Record a check to indicate correct pronunciations, write the substitutions or phonetic representations of incorrect responses, and designate 0 for no response.

4. At the end of each list, decide whether to go up or down to the next list or to stop. The flash scores are the most valid predictors of a contextual reading level (Morris et al., 2011). Morris suggests moving to the next word list when the student gets 50% or more on the flash test (follow the guidelines in your manual). Begin

the passage reading at the highest grade level where the student scored 80% or better on the flash word recognition (Morris, 2014).

Strategy for Giving Each Passage

1. Audio-record the entire passage administration.
2. Briefly prepare the student by asking a question that taps prior knowledge or by identifying the topic.
3. Ask the student to read the passage aloud or silently. *Remind the student to read carefully, because he or she will be asked to answer questions/retell at the end.*
4. If the student reads at mid-first-grade level or beyond, note the exact beginning time.
5. Code oral miscues as the child reads.
6. If the child hesitates too long (3–5 seconds; see your IRI manual), supply the word.
7. Discontinue the passage and do not ask the questions if:
   a. the passage is so difficult that you are reasonably sure it would be judged at the frustration level; or
   b. you have had to supply, in your judgment, too many words; or
   c. the reading rate has dropped significantly.
8. If you are recording reading rate, note the exact ending time.
9. Ask the child to retell the text as though he or she is telling it to someone who has not heard it. Take careful notes, or highlight your scoresheet text to document the retelling.
10. Ask the comprehension questions, giving partial credit where you feel it is warranted and rewording questions if you think it will help communicate what a given question asks. Give credit for questions that were reported in the retelling.
11. Use the appropriate formula below to calculate the words read correctly per minute (WCPM) for oral reading or words per minute (WPM) for silent reading. Then use fluency norms (such as Hasbrouck & Tindal's; see Chapter 6, Table 6.4, p. 161) to determine proficiency.

$$\text{WPM} = 60 \times \frac{\text{Number of words in passage}}{\text{Number of seconds needed to read passage}}$$

$$\text{WCPM} = 60 \times \frac{(\text{Number of words in passage} - \text{errors})}{\text{Number of seconds needed to read passage}}$$

12. Use the scoring guidelines to determine the level of the passage in terms of (a) oral accuracy and (b) comprehension. Come to an overall judgment as to whether the passage is at the child's independent, instructional, or frustration level. Sometimes this judgment may not be clear-cut. Use the data from the isolated word list, the reading rate, and the retelling data to inform your decision when the accuracy data and comprehension question scores are ambiguous.

Coding Oral Reading

As the child reads a passage, mark departures from the printed text. The goal is to create a record that can be "played back" later. These departures are often called *miscues,* rather than errors, because the reader may be using certain "cues" about a word (graphophonic, syntactic, or semantic). Major types of miscues include the following:

1. *Omission.* A word is skipped during oral reading.
2. *Insertion.* The reader says a word or phrase that is not in the text.
3. *Substitution.* The reader replaces a printed word with another.
4. *Reversal.* The reader changes the order of the printed words. (Changing the order of letters within a single word, such as saying *was* for *saw,* is a type of substitution.)
5. *Teacher-supplied word.* The reader hesitates long enough that the teacher steps in and pronounces the word in order to keep the process moving.
6. *Repetition.* The reader repeats a word or phrase, sometimes for better enunciation, sometimes to monitor comprehension.
7. *Ignoring punctuation.* The reader ignores commas, periods, question marks, and so forth, so that the oral reading is not meaningful and fluent, even though word accuracy may be quite high.
8. *Hesitation.* The reader hesitates, but not long enough that the teacher pronounces the word.
9. *Self-correction.* The child rereads one or more words in order to correct an error.

Not everyone agrees on how these miscues should be coded. The following examples represent conventional practice. In the end, it matters very little as long as (1) a teacher is consistent, and (2) teachers with whom coded passages may be shared are familiar with the system being used. As with all assessments, scoring must be complete, neat, and legible!

1. Text: Jim called me yesterday.
   Child: Jim called me.
   Coding: Jim called me ~~yesterday~~.

2. Text: Jim called me yesterday.
   Child: Jim called me up yesterday.

                       up
   Coding: Jim called me yesterday.
                       ^

3. Text: Jim called me yesterday.
   Child: Jim called me today.

                          today
   Coding: Jim called me ~~yesterday~~.

4. Text: Jim called me yesterday.
   Child: Jim called me me yesterday.
                              me
   Coding: Jim called me yesterday.
                           ^

5. Text: Jim called me yesterday.
   Child: Jim called me (*brief pause*) yesterday.
   Coding: Jim called me | yesterday.

6. Text: Jim called me yesterday.
   Child: Jim called me (*pause, word pronounced by teacher*) yesterday.
                              P
   Coding: Jim called me yesterday.

7. Text: Jim called me yesterday.
   Child: Yesterday Jim called me.
   Coding: Yesterday ⟍ Jim called me.

8. Text: Jim called me yesterday.
   Child: Jime called me yesterday.
              Jime
   Coding: Jim called me yesterday.
              (Or you could simply write a macron over the *i*.)

9. Text: Jim called me yesterday.
   Child: John phoned me sometime yesterday.
              John phoned sometime
   Coding: Jim called me yesterday.
                           ^

10. Text: Jim called me yesterday.
    Child: John Jim called me yesterday.
              John ✓
    Coding: Jim called me yesterday.

11. Text: Jim called me yesterday. We talked for an hour.
    Child: Jim called me yesterday we talked for an hour.
    Coding: Jim called me yesterday.   We talked for an hour.

Counting Miscues

Which miscues are tallied to determine the oral accuracy percentage? The answer to
this question may alter the results and lead to different conclusions about whether the
passage is on the child's independent, instructional, or frustration level. The question is

really twofold. First, can certain types of miscues be disregarded in counting the total? Conventional wisdom suggests that hesitations and ignoring punctuation should not be counted. This policy leaves the following:

1. Omissions
2. Insertions
3. Substitutions
4. Reversals
5. Teacher-supplied words
6. Repetitions

Authorities (including the authors of commercial IRIs) agree on the first five, but remain split on the issue of repetitions. Some studies indicate that counting them lends validity to the scoring criteria developed by Emmett Betts, who created the first IRIs (McKenna, 1983). Others argue that repetitions are healthy signs of comprehension monitoring and, in any case, involve no departure from the printed text. Perhaps the best advice is to adopt the policy recommended by the instrument a teacher is actually using, since it has probably been field-tested by professionals using that guideline.

The second question is whether to consider the semantic acceptability of a miscue in deciding whether to count it. When a child says *crimson* for *scarlet*, for example, it seems unjust to count it as an error. Unless the passage is from *Gone with the Wind*, the original meaning seems to have been preserved. Some authorities therefore recommend that the acceptability of any departure from the printed text be considered in arriving at an error tally. Our view is that the nature of miscues should be considered subjectively, as a source of potentially useful qualitative evidence, but that semantic acceptability should not be considered in arriving at an error count. There are several reasons for this policy. First, considering semantic acceptability is subjective; different examiners are likely to arrive at different tallies. Second, such a policy is time-consuming; IRIs already require a fair amount of time to administer and interpret, without compounding matters unnecessarily. Third, counting semantically acceptable miscues as correct would run counter to the findings of researchers who have determined that increased errors tend to alter the reading process, with reading becoming mechanical and less strategic (Clay, 2013; Killgallon, 1942; Kibby, 1979; McGee et al., 2015).

Applying Scoring Criteria

At the end of the examiner's copy of each passage are criteria for judging the child's performance. Separate criteria pertain to comprehension and to oral accuracy. Simple charts make it possible to arrive at rapid judgments, so that a teacher can decide which passage to administer next. These charts represent the error tallies and are tied to percentage criteria. Although authors differ about which criteria lead to the best estimates of reading levels, the most enduring are those suggested by Emmett Betts (1946; see Table 3.1).

The Betts criteria are somewhat strict, as we've discussed. Keep in mind that if more lenient criteria were used, the resulting estimate of a child's instructional level might be higher. Note also that the conjunction (*and* vs. *or*) is critically important. For example, for a passage to be judged on a child's independent reading level, the independent-level criteria for both comprehension *and* word recognition would need to be met. On the other hand, if either criterion for the frustration level is met, the passage is assumed to be at the frustration level. Later in this chapter, we reexamine how these criteria are applied.

GUIDELINES FOR INTERPRETING THE RESULTS OF AN IRI

The following guidelines may be useful for estimating a child's independent, instructional, and frustration levels after the IRI has been given.

1. Classify the student's performance on each passage given as independent, instructional, or frustration level. You may find it convenient to use the abbreviations IND, INST, and FRUS for this purpose. Use the lower level of word-recognition accuracy and comprehension, unless you are convinced to the contrary for reasons that are apparent during the testing.

   Examples:

Word recognition	Comprehension	Overall
IND	IND	IND
INST	INST	INST
FRUS	FRUS	FRUS
IND	INST	INST
INST	IND	INST
FRUS	IND	FRUS
INST	FRUS	FRUS

2. Estimate the independent level to be the highest level at which the overall judgment is IND.
3. Estimate the instructional level to be the highest level at which the overall judgment is INST.
4. Estimate the frustration level to be the lowest level at which the overall judgment is FRUS.
5. Ambiguous results are not unusual, especially above grade 2 when more factors are considered (oral and silent reading, narrative and expository text, familiar and unfamiliar content). Additionally, when scores fall in the gray area, we must dig more deeply into the other information that is available to us through the IRI process. We look at the isolated word-recognition data, the fluency performance, and retelling data for each passage. Example 3 provides a view of the comprehensive summary chart that allows the teacher to record and analyze the complete IRI data.

Example 1

Passage	Word recognition	Comprehension	Overall
PP	IND	IND	IND
P	IND	INST	INST
1	INST	INST	INST
2	INST	FRUS	FRUS

Independent level: PP

Instructional level: 1

Frustration level: 2

Example 2

Passage	Word recognition	Comprehension	Overall
PP	INST	IND	INST
P	INST	INST	INST
1	FRUS	INST	FRUS

Independent level: Not determined

Instructional level: P

Frustration level: 1

Example 3

| Levels | Word recognition in isolation (WRI) | | Oral reading in context | | | | Silent reading in context | | Overall judgment |
	Flashed	Untimed	Word recognition in context (WRC) accuracy	NAEP prosody	Rate/ %ile range	Comp.	Rate/ %ile range	Comp.	
PP	IND	IND							IND
P	IND	IND							IND
1	INS	INS	INS	4	>75	IND			INS
2, oral (narr.), silent (expo.)	GRAY	INS	INS	3	25–50	INS	50–75	IND	INS
3, oral (narr.), silent (expo.)	FRUS	INS	GRAY	2	11–25	Low INS	>75	FRUS	FRUS

Independent level: P

Instructional level: 2

Frustration level: 3

THE IMPORTANCE OF MISCUE ANALYSIS

Considering the nature of miscues can sometimes lead to (1) insights about how reading is developing and (2) indications of the kind of instruction a child needs. Looking for trends within and across passages is a subjective process that is informed by experience. Research can also help, and becoming knowledgeable about some of the major findings from studies of miscue analysis is useful. Here are just a few:

1. About half of first graders' miscues are omissions.
2. As children mature, substitutions become more common.
3. Initially, substitutions may amount to mere guesses, often with a word beginning with the same letter.
4. Substitutions gradually become more sophisticated, bearing greater phonic resemblance to the actual word.
5. Substitutions begin as real words (for beginning readers), but often become non-words (i.e., phonic approximations).
6. Insertions are rare (10% or fewer of all miscues).
7. Letter reversals (such as *was* for *saw*) are common in first grade, but typically disappear during second grade.
8. Reliance on context is heaviest for beginning readers and older poor readers.
9. Repetitions can be indications of a reader's using multiple sources of information to recognize a word, or attempting to make sense of what was read.
10. Word-perfect reading does not always mean good comprehension.

Form 3.2 (p. 78) is a worksheet that can be used to examine children's IRI miscues. Basically, we take each substitution and ask ourselves questions about it. First, we ask whether the miscue was graphically similar to the text word at the beginning (B), middle (M), or end (E) of the word. Next, we ask whether the word is syntactically similar to the text word, or whether it sounds right grammatically up to the point of the error. Then we ask whether the word has a similar meaning to the text word. For this, we use a fairly liberal criterion: whether the substitution would force the child to go back and correct the meaning. Thus a word can make sense, even if it is not a synonym for the text word. (For example, in the sentence "She wore a blue dress," substituting *beautiful* for *blue* would be semantically and syntactically consistent with the context.) Finally, we ask whether the word was self-corrected. We teach children to monitor their reading, and if a miscue does not make sense, we expect a child to notice and at least attempt to correct it. If a miscue does not make sense and the child does not attempt to correct it, it is likely that the child is not monitoring the reading for sense.

In the example given in Figure 3.1, taken from a first grader reading a preprimer passage at his frustration level, six of the eight miscues were graphically similar in the first position, four were syntactically similar, and three were semantically similar to the text word. This pattern suggests (1) that the child is relying on the first letter to identify words (because of the predominance of correct first letters), and (2) that the child is not using context to support or monitor word identification (since few of the words are syn-

Text says	Child says	Graphically similar?			Self-corrected?	Syntactically similar?	Self-corrected?	Semantically similar?	Self-corrected?
		B	M	E					
lost	like	✓				✓			
inside	in	✓				✓		✓	
looked	lood	✓		✓	Yes				
was	w-	✓							
he	him	✓						✓	
under	your			✓	Yes				
same	school	✓			Yes				
pony	horse					✓		✓	
Total		6		2	3	3	0	3	0

FIGURE 3.1. Sample miscue analysis.

tactically or semantically acceptable). This pattern is especially troublesome, because the passage had a clear, predictable pattern.

RUNNING RECORDS

Running records are coded notations of text reading, used as a vehicle for error analysis. After the student's reading is coded, the errors are evaluated to determine their type or reason. Although used widely in classrooms today, running records were originally used as daily progress-monitoring tools in Reading Recovery lessons (Clay, 1993). Running records share several characteristics with IRIs. However, running records can be generated from any text, not only prepared text. Unlike an IRI or a benchmark kit that is designed to be used two or three times a year, running records of novice readers should be administered frequently to monitor finer gradients of growth and progress.

Functions of Running Records

Teachers and researchers can use both types of assessments as authentic process measures of children's reading. In this case, *authentic* means that the measure duplicates reading that a child is likely to be doing in a classroom or independently. The one-on-one setting required for these measures may contribute to increased focus for some readers or to performance anxiety for others. A student is asked to read aloud, and the examiner records the student's reading of the text using a coding system. This procedure enables the researcher or teacher to get a "snapshot" of the reader engaged in the reading process, rather than the product evaluation obtained with commercially produced theme tests or standardized reading tests.

Errors are analyzed in relation to the reader's use of the semantic, syntactic, and graphic cues, called "meaning, syntactic, and visual (graphophonic) cueing systems" by Clay (2013). Although the examiner may ask a few comprehension questions after the reading, the miscue analysis constitutes the primary evaluation of meaningful reading. This information can be used to make immediate teaching decisions or to develop a plan of instruction at a later time.

Teachers who use leveled texts in reading instruction should use running records to track progress over time. By *leveled* texts, we mean any texts that increase in difficulty along a qualitative gradient that is sensitive to characteristics reflecting reading challenges. Teachers can use running records over time to demonstrate children's increasing competencies with increasingly difficult texts. Running records provide evidence of young children's developing knowledge of the reading process (see examples in Figures 3.2, 3.3, and 3.4).

Taking a Running Record

Texts

Two advantages of running records are their ease and flexibility of administration. The coding format of running records enables teachers to use them without a prepared typescript. However, because a typescript is not used, the coding of a running record is slightly more complex than the coding system employed for IRIs.

Text length is not dictated, but generally a sample should have between 100 and 200 words. This length enables teachers to conduct running records with a wide variety of texts. Running records of novice readers can be taken more frequently than a miscue analysis or an IRI can be used, because of their ease of use and adaptability to authentic settings where a variety of materials are used. Clay (1993, 2013) recommends that any texts that children can read with 90–95% accuracy be used to administer running records. Typically, authentic texts are used. "Little books" that contain complete, cohesive stories, or informational texts that have been leveled according to qualitative criteria (Peterson, 1991; Rhodes, 1981), are often selected as benchmark texts for systematic assessment. Running records may not be practical or appropriate for readers reading above 100 WPM. However, a teacher can get similar information from printing a 100-word sample of a text that a child is reading (e.g., textbook, trade book, novel).

Recording the Reading

Competence in recording running records requires time and practice. Clay (2000) advises beginners to practice tracking running records with average readers first. The fluency of good readers and the complex error patterns of struggling readers may be difficult for a beginner to record. It is a good idea for teachers to practice making running records with texts that are overly familiar to them. Although an examiner sits next to a child and looks at the text with him or her, it is less of a juggling act if the examiner has prior experience with the text and its challenges. Clay (2000) advises teachers to practice making running records until they feel comfortable and can get a "true account" of student reading with "any text, any time" (p. 6).

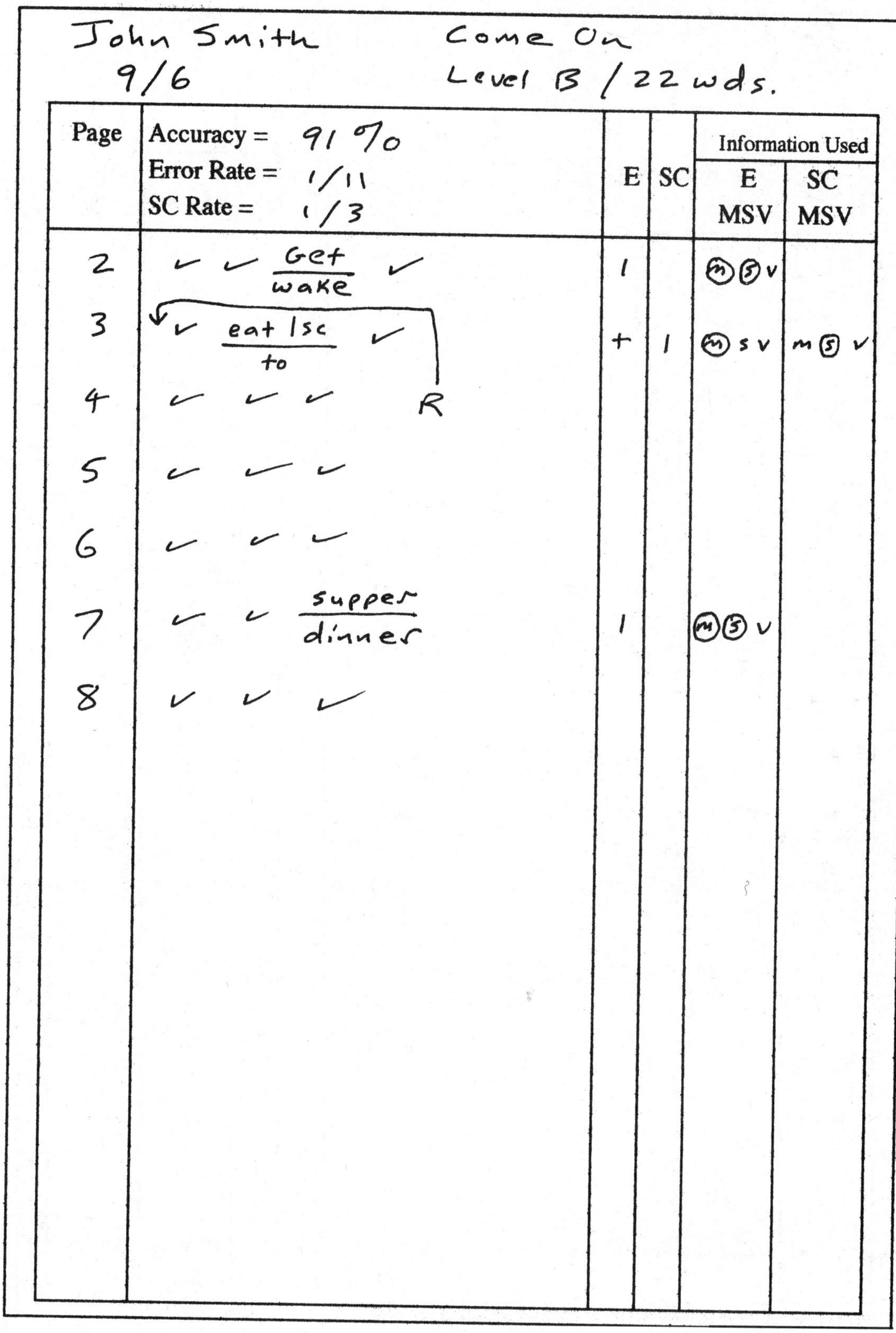

John Smith
   9/6

Come On
Level B / 22 wds.

Page	Accuracy = 91 % Error Rate = 1/11 SC Rate = 1/3	E	SC	Information Used	
				E MSV	**SC** MSV
2	✓ ✓ Get/wake ✓	1		ⓜⓢv	
3	✓ ✓ eat|sc/to ✓	+	1	ⓜ s v	m ⓢ v
4	✓ ✓ ✓ R				
5	✓ ✓ ✓				
6	✓ ✓ ✓				
7	✓ ✓ supper/dinner	1		ⓜⓢ v	
8	✓ ✓ ✓				

FIGURE 3.2. Running record taken at the beginning of the year.

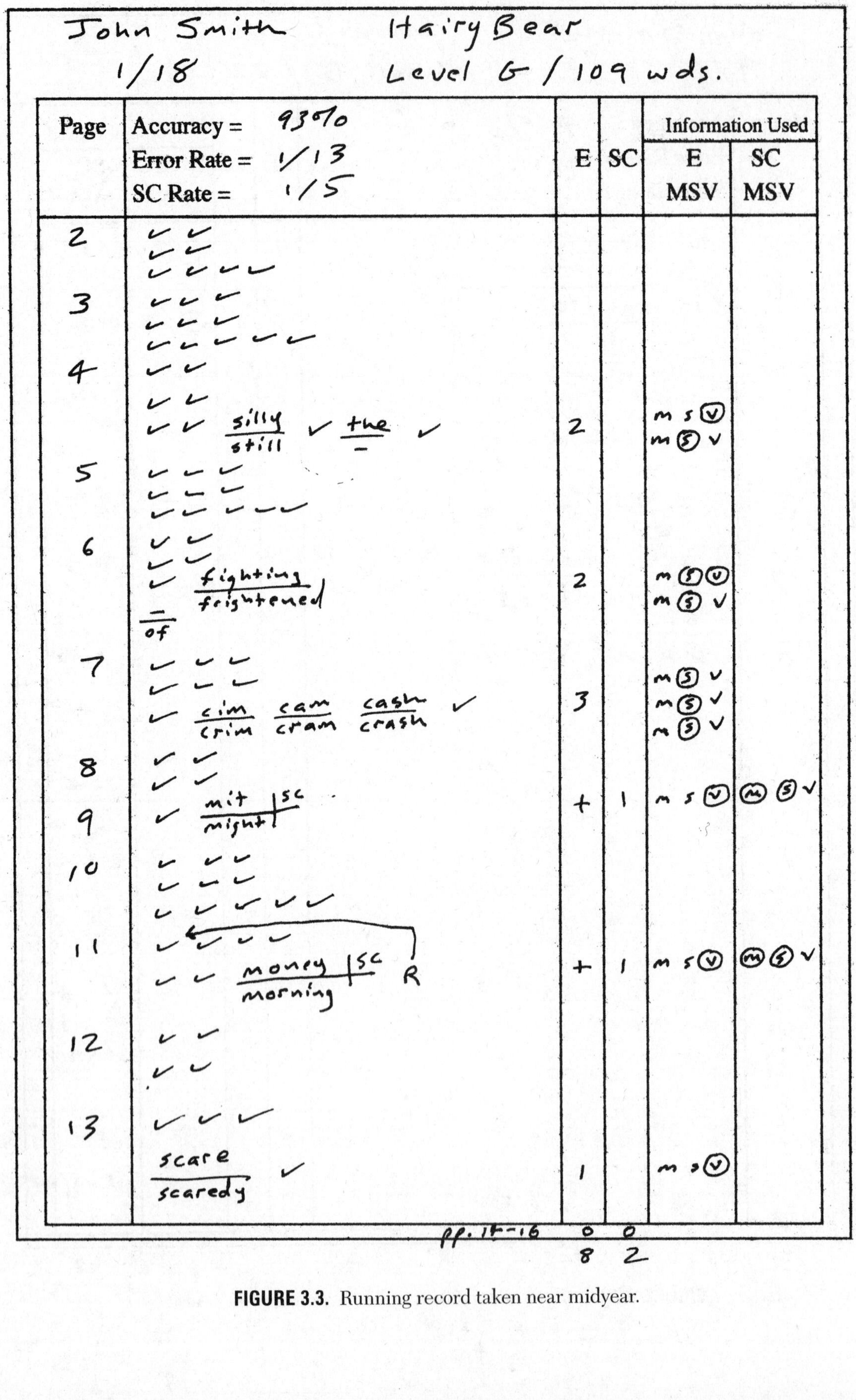
John Smith   Hairy Bear
1/18   Level G / 109 wds.

Page	Accuracy = 93% Error Rate = 1/13 SC Rate = 1/5	E	SC	Information Used E MSV	Information Used SC MSV
2	✓✓ ✓✓ ✓✓✓✓✓				
3	✓✓✓ ✓✓✓ ✓✓✓✓✓✓				
4	✓✓ ✓✓ ✓✓ silly/still ✓ the/— ✓	2		m s (v) m (s) v	
5	✓✓✓ ✓✓✓ ✓✓✓✓✓				
6	✓✓ ✓✓ ✓ fighting/frightened —/of	2		m (s)(v) m (s) v	
7	✓✓✓ ✓✓✓ ✓ cim/crim cam/cram cash/crash ✓	3		m (s) v m (s) v m (s) v	
8	✓✓ ✓✓				
9	✓ mit/might SC	+	1	m s (v)	(m) (s) v
10	✓✓✓ ✓✓✓ ✓✓✓✓✓✓				
11	✓✓✓✓ ✓✓ money/morning SC R	+	1	m s (v)	(m) (s) v
12	✓✓ ✓✓				
13	✓✓✓ scare/scaredy ✓	1		m s (v)	

pp. 14–16   0   0
8   2

FIGURE 3.3. Running record taken near midyear.

John Smith Frog & Toad Together – The Garden
5/12 Level K / 210 wds.

Page	Accuracy = 94% Error Rate = 1/16 SC Rate = 1/53	E	SC	Information Used E MSV	Information Used SC MSV
18	✓✓✓✓✓✓ ✓✓✓✓✓ ✓✓✓✓✓ ✓✓✓✓✓✓ ✓✓✓✓✓✓✓✓				
	✓✓✓ had/hand | SC R	+	1	m s (V)	(M) (S) v
	✓✓✓✓✓✓✓✓✓✓ ✓✓✓✓✓✓				
	✓✓✓✓✓ garden/ground ✓✓	1		(M) (S) v	
	✓✓✓✓✓✓✓✓✓				
19	✓ son/soon | SC ✓✓	+	1	m s (V)	(M) (S) v
	Quit/Quite ✓✓✓	1		m s (V)	
20	✓✓✓ ✓✓✓✓✓✓ ✓✓✓✓✓				
	stut | strat/start ✓	1		m s (V)	
	✓✓✓✓✓✓				
	—/a —/few —/times	3			
	✓✓✓✓ stat/start | A | T ✓✓	1		m s (V)	
21	✓✓✓ hand/head	1		(M) (S) v	
	✓✓✓ garden/ground	1		(M) (S) v	
	✓✓✓				
	New/Now ✓✓✓	1		m s (V)	
	✓✓✓✓✓✓✓ ✓✓✓✓✓✓✓✓✓				
	pp. 22–23	3	1		
		13	3		

FIGURE 3.4. Running record at the end of the year.

A teacher sets the stage for making a running record by asking a child to read to him or her and informing the child that the teacher will be writing down some notes. For *assessment* purposes, the text should be completely unfamiliar to the child; the examiner gives a brief introduction to the story and then asks the child to read. In an *instructional* setting, the selected book is more likely to be one previously introduced by the teacher and perhaps read once or twice the preceding day. For instructional decision making, children should be able to read a text at between 90 and 95% accuracy. This level enables a child to maintain fluent reading, but also allows the teacher to see what material challenges the child and how the child solves any difficulties with text.

Coding the Reading

Coding becomes easier with time and practice. The ability to code becomes refined with each running record you make on a child. It is okay to ask a child to hesitate before starting a new page if you need to catch up. While learning how to take running records, focus on recording the child's reading; you can go back later and record the text that was omitted or substituted. Among the variety of codes used to record errors, we use Clay's (2000, 2013). Standard coding procedures are important so that teachers can share information about a child. Coding can be done on a blank piece of paper, index card, or running record sheet. The book *Rosie's Walk* by Pat Hutchins (1968) is used below to demonstrate the coding system.

1. Mark every word read correctly with a check. Make lines of checks correspond to lines of text. Clay uses a solid line to indicate page breaks.

Rosie the hen went for a walk	✓ ✓ ✓ ✓ ✓ ✓ ✓
Across the yard	✓ ✓ ✓
Around the pond	✓ ✓ ✓
Over the haystack	✓ ✓ ✓

2. Record an incorrect response with the text under it. Each substitution is scored as an error.

Rosie the hen went for a walk	✓ ✓ <u>chicken</u> ✓ ✓ ✓ ✓ hen
Across the yard	<u>Around</u> ✓ ✓ Across
Around the pond	✓ ✓ ✓
Over the haystack	✓ ✓ <u>hay</u> haystack

3. Record an omission with a dash over the omitted word. Each omission is scored as an error.

Rosie the hen went for a walk	✓ ___ ___ ✓ ✓ ✓ ✓
	the hen
Across the yard	✓ ✓ ✓
Around the pond	✓ ✓ ✓
Over the haystack	✓ ✓ ✓

4. Record insertions by writing the word on top and putting a dash beneath. Each insertion is scored as an error.

Rosie the hen went for a walk	✓ ✓ ✓ ✓ ✓ long ✓
	—
Across the yard	✓ ✓ ✓
Around the pond	✓ ✓ fish ✓
	—
Over the haystack	✓ ✓ ✓

5. A self-correction occurs when a child has made an error and then corrects it. This self-correction is usually evidence that a child is cross-checking one set of cues against another (Johnston, 2000). A self-correction is recorded by using the abbreviation SC and is *not* considered an error.

Rosie the hen went for a walk	✓ ✓ chicken/SC ✓ ✓ ✓ ✓ ✓
	hen
Across the yard	Around/SC ✓ ✓ ✓
	Across
Around the pond	✓ ✓ ✓
Over the haystack	✓ ✓ ✓

6. A repetition is recorded with a line above the repeated segment of text but is *not* scored as an error. Repetitions may be demonstrations that a child is sorting out a point of some confusion—either because something did not make sense, because a word was difficult, or because the child needed to gain fluency and meaning (Clay, 2000; Johnston, 2000). A numerical superscript may be used to show multiple repetitions.

Rosie the hen went for a walk	✓ ✓ ✓ ✓ ✓ ✓ ✓
Across the yard	✓ R^2 ✓ ✓
Around the pond	Across/SC ✓ ✓ R
Over the haystack	✓ ✓ ✓

7. If a child hesitates for longer than 5 seconds because he or she has made an error and does not know how to correct it, or if the child stops and makes no attempts,

he or she is told the word. This pause is coded with a T (for *told*) on the bottom and is scored as an error.

Rosie the hen went for a walk	✓ ✓ ✓ ✓ ✓ ✓
Across the yard	<u>In</u> ✓ ✓ Across/T
Around the pond	<u>—</u> ✓ ✓ Around/T
Over the haystack	✓ ✓ ✓

8. If a child asks (A) for help, respond, "Try something," and wait 3–5 seconds for an attempt before telling the child the correct word. This strategy enables you as the teacher to observe what problem-solving strategies the child is likely to use when facing challenges in text.

Rosie the hen went for a walk	✓ ✓ ✓ ✓ ✓ ✓
Across the yard	— /A/ — ✓ ✓ Across/ /T
Around the pond	— /A/Across ✓ ✓ Around/ /T
Over the haystack	✓ ✓ ✓

9. Sometimes a child loses his or her place or goes off on a tangent that is far removed from the text. In such a case, say, "Try that again," and indicate the line, paragraph, or page where the child should restart. Record this by putting brackets around the faulty section of reading and coding it TTA. The entire section is coded as only one error.

Rosie the hen went for a walk	[✓ ✓ ✓ <u>wanted to get away</u>] went for a walk TTA ✓ ✓ ✓ ✓ ✓
Across the yard	✓ ✓ ✓
Around the pond	✓ ✓ ✓
Over the haystack	✓ ✓ ✓

10. Other behaviors may be noted but not scored. Pausing, sounding out parts of a word, fingerpointing, reading that is unusually fast or slow, and word-by-word reading should be noted on the running record and considered in the analysis, but should not be included in quantitative scoring. If there are alternative ways of scoring responses, the method that gives the fewest possible errors is usually chosen. According to Clay's (1993) system, with the exception of proper names, repeated errors are scored as errors each time. For example, if a child substitutes

will for *would* multiple times, each counts as a separate error. However, it only counts once if a child substitutes *Joey* for *Jerry* throughout a story.

Table 3.3 provides a review of the scoring of errors in a running record.

Analysis and Interpretation of the Running Record

Quantifying the Running Record

The *accuracy rate, error rate,* and *self-correction rate* are calculated. First, the number of running words (RW) in the text (excluding the title), the number of errors (E), and the number of self-corrections (SC) are counted. The accuracy rate is the percentage of words read correctly, or

$$RW - E = Difference/RW \times 100$$

We prefer the use of an accuracy rate rather than an error rate. An accuracy rate allows one to see the positive skills that readers have, instead of focusing on the errors they make. This rate relates to the independent, instructional, and frustration levels described earlier. The error rate is the ratio of errors to running words (E/RW). According to Clay (2000), error rates lower than 1:10 provide the best opportunities for observing children interacting with text. Students who have error rates higher than 1:9 with the text selection may be too frustrated to demonstrate their typical reading processes.

The *self-correction ratio* is the ratio of self-corrections to the total number of errors, or the proportion of times that a child self-corrects his or her errors:

$$E + SC = Sum/SC = 1:Ratio$$

Self-corrections may indicate the degree to which a reader is monitoring his or her reading or using multiple cueing systems to process text. Self-corrections can provide an important window into the reader's thinking. Which errors does the reader think need fixing? Some readers fix errors that interrupt meaningful reading. Other readers are more in tune with the visual system and only correct errors that don't look right. Typically, if readers have low error ratios, they are able to use multiple sources of information to self-monitor. However, higher error rates (above 1:5) may indicate that readers are neglecting information that they need to use to monitor and adjust their reading.

TABLE 3.3. Scoring of Errors in a Running Record

Scored errors	Non-error behaviors
Substitutions	Self-corrections
Omissions	Repetitions
Insertions	Hesitations
Told the word or told to "try that again"	Ignored punctuation
Repeated errors	

Miscue Analysis

The miscue analysis of an IRI is typically done on a separate worksheet. However, a running record worksheet usually includes columns for the miscue analysis. When an error is made, write the letters MSV (an abbreviation for *meaning, structure, visual*) in the error column, and circle the letters that indicate the source of information most likely used by the child up to the point of error. Miscues are analyzed by asking a series of questions about the miscues and any self-corrections. The questions may concern acceptability at the passage level, sentence level, partial-sentence level, and/or word level. The question areas include these:

- *Meaning (M)*. Did the reader choose a substitution or phrasing that makes sense in the passage or sentence or part of the sentence?
- *Structure cues (S)*. Did the reading sound like language that follows a grammatical form? (The grammatical form may be a dialect form used by the reader.) Did the reader follow the structure of the text? (Sometimes the reader continues with the earlier pattern in a predictable text, even when the structure of the text has changed.)
- *Visual (V)*. Did the child read a word that has graphic similarity or sound similarity to the word in the text? Was the graphophonic system being used?
- *Self-correction column (MSV; see above)*. What cueing systems did the reader use to fix the error?

Interpretation of Errors and Self-Corrections

The pattern of errors and self-corrections provides important insights into a child's developing awareness of the reading process. Do the child's errors reflect that he or she is reading for meaning or simply sounding out the words? Does the child's awareness of the graphophonic system extend to scanning the entire word and chunking, or is the child limited to saying the first sound and making a wild guess? A brief summary of observations and interpretations can be included on the running record sheet. A teacher who can observe these patterns in a written format possesses a powerful guide to instruction. Lesson plans for a child or small group of children should be based on behaviors represented in recent running records.

These records of observation are extremely important during reading acquisition. The shifts in how novice readers strategically use information can provide important insights into why some first graders struggle to read increasingly difficult text (McGee et al., 2015). These authors' research on 292 running records indicated that in order to successfully read books at the mid-first-grade level, novice readers must decrease their reliance on context and pictures, and increase their sophistication and utilization of the visual-alphabetic cues. Additionally, McGee et al. (2015) determined that less proficient readers relied on a single cueing system, while readers who made progress began using a chain of self-correction attempts, taking advantage of multiple cues until achieving a precise oral reading. These essential shifts in reading behaviors demonstrate why it is important for first-grade teachers to conduct running records and error analysis frequently, not just during the benchmark assessment screening periods.

Memories of even the most experienced, capable reading teachers are not always accurate. Observing by listening without recording may make it difficult to detect patterns of errors that require instructional attention. Furthermore, undocumented observations cannot be shared or used to trace changes over time. In an era when teacher accountability is becoming increasingly important in the lowest grade levels, the use of running records can be an effective tool for documenting student progress.

BENCHMARK TEXT KITS

A *benchmark text kit* is a hybrid between a running record and an IRI. Instead of containing reading passages, the benchmark text kit contains sets of leveled little books that are reserved for periodic testing. Unlike IRIs, which use quantitative readability formulas and Lexiles to gauge the difficulty of the passages, the books in benchmark kits level their texts according to a qualitative leveling system that incorporates features such as predictability, sentence complexity, organization, linguistic style, familiarity of content, genre, vocabulary, length, and text format features (e.g., font, layout, illustrations). These qualitative characteristics serve as sensitive gauges of increasing challenge for novice readers, but beginning in second grade, quantitative readability formulas tend to provide more reliable estimates of readability. Additionally, the CCSS and the assessments that are being used to measure achievement of the standards rely heavily on Lexiles for determining grade-level materials. In order for teachers to be informed about student performance in the intermediate grades and beyond, it is important to have an estimate of a student's Lexile reading range.

Most benchmark text kits provide a teacher worksheet to accompany each little book. The worksheet includes a typescript of the leveled text and guidelines for using a rubric to evaluate the reader's retelling. Generic comprehension questions are often used to prompt recall, but not as the primary means of judging comprehension. In kindergarten and first grade, this practice is acceptable, because the children may have limited experience retelling the events or ideas in a book from start to finish. Additionally, in these easy books there is minimal grist for inference generation and thought-provoking comprehension questions. Beyond first grade, however, it is important to be able to assess reliably how students are making sense of the texts that they are reading. Without clearly defined questions and retelling scoring guides, it is likely that the assessments will be scored with variations that destroy their reliability and validity as measures of reading comprehension.

ESTIMATING A CHILD'S LISTENING LEVEL

The *listening level* is conventionally defined as the highest passage at which comprehension of the passage read aloud to a child is at least 75%. Generally, a teacher first estimates the frustration level from the passages administered, and then selects the next-higher passage to administer on a listening basis. Both the passage and the questions are read aloud to the child. As with the reading passages, the teacher may need to administer more than one listening passage, either above or below the starting point, in order to determine the listening level.

Knowing a child's listening level can be useful in discerning whether comprehension difficulties are the result of decoding problems. In the following example, the listening level of this fourth grader is fourth grade, whereas the instructional level is only second grade. The teacher might justifiably conclude that this child's low reading level is primarily the result of inadequate word-recognition skills.

Example 1

Passage	Word recognition	Comprehension	Overall	Listening
1	IND	IND	IND	
2	INST	IND	INST	
3	FRUS	INST	FRUS	
4				80%

Independent level: 1
Instructional level: 2
Frustration level: 3
Listening level: 4

On the other hand, consider a hypothetical second grader whose listening level is no higher than the instructional level. In this case, the teacher first administered the second-grade passage on a listening basis. This task was clearly too difficult, however, so the teacher readministered the first-grade passage and then the primer passage, this time reading them to the child. (An alternate form at these levels might have been used.)

Example 2

Passage	Word recognition	Comprehension	Overall	Listening
PP	IND	IND	IND	
P	INST	INST	INST	80%
1	FRUS	INST	FRUS	60%
2				50%

Independent level: PP
Instructional level: P
Frustration level: 1
Listening level: P

For this student, it would be incorrect to conclude that merely improving decoding ability would lead to a substantial gain in reading level. More must be done. This student will require work in comprehension strategies and perhaps oral language development in order to make good progress.

ISSUES CONCERNING IRIs AND BENCHMARK KITS

IRIs and benchmark kits are among the best tools available for estimating reading levels. However, a number of issues surround their structure and use. The questions that follow continue to provoke debate, and authorities undoubtedly will continue to differ.

1. *Which question types should be included?* Studies have shown that different question sets covering the same passage can lead to very different interpretations of a child's comprehension (see McKenna, 1983). Field testing of the actual questions used can help, but there are no commonly accepted guidelines for question selection. We recommend using IRIs or kits that provide field-testing information about the norms for sets of questions and retelling means for each text passage. Before purchasing a benchmark kit, document that all comprehension questions have been field-tested. Be wary about making comprehension decisions based on benchmark kits that allow teachers to generate the comprehension questions "on the run."

2. *Are the questions dependent on having read the passage?* Sometimes children can answer questions on the basis of prior knowledge rather than having to understand the content of a passage. Ideally, each question should be answerable only after a child has read the passage, but it is difficult for test developers to predict what children in general might or might not know. We explore this issue further in Chapter 7.

3. *Which readability levels should be represented?* The higher the reading level of the passage, the more difficult it is to assert that a given passage represents a particular grade level. The difference, for example, between a sixth- and a seventh-grade passage is less than the difference between a second- and a third-grade passage. Again, we rely on field testing to assure an ordered sequence of passage difficulty, but the higher the passage, the greater the likelihood that anomalous results might occur. For example, if a child has more prior knowledge of the topic discussed in the sixth-grade passage than the topic in the fifth-grade passage, it might appear from the IRI that the child comprehends better at the sixth-grade level than at the fifth-grade level. Teachers must not be discouraged by anomalies of this kind, but they do need to interpret such results subjectively. Decoding, fluency, prior knowledge, genre, interest in the topic, vocabulary, working memory, and self-regulation all contribute to a child's comprehension threshold. The interaction of these pulse points can create seeming inconsistencies if a teacher is looking at a child's performance on one or two passages. That is why the data from a single IRI passage or benchmark text should not be used in isolation to make instructional decisions about a student.

4. *How long should the passages be?* The passages on some IRIs and benchmark texts gradually increase in length as grade level increases, on the rationale that fluency and attention span enable a student to handle longer samples of text. Authors of other instruments have elected to maintain the same length, except perhaps for the simplest passage, so that it is easier to apply scoring criteria and to compare a child's performance across passages of different difficulty levels.

5. *Do IRIs sufficiently reflect real-world abilities in the classroom?* Because the

experience of an IRI is so different from classroom activities, some have argued that IRI results may not adequately predict what a child is likely to do in the classroom. According to this argument, it would be preferable to observe and interpret reading performance during day-to-day classroom activities. We contend, however, that the IRI reveals the child's proficiency under more favorable circumstances (e.g., one-on-one engagement with the teacher, few distractions), and is therefore more likely to display what the child is truly capable of than classroom activities would. Therefore, it might serve as a useful preliminary screening tool. However, it is particularly important to use multiple assessments to build a more accurate representation of a student's comprehension abilities.

6. *Should a number of teacher prompts lead to discontinuing a passage?* When a child pauses at a difficult word, a teacher steps in to keep the process moving. The more times the teacher supplies unfamiliar words, however, the less representative the results will be of the child's ability. In extreme cases, the passage is more akin to a listening than a reading experience. The teacher must judge when this line is crossed and either halt the administration or discount the results afterward.

7. *Should IRI passages be narrative or expository?* Research tells us that, other factors being equal, expository prose is more difficult to process and comprehend than narrative prose. Some IRI developers approach this problem by intermingling narrative and expository passages, so that both types are represented in the inventory. (As we have noted in Chapter 2, this approach is also the one taken by developers of group achievement tests.) IRI authors who intersperse the two types rely on field testing to ensure a clear sequence of passage difficulty. An alternative approach is to separate expository and narrative passages into distinct strands. In the Qualitative Reading Inventory–6 (Leslie & Caldwell, 2016), for example, the teacher can choose in advance which passage type to present.

8. *Are questions of reliability and validity adequately addressed by the developers of IRIs and benchmark kits?* It is a concern that IRIs do not generally report reliability and validity evidence. Often their reliability is contingent on trust in the author rather than standardization. One study (Paris et al., 2004) found different forms of one popular IRI to be so different that the study authors needed to create their own scaling of the results. Teacher consumers of IRIs should examine, in advance, the evidence the IRI authors provide of the psychometric properties of their instruments. Form 3.3 (p. 79) can support a consumer review process when teachers are considering which IRI or benchmark kit to adopt as part of a school assessment system or for individual use.

9. *How do we ensure intertester reliability at our school?* When a school makes a commitment to use any assessment, including an IRI or benchmark kit, time must be devoted to training the teachers to administer the test, score it, and interpret the results with fidelity (Stahl & McKenna, 2013). Training must also include how to use the results to inform instruction. If prosody ratings, retellings, or written responses to text are used, grade-level teams must engage in a process that provides repeated practice with student samples in comparison to anchors until teachers reach a point of interrater consistency. This training must be thorough, and ideally the literacy coach will follow up the training with random drop-in fidelity checks (using a check sheet or test protocol) during

test administration. Test data should be transparent, so it is a good idea for grade-level teams to include the IRI results with other assessment data as part of the broader RTI decision-making process. See Stahl and McKenna (2013) for a thorough description of how to develop this process. Finally, booster sessions that provide a review of the trickier procedures (e.g., how many seconds before telling a child a word) should occur at team planning a week or two before each test administration.

STEPS TO A SHORTENED IRI

An IRI can be given on an abbreviated basis by limiting the assessment to a single passage. For example, a second-grade teacher may wish to know which students are reading at or near grade level by the end of the year. By administering only the second-grade passage to each child, the teacher can tell whether it falls at a given child's instructional or independent level. Of course, administering an IRI on this basis will not lead to estimates of the independent, instructional, and frustration levels. More than a single passage will be needed for that purpose.

In order to quickly categorize your students by administering an IRI on a shortened basis, we recommend the following steps:

1. Select the passage corresponding to your grade level or an appropriate Lexile level. If you teach first grade and will be testing during the spring, use the grade 1 or First Reader passage. In the intermediate grades, you may want to confirm that the Lexiles for the passages you select are aligned with the CCSS.
2. Duplicate one copy of the examinee's version per child. (You'll need these for marking the coding and notes.)
3. Assess each child individually.
4. Begin by reading the "prior-knowledge" questions, if any. Make a judgment call as to whether limited knowledge of the passage topic may prevent adequate comprehension. Usually the topics are relatively commonplace, and background knowledge is not an issue. If prior knowledge is, in your judgment, too limited, make a note of this absence.
5. Explain the procedure to the child, and give him or her the examinee's copy (the one containing only the passage and not the questions).
6. Code the miscues the child makes on the examiner's copy.
7. Use the scoring guide at the bottom of the examiner's copy to determine whether oral reading accuracy is at the independent, instructional, or frustration level.
8. If oral reading accuracy is at the frustration level, stop. Do not ask the questions; the passage is assumed to be at the frustration level.
9. If oral reading accuracy is above the frustration level, ask the comprehension questions.
10. Give full credit, partial credit, or no credit at your discretion. Reword questions to make them clearer, if you wish, but stop short of prompting.
11. Use the scoring guide at the bottom of the examiner's copy to determine whether comprehension is at the independent, instructional, or frustration level.

12. Compare the results of oral accuracy and comprehension. The passage is judged to be at the lower of these two results. For example, if oral accuracy is independent and comprehension is instructional, the entire passage is judged to be instructional.

13. On your class roster, note each child's performance level on the passage. That is, was each child's performance at the independent, instructional, or frustration level?

USING IRIs IN PROJECT AND SCHOOL EVALUATIONS

IRIs tend to provide more reliable information about reading growth than group standardized measures do. The fact that they are individually administered, and in a manner that is responsive to student performance, tends to produce valid results. Moreover, they can be administered much more flexibly than achievement tests can, so that pre–post comparisons can be made with reasonable confidence.

Several options are available for project evaluation, depending on the questions project personnel are interested in answering. The two options presented here offer a wide variety of evaluation opportunities.

Option 1: Full Pre–Post Administration

In the first option, IRI testing is done at the beginning and end of the project implementation. Our example is from Kashinkerry Elementary, a PreK–5 school. We assume that grades 1–5 have been involved in reading-related activities throughout the year. For grades 2–5, this reading activity includes one assessment in early fall and another in late spring. For first graders, however, the preassessment should be delayed until midyear, so that more children will be capable of reading at least a preprimer passage. Alternatively, if you are using benchmark texts in kindergarten and grade 1, particular levels can be translated into the numerical scale.

Two methods can be used to interpret the data. The first is to convert IRI instructional reading levels into continuous grade-level terms by using the following standard equivalencies, used in studies conducted at the National Reading Research Center:

Below preprimer	=	1.0
Preprimer	=	1.3
Primer	=	1.6
1st reader	=	1.8
2nd grade	=	2.5
3rd grade	=	3.5
4th grade	=	4.5
5th grade	=	5.5
6th grade	=	6.5
7th grade	=	7.5
8th grade	=	8.5

The advantage of this method is that parametric statistics (both descriptive and inferential) can be computed, and so growth can be plainly charted in terms of years gained. This indicator is far superior to the grade-equivalent scores produced through standardized achievement testing, because of the individual administration of the IRI and the fact that the data for children of differing chronological ages are not pooled as they are in achievement testing.

The results for Kashinkerry are summarized in Table 3.4. (These results are for a real school, located in an inner-city area and serving predominantly high-risk children.) In grades 2–5, the average gain is in the vicinity of 1 year. Growth at grade 1 reflects only the half-year since the January pretesting. Inferential statistics can be computed, if desired. In the case of Kashinkerry, growth at each grade was statistically significant ($p < .001$), and effect sizes (delta) ranged from 0.43 to 0.72. Such effects are considered moderately large and attest to the educational significance of reading growth at Kashinkerry. (Similar statistics might have been used to compare Kashinkerry with a contrast school in which project activities did not occur.)

A second method of data analysis is to represent the distribution of instructional reading levels at each grade and then, from these distributions, to compute the proportion of children at each grade level who finished the school year reading at or above grade level. These results for Kashinkerry are presented in Table 3.5.

Option 2: Single-Passage Administration

In the second approach, each child is given only one passage: the one at grade level. Only about 5 minutes per child are needed, compared with up to 20 minutes for a full IRI. (See the previous section for suggestions about how to administer an IRI in this way.) Although this approach does not reveal each child's instructional reading level, it can still be used to estimate the percentage of children who are reading at or above grade level versus the percentage who are reading below grade level.

Let's assume that Ms. Johnson, a third-grade teacher, administers the third-grade passage of an IRI to each child in the spring of the year. A child whose performance is judged to be instructional or independent on that passage is counted among those read-

TABLE 3.4. IRI Instructional Level Results for Kashinkerry Elementary

| | | Instructional reading level | | | | |
| | | Fall | | Spring | | |
Grade	N	M	SD	M	SD	Mean gain in years
1	123	1.4	0.7	1.9	0.9	0.5
2	106	2.0	1.1	3.3	1.8	1.3
3	79	2.9	1.8	4.3	2.2	1.4
4	97	4.7	1.9	5.7	2.3	1.0
5	92	5.0	1.9	6.1	2.0	1.1

TABLE 3.5. End-of-Year IRI Instructional Levels for Kashinkerry

Grade	None[a]	Preprimer	Primer	1st reader	2	3	4	5+
				Percentage of children at each level				
1	16	15	18	20	19	8	2	1
2	2	7	10	11	23	21	7	18
3	0	5	6	4	19	19	11	35
4	1	0	3	4	8	11	9	63
5	0	1	1	1	8	8	9	73

[a]No level could be determined.

ing at or above grade level. A child whose performance falls below the criteria for the instructional level is counted among those children reading below grade level.

Let's further assume that Ms. Johnson's students have been involved in a reading-related project, whereas Mr. Williams's students, who are demographically similar, have not participated. Mr. Williams's class can be used as a control group by means of the IRI assessment. Table 3.6 presents a hypothetical comparison. These results favor the class that took part in project activities, since fewer students were reading below grade level at year's end. These proportions can be compared statistically, if desired.

It should be noted that the teacher factor in this design has not been controlled. There is a possibility that Ms. Johnson's students might have produced similar results without benefit of the project. This possibility might have been countered by including more than one teacher in each group or by comparing two of Ms. Johnson's classes in successive years (e.g., the year before the project with the implementation year).

TABLE 3.6. IRI Results for Project and Nonproject Students

Class	Percentage of students reading below grade level	
	Fall	Spring
Project	72.3	30.3
Control	75.6	52.1

IRI Summary Form

Student's Name _____ Grade Level _____ Age _____

Examiner _____ Date(s) of Test _____

Levels	Word Recognition in Isolation (WRI)			Oral Reading in Context				Silent Reading in Context		Overall Reading Judgment	Listen. Comp.
	Flashed	Untimed	Total	Accuracy %age	Prosody	Rate in WCPM/ %ile	Comp. %age	Rate in WPM	Comp. %age		
Preprimer											
Primer											
First											
Second											
Third (Narrative)											
Third (Expository)											
Fourth (Narrative)											
Fourth (Expository)											
Fifth (Narrative)											
Fifth (Expository)											
Sixth (Narrative)											

(continued)

Levels	Word Recognition in Isolation (WRI)			Oral Reading in Context				Silent Reading in Context		Overall Reading Judgment	Listen. Comp.
	Flashed	Untimed	Total	Accuracy %age	Prosody	Rate in WCPM/ %ile	Comp. %age	Rate in WPM	Comp. %age		
Sixth (Expository)											
Upper Middle School											
(Optional) Leveled Reader Kit	×		×								×
Lv.	×		×								×
Lv.	×		×								×
Lv.	×		×								×

Independent Level ____/____/____ (Grade/Lexile/Lv.)	Instructional Level ____/____/____ (Grade/Lexile/Lv.)	Frustration Level ____/____/____ (Grade/Lexile/Lv.)
Justification:	Justification:	Justification:

(continued)

1. Strengths and Areas of Need

	Strengths	Areas of Need
Comprehension		
Fluency		
High-Frequency Word Recognition		
Decoding		
Writing in Response to Text		

2. Instructional Recommendations (rank in order of priority from 1 to 4 and identify instructional recommendations, including activities, strategies, and materials)

Comprehension and Vocabulary	Fluency	High-Frequency Word Recognition	Decoding	Writing

Miscue Analysis Chart

Text says	Student says	Graphically similar?			Self-corrected?	Syntactically similar?	Self-corrected?	Semantically similar?	Self-corrected?
		B	M	E					
Totals									

Shopping Guide When Purchasing an IRI or Benchmark Kit

Name of test:	Notes	Quality ranking: 1 (low) 5 (high)
Psychometric data about recent field testing is provided: • Number of students • Demographics		
How were passage readability levels determined? Also included: • Equivalency charts to other systems (e.g., Lexile, F&P). • Field-test data substantiating reliability of the assigned levels.		
Record-keeping and computation tools are teacher-friendly.		
Multiple forms are available at each level.		
Beyond mid-grade 1, questions are provided that are specific to each passage.		
For each passage, the number of comprehension questions answered (*mean*) on field tests by children meeting the reading accuracy instructional level is provided.		
Retelling score guides include the use of idea units or specified story grammar elements to ensure reliability of ratings between scorers.		
Field-test data are provided that include the mean % of retelling idea units or story grammar elements for each passage among children reading the passage at the instructional level.		
If older students must create written responses, anchor papers are included for each written response to ensure interrater reliability at the school level.		

FOUR

Emergent Literacy

During the years prior to school and into the primary grades as well, we expect to see young children develop behaviors that signal an adequate foundation for formal reading instruction. In order to monitor the development of these emerging literacy behaviors, teachers can apply simple, informal assessment techniques.

What do we expect children to be able to master before formal reading instruction? At one time, children were expected to have mastered certain prerequisite perceptual skills before they began a formal reading program. These discretely conceptualized skills—such as auditory discrimination, visual discrimination, and visual figure–ground discrimination—are now seen as relics of the past. Instead, we view a child as learning continuously about reading from the first exposure to print as an infant. This increasing knowledge of both print and oral language acquisition provides the foundation upon which successful reading is built.

Specifically, we examine some ways of assessing four major components of emergent literacy: concepts of print, alphabetic recognition, phonemic awareness, and the development of narrative comprehension.

CONCEPTS OF PRINT

It is easy to take for granted some of the conventions that surround how books are printed and how we read them. These conventions, or common understandings, have little or nothing to do with the processes of word recognition and comprehension. Instead, they are more basic, and we hope to see them developed long before formal reading instruction begins. Without them, children will be at a serious disadvantage and are sure to suffer frustration and confusion.

What are these concepts of print? As fluent readers of English, it has become second nature to us that when we hold a closed book, the spine is on our left. But this is not an inevitable, "natural" state of affairs. For example, closed books in Arabic or Hebrew are held with the spine to the right. Moreover, when we read a line of print in English, we start from the left and progress toward the right. Again, however, this is an arbitrary convention, and readers of Arabic and Hebrew, among other languages, begin at the right of each line. Furthermore, when we encounter a page of print, we know from long experience that we must begin reading the uppermost line and proceed downward. We must also understand that the letters and words are what convey the message, not the illustrations. A young child's first inclination is to focus on the pictures, which are the only components of a page that seem to have any meaning. Finally, in order to read a line of print, we must know that the white spaces between letter clusters mark the boundaries between *words*. This particular convention is extremely useful in the process of word recognition.

Concept of *Word*

One aspect of print concepts is the child's understanding that a word is represented by the marks within the spaces. This is a crucial concept, because it enables children to learn about letters and words through exposure to print (Flanigan, 2007). Several studies have found that acquiring concept of word in text, the ability to accurately match spoken words to printed words while reading a familiar text with fingerpointing, is an essential marker on the child's road to reading proficiency. Research suggests that children need to have some word knowledge and/or some phonological awareness before they are able to fingerpoint accurately (Ehri & Sweet, 1991; Morris, 1993; Uhry, 1999). Other studies have found that fingerpointing seems to be a prerequisite for learning about words from text (Clay, 1993; Morris et al., 2003).

The acquisition of the word concept in text, as indicated by fingerpointing, is generally measured by having a child memorize a simple rhyme, such as a nursery rhyme (e.g., "Baa, Baa, Black Sheep") or a simple song (e.g., "I'm a Little Teapot"). After the rhyme is memorized, the child is asked to read it in a book, pointing to each word as it is spoken.

The Concept of Word Scale (Gill, 2019) can be used with preschoolers or emergent readers in kindergarten to trace the development of a concept of word in text while reading. In its most abbreviated form, one can use two phrases from a poem to quickly gauge a child's concept of word. See Form 4.1 (p. 97). Model reading and fingerpointing the poem two or three times until the child can say the phrases with you. (This can be done with a whole class, followed by an individual assessment process.) Then ask the child to read and fingerpoint each word as he or she reads the phrases. Select the best descriptor from the Concept of Word Scale Key to identify where the child is on the developmental COW-T continuum. Repeat the assessment periodically, using different short poems or short pattern books, until the child can consistently track single-syllable and multisyllable words using one-to-one matching.

Assessing Concepts of Print

None of these understandings comes automatically. Children must learn them either through direct instruction or extensive teacher modeling. It is important to assess children's knowledge of these concepts. The following procedure quickly provides a great deal of information through a single, nonthreatening, informal encounter. As the child is seated at a table, place a closed picture book in front of him or her. Make sure that the book is not positioned in the traditional way. That is, don't place the book with the spine at the left and the front of the book uppermost. Ask the child to show you the front of the book. Then open the book to any page that has both a picture and at least two lines of print. Ask the child where you would begin reading. Ideally, the child will point to the leftmost word of the top line. (Do not be surprised, however, if the child points to the illustration or to some vague area within the text.)

Next, open the book to any page containing only a single line of print, and place two blank index cards at either end of the line. Using both hands, slide the cards toward each other and say to the child, "I want you to push these cards together until only one word shows. Show me one word." Repeat the process, asking the child to show you one letter. This entire procedure might last only a minute, but can give you a great deal of useful data. Simply record the child's responses in a convenient checklist form, making sure to date your entries. Such a checklist might look like the one in Form 4.2 (p. 98). Rather than using a single checkmark, however, you may want to write the date that a child has successfully demonstrated knowledge of a given concept, and to write nothing if the child fails to demonstrate it.

A more comprehensive approach involves the book-handling guidelines presented in Form 4.3 (p. 99).

ALPHABETIC RECOGNITION

It is vital for young children to learn letter names if they are to become proficient readers. Why is this true? It is certainly possible to learn to recognize words by memorizing them as whole units. For example, children with no alphabet knowledge at all could learn to say *cat* whenever they encounter the word in print. But learning words in this way would exert crippling demands on memory, and it would ignore the alphabetic nature of our language. Specifically, there are two important reasons for teaching children letter names at an early age. First, fluent readers do not recognize words as whole units. Rather, they do so by identifying the component letters. This process occurs at an unconscious level, but research leaves no room for doubt. The second reason is that teachers must have some means of referring to the letters during instruction. Although schools in the United Kingdom and some early reading programs teach sounds before letters, in the United States most young children are introduced to letter names first by parents singing the alphabet song, computer and iPad programs, and television. Therefore, in the United States it makes sense to take advantage of this preschool introduction to letter names.

The best way to assess alphabetic knowledge is to present a child with letters, one at a time, and ask him or her to say the name of each. Several questions arise about how best to implement this procedure.

1. *In what order should the letters be presented?* The best way to answer this question may be in the negative. That is, it is important only to avoid presenting the letters in alphabetical order. Doing so would provide the child with a built-in prompt that could lead to inaccurate results. Randomly ordering the letters is preferable.

2. *How should the letters be presented to the child?* We have found that the best way is to present all of the letters on a single sheet of paper in a grid format. Using a blank sheet as a placeholder for each row of letters, the teacher is able to observe the student's awareness of left-to-right directionality. If necessary, the teacher can simply point to each letter with one hand and record the child's response on a separate copy of the grid, using the other hand.

3. *Should capital letters or lowercase letters be assessed?* Because both forms of letters will be encountered continually in printed materials, both forms must be assessed. The random arrangement of letters on the grid should also randomize the appearance of each form. In other words, it would be a poor idea to put the capital and lowercase forms of the same letter next to each other.

4. *What font should be used?* There is probably no answer to this question on which everyone would agree. However, common sense suggests that a font that is plain and free of serifs (those extra, decorative marks, such as the short horizontal lines at the top and bottom of a capital *I* in many fonts) would be less likely to mislead the child. A related issue concerns the letters *a* and *g*. The lowercase forms of these letters often occur in two very different formats, so that children need to be assessed on their knowledge of both. They may encounter *a* or a, *g* or g.

Addressing all of the issues that we have just discussed results in a one-page grid displaying all of the letters, most of them in both their upper- and lowercase forms, plus an extra lowercase form for the letters *a* and *g*. This means that alphabet assessment should tap children's knowledge of 54 symbols. Using such a grid as a method of recording a child's responses is a convenient means of record keeping. By using different markings for repeated assessments, a teacher can document growth in alphabetic recognition on a single sheet of paper over the course of many months. Form 4.4 (p. 102) presents such a grid.

PHONEMIC AWARENESS

It is vital that prereaders become aware of the sounds that constitute spoken words. *Phonemes,* the smallest sounds we hear in words, are the building blocks of our spoken language, and becoming aware of their presence is vital to later successful phonics instruction. However, unlike phonics, phonemic awareness is entirely an auditory matter. It is not connected with written language in any direct way. A child may be phonemically aware and yet have no knowledge of the alphabet.

The research into phonemic awareness instruction is compelling. Findings clearly show that (1) children can be taught to become phonemically aware, and (2) there is a strong causal link between phonemic awareness and later abilities in phonics and spelling (National Reading Panel, 2000). This second finding makes perfect sense. After all, it is difficult to learn letter–sound correspondences if a child is unable to hear the component sounds of a spoken word. Thus, while a certain level of phonemic awareness is a prerequisite to successful phonics and spelling instruction, we recommend introducing letters into phoneme manipulation activities as soon as children are able.

Finally, let's examine a minor issue of terminology. Some experts prefer the term *phonological awareness* to *phonemic awareness*. The former term is broader and includes awareness of not just speech phonemes, but larger units of sound, such as rhymes, syllables, and word duration. For example, a teacher might ask a child to blend the following two sounds: /k/ and /at/. The child would then say the word *cat*. Technically, such an assessment activity is not purely a matter of phonemic awareness, because in this case the rime -*at* is larger than a single phoneme. It is a chunk of sound comprising two phonemes. Working with rimes and other chunks of sound that are larger than a single phoneme has led some to use the broader phrase *phonological awareness*. You are likely to encounter either phrase in the literature. It is a small but interesting distinction.

The word *cat* contains three phonemes, each represented by a letter. Learning about how these letters represent phonemes is a matter of phonics. Becoming sensitive to their presence in spoken words is something far more basic. Phonemic awareness should develop prior to school entry or in kindergarten.

How can we tell whether a child is aware of the component sounds of spoken words? How can we assess a child's phonological awareness? Form 4.5 (p. 103) can be used over time to document an emergent reader's increasing awareness of sounds in words.

Each task is entirely an oral activity, which is why such assessments can be done so readily with 4- and 5-year-olds. Phonological awareness activities often have game-like formats, and a child's responses can provide a teacher with useful information about the extent of that child's phonological awareness, even though the child is scarcely aware of being assessed. It is not recommended that all tasks be administered in one sitting unless the child is in first or second grade and experiencing difficulty with hearing sounds in words. At that point, the novice reader might be asked to perform several tasks to determine which behaviors are under the child's control and which types of awareness require additional instruction. Hearing and Recording Sounds in Words (Clay, 2013) is an instrument that appears in Form 4.6 (p. 106), along with some of the most recent norms. For a far wider array of norms, see Clay (2013). We include this instrument because invented spelling can be a useful way to evaluate phonological awareness. Although this dictation task provides a lens for viewing phonological awareness, alphabetic knowledge, and some print concepts, it can be a useful supplement to a "pure" test of phonological awareness. Furthermore, it can be given to small groups, as well as individually, thus making it an efficient screening tool.

Phonological Awareness Literacy Screening (PALS; Invernizzi, Meier, & Juel, 2007; Invernizzi, Sullivan, Swank, & Meier, 2004; Invernizzi, Swank, & Juel, 2007) is a set of assessments that may be used to test discrete phonological awareness and alphabetic knowledge. PALS-PreK and PALS-K focus on the earliest-developing skills, such as rhyming, initial sound awareness, name writing, and print concepts. PALS 1–3 include subtests of spelling, word recognition, and oral reading. Some of these assessments must be administered individually, and others, such as the spelling test, may be administered in a group setting.

Most commercially produced curriculum-based measures (CBMs) of early literacy include two widely used and easily accessible tests for assessing phonological awareness. The subtests are Initial Sound Fluency (ISF) and Phoneme Segmentation Fluency (PSF). These are timed, individual measures for determining a child's ability to identify and produce an initial sound of an orally produced word (ISF) and the ability to segment three- and four-phoneme words into their individual sounds. The DIBELS website (*https://dibels.uoregon.edu*) provides benchmark assessments, alternate forms for progress monitoring, and predictive data for evaluating students' scores. All DIBELS Next instruments can be downloaded at no cost. AIMSweb and FAST are other examples of commercial CBM packages that include these tests.

Recent research has indicated that segmentation tasks *reflect* rather than *predict* a child's spelling knowledge. If a child needs spelling knowledge to complete a task, then, not surprisingly, the task is highly correlated with other measures of word recognition, but it is not a pure task of phonological awareness. This is also true for phoneme deletion. Nevertheless, these tasks are included in many measures of phonological awareness, such as the Comprehensive Test of Phonological Processing—Second Edition (CTOPP-2; Wagner, Torgesen, Rashotte, & Pearson, 2013), which taps several phonological processing abilities across a wide age range. We feel that such measures should be interpreted carefully. The Test of Phonological Awareness—Second Edition: Plus (TOPA-2+; Torgesen & Bryant, 2004) is a norm-referenced measure that can be administered in individual or group settings. Although this instrument meets high standards of reliability and validity, classroom teachers also need to consider factors of cost and time effectiveness.

THE DEVELOPMENT OF NARRATIVE COMPREHENSION IN YOUNG CHILDREN

The CCSS have called increased attention to comprehension in the early grades. Although foundational skills are specified as targets for the early grades, comprehension dominates the Standards as early as kindergarten. Some states, such as New York, have written state prekindergarten English language arts (ELA) standards that align with the strong comprehension focus of the CCSS. This policy is theoretically sound because research has determined that a 4-year-old child's comprehension of videos and aurally presented stories is correlated with his or her reading comprehension at age 8 (Kendeou, Bohn-Gettler, White, & van den Broek, 2008). Most of the research with young children has been conducted with narratives.

The ways that emergent readers engage with familiar storybooks and wordless picture books can provide insights about their comprehension development before it becomes muddled with other complexities, such as decoding, fluency, multiple text structures, and novel technical content. The assessments in this section can provide windows into a child's awareness of narrative structure, self-regulation, strategy application, prior knowledge, oral language, and conceptual vocabulary. These dimensions are portrayed in the bottom two pathways of the cognitive model (see Figure 1.1).

Like many of the assessments in this chapter, these are administered individually. However, unlike the assessments for the foundational skills, these require more time to prepare and administer. They also require the expertise of a teacher who is sensitive to using a collection of developmental indicators to inform instruction, as opposed to using a formula for determining simple mastery or nonmastery. These assessments serve as gauges of a child's development of narrative comprehension. They can be used as school-entry screening tools or as assessments for children who are suspected of having early listening comprehension difficulties or language difficulties, based on a teacher's observations.

Emergent Storybook Reading

The Emergent Storybook Reading scale is based on Sulzby's (1985) research, which identified clear developmental trends in how children approach storybooks—moving from picture-governed attempts at reading to print-governed attempts, with the child finally moving toward near-accurate rendering of the text. Observing a child's attempt to read a storybook can provide valuable insights into the child's knowledge about how books work. It can likewise provide direction for how to help the child develop the knowledge needed to handle print.

The Emergent Storybook Reading scale can be used in a formal or informal setting. In a formal setting, the teacher might take the child aside, tell him or her to pick a favorite book, and then ask the child to "read" the book. It is important that the child be familiar with the book, so that more mature behaviors can be seen. A child who protests that he or she cannot read can be told to "read as best you can" or to "pretend to read the book." The teacher can encourage the child by making neutral comments, such as "What can I do to help? What do you want me to do? How will that help?" The scale also can be used informally while the teacher observes a child pretend-reading in a natural setting. Either way, understanding the stages that children go through as they learn to handle books will inform the teacher's instruction, by indicating the "next step" in the emergent reading process.

Sulzby (1985) found that children appear to go through nine stages in their approach to storybook reading, as they move from emergent to formal reading levels. This nine-stage scale has been validated repeatedly in her work. Form 4.7 (p. 108) can be used to document a child's approach to reading a familiar storybook.

Picture-Governed Attempts

1. *Labeling and commenting.* In this stage, the child looks at each picture and provides a name or descriptor, such as "doggie," "horse," or "bed," or makes a comment, such as "Go to bed," "That's ugly," or "He's a monster." Sometimes these comments are accompanied by a gesture or by slapping the page. Typically, the speech is less mature than the speech used in other contexts and may represent a storybook reading routine used by parents. In this and the following stage, each page is treated individually, and there are no attempts to link pictures to make a story.

2. *Following the action.* In this stage, children remark on the action in each picture as if it were occurring in the present moment. Comments might be similar to "There he goes. He's gonna get that monkey." The verbs used are typically present tense, present-progressive tense, or "gonna." Again, there is no attempt to link pictures to make a story.

3. *Dialogue storytelling.* This stage is a transition between the "labeling and commenting" and "following the action" stages and the more mature storytelling seen later. It may contain elements of the earlier stages, but also includes an attempt to bridge the pages, using dialogue between the adult and child. The "story" may seem disjointed, but a listener can perceive that the child is trying to make a story. Here is an actual example (Sulzby, 1985, p. 67):

CHILD: The children are looking for—for the other children (*turns page*) for one more children. And (*pause*) they looked all over the place (*pause*) for that little children (*turns page*). He went off to the _____. (*Turns page.*) He writed a note to—to the king—and they, uh (*pause*).

ADULT: They wrote a note to the king and then—

CHILD: Then they would. Then the boy bring the note to the king, and then he said to bring it back to here. (*Turns page.*) And then the little girl got peanuts and threw them at everybody.

ADULT: —Oh—

CHILD: And they're making stuff. And that, and that.

ADULT: —Oh—

CHILD: Pushed her into the peanuts.

4. *Monologue storytelling.* At this point, the child is clearly telling a story and uses a storytelling intonation that takes the form of an extended monologue stretching across the pages. The child makes reference to the picture content, but the major emphasis is on a continuous story. Sulzby (1985, p. 468) provides an example of this type of storybook reading:

"This is his house and he is going to sleep. He was reading a book and then after he was reading the book he saw pictures of the mountains up here. Here (*pause*) there's some pictures, here, and then he thought he was going exploring the mountains, he's going to, yeah, about the mountains and he thought I'm going to explore the mountains tomorrow. And then he asked his daddy . . . then he got out of the gate and he saw the mailman coming on the street. And then he went (*pause*) and then he went (*pause*) and then he said to him (*pointing to dog in picture*), Angus. Angus, 'cause that's his name, I know. After this we're gonna come to the mountains (*pause*) and then he got one of his, and then he stuck one flag in there and then this is gonna be his tree."

The story here is primitive, but there is a clear attempt to connect an ongoing plot across the different pages.

5. *Reading and storytelling mixed.* At this stage, the child's reading is still picture-governed. However, at times the story is told in a conversational register, and at other times the child uses the more formal written register. This more formal delivery may be likely to show up as the child's including some verbatim dialogue from the book or perhaps a repeated pattern. Patches of the story are repeated verbatim in this stage.

6. *Reading similar to original story and reading verbatim-like.* At this stage, the

child's awareness of "book talk" or written register dominate the pretend reading. There is evidence of adherence to genre devices and author's craft, such as patterns of three repetitions or "once upon a time," even if the particular book doesn't include that device. As the child continues to develop in this stage, the story the child is "reading" gets closer to being verbatim. A child may get frustrated and ask a caregiver to support a missing section that he or she can't remember. At this stage, the child knows that there is precise wording on the page and that the adult can retrieve it. However, the child's own reading is still driven by the pictures and the story's meaning, not by the print.

Print-Governed Attempts

7. *Print awareness.* This stage is a transition between the purely oral story, governed by picture interpretation, and reading. In this type of reenactment, the child inserts parts that sound like written language (in intonation, in wording, or in both) into parts that sound like oral language. The story may depart from the actual story, but the pretend reading shows a clear sense of audience and a concern with coherence that is missing in the excerpt above. This type of reading also contains parts that are decontextualized or are specified well enough that they can be understood without the pictures. At this stage, the child may refuse to read a section because he or she does not know the words. This stage is similar to Biemiller's (1970) conceptualization of the refusal stage, in which the child knows that print carries the information in the text and knows that he or she cannot read the print. In earlier stages, children may refuse to read, but in this stage the refusal is clearly based on the belief that they need to know more about the print in order to read. It is at this stage that it is useful to begin instructing the child with easy caption books and single-line, predictable pattern books.

8. *Aspect-governed reading.* In this stage, the child often uses the patterns of the original story or those in similar books. The child may focus on particular words that he or she knows or may overrely on a particular pattern. One child in Sulzby's (1985) study went through the book and read (pointing) "a," "the," "Grandpa," and "and," page after page. Other children focus their attention on sounding out individual words. Compared to the earlier stages, this may seem like a regression, but it is an important one. In this stage, the child is trying out new repertoires that will be integrated later with story knowledge.

9. *Text-governed reading.* In this type of reading, the child is clearly trying to create a verbatim rendering of the text. Sulzby divides this stage into two parts—reading with strategies unbalanced and reading independently—but we have merged these because both IRIs and running records made of children reading text are better ways to assess children's use of strategies during text-governed reading. What is significant here is that the child is clearly reading the text, not the pictures, often using fingerpointing. The child may skip unfamiliar words or insert nonsense words, but most of the words are text words, and the child is using a reading intonation.

The Emergent Storybook Reading scale can provide a great deal of information about a child's knowledge of how books work. If the child's "reading" does not fit clearly into one category or another, assume that the reading is in the lower of the two categories, and instruct the child in the next-higher category. For example, if the child's reading is between dialogue and monologue forms of storytelling, assume that the child is in the dialogue stage and prompt him or her to tell extended stories by asking for elaborations and clear transitions between pages.

Narrative Wordless Picture Book Task

Another approach to examining children's awareness of narrative is through the use of a wordless picture book, which enables a teacher to examine a child's knowledge of how stories work. This assessment is developmentally appropriate for emergent readers or novice readers who seem to be having comprehension difficulties. Paris and Paris (2003) provide evidence that it can be used with 5- to 8-year-olds. However, the comprehension components evaluated in this assessment are aligned with the CCSS. It can serve as an early indicator of comprehension difficulties that require an intervention that begins with simple stories and moves to more complex narratives.

Paris and Paris (2003) constructed a narrative comprehension assessment out of wordless picture books that consists of three parts: a "picture walk," story retelling, and prompted comprehension. To do this assessment, first choose a book that has a clear narrative that can be followed just by looking through the pictures. Paris and Paris used *Robot-Bot-Bot* by Fernando Krahn (1979), but any number of similar books could be used, such as those by Alexandra Day and Mercer Mayer. You want to select a book that has a clear, complete narrative structure. However, choose a book with more or fewer episodes, based on the child's age. For a young child, you might use an unfamiliar early leveled text that has a complete narrative structure and eliminate the text. The picture walk evaluates how the child approaches the text and handles the book; the language he or she uses; and his or her general familiarity with literate, "book-like" language, strategy use, and story structure. A convenient instrument for evaluating the picture walk appears in Form 4.8 (p. 110). Paris and Paris (2003, p. 44) use the picture walk to evaluate five behaviors:

- *Book-handling skills*—whether the child has a sense of the appropriate speed and order of reading, and whether pages are skipped or skimmed.
- *Engagement*—whether the child appears engaged in the story, as indicated by appropriate affect, attention, interest, and effort.
- *Picture comments*—whether the child makes comments about the pictures, including descriptions of objects, characters, emotions, actions, and so on (refers to looking at pictures individually).
- *Storytelling comments*—whether the child makes comments that integrate information across pictures, indicating that he or she is using the pictures to create a coherent story. Comments might include narration, dialogue, or the use of storytelling language.
- *Comprehension strategies*—whether the child uses strategies that indicate monitoring of comprehension. These strategies can include looking back or looking

ahead in order to make sense of something, self-correction of story elements or narrative, asking questions for understanding, or making predictions about the story.

Although scores are given for each skill, this procedure is better used as an informal means of assessing children's familiarity with storybooks. Used with an individual child, it can give insights into the child's knowledge of the function of books, experience of being read to, and knowledge of book conventions. These are the five categories provided by Paris and Paris; however, we suggest that you also look at the use of literary language. For example, does the child begin with "Once upon a time . . . " and conclude with "The End"? Does the child use language that sounds like story language, or does the child tell the story in vernacular terms? These observations also can be useful.

The retelling is given immediately after the picture walk. It is a free retelling, in which the child is asked to retell as much of the story as possible without looking back at the pictures. When the child has finished, give a neutral prompt, asking the child whether he or she remembers anything else about the story. Avoid pointing to specific pictures or asking specific questions about the story. During the retelling, note what is said, possibly making an audio recording to use later and refine the transcription for more accurate evaluation. The retelling is evaluated in terms of the number of story grammar elements included: settings, characters, goal/initiating events, problem/episodes, solution, and resolution/ending. We have provided an evaluation chart in Form 4.9 (p. 111).

Again, this retelling can provide some information about the child's experience with narratives. Children who have a strong story sense, as evidenced by their use of story grammar elements in their retelling, are likely to do better in reading stories than children who lack such a sense. Furthermore, the retelling should be evaluated for overall coherence. Is a child clearly telling a story, or merely recalling bits and pieces of unrelated information? Children without a clear story sense will need additional practice in listening and responding to stories.

Paris and Paris (2003) provide a set of comprehension prompts as the third part of the assessment. Although these prompts are specific to the story that Paris and Paris used, they might be useful in guiding recall for most stories. They are listed below, with directions for conducting the prompted comprehension component of the Narrative Wordless Picture Book Task.

Explicit Questions

1. [Book closed; characters] "Who are the characters in this story?" [Replacement words: *people, animals*]
2. [Book closed; setting] "Where does this story happen?" [Replacement words: *setting, take place*]
3. [Book open to initiating event, usually the first page] "What happens at this point in the story? Why is this an important part of the story?"
4. [Book open to problem] "If you were telling someone this story, what would you say is going on now? Why did this happen?"
5. [Ending] "What happened here? Why did this happen?"

Implicit Questions

1. [Feelings] "Tell me what the people are feeling in this picture. Why do you think so?"
2. [Causal inference] "Why do you think this happened?"
3. [Go to page with people speaking] "What do you think the people would be saying here? Why would they be saying that?"
4. [Go to last page of the book] "This is the last picture in the story. What do you think happens next? Why do you think so?"
5. [Close the book; theme] "In thinking about everything that happened in this book, what have you learned from this story?"

Overall, this evaluation will give you a sense of the skills that precede being able to read with comprehension. Many of the skills assessed in this test are directly aligned with the CCSS in the early grades, particularly the child's ability to link the events in a story, generate inferences, and identify the theme.

WHAT TO DO WITH ASSESSMENT RESULTS?

Teaching children in the emergent literacy stage involves providing experience with books and book handling, as well as direct instruction in the skills needed for the next stage. It is important that children develop a foundation in print concepts and book handling, because this foundation is the basis for learning how to read connected text. Although we believe very strongly in decoding instruction, placing too much emphasis on decoding too early will lead to confusion later. Instead, we believe that a program for early readers should involve a balance among word work, text experience, and oral language development. A typical program for children reading at the emergent level would involve experience with predictable books, general book handling, phonological awareness instruction, word-recognition work, and responding to a wide variety of teacher read-alouds. It's important to keep in mind that the National Reading Panel (2000) determined that over a school year, instruction in phonemic awareness should take no more than 20 hours (that's about 6 minutes per day). In addition, they recommended using assessment to determine whether instruction should engage students in the easier tasks, such as rhyming and initial sound identification, or the more difficult manipulation and segmentation tasks. We offer suggestions in the following material.

Predictable Books

Predictable books are books that have a repetitive pattern, which supports children in learning print conventions (COW-T, fingerpointing, left-to-right progression, etc.) and provides what we call "book success." Experiencing book success is essential for children who have initially failed to learn to read, because it convinces them that they *can* learn to read.

Consider a book such as *Brown Bear, Brown Bear, What Do You See?* (Martin, 1967).

It is a simple pattern, with the pictures supporting the text. On one page is the pattern "[Color, animal], [color, animal], what do you see?" (the animals include a brown bear, a goldfish, a red bird, etc.). These animals are pictured. On the following page is "I see a [color, animal] looking at me." Thus reading is propelled by the pattern, which provides an excellent opportunity to teach both directionality and fingerpointing during the joint reading. It is easy to memorize the book, so that children can bring it home and demonstrate their "reading" skills to their parents as they develop facility with the alphabetic system.

Following the reading of a predictable book, a teacher can put some of the words on word cards and use these as the basis of word-reading or word-sorting lessons (see Chapter 5). Over the course of the child's program, the teacher works with progressively less predictable books. Among the available metrics for predictability are the Reading Recovery levels or the Fountas and Pinnell levels, now widely used to gauge book levels. These texts are important because the act of reading propels children's ongoing understanding about how the alphabetic system works (Morris et al., 2003).

In addition to predictable books, we recommend that daily literacy instruction should include some exposure to sophisticated storybooks and informational texts, used for comprehension. It is important for all children to continue to develop the vocabulary and comprehension skills needed for success in the later grades. Facilitating the acquisition of these skills might involve an interactive reading session, during which the teacher reads the book and pauses at key points to ask questions, model strategies, or prompt a discussion about the story.

Developing Phonological Awareness

Phonological awareness stems from the insight that words can be thought of as an ordered set of sounds. In normal development, this is learned through play or experimentation. For a child with reading problems, however, this experimentation should be directed through activities that encourage the child to think actively about sounds in words. Some of these activities are described in the following material.

Nursery Rhymes

Teaching common nursery rhymes should be part of every preschool and kindergarten class. We recommend that nursery rhymes be presented on charts, so that the children can learn basic print concepts as well as the rhyme. Rhymes can be chanted chorally by groups or memorized individually. Children should be encouraged to predict rhymes, write (or orally compose) another line in the rhyme, and so on.

Picture Sorting

Sorting pictures is an effective phonological awareness task. Teachers can gather pictures of objects that begin with the same sound, or, after children are proficient in beginning sounds, that end with the same sound. For example, children can sort pictures that begin with the same beginning as *bear* or *mom*. They can start with sorting two sounds, then move to three sounds. This exercise can be integrated with letter work, so that after a letter has been taught, the children can sort pictures that begin with the new sound from pictures that begin with previously taught sounds.

Oddity Tasks

Tasks that require students to identify the "odd one out" from a set of words can also improve phonemic awareness. A teacher might begin with rhyming words, progress to words that differ in beginning consonants, then move on to words differing in final consonants. Words that differ in medial consonants can be used, but may be too difficult at this level.

Stretch Sounding

Children can also be taught to stretch a word out so that phoneme changes can be heard clearly. For example, *dog* may be stretched to *d-d-d-o-g-g-g-g*. Teachers can do this by first modeling it, then having the students repeat what they have vocalized. Once students are proficient at stretching out words, a teacher can try having them clap or place a token in a box as they hear new sounds. For example, if the word is *sad,* the teacher would draw a row of three boxes. Students put a token into a box (moving from left to right, of course!) when they hear the phonemes change. As soon as students are able, the manipulation of letters should be incorporated in place of tokens. A Russian psychologist, Elkonin (1973), introduced this effective technique.

  Caution: Although we are using the term *phoneme* for clarity, we advise against teaching it or any other technical term to students. *Sound* can be used instead, but teachers should be clear in their own minds what they mean.

Invented Spelling

Stretch sounding should serve as a natural bridge to invented spelling, since one must stretch a word out in order to spell it. Invented spelling appears to improve phonemic awareness, among other skills. This point is discussed more thoroughly in Chapter 5.

Tongue Twisters

Students can repeat a tongue twister (from Wallach & Wallach, 1979), first in a regular fashion, then separating onset and rime. For example, for the /h/ sound, the tongue twister *Harry had a horrible headache and hated to hear Henry howl* might be separated out as *H-arry h-ad a h-orrible h-eadache and h-ated to h-ear H-enry h-owl.*

Adding Sounds

Teachers can take a common rime (*-ear, -ake, -all,* etc.) and have students add and subtract sounds. For example, a teacher might start by saying, "If I have *ear* and I add /h/, what do I have now? Then, if I take away the /h/ and add /w/, what do I have?" And so forth. This can be done later, using words on the blackboard.

Deletion Tasks

Teachers can have students say *burn* without the *b, pink* without the *p,* and so forth. Rosner (1975), who invented this task, chooses each word so that the result is a real word, but we do not employ this limitation—especially after the children get the hang of it.

The Troll

A teacher might use a troll puppet (or any other type of puppet) and say, "The troll will only allow people whose name begins with [or ends with, or has in it] the sound of ____ to cross the bridge." Then the teacher can give names (from the class or outside) and have students determine whether the troll will let this person cross the bridge. If this task proves too difficult, teachers can begin with syllables, using the same type of activity. The game can begin with continuant consonants (*m, s, n, f, z, v*) and vowels, because these can be sounded by themselves. Stop consonants (such as *t, d, b, c*) should be saved until later.

Alphabet Books

Today there are alphabet books based on myriad themes and topics. Using these books as shared reading or interactive teacher read-alouds is an excellent way to extend phonemic awareness and provide reinforcement for letter instruction. Children should be encouraged to repeat some of the words representing letter sounds and to generate their own words for selected pages. Alliterative word play is suggested. Books that draw attention to a clear letter–sound correspondence or letter–picture correspondence are likely to be more effective in teaching about letters and sounds than books that present letters as story characters or within the context of a story (Bradley & Jones, 2007). Alphabet books can provide opportunities for cross-curricular connections and vocabulary development. Children might be encouraged to create pages for a class alphabet book using science and social studies themes.

Alphabetic Work

Children in the United States and Canada are typically introduced to letter names and uppercase letters in their homes through songs, games, and television. In these countries, it makes sense to build on this knowledge in teaching young children about the alphabet.

There are many approaches to teaching letters individually. Recent research seems to suggest that systematically teaching a "letter of the day" (rather than one a week) allows for more distributed practice of the letters that are more difficult to learn (Jones & Reutzel, 2012; Piasta & Wagner, 2010b). We recommend continually reviewing all the letters taught, rather than placing them on the back burner, in essence, at the end of each week. Quickly and repeatedly reviewing previously introduced letters takes advantage of

a powerful learning principle: that of distributed review. In addition, combining phonological awareness training with instruction in letter names, formations, and sounds works
the best. We have children cut out pictures of items that contain the targeted letter from
old magazines, do picture sorts (see above), do the troll activity using letters rather than
sounds, and so on. We also integrate writing into these lessons, because learning to form
the letters provides writing practice as well as important reinforcement for learning the
names of the letters.

New evidence suggests that letter name knowledge is the strongest predictor of
letter–sound knowledge. Certain characteristics of children as well as letters make some
letters easier or harder to learn. Children who have stronger levels of phonological awareness are likely to learn letter sounds more easily than children who cannot separate the
onset from the rime. Additionally, not all letters need equal effort (Evans, Bell, Shaw,
Moretti, & Page, 2006; Huang, Tortorelli, & Invernizzi, 2014; Piasta & Wagner, 2010a,
2010b). These advantages should be considered in planning which letters to introduce
first and which letters will be likely to require the most instruction. Robust evidence
indicates that the letters that come first in children's own names, letters in the beginning
and ending of the alphabet, and the letters that have their own sound within the letter
name (*b, d, j, k, p, t, v, z, f, l, m, n, r, s*) are learned most easily. On the other hand, some
letter names have no association with their sounds (*h, w, y*) or an ambiguous association
(*c, g*, and vowels). These are among the most difficult letters for children to learn, even
for those who have attained high levels of phonological awareness. Teachers should plan
to spend more time teaching these letters than those that are more easily learned.

Word Work

Finally, at this emergent stage, we feel that some word learning is useful. A word-learning
activity might involve asking the children to pick out words that they want to learn or
words from the books they are reading. These words can be printed on index cards to be
practiced in isolation at home and in school. For older children, we have found that the
Three Strikes and You're Out procedure, described in Chapter 5, works well. If a word is
read correctly in three separate sessions, the word is "retired" or placed in some form of
word bank. Word cards also can be used for word sorting (see Chapter 5). In using these
sorts, we want the children to notice the features of words, not necessarily be able to spell
those words.

We also want children to write using invented spelling. This "writing" might be a
sentence or a story. In a typical classroom setting, a teacher might encourage the children to attempt to write daily about a topic of their choice. When time permits, a more
structured approach might be used. In Reading Recovery (Clay, 1993), for example, the
teacher and student agree on a sentence and work on writing the sentence together in a
writing notebook. When a challenge arises, the child writes what he or she can on a practice page. The teacher fills in what the child does not know, or may use Elkonin (1973)
boxes to break the word into sounds and add letters for the sounds that fit in the boxes.
Again, the child can be encouraged to do this by him- or herself or with teacher assistance. Making and breaking words that the teacher has modeled with magnetic letters is
also a good way for emergent readers to learn words.

It is important to remember that we want to provide a foundation for these young children, so that later reading will be successful and at the same time prepare the children quickly for formal reading instruction. For children at the emergent stage in first grade and beyond, we want to be efficient, so that we can get the children at this stage ready to work with their peers; often these children need to make more than a year's progress in a year's time. Indeed, they need to make "accelerated progress," in Clay's (1993) words, learning more material than they ordinarily might in the same amount of time. Programs such as Reading Recovery are designed to help children make such progress and should be considered as potential learning resources for any child with reading problems at this level.

Concept of Word Scale

Child's Name: _____ Grade: _____

Teacher: _____ Date _____

H						
G						
F						
E						
D						
C						
B						
A						
Session/ Date	1	2	3	4	5	6

Firm COW (G–H)

Rudimentary COW (E–G)

Developing COW (A–E)

Key: *What is the reader <u>pointing to</u>? What is the reader <u>saying</u> each time he or she points?*

A = <u>Points to</u> no discernible unit in any particular direction.

B = <u>Points to</u> no discernible unit in a left-to-right sweep.

C = <u>Points to</u> letters while <u>saying</u> each stressed unit

D = <u>Points to</u> a word while <u>saying</u> each stressed unit.

E = <u>Points to</u> a word while <u>saying</u> each syllable (gets off track on two-syllable words).

F = <u>Points to</u> a word while <u>saying</u> each syllable (gets off track on two-syllable words), but may self-correct (may or may not pick up a few words from reading).

G = Mostly accurate <u>pointing</u> while <u>saying</u> the correct word simultaneously; self-corrects when needed; picks up some words from reading.

H = Consistent and accurate <u>pointing</u> while <u>saying</u> the correct word simultaneously; picks up many/most words from reading.

From Gill (2019). Adapted with permission.

Checklist for Concepts of Print

Concept	Date / /	Date / /	Date / /	Date / /	Date / /	Date / /
Directionality (specify: book orientation, page, left to right, top to bottom, return sweep)						
Print carries message						
Word-by-word pointing						
Function of punctuation (specify known and unknown)						
Concept of first and last						
Concept of word and concept of letter						
Concepts of capital and lowercase letters						

Book-Handling Knowledge Guidelines

Name: _____ Age: _____ Grade: _____ Date: _____

> Before you begin, make sure that you are familiar with the test and the book you will be using. Make sure you select a book that has both pictures and a written story that includes the required punctuation marks. When you begin, be sure to make the child feel comfortable. If you quickly establish rapport, the results will be more valid. If a child shows mastery of a concept, check the provided space. If a child does not show mastery of a concept, leave the space blank or write what the child did.

Say: **I'm going to read you this story, but I want you to help me.**

1. Test: For orientation of book.

   Pass the book to the child. Hold the book vertically by its outside edge, spine toward the child. Say:

   Show me the front of the book

   Orientation of book

   Concept _____

2. Test: For the concept that print, not pictures, carries the message.

   Turn to the first page of the story. Say:

   I'll read this story. You help me. Show me where to start reading.

   Where do I begin?

   Print carries message

   Concept _____

   Read the page. Turn to the next page.

3. Test: For directional understanding (left to right, return sweep). Say:

   Show me where to start.

   (If child goes back to the beginning of the book, turn back to the page under discussion and provide the next prompt.)

   Show me where to start on this page.

   Which way do I go? (Child should indicate left-to-right motion.)

   Where do I go after that? (Child should go to beginning of next line.)

   Directional understanding

   Concept _____

   Read the page.

(continued)

4. Test: For speech-to-print match/word-by-word pointing. Say:
   Point to it while I read it.

   Read the page slowly but fluently.   Speech-to-print match

                                                               Concept _____

5. Test: For concept of first and last.

   Read the page. Say:
   Show me the first part of the story.
   Show me the last part of the story.   First and last (must have both)

                                                               Concept _____

6. Test: A left page is read before a right page.
   Read text until you come to a page that has print on both left and right sides
   of the page. Then ask:
   Where do I start reading?   Left page read before right

                                                               Concept _____

7. Test: Punctuation.
   Read text, then point to period and ask:
   What is this for?   .   Period recognition

                                                               Concept _____

   Read text, then point to question mark and ask:
   What is this for?   ?   Question mark recognition

                                                               Concept _____

   Read text, then point to exclamation point and ask:
   What is this for?   !   Exclamation point recognition

                                                               Concept _____

   Point to comma and ask:
   What is this for?   ,   Comma recognition

                                                               Concept _____

   Point to quotation marks and ask:
   What is this for?   " "   Quotation mark recognition

                                                               Concept _____

(continued)

8. Test: Lowercase letters.

   Point to a capital letter. Say:

   Find a little letter, or a lowercase letter, like this.

   Demonstrate correct match if child does not succeed.

   Point to a different capital letter. Say:

   Find a little letter, or a lowercase letter, like this.   Lowercase letter

   Concept _____

9. Concept of letter, word, first and last letter, capital letter.

   Use two index cards or small pieces of paper that a child can slide easily.
   To start, lay the cards on the page, but leave all the print exposed. Open the
   cards between questions.

   Read the last page of the book, then say:

   I want you to push the cards across the story like this. Demonstrate how
   you can move the cards across the page, coming from opposite directions.

   **Now I want you to push the cards across the page so all you can see is
   just one letter.**

   Now show me two letters.

                                                     Letter concept _____

   Now show me just one word.
   Now show me two words.

                                                     Word concept _____

   Take the cards again and show me the first letter of a word.

   Now show me the last letter of a word.   First and last _____

   Show me a capital or uppercase letter.   Capital letter _____

Alphabet Recognition Chart

A S D F C B E

R G T Y U H J

M Z P K V Q W

N O I X L

a s d f c b e

r g t y u h j

m z p k v q w

n o i x l α g

Tests of Phonological Awareness

Administration

For each subtest, provide one or two examples with feedback to be certain that the task is clear to the child. Then assess the student using five items without feedback. Mastery is indicated if the student is able to correctly complete four of the five items. All tasks are performed orally without the use of printed letters or words.

	Task description	Mastery 4/5 or 80%
Rhymes	a. Identifies teacher-generated words that rhyme or don't rhyme. b. Generates words that rhyme with a teacher prompt.	a. b.
Phoneme isolation	Isolates particular sounds from the remainder of the word. The child can identify /k/ as the first sound in the word *cake*.	
Phoneme identity	Given three words, the child can identify a common sound in all three words.	
Phoneme categorization	Say three words to the child, two of which have a common phoneme, such as an initial sound (e.g., *dog, horse, duck*). Ask the child to tell which of the three words does not belong with the other two.	
Blending	Tell the child that you are going to say a word in your own "secret code." Then pronounce the word by saying each phoneme in succession. For example, say "/k/ /a/ /t/." The child must blend these sounds to form the word *cat*.	
Phoneme addition	Provide the child with a common rime. Ask the child to make a word by adding a sound (e.g., add /sh/ to the beginning of *-ake*).	
Phoneme deletion	Say a common one-syllable word, such as *cake*. Ask the child to remove the beginning sound, so that the child says *ake*.	
Phoneme substitution	Ask the child to substitute one phoneme for another to make a new word. The word is *shake*. Change /k/ to /d/ to make a new word.	
Phoneme segmentation	a. Segments a word beginning and ending with single consonant into its individual sounds. (7/8) b. Segments a word beginning with a consonant cluster into its individual sounds. (10/12) c. Segments a word ending with a consonant cluster into its individual sounds. (11/13)	a. b. c.

(continued)

Skill	Sample Tasks	Score
Rhymes	a. *Pat* and *mat* go together because they rhyme. Which word doesn't belong? OR which two words rhyme? lit bun run fed eat wed rip clip tear pat pack tack hop rabbit stop b. *Pat* and *mat* rhyme. Tell me a word that rhymes with the words that I say. he say can mug fit	a. /5 b. /5
Phoneme isolation	The first sound that I hear in fish is /f/. Tell me first/last sound that you hear in each word that I say. First sound Last sound dime go kite buzz patch rag mail beef soup cone	/5
Phoneme identity	What is the same about the three words that I say? lamp list ladder vase vote visit tired toast tickle brown badge bother rusty real relative	/5
Phoneme categorization	Listen to the beginning sounds of the words I say. Which word doesn't belong with the other two words? sing Suzie shut happy joy jungle dig taste doll hug gown ghost wink wagon yellow	/5

(continued)

Skill	Sample Tasks	Score
Blending	I am going to say some words to you in a secret code. I want you to put the sounds together and tell me what word I said. For example, I say /k/ /a/ /t/ and you put those sounds together. What word would does it make? Right, it makes the word *cat*. /p / /ī/ (pie) (kindergarten only) /n/ /ō/ /s/ (nose) /s/ /i/ /k/ (sick) /b/ /u/ /g/ (bug) /ch/ /o/ /p/ (chop) /f/ /l/ /a/ /g/ (flag)	/5
Phoneme addition	Say *ake*. Now put /sh/ at the beginning of *-ake*. What word did you make? Yes, *shake*. Let's make more words like that. Say *oat. Now put* /k/ *at the beginning of -oat* (coat). Say *an. Now put* /m/ *at the beginning of -an* (man). Say *ate. Now put* /d/ *at the beginning of -ate* (date). Say *oke. Now put* /j/ *at the beginning of -oke* (joke). Say *and. Now put* /st/ *at the beginning of -and* (stand).	/5
Phoneme deletion	Say *shake*. Now say *shake* without the /sh/. What is left? Yes, *ake*. Say *pant* without the /p/ (ant) Say *shout* without the /sh/ (out) Say *tape* without the /t/ (ape) Say *cow* without the /k/ (ow) Say *crow* without the /k/ (row)	/5
Phoneme substitution	Say the word *shake*. Change /k/ to /d/ to make a new word. Say the word *shake*. Change /sh/ to /m/ to make a new word. Say the word *heat*. Change /t/ to /p/ to make a new word. Say the word *heat*. Change /h/ to /b/ to make a new word. Say the word *heat*. Change /ē/ to /i/ to make a new word. Say the word *couch*. Change /k/ to /p/ to make a new word.	/5

Phoneme segmentation	I am going to say a word to you, and I would like you to break the word apart. Say each sound separately and in order. For example, if I say *bat,* should say /b/ /a/ /t/. Now you do one—say each sound in *bike*. Yes, /b/ /ī/ /k/. (Score 1 point for each correct sound unit.)
	a. hay /h/ /ā/
	    lid /l/ /i/ /d/
	    feet /f/ /ē/ /t/
	b. step /s/ /t/ /e/ /p/
	    grub /g/ /r/ /u/ /b/
	    flake /f/ /l/ /ā/ /k/
	c. mask /m/ /a/ /s/ /k/
	    soft /s/ /o/ /f/ /t/
	    blast /b/ /l/ /a/ /s/ /t/
		a. /8
		b. /12
		c. /13

Hearing and Recording Sounds in Words

I am going to read you a story. When I have read it through once, I will read it again very slowly so that you can write down the words in the story. Read the sentences in Form A, B, or C. Then say to the child: *Some of the words are hard. Say them slowly and think how to write them. Just do your best to write the sounds that you hear.* Slowly dictate the two sentences, maintaining a pace that allows the child to write the words as you go, repeating phrases as needed.

Form A I   h a v e   a   b i g   d o g   a t   h o m e.   T o d a y

     1   2 3 4   5   6 7 8   9 10 11   12 13   14 15 16   17 18 19 20

 I   a m   g o i n g   t o   t a k e   h i m   t o   s ch oo l.

 21 22   23 24 25 26 27   28 29 30   31 32 33   34 35 36 37

Form B M o m   h a s   g o n e   u p   t o   th e   sh o p.

     1 2 3   4 5 6   7 8 9   10 11   12 13   14 15   16 17 18

 Sh e   w i ll   g e t   m i l k   a n d   b r ea d.

 19 20   21 22 23   24 25 26   27 28 29 30   31 32 33   34 35 36 37

Form C Th e   b oy   i s   r i d i n g   h i s   b i k e.   H e

     1 2   3 4   5 6   7 8 9 10 11 12   13 14 15   16 17 18   19 20

 c a n   g o   v e r y   f a s t   o n   i t.

 21 22 23   24 25   26 27 28 29   30 31 32 33   34 35   36 37

Score 1 point for each phoneme that the child represents appropriately that is numbered 1–37. It is not necessary that the phoneme be spelled correctly, only that it is represented. For example, a child who writes *skol* should receive 4 points for the word *school*. A child who represents the word *very* as *vare* should be scored 1 + 0 + 1 + 1 = 3. Deduct 1 point for a change in letter order (*hva*/have 3−1 = 2).

(continued)

National Percentile Ranks for First-Grade Students in the United States

Raw Score	Fall	Mid-Year	Year-End
0–1	1	1	1
2–4	1	1	1
5–6	2	1	1
7–8	3	1	1
9	4	1	1
10	5	1	1
11	6	1	1
12	7	1	1
13	8	1	1
14	9	1	1
15	10	1	1
16	12	1	1
17	13	1	1
18	14	1	1
19	16	1	1
20	18	1	1
21	20	1	1
22	22	1	1
23	24	2	1
24	26	2	1
25	29	2	1
26	33	3	1
27	37	4	1
28	41	5	1
29	45	6	2
30	50	8	3
31	56	11	3
32	63	16	5
33	69	22	8
34	76	30	13
35	83	43	24
36	90	63	45
37	99	99	99

Modified Emergent Storybook Reading Scale

Stage	Characteristics	Notes
Picture-Governed		
Labeling and commenting	1. Each page is treated as a separate unit. 2. Child either names or describes person/animal on each page or comments on it.	
Following the action	1. Each page is treated as a separate unit. 2. Child describes the action on each page.	
Storytelling in dialogue format	1. Child begins to make links between pages. 2. Overall, the listener can perceive a story, although it is disjointed. 3. Storytelling is in dialogue form, propelled by prompts from adult.	
Storytelling in monologue format	1. Child bridges plot between pages. 2. Tends to take the form of a monologue.	
Reading and storytelling mixed	Speech varies from storytelling to written register.	
Reading similar to original story and reading verbatim-like	1. Intonation sounds like reading. 2. Reading matches story events. 3. Attempt to recreate verbatim reading from pictures and memory.	

(continued)

After Sulzby (1985).

Stage	Characteristics	Notes
Print-Governed		
Print awareness	1. New awareness that we read printed words. 2. Child may refuse to read based on lack of print knowledge.	
Aspectual reading	1. Child attends to one or two aspects of printed words. 2. Beginning efforts to balance letter sounds and meaning. *Shift to leveled text reading assessment*	
Reading with strategies imbalanced	1. Developing balance in use of word recognition, syntax, and meaning. 2. May recognize errors, but unsure how to fix.	
Reading independently	1. Effective balance of word recognition, syntax, and meaning to arrive at accurate reading of print. 2. Self-corrections provide cues to processing.	

Picture Walk Scoring Guidelines

This book is called _____. In this book the pictures tell the story. There aren't any words written. I'd like you to look at the pictures in the book and use your own words to tell me the story.

Picture walk element	Score description	Score
1. Book-handling skills: Orients book correctly, has sense of appropriate viewing speed and order; viewing errors include skipping pages, speeding through pages, etc.	Incorrectly handles book and makes more than two viewing errors.	0
	Makes one to two viewing errors.	1
	Handles book appropriately, making no viewing errors.	2
2. Engagement: Displays behavioral and emotional involvement during the picture walk, as indicated by attention, interest in book, affect, and effort.	Displays off-task behavior or negative comments.	0
	Displays quiet, sustained behavior.	1
	Shows several examples of attention, affect, interest, or effort (i.e., spontaneous comments).	2
3. Picture comments: Makes discrete comments about a picture, including descriptions of objects, characters, emotions, actions, and options, as well as character vocalizations.	Makes no picture comments.	0
	Makes one picture comment or verbalization.	1
	Makes two or more comments or verbalizations about specific pictures.	2
4. Storytelling comments: Makes comments that encompass several pictures, demonstrating an understanding that the pictures tell a coherent story—can include narration, dialogue, using book language, and storytelling voice.	Makes no storytelling comments.	0
	Provides storytelling elements, but not consistently.	1
	Through narration or dialogue, connects story events and presents a coherent storyline.	2
5. Comprehension strategies: Displays vocalizations or behaviors that show attempts at comprehension, such as self-correcting, looking back/ahead in book, asking questions for understanding, making predictions about story.	Demonstrates no comprehension strategies.	0
	Exhibits one instance of comprehension strategies.	1
	Demonstrates comprehension strategies at least two or more times.	2

From Paris and Paris (2003). Copyright © John Wiley and Sons, Inc. Reprinted by permission.

Retelling Evaluation Guidelines

Did the child include . . .	Yes/No
Setting	
Characters	
A goal or initiating event	
A problem faced by a character, or episodes involving that character	
A solution to the problem	
A clear ending	

FIVE

Word Recognition and Spelling

Monitoring the development of word-recognition ability is one of the most important tasks of teachers in the primary grades and teachers of struggling readers in the upper grades. The broad area of word recognition is complex, however. There are many contributing skills to track, so it is important that teachers have a solid understanding of the skill areas underlying a student's ability to recognize words.

A useful way of organizing both assessment and instruction in this complex area is to divide it into three components: phonics, sight words, and morphological analysis. Let's look at each of these areas in turn.

PHONICS

Phonics refers to the ability to use letter–sound correspondences to derive the pronunciation of words. Good phonics assessments are nearly always individually administered, because the application of phonics skills requires that students produce pronunciations. Teachers obviously cannot monitor pronunciations in a group setting.

Phonics inventories are representations of what we know about the development of decoding skills. They are usually organized to test a set of skills in order from least to most difficult, or to assess a particular skill across examples. They may begin at the beginning—with individual consonant sounds, then single-syllable short-vowel words, then words with consonant blends and digraphs, for example. Keep in mind that we must consider the results of any assessment in light of the number of examples it uses. If a child can read the word *can*, does that mean that he or she can read *pan* and *man*? *Cat* and *cap*? Since individual words become sight words fairly quickly, it makes sense to test a particular skill with multiple probes.

Three phonics assessments are reviewed in this chapter. We begin with the Z-Test, an assessment that can reveal whether a child is able to decode one-syllable words quickly. If a problem is detected, one of the more detailed assessments can be given. The first of these is the Informal Phonics Inventory, which begins at the most basic level of phonics knowledge: consonant sounds. The other is the Informal Decoding Inventory, which begins with CVC words and continues through two-syllable words.

Z-Test

The Z-Test is a phonics assessment that targets a child's ability to make analogies to known words based on familiar rimes. The word *rime* has a technical meaning in this case. In a one-syllable word, it refers to the vowel and the consonant(s) following it. In the word *cat, -at* is the rime; in *date,* the rime is *-ate.* The Z-Test (Form 5.1, p. 131) presents the child with the 37 most familiar rimes, using the same onset, in order to focus the child's attention on the rime itself. The result is a series of pseudowords, all beginning with the /z/ sound. Children who recognize common rimes as word chunks will be able to pronounce most or all of these pseudowords as whole-word units. Students who are not proficient at making such comparisons may be able to pronounce many of the words by blending the phonemes individually. Their reliance on this strategy will be obvious. There are no norms or scoring criteria for interpreting the results of this test. Subjective judgment is required. On the other hand, pre- and postintervention administrations of this simple test will provide an enlightening indicator of improved decoding skills. We recommend timing the test to increase its level of sensitivity in quantifying the child's developing word-recognition processes.

Informal Phonics Inventory

The Informal Phonics Inventory (Form 5.2, p. 134) provides a convenient means of monitoring specific skill acquisition. The first three subtests (Consonant Sounds, Consonant Digraphs, and Beginning Consonant Blends) present children with individual letters or two-letter combinations and ask them to provide pronunciations. Some educators may object to such a task on the grounds that individual consonants cannot be pronounced without attaching a vowel sound. This may be true, but it is of very little importance, and taking such an objection too seriously deprives us of a valid means of assessing phonics knowledge. When children see the letter *b,* for example, they can be expected to say something like "buh." We treat these items as specific, constrained skills. If a child knows them, we do not have to teach them. If a child doesn't, we do.

The next two subtests use real words. On the Final Consonant Blends subtest, the children are scored for their ability to read each blend as part of the real word. Notice that all of the words contain short vowels. This is because short vowels are typically mastered first. However, children need only pronounce the blend correctly to get credit for each item. You will see that some children can pronounce the blend but confuse the short-vowel sounds. We test short-vowel knowledge next. In the Short Vowels in CVC Words subtest, the item is scored correctly as long as the correct vowel sound is read. For example, reading *tim* for *tin* is considered correct. The Rule of Silent *e* subtest is more difficult, because it seems to require that the child consciously apply the rule rather than simply read the words.

We recommend that you use the Informal Phonics Inventory in Form 5.2 in two steps. Use it first as a diagnostic assessment to determine areas on which to focus instruction. The scoring table will help you identify these areas. After you have provided instruction, you can then use it to track the progress of individual students as they learn specific skills. The chart included in Form 5.2 is designed to help you keep track of skill mastery as you readminister portions of the Informal Phonics Inventory from time to time.

Informal Decoding Inventory

Beginning at a more advanced level, the Informal Decoding Inventory (Walpole & McKenna, 2017) consists of a series of short progressive subtests that follow the sequence in which decoding skills are typically acquired (see Form 5.3, p. 141). The teacher gives only the subtests that are likely to be near a child's level of development. Using available information, such as classroom performance, the teacher starts at the appropriate point and proceeds upward (and occasionally downward) in search of the first level at which mastery has not been attained.

Each subtest consists of two sets of 10 words representing a particular skill. The first set contains real words; the second consists of pseudowords. For example, in the initial subtest, Short Vowels, the first real word is *sat,* and the first pseudoword is *mot.* Including pseudowords provides a second window into decoding and, as in the Z-Test, prevents the possibility that sight-word knowledge will inflate performance. The Multisyllabic Words subtest contains only real words that differ in syllable type. As in the Informal Phonics Inventory, an 80% criterion is used for real words, though a more lenient 60% criterion is used for pseudowords. The teacher weighs these two in tandem. The first test at which the child falls below the criteria becomes the target of instruction.

KNOWLEDGE OF HIGH-FREQUENCY WORDS

Let's begin with a common confusion in terminology. It concerns the distinction between a *sight word* and a *high-frequency word.* These terms are often used interchangeably, but there is a difference. A sight word is any word that an individual reader can read and pronounce automatically, without conscious analysis. Believe it or not, nearly every word in this book is a sight word for you. As a skilled reader, you rarely stop and sound out words. In fact, when you have to, you may become a bit irritated. However, not every word in this book would be a sight word for a beginning reader (e.g., a beginning reader might struggle with the word *could,* but you would not). Thus sight words are individual to each reader.

In contrast, not all of the words in this book are high-frequency words—that is, those words that occur most often in written English (such as *of, but, can,* etc.). There is a tendency to confuse the notion of sight words (which are specific to an individual reader) with that of high-frequency words (which are specific to a language, but are the same for every reader in that language). It is true that all high-frequency words must eventually become sight words if a reader is to be fluent. However, even a reader's initial sight vocabulary must include many low-frequency words, such as his or her last name. Sight vocabularies, therefore, differ considerably from one student to the next (you might be able to automatically recognize the word *could,* but a beginning reader might not), while high-frequency words are the same for everyone who reads in a particular language. The word *could* is the 68th most frequent word in English, regardless of the fact that you can read it and a beginning reader might struggle with it (Zeno, Ivens, Millard, & Duvvuri, 1995).

Knowledge of high-frequency words as sight words is essential for fluent reading. According to Carroll, Davies, and Richman (1971), 109 of the most frequent English words make up 50% of all words found in reading material for grades 3–8. If you are skeptical, just go back over the preceding paragraph, and you'll note that nearly every other word is a high-frequency word like *as, is her, that,* and *the*. It's no wonder, then, that teachers hope that all of their students eventually master these high-frequency words as individual sight words; without automatic sight-word knowledge of English's most frequent words, no one would be able to read anything fluently.

In order to assess high-frequency words, a teacher must begin with a target list. Primary teachers typically use the Dolch (1936) or Fry (1980) list or some other compilation of high-frequency words. Next, the teacher must decide on an assessment format in order to gain knowledge about how many of these words each child can pronounce automatically, or at sight.

One way—a very efficient one—is to assess children as a group. The format presented below is designed for such a group assessment. Some standardized tests, such as i-Ready, test high-frequency words in this way. The children are presented with row after row of words, each row containing four words. In the first example, the teacher leads the children from one row to the next, instructing them to circle one of the words.

Example 1

Teacher says, "Circle *book*." Child sees row of four words.

pear   book   bolt   napkin

The time saved through group assessment is considerable, of course. However, the accuracy of the results may be compromised, as it often is in group assessments. For example, a child who is familiar with the sound made by the letter *b* will be able to eliminate the first and fourth words of the sample item, even though the word *book* may not yet be a sight word for that child. Reading the word is a higher skill level than identifying a spoken word in text.

In contrast, consider the format presented in Example 2, designed for individual administration. In this case, the teacher shows the child a word and asks for a pronunciation. The words can be presented on flash cards in list form. We recommend placing the words on PowerPoint slides that are timed at 1 second per slide for kindergarten and first grade, and 0.5 second per slide for older students.

Example 2

Teacher says, "Say this word." Child sees flash card.

book

It is important that the teacher remember that a sight word is one that can be pronounced immediately, without analysis. If a student takes more than 0.5 second (1 second in K–1) to produce the pronunciation or perceptibly "sounds it out," then that word cannot reasonably be judged a sight word. In fact, words that are in a skilled reader's sight vocabulary are recognized in less than 0.25 second (Rayner et al., 2012).

It is easy to construct a sight-word inventory once you have decided on which target words to include. Many lists are available. Some include shorter, high-frequency word lists (e.g., the Dolch [1936] list of 220 and Fry [1980] lists of 300 and 600 "instant" words). Some are longer lists that include words of lower frequency. Though these lists were constructed with different procedures, you will see that they have many words in common. Form 5.4 (p. 145) presents Fry's list of 300 instant words in the form of a sight-word inventory. Form 5.5 (p. 152) displays Dolch's list of 220 words categorized by approximate level. Although the personnel at some schools may prefer to construct a simple sight-word inventory based on their reading programs, we recommend using the more popular Dolch or Fry lists. Keep the big picture in mind. A sight-word inventory is a sampling of items; it is not a full examination of a child's sight-word knowledge.

For older students, it is a good idea to use a normed list to compare their results with the results of other students their age. They know many sight words, so it can be difficult to determine whether their sight-word knowledge is hindering their reading fluency and comprehension. The Test of Word Reading Efficiency—Second Edition (TOWRE-2) is a measure of word-reading accuracy and efficiency (Torgesen, Wagner, & Rashotte, 2012). The TOWRE-2 Sight Word Efficiency task is a list of high-frequency words that students read individually in 45 seconds. Raw scores can be converted into percentiles, scale scores, and age and grade equivalents.

Regardless of the list you use, it is important to keep in mind that sight-word knowledge consists of a set of individual words. That is to say, each word is a separate skill! Were you to administer a sight-word inventory, it would therefore make little sense to tally the number of words a child can pronounce at sight, except as a general measure of growth. Rather, each of the words represents a distinct skill—a word worth knowing in its own right. A sight-word inventory, then, is a clear example of a diagnostic test. It provides a specific instructional target.

Essential Words

For older children, it is useful to know what they know about *survival words* or *essential words*. These are words that children (and adults) need to know to survive in the real world. We present two lists of essential words, but these are only a beginning and are by no means comprehensive. Teachers of older students with special needs and of students with severe learning disabilities may need to prioritize the instruction of words selected from our essential-word lists. The first list (Table 5.1) contains an older set of words; the next list (Table 5.2) is an updated version by Davis and McDaniel (1998). There may be others that are important in your town or for particular children. Again, use our lists as a starting point.

TABLE 5.1. The Original Essential Vocabulary

adults only	flammable	noxious
antidote	found	nurse
beware	fragile	office
beware of the dog	gasoline	open
bus station	gate	out
bus stop	gentlemen	out of order
caution	handle with care	pedestrians prohibited
closed	hands off	poison
combustible	help	poisonous
condemned	high voltage	police (station)
contaminated	inflammable	post no bills
deep water	information	post office
dentist	instructions	posted
do not cross, use tunnel	keep away	private
do not crowd	keep closed at all times	private property
do not enter	keep off (the grass)	pull
do not inhale fumes	keep out	push
do not push	ladies	safety first
do not refreeze	live wires	shallow water
do not shove	lost	shelter
do not stand up	men	smoking prohibited
do not use near heat	next (window) (gate)	step down (up)
do not use near open flame	no admittance	taxi stand
doctor (Dr.)	no checks cashed	terms cash
don't walk	no credit	thin ice
down	no diving	this end up
dynamite	no dogs allowed	this side up
elevator	no dumping	up
emergency exit	no fires	use before [date]
employees only	no fishing	use in open air
entrance	no hunting	use other door
exit	no loitering	violators will be prosecuted
exit only	no minors	walk
explosives	no smoking	wanted
external use only	no spitting	warning
fallout shelter	no swimming	watch your step
fire escape	no touching	wet paint
fire extinguisher	no trespassing	women
first aid	not for internal use	

MORPHOLOGICAL ANALYSIS

Morphemes are the smallest units of meaning in a word. The word *cat* has just one morpheme, but *cats* has two (*cat-s*) and so does *cattail* (*cat-tail*). Following are five types of morphemes we want our older students to work with and understand; for older students, we strongly recommend posting an anchor chart in your classroom with these five word parts highlighted, for reference throughout the year.

1. *Prefixes:* Units of meaning that are attached *before* a base word or root (e.g., *pre-*, *in-*). Prefixes can modify the core meaning of a base word or root (*preview* is "to view before"; *inhuman* is "not human").
2. *Suffixes:* Units of meaning that are attached *after* a base word or root (e.g., *-ion*, *-ist*, *-ous*). Suffixes can change a word's part of speech (e.g., *-ion* changes the verb *elect* to the noun *election*).

TABLE 5.2. Updated List of Essential Words

10 items or less	falling rock	pay cashier before pumping
30 days same as cash	fasten seat belt	pay here
911	fax machine	pedestrian crossing
airbags	fire alarm	polluted area
alternate route	fire exit	prepare to stop
aluminum cans only	flagger ahead	quiet please
ambulance	flush	radiation hazard
asbestos hazard	for help dial	radioactive materials
automatic	form line here	radioactive waste
biohazard	handicapped parking	railroad crossing
biohazardous waste	hard hat area	read directions before using
blasting zone	harmful	recyclable
bomb threat	hazard	recycle
breakable	hazardous	refrigerate
bridge ices before road	hazardous area	restricted area
buckle up	hazardous chemicals	restrooms
bump	hazardous waste	resume safe speed
business route	help wanted	right of way
by-pass	hospital	right turn only
caffeine	ID required	road closed
cancerous	if swallowed, induce vomiting	school crossing
cash only	in case of fire	school zone
cellular phones prohibited	incinerate	service engine
chemicals	incinerator	self-service
children at play	infectious area	shake well
clearance	insert card (ATM)	shirt and shoes required
construction ahead	irritant	signature
consult physician before use	keep away from water	slippery when wet
danger	keep frozen	slow down
dangerous	keep out of reach of children	soft shoulders
deer crossing	keep refrigerated	speed limit
delay	kerosene	stairs (stairway)
deliveries	lifeguard on duty	stop ahead
detour	loading zone	subway
diesel fuel	makes wide turns	Surgeon General warning
directions	manager	take with food
dispose	may cause birth defects	teller machine
do not bend	may cause dizziness	through traffic
do not block intersection	may cause drowsiness	timecard
do not enter	microwave in use	time clock
do not get in eyes	microwave safe	tornado warning
do not ingest	minimum speed	tornado watch
do not mix	must be 21 years of age	tow away zone
do not take if allergic to . . .	no jet skis allowed	tow zone
do not take with milk	no left turn	toxic
do not use near water, fire, etc.	no littering	toxic waste
dosage	no outlet	turn off cellular phones
drive in	no pagers	turn signal
drive through	no parking	uneven shoulder
drive-up window	no pets	use only as directed
electrical hazard	no photographs permitted	ventilation required
Emergency Medical Services	no refunds	video camera in use
enter only	no returns	video monitor in use
escalator	no through traffic	watch for falling rocks
exact change (needed)	no turn on red	watch for trucks
exit only	no video cameras allowed	wear protective eye gear
expect delays	nonalcoholic	wear safety glasses
expiration	nontoxic	weight limit
expires (EXP)	nuclear waste	wide load
explosives	one way	wrong way
express line	order here	X-ray
evacuate	oxygen in use	yield

3. *Affixes:* The collective term for prefixes and suffixes.
4. *Base words:* Words that can stand alone as English words. For example, in the word *ungovernable, govern* is a base word because it can stand as a word by itself. *Un-* ("not") is the prefix, and *-able* ("capable of") is the adjective-forming suffix.
5. *Roots:* Word parts, often of Greek or Latin origin, that combine with affixes to form words. A root *cannot* stand alone as a word (e.g., the *-spect* in *retrospect* is a Latin root that means "look"). *-Spect-* is not a word in English, but when combined with the prefix *retro-*, it creates a word. In contrast to many programs, we prefer the term *root* to the more commonly used *root word*, because, as one of our students asked us, "Why do they call it a root word when it's not even an actual word?" Remind your students that Latin and Greek roots, like *-spect*, need to be attached to other word parts to "live" as stand-alone words in English—just as plant roots need to be attached to other plant parts, like stems and leaves, to stay alive.

Morphological analysis is the act of breaking down words into these various units of meaning (e.g., prefixes, suffixes, roots). Children are required to use morphological analysis from an early age, as when they differentiate singular from plural forms or past and present tenses of verbs. As the material they read becomes more complex, a greater array of affixes confronts them. The ability to take apart an unfamiliar word in order to determine its meaning is of increasing importance.

Just how powerful is this morphological system? Is it worth teaching? Consider this: 90% or more of upper-level English vocabulary words are of Latin or Greek origin (Green, 2008). When we teach just one powerful root (e.g., the Greek root *-arch/-archy*, meaning "rule" or "chief"), we are giving our students the key to unlock scores of related word meanings (e.g., *monarch/monarchy, anarchy, patriarch, matriarch, oligarchy, archetype, hierarchy, archbishop, archangel, architect*), all sharing the core meaning of "rule" or "chief." With morphology, a little goes a long way. When we teach affix and root knowledge like this, we are not just giving our students fish so they can eat for a day; we are teaching them how to fish for words for the rest of their lives. This is an incredibly powerful and efficient way to boost vocabulary knowledge.

Assessing Affix and Root Knowledge

However, assessing a child's proficiency in the area of affix/root knowledge can be problematic. One way would be to show the child a sentence containing a word that is subject to structural analysis (i.e., a word that can be structurally analyzed). This approach allows the teacher to see if the student can apply his or her affix and root knowledge in context. For example, let's say the child is shown this sentence:

The hot sun made the man uncomfortable.

The teacher asks the child what the word *uncomfortable* means, or perhaps how the man felt. If the child responds by saying that the man felt bad, or words to that effect, would the teacher be justified in assuming that the child has used structural analysis? Perhaps, but the word *uncomfortable* is so common that it might well already be a sight word for that particular child.

Another approach to assessment is simply to ask the meanings of common prefixes and suffixes, such as those shown in the following charts. That is, if the child understands that the prefix *un-* means "not," then this knowledge can be tested the way we might test other vocabulary knowledge. For example, a teacher could simply inventory a child's ability to supply the meanings of familiar affixes. The problem with this approach, however, is that it in no way guarantees that the child can apply this knowledge of affixes to the words encountered in real reading and writing.

Assessing Application and Depth of Affix and Root Knowledge: Generating Related Words Task

To solve this problem of assessing affix/root knowledge in isolation, you can add a simple task called Generating Related Words to the affix/root assessment described above, to assess whether students can actually apply their affix or root knowledge to English words (as opposed to simply knowing that the prefix *sub-* means "below," but not being able to apply it to related words like *submarine* or *subatomic*). Following is a sample assessment task you can use to assess a learner's affix or root knowledge (Templeton et al., 2015). For each affix or root, the student is presented with the target word part (which is not defined) and an example word that contains that target word part (e.g., *re-*, *return*). For each affix/root, ask the student to (1) think of and write four (or more) related words with the same prefix or root as the example word, and (2) then write the meaning of the prefix or root.

Prefixes and Roots

re- (example: *return*) redo, reuse, replay, rerun
re- means: again

inter- (example: *international*) intermission, interact, intercontinental railroad
inter- means: between

-tract- (example: *distract*) retract, traction, tractor, contract
-tract- means: pull

While this assessment may be somewhat challenging for students, it is one of our favorite ways to assess morphological knowledge with older students, for a number of reasons. First, we can quickly and efficiently gauge the depth of learners' knowledge of a target morpheme by the quantity and sophistication of the related words they can generate. Second, we can administer this assessment quickly and efficiently in a whole-group setting. Third, this task taps learners' ability to apply their affix/root knowledge in writing. Finally, we've found that students are often better able to determine an affix or root's meaning after generating the related words. We can also dig deeper later by asking students to define the actual words they've generated. Periodically assess these same affixes and roots as a postintervention assessment to measure growth in morphological knowledge.

The three lists below include (1) high-utility prefixes and their meanings, (2) high-utility suffixes and their meanings, and (3) high-utility Latin and Greek roots and their meanings. You can assess and teach these in the upper elementary grades and beyond. Use the Generating Related Words task described above for these affixes/roots. Those the child cannot define and/or generate related words for can be taught, and the list becomes an informal diagnostic assessment.

We strongly recommend posting these affixes/roots and their meanings in your classroom as you teach them, and providing individual affix/root reference sheets your students can refer to while reading, writing, and learning across the content areas. You and your students will be amazed at how often these roots come up across the day in math, science, social studies, and ELA. It is one of the best ways we know to make connections across the content areas, as these meaning parts are already naturally embedded in the vocabulary of your curriculum.

Common Prefixes and Their Meanings

un-	not	ir-	not	ex-	out
in-	not	il-	not	ante-	before
im-	not	a-	not	anti-	against
sub-	below	kilo-	1,000	de-	away
super-	above	mega-	large	dis-	apart from
mono-	one	micro-	small	dis-	opposite
uni-	one	multi-	many	extra-	beyond
bi-	two	over-	above	fore-	in front of
di-	two	poly-	many	mal-	bad
tri-	three	prim-	first	magni-	large
quad-	four	proto-	first	medi-	middle
tetra-	four	sol-	along	mid-	middle
quint-	five	tele-	far	mis-	wrong
penta-	five	under-	below	neo-	new
hexa-	six	ab-	away from	omni-	all
septa-	seven	ad-	to	post-	after
oct-	eight	auto-	self	pre-	before
deca-	ten	bene-	good	pro-	forward
cent-	hundred	circ-	around	re-	again
ambi-	both	con-	with	trans-	across
semi-	half	com-	with	ultra-	beyond
hyper-	over	con-	against		

Common Suffixes and Their Meanings

-less	without	-ness	state of	-ment	state
-er	more	-ous	like	-itis	disease

-est	most	-ish	like	-phobe	one who fears
-ette	small	-logy	study of	-ism/-ist	belief/one who
-trix	woman	-ly	like		believes in

Suffixes can be difficult to define. We recommend that suffixes be presented in words, rather than in isolation.

Common Greek and Latin Roots and Their Meanings

micro, min	small	macro	large	aud	hear
scope	watch	spec/spic	see	gram/graph	write
scrib/script	write	voc	call	fract, rupt	break
struct	build	bio	life	geo	earth
therm	heat	photo	light	port	carry
tract	pull	hydra/hydro	water	aster/astr	star
dem	people	jur, leg	law	spir	breathe
fid	faith	soph	wisdom	polis	city, state, citizen

SPELLING

Since the pioneering work of Edmund Henderson (1981), Charles Read (1971), and Carol Chomsky (1979), educators have known that the invented spelling of young children follows a clear developmental pattern. As children learn about written words, their attempts at spelling reflect this growing sophistication of their knowledge of orthographic patterns. We follow the stages outlined by Henderson as we examine this growth. Different authors may use different names to describe the developmental stages. We apply the stage names used by Bear and colleagues (2020).

Emergent Spelling

Children's initial attempts at writing are generally nonalphabetic; sometimes these first attempts are pictures but are called "writing" by the children. Later attempts are scribbles that, although illegible to observers, can be "read" by the young writers. Harste, Burke, and Woodward (1982), working with children of different cultures in a university day care center, found that their scribbles reflected the print to which they were exposed. Thus children from Arab families produced scribbles that resembled Arabic, children from Chinese families made scribbles that resembled Chinese characters, and so on. This correspondence suggests that scribbles represent an early understanding of the form of print.

When children learn letters, they incorporate those letters into their spelling. At first, these letter strings have nothing to do with the sounds in the word itself. So *bear* might be represented by MSDF.[1] We have to learn to view early writing as a demonstra-

---

[1] We use all caps to note invented spelling, regardless of how a "word" was written.

tion of what children do know rather than what they don't. The use of letters, rather than scribbles, suggests that the children (1) know the convention that words must be made up of letters, and (2) know at least some letters. At this stage, children often begin to write words logographically. That means that they may be spelling a learned word as a unit, such as their names, MOM, or STOP.

As children continue to learn letters and develop some phonemic awareness, their spellings begin to reflect their emergent analysis of words. Children's spellings may consist only of a letter representing an initial or final sound, such as *J* for *jam* or *S* for *sun*. Sometimes a child at this stage may put down a letter representing a single sound and then add others, such as the girl we worked with who first put down an *f* for *fish* and then added additional letters—FZTHSLT—saying that "*f*-words were always long." Children who can represent a sound in a word with a letter are developing rudimentary phonemic awareness. Our research shows that such children nearly always use initial sounds to identify written words (Stahl & McKenna, 2001). Spelling development closely follows the development of word recognition but lags a little behind, because spelling is a production task, and production tasks are more difficult than recognition tasks. This level, however, seems necessary for children to make sense of the alphabetic system.

As children continue to analyze words in terms of phonological awareness as well as written word recognition, their spellings become increasingly complex. First they add final consonants, so that *bear* becomes BR or *hen* becomes HN. Often their spellings reflect the way they analyze the words as they are saying them. So blends such as *dr*, as in *dragon*, may be represented by JR, because that is how the child may hear it. Other blends may be represented by single consonants.

Letter Name–Alphabetic Spelling

Learning about vowels is the next large conceptual leap for children. Emergent spellings do not include vowels. The inclusion of vowel markers, whether correct or incorrect, represents a child's beginning knowledge of the alphabetic principle. Spoken words fold consonants around the vowel, so that they are copronounced; a consonant is pronounced slightly differently with each vowel. Children can be aware of consonants through sensitivity to articulatory gestures (Byrne, 1998); still, consonants are difficult to isolate within words (Shankweiler & Liberman, 1972).

Children generally begin to include vowels in their spellings by about first grade. Whether this inclusion is due to instruction or experience with language is not clear, but the shift is an important one for children learning to read and spell. At this point, *bear* may be represented as BAR, with the child using the letter name "AY" to represent the long-vowel /A/ sound; similarly, *hen* may be spelled HAN.[2] As the name of this stage indicates, children at this stage use the letter name strategy when spelling words. This

---

[2] The substitution of *a* for short *e* may be due to a letter name. The sound of long *a* is really a diphthong of /ey/. When children want the short-*e* sound, they find it in the sound of the letter name "a," which actually begins with a short-*e* sound! Although this hypothesis seems to be a stretch, the substitution of short *a* for short *e*, and *i* for short *a* (/ay/), is common enough that it seems a plausible explanation. Another explanation is that short *e* and long *a* both "feel" similar because they are both *front* vowels (i.e., both sounds are made in similar places of articulation in the vocal tract).

means that they use the *names* of the letters as clues to the *sounds* these letters represent. This works for many letters (e.g., the use of "bee" for the letter *B* and the long vowels such as "ee" for the letter *E* makes sense), but not for a number of other letters (e.g., the letter name "WIE" for *Y* actually makes the /w/ sound; the short vowel "eh," like all the short vowels, has no correlating letter name in the alphabet).

At the earlier points of this stage, children may use the letter name to represent a syllable—GRL and LETR are common—but most typical is the emergence of vowels. Consistently representing vowels in words indicates that the child understands the alphabetic principle: namely, that letters represent the sounds that make up spoken words.

Within Word Pattern Spelling

The letter name spelling stage is fueled by acquisition of the alphabetic principle. The within word pattern stage involves the learning of high-frequency spelling patterns—or sequences of letters—that occur in written words (e.g., "ai" in *rain*, "ay" in *day*). At this point, children (1) consistently spell words with short vowels correctly; (2) begin to show sensitivity to patterns in words; (3) make distinctions between long and short vowels; and (4) use long-vowel markers, although not always correctly. Thus *bake* might be BAIK but not BAK; *like* is spelled LIKE or LEIK not LIK. In addition, children use *-ed* and *-ing* endings. This stage, which is usually achieved by the end of second or early third grade, is characterized by mastery of basic sound–symbol spelling conventions and a growing knowledge about the large variety of spelling patterns that represent single sounds. Due to the different representations of the same sound, instruction must incorporate distributed practice over time that allows students to practice spelling and reading a collection of words beyond the small list of words that were taught.

Further growth in spelling moves from the purely sound–symbol and pattern levels to the morphological level, as children master the basic orthographic patterns and display an emerging awareness of spelling–meaning relationships.

Syllables and Affixes Spelling

The next stage might also be called the *syllable juncture stage,* because it represents children's knowledge of how syllables fit together. The most obvious marker is the consonant-doubling rule; children during this stage develop consistency in spelling words that end with *-ing* or *-ed,* and in knowing when the consonants have to be doubled and when they do not (e.g., *bat–batted* vs. *bait–baited*). Children learn other conventions at this stage, such as the use of *-y* or *-le* at the end of words, but they may not consistently apply them. This stage signals that children are ready to work with strategies for approaching multisyllabic words.

This stage represents children's initial use of morphological knowledge to spell words. During this time period, children master *bound morphemes,* or morphemes that do not stand alone as words (affixes and roots). The morphemes mastered also tend to function as syntactic markers, such as tense or number (e.g., the plural formed by adding *-s* or *-es*). Children can usually be observed in this stage between grades 3 and 8.

Derivational Relations Spelling

At the stage of derivational constancy or derivational relations, children learn to use spelling to recognize and represent semantic relationships between words, even words that are pronounced differently. Thus children may use knowledge that words are derived from a common root to spell them conventionally. For example, children may use the relationships between words like *fantasy* and *fantastic* and *fantasize,* or *inspire* and *inspiration,* to help spell them conventionally. This stage may continue through adulthood as the derivational relationships between words provide a means of connecting spelling and meaning.

Spelling Inventories

There are multiple spelling assessments available to determine and analyze a student's spelling stage. Among the most popular are those by Ganske (2014) and Bear and colleagues (2020). We have included the Developmental Spelling Analysis (DSA) Screening Inventory from *Word Journeys, Second Edition* (Ganske, 2014) in Form 5.6 (p. 154). The purpose of the DSA Screening Inventory is to identify a student's spelling stage. It is designed to be followed by one of the 25-item stage feature inventory lists for a precise analysis of a student's performance on specific word features within a particular stage. As the student progresses, different forms of the feature inventories are used to trace developmental growth. In *Words Their Way* (Bear et al., 2020), each of three inventories (primary, elementary, upper-level) has an accompanying feature guide to identify spelling patterns that require instruction.

This discussion is only preliminary; the interested reader is referred to the books by Ganske (2014) and Bear and colleagues (2020) for more in-depth assessments, discussions of how spelling analysis can be used for planning instructional programs, and developmentally appropriate teaching activities.

TEACHING WORD RECOGNITION AND SPELLING

Entire books have been written about techniques for teaching children to recognize words (e.g., Bear et al., 2020; Cunningham, 2012; Ganske, 2014; Hayes & Flanagan, 2014; O'Connor, 2014). In this section, we highlight a few techniques that we use often in the clinic.

The first rule of clinical practice in working with a struggling reader is to "find out what has been done before, and don't do it." This is truer in the area of word recognition than in any other area. A first-grade child with whom Kay worked as a teacher had come from another school and read at a preprimer level. He had worked very diligently and had reached a point where he was ready to use a particular phonics workbook for additional practice. At his then-current stage of development, this would have been an easy review, for he had already mastered the material. However, because he had used that particular book in his previous school and had failed miserably with it, he recoiled and would not touch it. Perhaps this is an extreme example, but the principle holds: Do not use an approach that has failed in the past, whether or not it is appropriate, because it will not work now.

Numerous different approaches to teaching word recognition are currently available. Stahl, Duffy-Hester, and Stahl (1998) divide phonics instruction into traditional, constructivist, and spelling-based approaches. Hence we briefly review synthetic phonics (a traditional approach); compare–contrast (a constructivist approach); and making words (Cunningham & Cunningham, 1992) and word sorts (Bear et al., 2020) (spelling-based approaches). We begin with a description of word banks, a tried-but-true method of building sight vocabulary based on the principle of distributed review.

Word Banks

Words missed on a high-frequency word inventory, causing trouble during oral reading, or partially known but not yet solidly stored in memory can be used to develop a word bank or as an informational source for planning additional instruction. Words can be written on 3" × 5" index cards and used for practice in a game called Three Strikes and You're Out. Words correctly identified by a child on three different occasions are retired from the word bank; a growing number of "retired" words can be highly motivating. Children can practice words from each other's word banks during individual reading time.

Synthetic Phonics

Synthetic phonics instruction starts with teaching letter sounds and then supporting students as they blend these sounds to form words. The word *synthetic* refers to the fact that students build, or synthesize, words by blending the phonemes. The student begins by sounding out words, first in lists and then in texts (often decodable texts). The hallmark of synthetic phonics is that children are taught to *blend* sounds together to make words. An example:

1. If the letter *e*, representing the short sound of *e*, is to be taught, the teacher presents the letter *e* on the blackboard or on a note card. The teacher may say, "This is the letter *e*. It says /e/."

2. Next, the teacher writes the word *pet* on the board or presents three note cards with the letters *p*, *e*, and *t* on them. (The use of note cards allows a physical demonstration blending.) The teacher demonstrates the blending of the letters to make the word *pet* by running his or her finger under the letters (if the blackboard is used) or pushing the cards together.

3. Students practice blending the word *pet* as a group.

4. The teacher then writes or shows a list of words, such as these:

| pen | bet | deck | mesh | then | peck | let |
| send | less | yet | fed | bent | shed | tell |

The students blend the words together, at first as a group and then individually.

5. Next, the students read a decodable text that contains words with the short sound of *e*.

6. We find that an especially effective follow-up, either later in the lesson or immediately following the reading of the decodable text, is to have children write short-*e* words from dictation.

7. Following this lesson, the teacher may further follow up on the short sound of *e* by using a compare–contrast approach, having each student practice on short-*e* words with a partner, or having students use a computer program that provides practice on short-*e* words.

Synthetic phonics is used in a number of commercial programs, but the basic lesson can be done quite easily. The steps described above should be done at a brisk pace to ensure engagement. This foundational approach can be used to introduce patterns that a child has missed on the Informal Phonics Inventory or on one of the other measures presented in this chapter.

Compare–Contrast Approaches to Phonics

In the compare–contrast approach, children are taught to compare new words to already known words. This method is used at the Benchmark School in Media, Pennsylvania (Gaskins et al., 1988; Gaskins, Ehri, Cress, O'Hara, & Donnelly, 1996). In synthetic phonics, teachers help children learn to sound out words; in the compare–contrast system, teachers help children learn how to use analogies to decode unknown words. Since adult learners use both types of knowledge, these approaches, in our view, are not mutually exclusive. Instead, we feel that once children have acquired some sound–symbol knowledge, possibly through synthetic phonics instruction, they should learn to compare new words to already known words. Compare–contrast approaches are also particularly useful for teaching students to decode polysyllabic words.

The basic compare–contrast lesson consists of a dialogue aimed at helping children internalize the process of identifying words by (1) identifying known words (clue words) that resemble an unknown word, (2) seeing what is similar between the two, (3) using what is similar to make a tentative identification of the word, and (4) checking to make sure that the identified word makes sense in context. A simple version of a compare–contrast lesson follows:

1. Give students six index cards. Have them print the following six words on the cards so that you can see them. These words become the students' key words, and students must be able to recognize them automatically.

black   hold   kind   play   rain   run

Now display words from the following group. Have each child find the word that looks most like the presented word. At a signal from you, have all the students display their "look-alike" word. Students should respond to questions such as "Where are the two words alike? Where are they different?" Ask a volunteer to pronounce both words.

mind	crack	blind	hind	fold	lack	runt
pain	smack	hay	main	blast	slack	stack
gold	rind	bind	mold	tack	bay	bun
gain	gray	plain	raid	pray		

2. On the following day (or when you feel the students are ready), add three words to their key word list: *man, less, her.* Match these nine words to the following group.

clay	per	ban	lent	fan	bless	pan
led		press	sun	sold	sack	stain

You can make up other words (with or without students' help) to add to any of these matching lists.

The compare–contrast approach can be used with the phonograms in the Z-Test, described earlier in this chapter. For words that are not known, a key word can be taught, using the same procedures as above. Additionally, multisyllabic words that contain one or more of the key rimes can be introduced by using the procedures suggested in Step 1. These difficult words may be drawn from wide-ranging reading contexts. Whether or not you use the technique with words in context, you should make a significant effort to help students see the relationship between what they do during the exercises and how they can use the new skills during their independent reading.

Making Words

Making words is a spelling-based decoding activity. In this activity, children learn to think about letters in words by manipulating letters in a spelling task. An example:

1. The teacher might take 1-inch-square index cards containing the following letters:

    a   i   o   d   n   s   r   u

2. The teacher announces, "I want you to make a two-letter word [signals with two fingers]—*an.*" As children move letters to make the word, the teacher checks their efforts and offers praise.

3. After all children have spelled the word, the teacher displays the word on a word card and puts it in a pocket chart.

4. The teacher proceeds through other two-letter words (e.g., *do, is, in*), three-letter words (e.g., *run, sad, rid, nod*), four-letter words (e.g., *said, rods, rind*), five-letter words (e.g., *sound, round*), and up to an eight-letter word (e.g., *dinosaur*).

Patricia Cunningham and her colleagues have written several books with lesson plans for making words (short words, appropriate for students through second grade; e.g., Cunningham & Hall, 2008) and making big words (appropriate for students in third to sixth grade; e.g., Cunningham & Hall, 2001).

Word Sorts

Word sorts are another spelling-based approach to teaching children how to decode. With this method, children are given lists of words and asked to sort them. In *closed* sorts, children are given categories; in *open* sorts, children are asked to come up with their own categories. Open sorts can be difficult for children who have reading problems or who have minimal experience working with particular patterns; however, the extra challenge of figuring out the patterns and categories is often extremely motivating. We recommend beginning with closed sorts, introducing open sorts only after children have had ample practice with the easier task or as a review of several previously taught patterns. When introducing open sorts, the teacher needs to provide needed modeling to the group.

A list of words like the following word group might be used for children who are learning to contrast *sh* and *st*, first in the initial and then in the final position:

stand	shop	step	shut	stamp
shall	shed	stub	ship	stun
rest	trash	last	mush	list
fist	fast	fish	just	rash
past	mist			

In a closed sort, these words might be sorted as words with *sh-*, as in *she*, and words with *st-*, as in *stop*. Or they might be sorted as having *st* and *sh* at the beginning or at the end.

SMART Boards provide a touch-and-drag digital option for sorting, though the low-tech pocket chart is still an effective mainstay in many classrooms. Bear and colleagues (2020) and Ganske (2014) provide many suggestions for word-sorting activities that are tied to children's spelling and decoding knowledge.

WORD-STUDY INSTRUCTION: PUTTING IT ALL TOGETHER

We believe that deep-rooted, robust word knowledge best develops when we provide learners a variety of ways to work with words. Using just one approach or method often won't work, particularly with struggling readers. We want readers and writers to be able to (1) break whole words into word parts (analytic phonics), (2) put word parts together to build words (synthetic phonics), (3) compare new words to known words (analogies), (4) and apply their word knowledge in context. With this in mind, Hayes and Flanigan (2014) recommend choosing activities across a week that provide your students opportunities to learn about words in four different ways:

1. Read words (e.g., word sorts, word banks, compare–contrast methods).
2. Write/spell words (writing sorts; generating as many words as possible that follow a pattern).

3. Manipulate words/word parts (making words, synthetic phonics).
4. Transfer word knowledge to reading/writing (word hunts—hunting for target word patterns in familiar books, writing dictated sentences with target words).

WORD STUDY OVER TIME

The foundation for word recognition begins in the preschool years and it plays an important role in teaching children to read in the primary grades. However, we are doing students a disservice if a systematic, explicit approach to word study stops at third grade. In the intermediate grades, students will benefit from continuing to increase automaticity with the top 1,000 Fry high-frequency words that can be obtained online. This is particularly true for older students in special education, who may have phonological processing and/or word recognition problems. Additionally, a systematic approach to the complexities of multisyllabic words and morphological analysis is key within a school. A systematic, schoolwide approach ensures that students are receiving deliberate, comprehensive instruction in high-utility affixes and roots, which will also support their vocabulary growth. Finally, all instruction of early or complex word recognition skills should be developmentally driven, engaging, and cognitively active.

Z-Test

Name _____ Teacher/Clinician _____

Directions. Tell the student you are going to show him/her some pretend words and that you would like for him/her to pronounce each one. Say that all of the words begin with "/z/, like *zebra*." Then expose the words on the student form, one at a time. Place a check in the blank under the date of testing if the child pronounces a pseudoword accurately. Option: For progress monitoring, time each administration of the Z-Test.

Date of Testing   _____ _____ _____ _____

zit	____	____	____	____
zay	____	____	____	____
zin	____	____	____	____
zap	____	____	____	____
zan	____	____	____	____
zill	____	____	____	____
zack	____	____	____	____
zing	____	____	____	____
zip	____	____	____	____
zat	____	____	____	____
zore	____	____	____	____
zug	____	____	____	____
zell	____	____	____	____
zink	____	____	____	____
zump	____	____	____	____
zash	____	____	____	____
zank	____	____	____	____
zice	____	____	____	____
zoke	____	____	____	____
zick	____	____	____	____
zock	____	____	____	____
zunk	____	____	____	____

(continued)

_____

zake	___	___	___	___
zame	___	___	___	___
zaw	___	___	___	___
zide	___	___	___	___
zeat	___	___	___	___
zop	___	___	___	___
zot	___	___	___	___
zuck	___	___	___	___
zight	___	___	___	___
zale	___	___	___	___
zest	___	___	___	___
zail	___	___	___	___
zain	___	___	___	___
zate	___	___	___	___
zine	___	___	___	___
Time	_____	_____	_____	_____

These words are arranged in order of increasing difficulty, as determined empirically. See J. W. Cunningham et al. (1999).

(continued)

zit	zell	zaw
zay	zink	zide
zin	zump	zeat
zap	zash	zop
zan	zank	zot
zill	zice	zuck
zack	zoke	zight
zing	zick	zale
zip	zock	zest
zat	zunk	zail
zore	zake	zain
zug	zame	zate
		zine

Informal Phonics Inventory

Directions for Administration

Consonant Sounds
Point to **S**. Say, "What sound does this letter say?" Go from left to right, repeating this question. It is fine if the child reads across a line without prompting. For **C** and **G**, have the child give both sounds. [**Note**: If the child cannot pass this subtest, consider giving an alphabet inventory.]

Consonant Digraphs
Point to **th**. Say, "What sound do these letters say?" Go from left to right, repeating this instruction. It is fine if the child reads all five without prompting.

Beginning Consonant Blends
Point to **bl**. Say, "What sound do these letters say?" Allow child to proceed with or without prompting.

Final Consonant Blends and ng
Point to **bank**. Say, "What is this word?" Allow child to proceed with or without prompting.

Short Vowels in CVC Words
Point to **fit**. Say, "What is this word?" Allow child to proceed with or without prompting.

The Rule of Silent e
Point to **cap**. Say, "If this is **cap**, what is this?" Point to **cape** as you say the second part of this sentence. Go from left to right, repeating the question for each pair.

Vowel Digraphs, Diphthongs, r-Controlled Vowels, and -al
Have the child read each word across each line, from left to right.

Scoring

For all subtests and for the total test, use the following criteria:

Mastery	80%+
Needs Review	60–79%
Needs Systematic Instruction	Below 60%

The table below gives the number of correct answers that roughly corresponds to these percentages.

Subtest	Total possible	Mastery	Review	Systematic instruction
Consonant Sounds	20	16–20	12–15	0–11
Consonant Digraphs	5	4–5	3	0–2
Beginning Consonant Blends	20	16–20	12–15	0–11
Final Consonant Blends and *ng*	12	10–12	8–9	0–7
Short Vowels in CVC Words	10	8–10	6–7	0–5
The Rule of Silent *e*	4	4	2–3	0–1
Long-Vowel Digraphs	10	8–10	6–7	0–5
Diphthongs	6	5–6	4	0–3
r-Controlled Vowels and *-al*	6	5–6	4	0–3
Total	**93**	**75–93**	**56–74**	**0–55**

(continued)

Phonics Skills Record

Use a checkmark to note specific skills that still require instruction.

Phonics Skills		Date							
Consonant Sounds	S								
	D								
	F								
	G								
	H								
	J								
	K								
	L								
	Z								
	P								
	C								
	V								
	B								
	N								
	M								
	Qu								
	W								
	R								
	T								
	Y								
Consonant Digraphs	th								
	sh								
	ch								
	wh								
	ph								

(continued)

Phonics Skills		Date							
Beginning Consonant Blends	bl								
	fl								
	fr								
	gl								
	br								
	gr								
	pl								
	pr								
	cl								
	sk								
	sl								
	sm								
	cr								
	sn								
	sp								
	tr								
	dr								
	st								
	str								
	sw								
Final Consonant Blends and *ng*	nk								
	pt								
	mp								
	nd								
	ct								
	lt								
	ng								
	ft								
	sp								
	sk								
	nt								
	st								

(continued)

136

Phonics Skills		Date							
Short Vowels	a								
	e								
	i								
	o								
	u								
Rule of Silent e	a								
	o								
	u								
	i								
Long-Vowel Digraphs	oa								
	ea								
	ai								
	ee								
	ay								
	ue								
Diphthongs	ow								
	ou								
	oy								
	ew								
	oi								
	aw								
r-Controlled Vowels	ar								
	ir								
	or								
	ur								
	er								
-al	al								

(continued)

Informal Phonics Inventory

Name _____ Date _____

____/20   Consonant Sounds

S	D	F	G	H	J
K	L	Z	P	C	V
B	N	M	Qu	W	R
T	Y				

____/5   Consonant Digraphs

th	sh	ch	wh	ph

____/20   Beginning Consonant Blends

bl	fl	fr	gl
br	gr	pl	pr
cl	sk	sl	sm
cr	sn	sp	tr
dr	st	str	sw

____/12   Final Consonant Blends and *ng*

bank	apt	limp
band	pact	lilt
bang	lift	lisp
bask	lint	list

____/10   Short Vowels in CVC Words

fit	led	sup	lap	hug
rot	tin	rag	wet	job

____/4   The Rule of Silent *e*

cap	tot	cub	kit
cape	tote	cube	kite

____/10   Long-Vowel Digraphs

loaf	heat	aim	weed	ray
gain	fee	coal	leaf	due

____/6   Diphthongs

town	loud	joy	threw	oil	law

____/6   *r*-Controlled Vowels and -*al*

tar	hall	sir	port	hurt	fern

____/93   **Total**

(continued)

S	D	F	G	H	J
K	L	Z	P	C	V
B	N	M	Qu	W	R
T	Y				

th	sh	ch	wh	ph

bl	fl	fr	gl
br	gr	pl	pr
cl	sk	sl	sm
cr	sn	sp	tr
dr	st	str	sw

(continued)

bank	apt	limp
band	pact	lilt
bang	lift	lisp
bask	lint	list

fit	led	sup	lap	hug
rot	tin	rag	wet	job

cap	tot	cub	kit
cape	tote	cube	kite

loaf	heat	aim	weed	ray
gain	fee	coal	leaf	due

town	loud	joy	threw	oil	law

tar	hall	sir	port	hurt	fern

Informal Decoding Inventory

This inventory includes six subtests that progress in difficulty. The first five address single-syllable decoding; the last addresses multisyllabic decoding. Grouping decisions are based on the first subtest the student fails to pass. It is not necessary to total scores across subtests but simply to identify the highest level of proficiency. Use a criterion of 8 correct for real words and 6 for nonsense words as proficiency with a particular word type.

Directions for Administration

Short Vowels

Point to **sat.** Say, "What is this word?" Go from left to right on the scoring form (top to bottom for the child), repeating this question for each word in row 1. It is fine if the student reads across the line without prompting. Repeat the procedure for row 2 (nonsense words). (Note: If the student cannot pass this subtest, consider placing the student in a Tier 3 intensive intervention program and using the assessments that accompany that program.)

Consonant Blends and Digraphs

Point to **blip.** Say, "What is this word?" Go from left to right on the scoring form, repeating this question for each word in row 1. It is fine if the student reads across the line without prompting. Repeat the procedure for row 2 (nonsense words).

r-Controlled Vowel Patterns

Point to **card.** Say, "What is this word?" Go from left to right on the scoring form, repeating this question for each word in row 1. It is fine if the student reads across the line without prompting. Repeat the procedure for row 2 (nonsense words).

Vowel–Consonant–e

Point to **stale.** Say, "What is this word?" Go from left to right on the scoring form, repeating this question for each word in row 1. It is fine if the student reads across the line without prompting. Repeat the procedure for row 2 (nonsense words).

Vowel Teams

Point to **neat.** Say, "What is this word?" Go from left to right on the scoring form, repeating this question for each word in row 1. It is fine if the student reads across the line without prompting. Repeat the procedure for row 2 (nonsense words). For nonsense words *feap* and *tead* accept either the long or short /e/ sound.

Multisyllabic Words

This subtest contains only real words, and they progressively differ in syllable type. Point to **flannel.** Say, "What is this word?" Go from left to right on the scoring form, repeating this question for each word.

(continued)

Informal Decoding Inventory: Teacher Protocol

Name: _____ Date: _____

Short Vowels									
sat	pot	beg	nip	cub	pad	top	hit	met	nut
								Total	
mot	tib	han	teg	fet	lup	nid	pab	hud	gop
								Total	

Consonant Blends and Digraphs									
blip	check	clam	chin	thick	frank	mint	fist	grab	rest
								Total	
clop	prib	hest	chot	slen	bund	bist	hald	slub	shad
								Total	

r-Controlled Vowel Patterns									
card	stork	term	burst	turf	fern	dirt	nark	firm	mirth
								Total	
fird	barp	forn	serp	surt	perd	kurn	nirt	mork	tarst
								Total	

(continued)

Vowel–Consonant–e

stale	hike	dome	cube	blame	chive	cute	prone	vane	brine
							Total		
bame	neme	hile	pome	rute	nube	vope	clate	vike	pene
							Total		

Vowel Teams

neat	spoil	goat	pail	field	fruit	claim	meet	beast	boast
							Total		
craid	houn	rowb	noy	feap	nuit	maist	ploat	tead	steen
							Total		

Multisyllabic Words

flannel	submit	cupid	spiky	confide	cascade	varnish	surplus	chowder	approach
							Total		

Informal Decoding Inventory: Student Materials

sat	blip	card	stale	neat	flannel
pot	check	stork	hike	spoil	submit
beg	clam	term	dome	goat	cupid
nip	chin	burst	cube	pail	spiky
cub	thick	turf	blame	field	confide
pad	frank	fern	chive	fruit	cascade
top	mint	dirt	cute	claim	varnish
hit	fist	nark	prone	meet	surplus
met	grab	firm	vane	beast	chowder
nut	rest	mirth	brine	boast	approach
mot	clop	fird	bame	craid	
tib	prib	barp	neme	houn	
han	hest	forn	hile	rowb	
teg	chot	serp	pome	noy	
fet	slen	surt	rute	feap	
lup	bund	perd	nube	nuit	
nid	bist	kurn	vope	maist	
pab	hald	nirt	clate	ploat	
hud	slub	mork	vike	tead	
gop	shad	tarst	pene	steen	

Fry Sight-Word Inventory

This instrument surveys a child's ability to recognize 300 frequently occurring words, as selected by Edward B. Fry (1980). The words are grouped into three sets of 100 by relative difficulty, and each group of 100 words is, in turn, grouped into sets of 25.

Directions for Administration

Place the student version of the First 100 Words in front of the child. Position the teacher's version so that you can make notations on it. There are three blanks for each word, for repeated administrations. You may want to record the date at the top of each column of blanks. Explain that you will be showing the child some words and that you want the child to say them aloud. Use the window card below to reveal the words one at a time, or make your own from a 3" × 5"-inch index card with an X-Acto knife. A window card screens the other words and helps the child focus.

For each word, write a plus (+) in the blank next to it if the child correctly pronounces it in less than 1 second (informally timed). If the child takes more time but eventually pronounces the word accurately, write *D*, for *decoded*. That is to say, the word was not identified automatically and is therefore not yet a sight word. If the child mispronounces the word, try to spell the response phonetically. If there is no response, write *NR*. Move the window card to each word in succession while, with your other hand, you record the response. Proceed through each of the five columns.

Repeat these steps with the Second 100 and the Third 100. Discontinue testing if, in your judgment, the words become too difficult.

If you readminister the inventory, return only to those words not automatically recognized during previous testing.

Scoring and Interpretation

There is no cumulative score. Each word is actually a separate "skill," which means that there is a very direct link between testing and teaching. Any word that is not pronounceable automatically simply requires more practice!

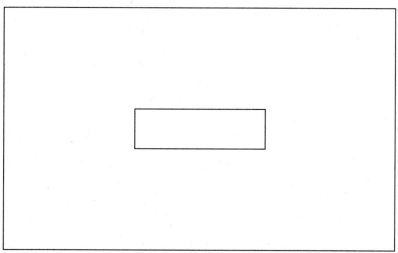

(continued)

First 100 Words

the	or	will	number
of	one	up	no
and	had	other	way
a	by	about	could
to	word	out	people
in	but	many	my
is	not	then	than
you	what	them	first
that	all	these	water
it	were	so	been
he	we	some	call
was	when	her	who
for	your	would	oil
on	can	make	now
are	said	like	find
as	there	him	long
with	use	into	down
his	an	time	day
they	each	has	did
I	which	look	get
at	she	two	come
be	do	more	made
this	how	write	may
have	their	go	part
from	if	see	over

(continued)

First 100 Words

the _____	or _____	will _____	number _____
of _____	one _____	up _____	no _____
and _____	had _____	other _____	way _____
a _____	by _____	about _____	could _____
to _____	word _____	out _____	people _____
in _____	but _____	many _____	my _____
is _____	not _____	then _____	than _____
you _____	what _____	them _____	first _____
that _____	all _____	these _____	water _____
it _____	were _____	so _____	been _____
he _____	we _____	some _____	call _____
was _____	when _____	her _____	who _____
for _____	your _____	would _____	oil _____
on _____	can _____	make _____	now _____
are _____	said _____	like _____	find _____
as _____	there _____	him _____	long _____
with _____	use _____	into _____	down _____
his _____	an _____	time _____	day _____
they _____	each _____	has _____	did _____
I _____	which _____	look _____	get _____
at _____	she _____	two _____	come _____
be _____	do _____	more _____	made _____
this _____	how _____	write _____	may _____
have _____	their _____	go _____	part _____
from _____	if _____	see _____	over _____

(continued)

Second 100 Words

new	great	put	kind
sound	where	end	hand
take	help	does	picture
only	through	another	again
little	much	well	change
work	before	large	off
know	line	must	play
place	right	big	spell
year	too	even	air
live	mean	such	away
me	old	because	animal
back	any	turn	house
give	same	here	point
most	tell	why	page
very	boy	ask	letter
after	follow	went	mother
thing	came	men	answer
our	went	read	found
just	show	need	study
name	also	land	still
good	around	different	learn
sentence	form	home	should
man	three	us	America
think	small	move	world
say	set	try	high

(continued)

Second 100 Words

new _____	great _____	put _____	kind _____
sound _____	where _____	end _____	hand _____
take _____	help _____	does _____	picture _____
only _____	through _____	another _____	again _____
little _____	much _____	well _____	change _____
work _____	before _____	large _____	off _____
know _____	line _____	must _____	play _____
place _____	right _____	big _____	spell _____
year _____	too _____	even _____	air _____
live _____	mean _____	such _____	away _____
me _____	old _____	because _____	animal _____
back _____	any _____	turn _____	house _____
give _____	same _____	here _____	point _____
most _____	tell _____	why _____	page _____
very _____	boy _____	ask _____	letter _____
after _____	follow _____	went _____	mother _____
thing _____	came _____	men _____	answer _____
our _____	went _____	read _____	found _____
just _____	show _____	need _____	study _____
name _____	also _____	land _____	still _____
good _____	around _____	different _____	learn _____
sentence _____	form _____	home _____	should _____
man _____	three _____	us _____	America _____
think _____	small _____	move _____	world _____
say _____	set _____	try _____	high _____

(continued)

Third 100 Words

every	left	until	idea
near	don't	children	enough
add	few	side	eat
food	while	feet	face
between	along	car	watch
own	might	mile	far
below	close	night	Indian
country	something	walk	real
plant	seem	while	almost
last	next	sea	let
school	hard	began	above
father	open	grow	girl
keep	example	took	sometimes
tree	begin	river	mountain
never	life	four	cut
start	always	carry	young
city	those	state	talk
earth	both	once	soon
eye	paper	book	list
light	together	hear	song
thought	got	stop	leave
head	group	without	family
under	often	second	body
story	run	late	music
saw	important	miss	color

(continued)

Third 100 Words

every _____	left _____	until _____	idea _____
near _____	don't _____	children _____	enough _____
add _____	few _____	side _____	eat _____
food _____	while _____	feet _____	face _____
between _____	along _____	car _____	watch _____
own _____	might _____	mile _____	far _____
below _____	close _____	night _____	Indian _____
country _____	something _____	walk _____	real _____
plant _____	seem _____	while _____	almost _____
last _____	next _____	sea _____	let _____
school _____	hard _____	began _____	above _____
father _____	open _____	grow _____	girl _____
keep _____	example _____	took _____	sometimes _____
tree _____	begin _____	river _____	mountain _____
never _____	life _____	four _____	cut _____
start _____	always _____	carry _____	young _____
city _____	those _____	state _____	talk _____
earth _____	both _____	once _____	soon _____
eye _____	paper _____	book _____	list _____
light _____	together _____	hear _____	song _____
thought _____	got _____	stop _____	leave _____
head _____	group _____	without _____	family _____
under _____	often _____	second _____	body _____
story _____	run _____	late _____	music _____
saw _____	important _____	miss _____	color _____

Dolch Words Organized by Level

Teacher Version

Preprimer		Primer		First grade		Second grade		Third grade	
a		all		after		always		about	
and		am		again		around		better	
away		are		an		because		bring	
big		at		any		been		carry	
blue		ate		as		before		clean	
can		be		ask		best		cut	
come		black		by		both		done	
down		brown		could		buy		draw	
find		but		every		call		drink	
for		came		fly		cold		eight	
funny		did		from		does		fall	
go		do		give		don't		far	
help		eat		going		fast		full	
here		four		had		first		got	
I		get		has		five		grow	
in		good		her		found		hold	
is		have		him		gave		hot	
it		he		his		goes		hurt	
jump		into		how		green		if	
little		like		just		its		keep	
look		must		know		made		kind	
make		new		let		many		laugh	
me		no		live		off		light	
my		now		may		or		long	
not		on		of		pull		much	
one		our		old		read		myself	
play		out		once		right		never	
red		please		open		sing		only	
run		pretty		over		sit		own	
said		ran		put		sleep		pick	
see		ride		round		tell		seven	
the		saw		some		their		shall	
three		say		stop		these		show	
to		she		take		those		six	
two		so		thank		upon		small	
up		soon		them		us		start	
we		that		then		use		ten	
where		there		think		very		today	
yellow		they		walk		wash		together	
you		this		were		which		try	
		too		what		why		warm	
		under		when		wish			
		want				work			
		was				would			
		well				write			
		went				your			
		white							
		who							
		will							
		with							
		yes							

From Dolch (1936). Copyright © University of Chicago Press. Reprinted by permission.   *(continued)*

Child Version

a	all	after	always	about
and	am	again	around	better
away	are	an	because	bring
big	at	any	been	carry
blue	ate	as	before	clean
can	be	ask	best	cut
come	black	by	both	done
down	brown	could	buy	draw
find	but	every	call	drink
for	came	fly	cold	eight
funny	did	from	does	fall
go	do	give	don't	far
help	eat	going	fast	full
here	four	had	first	got
I	get	has	five	grow
in	good	her	found	hold
is	have	him	gave	hot
it	he	his	goes	hurt
jump	into	how	green	if
little	like	just	its	keep
look	must	know	made	kind
make	new	let	many	laugh
me	no	live	off	light
my	now	may	or	long
not	on	of	pull	much
one	our	old	read	myself
play	out	once	right	never
red	please	open	sing	only
run	pretty	over	sit	own
said	ran	put	sleep	pick
see	ride	round	tell	seven
the	saw	some	their	shall
three	say	stop	these	show
to	she	take	those	six
two	so	thank	upon	small
up	soon	them	us	start
we	that	then	use	ten
where	there	think	very	today
yellow	they	walk	wash	together
you	this	were	which	try
	too	what	why	warm
	under	when	wish	
	want		work	
	was		would	
	well		write	
	went		your	
	white			
	who			
	will			
	with			
	yes			

Developmental Spelling Analysis (DSA) Screening Inventory

Directions for Administration and Scoring

1. Dictate the words and sentences as long as students can spell two words in each set of five words. A student who spells only one word or none in any set of five words may stop the test.

2. Award 1 point for each correctly spelled word.

3. If a child spelled any words correctly in sets beyond the guidelines specified for stopping, those words receive 0 points. (In order to score a point, two or more words in the set must be spelled correctly.)

4. Use the Spelling Stage Prediction Chart to identify the child's developmental stage.

5. The feature inventories provide insights into the needs of students who appear to straddle two stages.

DSA Screening Inventory

Directions: I am going to say some words that I want you to spell for me. Some of the words will be easy to spell, and some will be more difficult. When you don't know how to spell a word, just do the best you can. Each time, I will say the word, then use it in a sentence, and then I will say the word again.

1. hen	The hen sat on her eggs.
2. wish	The boy made a wish and blew out the candles
3. trap	A spider web is a trap for flies.
4. jump	A kangaroo can jump high.
5. brave	A brave dog scared the robbers.

* * *

6. smile	A smile shows that you are happy.
7. grain	One kind of grain is called wheat.
8. crawl	The baby can crawl but not walk.
9. clerk	The clerk sold some shoes to me.
10. clutch	The lady had to clutch her hat to keep it from flying off.

* * *

11. palace	The king and queen live in a palace.
12. observe	I like to observe birds at the feeder.
13. shuffle	Please shuffle the cards before you deal.
14. exciting	The adventure story I'm reading is very exciting.
15. treason	The man was found guilty of treason.

* * *

16. column	His picture was in the first column of the newspaper.
17. variety	A grocery store has a wide variety of foods.
18. extension	The workers need an extension ladder to reach the roof.
19. competition	There was much competition between the two businesses.
20. illiterate	An illiterate person is one who cannot read.

Stop when a student has spelled no words or one word correctly out of any set of five.

(continued)

From Ganske (2014). Copyright © The Guilford Press. Reprinted by permission.

DSA Screening Inventory Spelling Stage Prediction Chart

Inventory score	Predicted stage(s)
20	DC
19	DC
18	DC
17	DC
16	SJ/DC
15	SJ/DC
14	SJ
13	SJ
12	SJ
11	WW/SJ
10	WW/SJ
9	WW
8	WW
7	WW
6	LN/WW
5	LN/WW
4	LN
3	LN
2	LN
1	LN*
0	LN*

Note. DC, derivational constancy; LN, letter name; SJ, syllable juncture; WW, within word pattern.

*Children who achieve scores of 1 or 0 may or may not be letter name stage spellers.

SIX

Fluency

If fluency was once the "neglected reading goal" (Allington, 1983), it is no longer. There has been an increased interest in developing fluency, as indicated by research findings confirming the effectiveness of guided oral reading approaches in developing comprehension (Kuhn & Levy, 2015; Kuhn & Stahl, 2003; National Reading Panel, 2000).

There are three well-established components to fluency: Fluent reading should involve *accurate* and *automatic* word recognition, with appropriate *prosody* or inflection. Each component affects comprehension in its own way. To these three, some have suggested adding a fourth component: *endurance* or *stamina*, the ability to read extended texts (e.g., Marcell, 2011). The importance of reading with endurance grows as students move into the upper grades.

Obviously, if children cannot read the text relatively accurately, their comprehension will suffer. As noted in Chapter 3, the reading does not have to be word-perfect. A child can misread 5 words out of 100 (95% accuracy) and still be within the instructional range. With more instructional support, such as that found in some of the fluency-oriented approaches discussed at the end of this chapter, the child can read initially with less accuracy. However, word-recognition accuracy will continue to affect comprehension.

Automaticity is also important for comprehension. By *automaticity,* we mean the ability to read words without conscious effort, as you are doing now. Unless we throw in a word in a crazy font, like ketchup, your reading proceeds without your having to think about the words; instead, you continue to focus on comprehension. If a child reads accurately but has to sound out or stumble over too many words, comprehension also will suffer. Readers have just so much mental energy to devote to a cognitive task such as comprehension. If they have to put extra mental energy into decoding the words, that energy or focus will not be available for comprehension. We find that many struggling readers who have experienced successful remediation of their word-recognition skills often have difficulty with automaticity.

Prosody is the ability to read with some sort of expression. When we read aloud, our voices go up and down, depending on the part of each sentence we are reading. We tend to drop our voices (slightly, but perceptively) at the ends of statements and to raise our pitch at the ends of questions. We pause for punctuation and use appropriate phrasing.

We see prosody as an indicator that children are understanding the meaning of a sentence—in essence, a low-level type of comprehension.

JUDGING ORAL FLUENCY

When we consider fluency, we are interested in all three components: accuracy, automaticity, and prosody. We can judge accuracy by applying the procedures of IRIs, as discussed in Chapter 3. Automaticity is usually assessed in terms of a student's rate of reading. This can be documented for children reading at or beyond mid-first-grade level by using an IRI and the calculation procedures explained in Chapter 3. We provide guides for reading rates later in this chapter. Prosody is the most difficult of these components to assess. For example, in using benchmark kits, we have found that it is difficult to get agreement on variations in appropriate phrasing. Judging whether a child uses inflection well can be even more difficult. The NAEP rubric is a simple 4-point scale that can give only the broadest indication of a child's fluency, but it can be used easily. This scale can be applied to any oral reading sample, from either an IRI or a classroom reading. You can record individual students to observe growth over time. Recorded reading samples can be used for parent–teacher conferences and can be a powerful demonstration of a child's progress over time.

NAEP Rubric

Table 6.1 shows the fluency scale used in the NAEP oral reading study, updated in 2005 and given in the most recent administrations of NAEP. We have found this scale to be fairly easy to apply to a child's oral reading sample. Listen as the child reads a selection, and give an overall rating, using the four levels described in Table 6.1. We strongly recommend that you meet with another teacher or your grade-level team to establish interrater agreement before doing this on your own. You can use recorded examples for this purpose. Our experience is that interrater reliability is easy to establish on this scale, because it is straightforward—and it is an important part of the process. School teams

TABLE 6.1. The NAEP Oral Reading Fluency Scale

Level 4 *Fluent*	Reads primarily in larger, meaningful phrase groups. Although some regressions, repetitions, and deviations from text may be present, these do not appear to detract from the overall structure of the story. Preservation of the author's syntax is consistent. Some or most of the story is read with expressive interpretation.
Level 3 *Fluent*	Reads primarily in three- or four-word phrase groups. Some smaller groupings may be present. However, the majority of phrasing seems appropriate and preserves the syntax of the author. Little or no expressive interpretation is present.
Level 2 *Nonfluent*	Reads primarily in two-word phrases with some three- or four-word groupings. Some word-by-word reading may be present. Word groupings may seem awkward and unrelated to larger context of sentence or passage.
Level 1 *Nonfluent*	Reads primarily word by word. Occasional two-word or three-word phrases may occur, but these are infrequent and/or they do not preserve meaningful syntax.

Note. From National Center for Education Statistics (2005).

may wish to create recordings to use as examples of each level to ensure consistency, especially between Level 3 and Level 2.

Multidimensional Scale

The Multidimensional Scale (Zutell & Rasinski, 1991), shown in Table 6.2, provides a more refined measure of fluency than the NAEP rubric. It provides a summative quantitative score for multiple dimensions of prosodic reading. However, the individual dimensions provide formative information that can be used to guide instruction. In addition,

TABLE 6.2. Multidimensional Fluency Scale

Use the following scales to rate reader fluency (expression and volume, phrasing, smoothness, and pace). Scores range from 4 to 16. Generally, scores below 8 indicate that fluency may be a concern. Scores of 8 or above indicate that the student is making good progress in fluency.

Dimension	1	2	3	4
A. Expression and volume	Reads with little expression or enthusiasm in voice. Reads words as if simply to get them out. Little sense of trying to make text sound like natural language. Tends to read in a quiet voice.	Some expression. Begins to use voice to make text sound like natural language in some areas of the text, but not others. Focus remains largely on saying the words. Still reads in a quiet voice.	Sounds like natural language throughout the better part of the passage. Occasionally slips into expressionless reading. Voice volume is generally appropriate throughout the text.	Reads with good expression and enthusiasm throughout the text. Sounds like natural language. The reader is able to vary expression and volume to match his or her interpretation of the passage.
B. Phrasing	Monotonic with little sense of phrase boundaries, frequent word-by-word reading.	Frequent two- and three-word phrases giving the impression of choppy reading; improper stress and intonation that fail to mark ends of sentences and clauses.	Mixture of run-ons, midsentence pauses for breath, and possibly some choppiness; reasonable stress/intonation.	Generally well phrased, mostly in clause and sentence units, with adequate attention to expression.
C. Smoothness	Frequent extended pauses, hesitations, false starts, sound-outs, repetitions, and/or multiple attempts.	Several "rough spots" in text where extended pauses, hesitations, etc., are more frequent and disruptive.	Occasional breaks in smoothness caused by difficulties with specific words and/or structures.	Generally smooth reading with some breaks, but word and structure difficulties are resolved quickly, usually through self-correction.
D. Pace (during sections of minimal disruption)	Slow and laborious.	Moderately slow.	Uneven mixture of fast and slow reading.	Consistently conversational.

Note. From Zutell and Rasinski (1991). Copyright © 1991 The Ohio State University College of Education and Human Ecology. Adapted by permission.

you can use the scale to help students increase their awareness of specific aspects of their own reading fluency. Eventually, students may use the scale to evaluate their own reading fluency.

CURRICULUM-BASED MEASUREMENTS

Another way of using oral reading to determine a child's achievement is through CBMs. Originally, this approach used passages taken from texts that were used in a child's class. Today, most CBMs are commercially produced packages of materials that have been pilot-tested and normed on thousands of previous administrations. Typically, CBM products consist of standardized administration directions, scoring rules, standards for judging performance, and record-keeping charts. One advantage of using timed CBMs is that they are sensitive to small intervals of growth. Like many other CBM measures, oral reading fluency (ORF) CBMs are general outcome measures. This means that this type of assessment is a holistic test that consolidates contributing subskills (e.g., decoding, high-frequency word recognition) that students are expected to employ while reading meaningful, connected text. It also means that ORF CBMs consist of sets of passages that are all at the end-of-year reading level.

Due to the consistency in each CBM administration and text difficulty, improvements over time should be observable. ORF CBMs are typically administered to all students as benchmark screenings three times a year. For those students whose scores indicate that they are at moderate or high risk for reading difficulties, or who are performing at low levels compared to their grade-level peers, ORF CBM progress monitoring should be done biweekly or weekly.

When a child is given an ORF CBM, the child is asked to read the passage and is judged on the basis of rate and accuracy. The procedures for administering and scoring such CBMs are presented in Table 6.3.

Hasbrouck and Tindal (2006, 2017) have developed norms for CBMs that can also be used for judging ORF rates in other materials. To use the norms in Table 6.4, calculate the number of words correctly read per minute (WCPM[1]). To do this for a CBM, stop the child after 1 minute, and simply count the number of words correctly pronounced. For benchmark screening, it is recommended that you repeat this process with three different passages and record only the median score, the middle number. This policy makes sense because it increases reliability.

Hasbrouck and Tindal (2006, 2017) give the median scores at the 10th, 25th, 50th, 75th, and 90th percentile ranks at three testing times (fall, winter, and spring). Compare the score you obtain to the scores in Table 6.4. Scores between the 25th and 75th percentiles can be considered roughly average; scores above or below would be considered above or below average. Most commercially produced CBM packages also include tests that measure the fluency of other early literacy skills, such as letter identification, phoneme segmentation, and decoding nonsense words. This set of tools can be a convenient

---

[1] This metric is sometimes referred to as words correctly read in 1 minute, or WC1M.

TABLE 6.3. Curriculum-Based Measurement Procedures for Assessing and Scoring Oral Reading Fluency

Say to the student: *"When I say 'start,' begin reading aloud at the top of this page. Read across the page* [demonstrate by pointing]. *Try to read each word. If you come to a word you don't know, I'll tell it to you. Be sure to do your best reading. Are there any questions?"*

Say, *"Start."*

Follow along on your copy of the story, marking the words that are read incorrectly. If a student stops or struggles with a word for 3 seconds, tell the student the word and mark it as incorrect.

Place a vertical line after the last word read and thank the student.

The following guidelines determine which words are counted as correct:

1. *Words read correctly.* Words read correctly are those words that are pronounced correctly, given the reading context.
   a. The word *read* must be pronounced *reed*, not as *red*, when presented in the context of "He will read the book."
   b. Repetitions are not counted as incorrect.
   c. Self-corrections within 3 seconds are counted as correctly read words.
2. *Words read incorrectly.* The following types of errors are counted: (a) mispronunciations, (b) substitutions, and (c) omissions. Furthermore, words not read within 3 seconds are counted as errors.
   a. *Mispronunciations* are words that are misread: *dog* for *dig*.
   b. *Substitutions* are words that are substituted for the stimulus word; this is often inferred by a one-to-one correspondence between word orders: *dog* for *cat*.
   c. *Omissions* are words skipped or not read; if a student skips an entire line, each word is counted as an error.
3. *Three-second rule.* If a student is struggling to pronounce a word or hesitates for 3 seconds, the student is told the word, and it is counted as an error.

Note. From Shinn (1989, pp. 239–240). Copyright © 1989 The Guilford Press. Adapted by permission.

and time-efficient means of monitoring many early literacy skills. A list of the most commonly used commercial CBM packages is found in Table 6.5.

WHEN SHOULD YOU FOCUS ON FLUENCY?

For children making good progress along the road to proficiency, fluency activities are an important part of their instructional diet. For students who struggle, however, some extra attention may be needed. A child judged to be at risk in ORF could benefit from small-group work that targets this area. Before we describe a variety of evidence-based approaches to developing fluency, let's revisit the cognitive model. This model is grounded in the idea that fluent reading requires a range of decoding skills and an adequate sight vocabulary. If there is a substantial gap in either of these, fluency instruction that focuses only on connected text approaches is not likely to be very effective. Figure 6.1 reproduces the upper portion of the cognitive model, and as we return to it, we can now reference many of the instruments we have examined.

TABLE 6.4. Hasbrouck and Tindal's Oral Reading Fluency (ORF) Norms

Grade	Percentile	Fall WCPM	Winter WCPM[a]	Spring WCPM[a]	Avg. weekly improvement[b]
1	90		97	116	1.1
	75		59	91	2.0
	50		29	60	1.9
	25		16	34	1.1
	10		9	18	0.6
2	90	111	131	148	1.2
	75	84	109	124	1.3
	50	50	84	100	1.6
	25	36	59	72	1.1
	10	23	35	43	0.6
3	90	134	161	166	1.0
	75	104	137	139	1.0
	50	83	97	112	0.9
	25	59	79	91	1.0
	10	40	62	63	0.7
4	90	153	168	184	1.0
	75	125	143	160	1.1
	50	94	120	133	1.2
	25	75	95	105	0.9
	10	60	71	83	0.7
5	90	179	183	195	0.5
	75	153	160	169	0.5
	50	121	133	146	0.8
	25	87	109	119	1.0
	10	64	84	102	1.2
6	90	185	195	204	0.6
	75	159	166	173	0.4
	50	132	145	146	0.4
	25	112	116	122	0.3
	10	89	91	91	0.1
7	90	180	192	202	0.7
	75	156	165	177	0.7
	50	128	136	150	0.7
	25	102	109	123	0.7
	10	79	88	98	0.6
8	90	185	199	199	0.4
	75	161	173	177	0.5
	50	133	146	151	0.6
	25	106	115	124	0.6
	10	77	84	97	0.6

Note. Hasbrouck and Tindal have completed extensive studies of ORF, the results of which were published in technical reports that are available on the University of Oregon's Behavioral Research and Teaching website (*www. brtprojects.org*) and in Hasbrouck and Tindal (2006). The table shows the mean ORF of students in grades 1–6, as determined by Hasbrouck and Tindal's data (2017). The norms for grade 7 and grade 8 are based on the 2006 results.

You can use the information in this table to draw conclusions and make decisions about the ORF of your students. Students scoring 10 or more words below the 50th percentile when the average score of two unpracticed readings from grade-level materials is used need a fluency-building program. In addition, you can use the table to set the long-term fluency goals for struggling readers.

Average weekly improvement is the average increase in words per week you can expect from a student. It is calculated by subtracting the fall score from the spring score and dividing the difference by 32, the typical number of weeks between the fall and spring assessments. For grade 1, since there is no fall assessment, the average weekly improvement is calculated by subtracting the winter score from the spring score and dividing the difference by 16, the typical number of weeks between the winter and spring assessments.

[a]WCPM, words correct per minute.
[b]Average words-per-week growth (see above).

TABLE 6.5. Commercially Produced CBM Materials

Test	Grade levels	Content	Notes
AIMSweb *www.pearsonassessments.com/* *professional-assessments/digital-* *solutions/aimsweb/about.html*	PreK–12	Reading, Math, Social-Behavioral, Dyslexia Screener (rating scale)	Benchmark and progress monitoring (PM)
DIBELS 8th Edition *https://dibels.uoregon.edu*	K–8	Reading, Spanish (IDEL)	Benchmark and PM; DIBELS 6th Edition is free (K–6)
easyCBM *https://easycbm.com*	K–8	Reading, Math, Spanish; Intervention Toolkit	Free PM tools; benchmark and intervention toolkit for a fee
FastBridge Learning *www.fastbridge.org*	CBM 1–8 Adaptive K–12	Reading, Math, Social-Emotional Behavior	Benchmark and PM; also includes adaptive comprehension tests
Intervention Central *www.interventioncentral.org*	Create your own CBMs	Reading, Math, Written Expression	Free

Once you have determined the influence of decoding or sight-word deficits, you can develop a proper plan for fluency remediation. If decoding and sight-word reading weaknesses exist, create a plan that includes isolated skill practice in the deficit areas, combined with connected text fluency approaches. If the foundational skills are strong, but only fluency assessments indicate below grade-level performance, then focus on a variety of the connected text approaches described in the following sections.

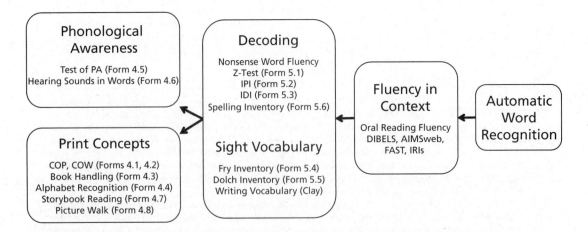

FIGURE 6.1. Cognitive model and assessments useful for foundational skills. COP, concepts of print; COW, concept of word; IDI, Informal Decoding Inventory; IPI, Informal Phonics Inventory.

INSTRUCTIONAL APPROACHES FOR IMPROVING FLUENCY

A rule in our clinical work is that children need to spend the majority of the time during tutoring sessions reading a wide variety of connected text aloud for different purposes. Novice readers who are still learning the alphabetic system need to be held accountable for reading some texts that are tightly bound to their identified instructional reading level. Additionally, they should practice reading some decodable texts and controlled vocabulary texts for high-density practice of specific word-study targets. As all students move beyond the mid-first-grade reading level, in addition to reading in instructional-level texts, their connected text reading practice needs to broaden to include fluency practice and reading stretch texts that incorporate rich conceptual vocabulary, complex themes, and new information. This reading can be challenging, but still within what Vygotsky (1978) referred to as the ZPD (see Chapter 3). Unlike texts at the instructional level, these texts require more supportive scaffolding by the more knowledgeable other. Repeated readings or any variation of fluency-oriented instruction can be employed. We find that repeated or assisted reading gives children the support they need to read increasingly difficult texts. Research suggests that assigning children a passage to read repeatedly is more effective when it is complemented by assisted reading, in which an adult actively models reading (Kuhn & Stahl, 2003, Lee & Yoon, 2017; Swain, Leader-Janssen, & Conley, 2017).

Several approaches to fluency development are described below. These approaches are most useful for children who already have good oral language comprehension but either poor or slow word recognition. Some techniques, like charted repeated reading, can be used in isolation to increase reading rate. Other assisted reading techniques, like echo reading or paired reading, are better suited to exposing lower-level readers to stretch texts with high volumes of words and conceptual density. Finally, fluency repertoire protocols combine assisted reading, repeated reading, and comprehension activities. These work well as universal design instruction within shared reading contexts to support all students in reading complex texts, including English learners, special education students, and students who are reading below grade level.

For this targeted fluency work, we suggest choosing material that is a stretch for a child, although not beyond his or her level of comprehension—perhaps one level above the child's instructional level, but not so far above it that he or she cannot cope. We have found that children can benefit from reading material with as low as 85% accuracy, if they are given adequate support. If a student does not demonstrate improvement in rate and/or accuracy by the third or fourth reading, the text selection may have been too difficult. Some suggested activities follow.

Charted Repeated Reading

Students read the same text repeatedly until a desired level of fluency is attained. We use a specific procedure in the reading clinic, as follows:

1. Choose a passage to read that is slightly above the child's instructional level, but one that the child might be interested in reading. (This method can be used with

grade-level materials for a child who is reading below grade level. Many websites and educational publishing houses produce texts explicitly for fluency practice.)

2. Take a 100-word excerpt from this passage. (You can use different lengths, but the math is more difficult!)

3. Have the child read the passage aloud, marking all his or her miscues. Time the reading, using a stopwatch or watch with a sweep secondhand. Mark the child's speed and error rate on a chart.

4. Review the child's miscues with him or her.

5. Have the child reread the passage, and mark his or her errors and time on the chart.

6. Have the child continue until a speed of 100 WPM, with at most one miscue, is achieved. If achieving this goal takes more than four tries, you might want to use an easier passage. This process should be done two to three times within one session; chart each attempt.

7. Proceed to another section at the same level. When the child can read relatively fluently for the first time, select a more difficult passage.

An Alternate Approach

This instructional method can be used with small groups or an entire class, as well as with an individual child. Take a book or passage, and have the child(ren) read orally for 1 minute. At the end of that time, ask the child(ren) to mark with a pencil the last word read. You might discuss words with which the child(ren) had problems. Immediately, chart the number of words read correctly. Then have the child(ren) reread the passage from the beginning, again for 1 minute, and ask him, her, or them to mark the last word read. There should be more words read during the second attempt. Again, chart the number of words read correctly.

Studies of repeated reading seem to indicate that four repetitions yield significantly greater improvement than three repetitions (Lee & Yoon, 2017). Surprisingly, error corrections by a teacher or peer don't seem to make a difference (Lee & Yoon, 2017). This should lower the concern of teachers who worry about using this technique in student stations or peer partnerships. Using this charted repeated reading even once a week has the potential to yield gains beyond typical growth expectations (Swain et al., 2013).

Echo Reading

In echo reading, the teacher reads a section of the text aloud while the students read silently in their own texts. This section could be a paragraph or a longer passage. Students "echo" the section back. Sections of text need to be long enough that students are required to rely on reading their texts and not just remembering what the teacher said. This is a useful introduction to a difficult text. After echo-reading a passage, teachers may do a think-aloud of decoding strategies for reading a difficult word in the passage. This technique may be used with children reading at first- and second-grade levels, but it is less appropriate for older students, and it is not appropriate for chapter books.

Choral Reading

Choral reading, which involves the simultaneous reading of a passage, can be done individually or in groups. In classes, it is often fun to use the choral reading format with poems. Anthologies of poems by authors such as Shel Silverstein and Jack Prelutsky are popular choices. In a choral reading session, it is important to monitor children's reading to ensure that *all* children are participating.

For individual work, choral reading can be applied to any passage and can be done repeatedly. In repeated choral reading, a teacher might lower his or her voice with each repeated reading, thus phasing him- or herself out and gradually releasing responsibility to the student.

Recorded Reading

The teacher records a longer passage or uses a commercially available version. Again, the passage should be a bit beyond the child's instructional level. The student reads along until he or she can read the story comfortably and fluently. Then the student reads to the teacher, who evaluates whether or not the reading is adequate. Teachers need to make sure that students are responsible for reading the text themselves. Too often, these "read-along" opportunities turn into listening opportunities. Children who need fluency practice generally have good language abilities and do not benefit as much from listening as they do from reading practice. We cannot stress too strongly that *unless students are held accountable for reading what they have practiced to an adult, reading along with a recording is a waste of time.*

Partner Reading

Students choose partners and read an entire story, taking turns. Usually, turn taking proceeds page by page, but partners can negotiate differently. During reading, one partner reads while the other monitors the reading and helps if needed.

An alternative to partner reading is a team effort in which partners or a group work together as problem solvers. The children work on a difficult text, paragraph by paragraph, striving together to understand the meaning of the passages. In such a group, three older children with reading problems might be working with a text that might be far too difficult for any one of them to work on alone. One child would read a section of the text, and the group members would discuss any difficulties they might have with that section, such as difficulties with words, with the meaning, or with specific vocabulary. After the section is discussed, the student who read it now paraphrases the section. The next student reads the next section, and so it goes.

Another variation is radio reading (Rasinski, 2010). The students each rehearse a section of informational text and then read it aloud to their group. Each child has a copy. They discuss the meaning, and the reader also asks a comprehension question about his or her passage.

Paired Reading

Paired reading, a program developed by Keith Topping (1987) in Scotland, is widely used in the United Kingdom and Canada. In paired reading, a more capable reader, usually an adult, works one on one with a struggling reader. A paired reading session begins with the tutor and child choosing a book together. The only selection requirement is that the book be of interest to the child. There should be no readability limits (although our experience is that children rarely choose material that is far too difficult). The two begin by reading in unison, until the child signals the tutor (by touching the tutor, raising a hand, or using some other prearranged signal) when he or she wants to read solo. The solo reading continues until the child makes an error. The tutor provides the word, they repeat the sentence in unison, and the procedure begins again. The tutor asks intermittent comprehension questions to monitor meaning making. (See Topping, 1987, for more details.) This technique works exceptionally well with students reading at third-grade level and beyond. The Northern Alberta Reading Specialist's Council video may be old, but it provides the most accurate description and representation of Topping's version of paired reading as described in his study, which yielded powerful results (*www.youtube.com/watch?v=RJXbsTGLhOc*).

Buddy Reading

Children with reading problems benefit from working with younger children as readers or tutors. Reading to younger students is a good way for children to practice their own reading in a natural setting. With teacher guidance, an older student picks a book that might be interesting to younger children. It should be short and colorful, with few sentences on each page. The student practices the book until he or she feels comfortable. Then he or she reads the book to a younger child or to the class, to the benefit of both. In the case of older children who read at a very low level (e.g., a sixth grader reading at a first-grade level), allowing them to select books to read to kindergartners, say, is a practical way of allowing them to practice appropriate material while maintaining their self-esteem. They might also do repeated reading as rehearsal for creating audiobooks for young readers.

Plays, Reader's Theater, and Famous Speeches

Plays and famous speeches are two popular approaches for engaging children in reading practice. Having children practice parts is an excellent way of getting them to read text repeatedly until they reach a desired level of fluency. One guideline: In order to benefit the readers who demonstrate weak reading skills, they must be assigned the most substantial roles and have adequate practice prior to performance. However, Reader's Theater is the least time-efficient technique for a busy classroom, and the fluency improvement is difficult to assess. Speeches work well for older students. They can be easily connected to disciplinary content-area units. Two websites serve as good sources: *www.powerfulwords.info/speeches* and *www.americanrhetoric.com/top100speechesall.html*.

Walpole–McKenna Differentiated Fluency

A small-group approach developed first for the primary grades (currently described in Walpole & McKenna, 2017), and later extended to the upper grades (Walpole, McKenna, Philippakos, & Strong, in press), involves a 15-minute daily session during which a selection is read twice. The first reading involves a higher level of support (either echo or choral reading), and the second involves less support (partner or whisper reading). (See Figure 6.2.) In this way, repeated readings are combined with other effective approaches to building fluency. A student's ORF is progress-monitored until it reaches benchmark level.

Oral Recitation

The oral recitation lesson (Hoffman, 1987) has two parts: a direct teaching phase and a mastery phase.

Direct Teaching Phase

1. For a regular-length story, the teacher begins by reading the entire story to the group. Then the teacher discusses the story as a whole, either asking questions or developing a group story map.
2. Then the teacher rereads the story, either sentence by sentence or paragraph by paragraph (whichever seems more suitable), as students follow along in their books, after which students echo back the portion read. Teacher and students proceed through the story in this way.
3. The teacher divides the story into parts and assigns a section to each student. Students practice their assigned sections and perform the story for the group. As an alternative to assigned parts, students can choose parts in which they are interested.
4. Teacher and students proceed to the next story. The teacher could assign worksheets, work on skills, and so on here.

Mastery Phase

Students practice stories covered in the direct teaching phase until they are able to read them with 99%+ accuracy and at a rate of at least 85 WPM (or another acceptable level of fluency). This practice is done on their own. The teacher works with them when they feel they are ready.

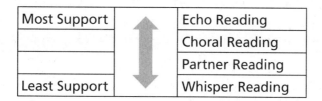

Most Support		Echo Reading
		Choral Reading
		Partner Reading
Least Support		Whisper Reading

FIGURE 6.2. Level of teacher support provided by fluency approaches.

Students progress more quickly through the direct teaching phase than the mastery phase, so that a child may be on a fifth story in the direct teaching phase but may only have mastered the first three stories. Students engage in mastery work during independent work time, in place of generic seatwork.

Fluency-Oriented Reading Instruction

Fluency-Oriented Reading Instruction (FORI) is a research-validated approach to fluency that also emphasizes comprehension and motivation (Schwanenflugel et al., 2009; Stahl & Heubach, 2005). FORI involves 5-day lesson sequences that incorporate several evidence-based approaches.

Day 1

- Preteach two or three key words.
- Discuss the book to build and activate prior knowledge.
- Read aloud expressively as children follow in their copies.
- Stop and question intermittently.
- For information books, use a graphic organizer.
- Conduct a postreading discussion, focusing on themes and summarizing.

Day 2

- Echo-read the book, pausing after each paragraph or page (depending on your students and the text).
- During reading, intermittently target and review key vocabulary. Coach the use of decoding strategies for the most difficult words.
- Ask questions that focus on specific points of comprehension.
- If possible, send the book home for each child to practice with a caregiver.

Day 3

- Lead the children in a choral reading of the entire book.
- Model expressive reading, and stress to the children that how you read aloud should reflect the text's meaning.

Day 4

- Students partner-read the book.
- If appropriate, tie the reading to a comprehension strategy, such as student-generated questioning or summarizing. For example, after one partner reads a text segment, the other might ask a question.
- For information books, students collaboratively summarize the most important ideas.

Day 5

Possible extension activities include the following:

- *Conversation groups.* By now, all students have a good understanding of the text and can benefit from sharing comments with their classmates.
- *Writing.* This activity might involve a brief response to the book or an extended composition that focuses on the writing process. It involves creative applications such as writing captions for illustrations.
- *Inquiry projects.* Students can explore other books to follow a related topic and write about it.

Wide Reading FORI

Although FORI employs a range of effective strategies, some teachers prefer an approach that confronts children with a greater variety of text. Wide Reading FORI is a modification of FORI that accomplishes this goal, but the tradeoff is less reliance on repeated readings. The approach requires 5 days. The first 2 days are identical to those in FORI. The third day incorporates the extension activities that make up the fifth day in FORI. It is during the fourth and fifth days that the approaches differ.

Day 4

- Introduce and echo-read a *second* book, pausing after each paragraph or page (depending on your students and the text).
- During reading, intermittently target and review key vocabulary.
- Ask questions that focus on specific points of comprehension.
- If possible, send the book home for children to read with a caregiver.

Day 5

- Introduce and echo-read a *third* book, pausing after each sentence, paragraph, or page (depending on your students and the text).
- During reading, intermittently target and review key vocabulary.
- Ask questions that focus on specific points of comprehension.
- If possible, send the book home for each child to read with a caregiver.

Figure 6.3 shows the differences between the two approaches and the tradeoff they involve. An excellent discussion of the two approaches appears in Kuhn and Levy (2015). Both FORI and Wide Reading FORI have proven extremely effective in second-grade classrooms, demonstrating reading achievement increases of more than 1.5 years in just a year (Schwanenflugel et al., 2009; Stahl & Heubach, 2005). The techniques have been effectively employed during whole-class shared reading with children from late first grade through third grade.

Peer-Assisted Learning Strategies

Peer-Assisted Learning Strategies (PALS) has been demonstrated to be an effective strategy for students from elementary through secondary grade levels (Fuchs & Fuchs, 2005; Fuchs, Fuchs, Mathes, & Simmons, 1997). PALS is a fast-paced, engaging 32-minute pro-

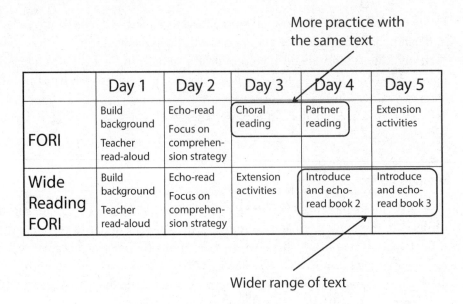

More practice with
the same text

	Day 1	Day 2	Day 3	Day 4	Day 5
FORI	Build background Teacher read-aloud	Echo-read Focus on comprehension strategy	Choral reading	Partner reading	Extension activities
Wide Reading FORI	Build background Teacher read-aloud	Echo-read Focus on comprehension strategy	Extension activities	Introduce and echo-read book 2	Introduce and echo-read book 3

Wider range of text

FIGURE 6.3. FORI versus Wide Reading FORI.

tocol designed to improve fluency and comprehension. It is designed to be used as a Tier 1 whole-class intervention, including in middle school content-area classrooms. Begin by rank-ordering the students, using any available data, in terms of their overall reading proficiency. Then divide the list in half and form partners, pairing the highest-ranking student with one in the middle. In a class of 20, for example, Student 1 would be paired with Student 11, Student 2 with Student 12, and so forth. This system ensures that the difference in proficiency is about the same for all pairs.

PALS is most effective if it is implemented every other day for 12–18 weeks. Some middle schools that we have worked with have trained content-area teachers to use PALs and divide the days of PALS between content areas such as science and social studies. Each content area uses PALS 1 or 2 days a week. You can use one common text, or each pair can read an individual text. The important thing is that the text has to be within both students' ZPD, so that the students can read it aloud (with support from one another) without getting frustrated. PALS consists of four activities:

1. *Partner reading (10 minutes).* The first student reads aloud for 5 minutes while the other coaches. They then switch roles. The teacher provides points to each pair for focus, cooperation, catching mistakes, and providing help to one another.

2. *Story retell (2 minutes).* For 2 minutes, the partners take turns reviewing what they've read in partner reading. They use sentence frames, such as these:

- "The first thing that happened was . . ."
- "The next thing that happened was . . ."

They can also look back in the text.

3. *Paragraph shrinking (10 minutes).* Students alternate reading paragraphs and then retelling what happened in each paragraph. Some recurring prompts include these:

- "Name the who or what."
- "Tell the most important thing about the who or what."
- "Say the main idea in 10 words or less."

4. *Prediction relay (10 minutes)*. The final 10 minutes combine the prediction and paragraph-shrinking procedures. The partners begin by asking what they think will happen next. Then they read about half a page to test their predictions.

In PALS for younger students, the stronger reader reads for 5 minutes, and then the weaker reader rereads the same section; for older readers, the reading is new text. Additionally, the time allocation may need to be shortened. PALS has three main management tools:

1. Students share a text to compel them to work together.
2. Students use scripts and procedures to respond to one another, to ensure that they provide feedback.
3. The teacher circulates, constantly providing positive feedback (through points) to students for engaging in the procedures.

PALS definitely works. Our own experiences in schools confirm the evidence of controlled studies. You can learn more about the approach by visiting the PALS section of the Fuchs Research Group website *(https://vkc.mc.vanderbilt.edu/frg)*. Additionally, we highly recommend the free IRIS Center modules, which provide a thorough training in implementing PALS for differentiated grade-level bands *(https://iris.peabody.vanderbilt.edu/#content)*.

SEVEN

Vocabulary

Vocabulary knowledge is consistently correlated with reading comprehension. This is why it is important to assess vocabulary needs and provide instruction accordingly. Many schools find it difficult to form a strategic alignment of the assessment and instruction of vocabulary. As a result, many schools administer few if any assessments in this key area.

It is important to keep in mind that every child has not one but several vocabularies. In this chapter, we focus on the assessment of *conceptual vocabulary,* which consists of a learner's knowledge of word meanings (e.g., knowing that *scowl* means to frown with displeasure). This is in contrast to sight vocabulary and high-frequency vocabulary, which we have discussed in Chapter 5 in relation to word recognition. Sight words are those words that children recognize immediately, at sight, without the need for analysis; high-frequency words are those words that occur most frequently in English language texts. Because it is important for children to recognize the high-frequency words automatically, these words are taught until they become sight words. For beginning readers, sight words are nearly always high-frequency words (with a few exceptions, such as a child's name), and high-frequency words are typically familiar in meaning when the child hears them in context (e.g., *the, like, and*). Figure 7.1 shows the relationship among these three types of vocabulary.

When we refer to conceptual vocabulary, we are concerned with word meaning. Conceptual vocabulary is acquired across a lifetime. Our *breadth* of vocabulary knowledge continues to grow as we continue to learn more and more words. Think about the new technology words that you have added to your vocabulary in the last 10 years! Also, our experiences with a particular word across a range of contexts contribute to our *depth* of knowledge—that is, to our increasingly nuanced understandings of a word. In Figure 7.2, we've taken the circle representing conceptual vocabulary in Figure 7.1 and tilted it a bit. In this three-dimensional view, you can see how breadth and depth are two separate dimensions. When we think about the assessment of vocabulary, we want assessment tools that serve as gauges of the breadth *and* depth of our students' vocabulary development.

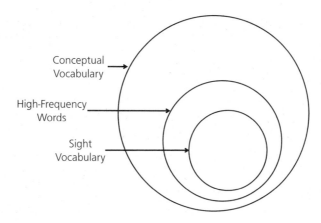

FIGURE 7.1. Relationship of sight words, high-frequency words, and conceptual vocabulary.

COMPLEXITY OF WORD KNOWLEDGE

Although we may perceive a word as a single unit of study, acquisition of conceptual vocabulary is actually associated with five aspects of word knowledge (Nagy & Scott, 2000). This complexity contributes to the challenge of assessing vocabulary.

- *Incrementality.* Knowledge about a word grows over time as the learner experiences the word in a variety of contexts.
- *Polysemy.* Many words have multiple meanings. Everyday words, such as *make*, tend to have more meanings than less common words like *polysemy*. Words can have distinctly different definitions or different shades of meaning for the same definition that depend on text, purpose, and context (e.g., *drinking water, drinking at the bar, drinking in knowledge*).
- *Interrelatedness.* Words are not learned in a vacuum. Knowing a word involves knowing how it connects with other words and where it fits within the networks that make up semantic memory.
- *Multidimensionality.* As incremental knowledge of a word develops, multiple dimensions of knowledge about the word are expanded, such as semantic and

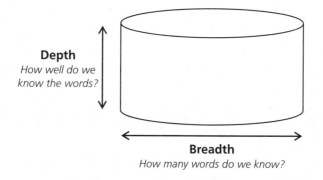

FIGURE 7.2. Depth and breadth of knowledge.

morphological relations (derivations and affixes), stylistic register (e.g., *weed* as *marijuana*), connotations (e.g., *golf* implying wealth), and collocational behavior (i.e., other words that tend to occur with a focus word; e.g., novelists *write* novels—they do not *invent* or *build* them). So far, research indicates that this incremental pathway follows an individual course. But assessment limitations still leave room for uncertainty about individual differences in what students know about the multidimensional characteristics of words.

- *Heterogeneity.* Not all words and not all word meanings are of equal usefulness. Given the limited time for instruction, it is important for teachers to teach and test the most useful words.

COMPREHENSION AND VOCABULARY

Not surprisingly, the relationship between vocabulary and comprehension is also complex. Anderson and Freebody (1985) proposed three hypotheses to explain the strong association. The *general aptitude* hypothesis states that general verbal abilities are at the root of both vocabulary acquisition and the ability to make sense of a text and the world. General aptitude includes how easily one can remember and retrieve knowledge. Stahl and Nagy (2006) refined the general aptitude hypothesis to include the *metalinguistic hypothesis:* That is, the ways that children think about language and their awareness of how the language system works contribute to (or limit) their ongoing language acquisition. The *instrumental hypothesis* suggests that simply knowing more words is going to result in a greater likelihood of comprehending a piece of text. And third, the *knowledge hypothesis* proposes that both vocabulary and comprehension are reliant on, and associated with, a reader's world knowledge and experience.

Taken together, these hypotheses have major instructional implications that further highlight the importance of assessment. First, children who know more of the words in the texts that they are reading or hearing will have a greater likelihood of being able to make sense of the text. That is, their word knowledge is *instrumental* in their comprehension. One of the actions that we can undertake as teachers is to ensure that we provide both definitions and contextual experiences for the words that children are likely to encounter (Stahl & Fairbanks, 1986). Systematic, explicit attention is just as important in teaching vocabulary as it is in teaching phonics. Identifying which words to teach, such as sophisticated words in literary texts or disciplinary terms and academic language in informational texts, is the first step.

Teaching words during integrated disciplinary content units provides children with hands-on experiences applying discipline-specific vocabulary. They see the words in print, and they use the words in speech and writing. In essence, disciplinary units provide repeated exposures to words and create an authentic context for building semantic networks of words, so that concepts are learned in tandem. These experiences and the networks of associations they help to extend are the foundations of disciplinary *knowledge.*

Finally, it is important to recognize students' individual differences in both prior knowledge and cognitive abilities. Vocabulary knowledge is an unconstrained ability and thus tends to be incremental rather than all or nothing. Dale (1965) identified four stages of word knowledge:

- Stage 1: Has never seen the word before.
- Stage 2: Has heard (or seen) the word, but doesn't know the meaning of the word.
- Stage 3: Has vague or general knowledge of the word or knowledge of the word's meaning in a single context.
- Stage 4: Knows the word well in multiple contexts.

Students come to our classes with different networks of knowledge (see Figure 7.3). Although two children in a prekindergarten class seem to exhibit familiarity with the

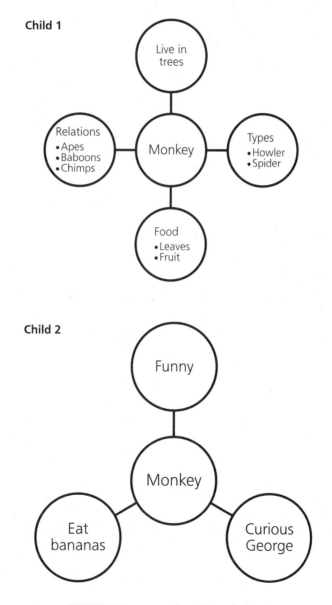

FIGURE 7.3. Networks of knowledge.

word *monkey* during a teacher read-aloud, if we could peer into their minds, we would see two different networks of knowledge surrounding the word *monkey*. As teachers, we want to expand each child's existing knowledge of a word. Regardless of whether a child knows a lot or a little about a word, we can always help him or her learn more. However, both the rate of learning and number of exposures that it takes a child to learn a word will vary by individual. Sensitive assessments help us (1) identify where students are located along this continuum of knowledge, (2) target instruction to students' needs, and (3) quantify students' vocabulary growth so that we can monitor it.

Vocabulary Knowledge Scale

A common way to assess children's knowledge of the targeted vocabulary in an upcoming classroom book selection or a disciplinary content unit is to administer a vocabulary knowledge rating scale. The Vocabulary Knowledge Scale (VKS), mentioned previously, is a self-report assessment that is easy to administer and score. It employs Dale's (1965) stages of word learning. Although it will not reveal a student's knowledge of the particular nuances of each word's use, Wesche and Paribakht (1996) found that the assessment is a reliable guide to a student's knowledge of a set of words, and that it is sensitive enough to quantify incremental growth over a short period of time. Wesche and Paribakht also determined that their students' self-assessment of their knowledge of a word was highly correlated with a test score that reflected their actual knowledge of the words. This form of assessment can be used with both English-only students and English learners.

For elementary students, it is possible to use a table format that lists the targeted words and then asks children to identify their level of knowledge about each word with a checkmark in the appropriate cell (see Figure 7.4). For the youngest students or for certain topics, it might be helpful to refine the particular descriptions for each stage of knowledge. For older students, teachers might include additional columns to invite students to generate a written response for examples or definitions of a word (Brozo & Afflerbach, 2011). This constructed response format, which will yield richer informa-

	I have never heard of this body part.	I have heard of this body part, but I can't tell you what job it does.	I can tell you where this body part is in my body and what job it does.
saliva			
colon			
appendix			
intestines			
pancreas			
liver			
esophagus			
stomach			

FIGURE 7.4. Vocabulary Knowledge Scale (VKS) assessing a unit on digestion.

tion about a learner's vocabulary knowledge, can be used as a pre- and postintervention assessment.

Wesche and Paribakht (1996) describe another assessment variation geared toward gathering a more detailed analysis of older learners' vocabulary knowledge. This assessment includes a constructed response to provide evidence of levels of familiarity with the target vocabulary. Collecting this amount of detail requires more discrimination when selecting which words to assess.

I. I don't remember having seen this word before. (1 point)
II. I have seen this word before, but I don't think I know what it means. (2 points)
III. I have seen this word before, and I think it means _____. (synonym or translation) (3 points)
IV. I know this word. It means _____. (synonym or translation) (4 points)
V. I can use this word in a sentence: _____. (If you do this section, please also do Section IV.) (5 points)

Any incorrect response in Category III yields 2 points for the total item, even if the student has attempted Categories IV and V unsuccessfully. If the sentence in Category V demonstrates the correct meaning, but the word is not used appropriately in the sentence context, a score of 3 is awarded. A score of 4 is awarded if the wrong grammatical form of the target word is used in the correct context. A score of 5 reflects semantically and grammatically correct use of the target word. The VKS is administered as a pretest before a text or unit is taught, and then after instruction to assess growth.

EXPRESSIVE AND RECEPTIVE VOCABULARY

One of the challenges of assessing vocabulary is that there are four types of vocabulary knowledge to assess. Listening vocabulary and reading vocabulary are both receptive forms of vocabulary knowledge. *Listening vocabulary* refers to the words we understand when we are listening. *Reading vocabulary* refers to the words we understand when we are reading. Speaking and writing vocabularies are both considered expressive vocabularies. *Speaking vocabulary* consists of the words we use when we speak, and *writing vocabulary* consists of the words we use when we write. Figure 7.5 provides a helpful breakdown.

These vocabularies are not identical! Just because we can match a definition to a word does not mean that we know other definitions or different contextual applications for the same word, or that we have expressive control of the word. Most people have larger receptive than expressive vocabularies (Pearson, Hiebert, & Kamil, 2007). For example, each of us has a bank of words that we know well enough to understand when we read the word in a book or hear it articulated in speech. However, we might not know the word well enough to retrieve it spontaneously to use in conversation, or be confident enough with the pronunciation or meaning nuances to use the word publicly with colleagues.

Most normed assessments and most summative assessments used by teachers only

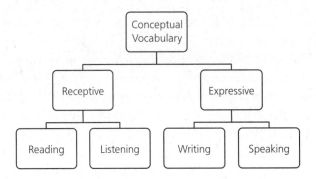

FIGURE 7.5. Receptive and expressive vocabulary.

assess written receptive vocabulary (Pearson et al., 2007). The most common assessments call for children to match words to a definition or to identify the best vocabulary word to fill in a blank within a sentence. Multiple-choice items may ask a child to select a synonym or brief definition for a highlighted word in a sentence. These modes of assessment are shallow gauges of word knowledge.

Formative classroom assessments present a better opportunity to document students' expressive vocabulary. Additionally, in order to assess the depth of vocabulary knowledge, we must use more than a single item to document a student's use of a target word. Cronbach (1942) articulated the following dimensions of word knowledge that we want to consider as we evaluate what our students know about word meanings:

- *Generalization:* The ability to define a word.
- *Application:* The ability to select an appropriate use of the word.
- *Breadth:* Knowledge of multiple meanings of the word.
- *Precision:* The ability to apply a term correctly to all situations.
- *Availability:* The ability to retrieve the word and use it productively.

You can create formative vocabulary assessments that range across a continuum of standardization in administration and scoring. Here are some possibilities.

Word Wizard Charts

A *word wizard chart* is among the most informal means of documenting the ways and numbers of times that children in a classroom use the targeted vocabulary. Beck, Perfetti, and McKeown (1982) originated the use of the word wizard activity to sensitize children to new vocabulary words that had been taught, and as an incentive for them to use the words expressively in their speech and writing. A teacher lists the children's names down the left side of the word wizard chart and lists target words (10–15) across the top. Whenever a child uses the target word in his or her speech or writing, the child receives a check on the word wizard chart.

Typically, teachers select sophisticated words that children are taught during a teacher read-aloud or a shared reading of literary text. Beck and McKeown (2001) call these words *Tier Two* words. Children know the concepts for these words but are unfamiliar with the actual words (e.g., *bellow, amber, treacherous*). Teachers need to be intentional in providing repeated exposures to high-utility Tier Two words. However, because children already know the concept, learning the word requires less instructional attention than words requiring conceptual development. Nevertheless, providing children with explicit instruction and repeated exposures to Tier Two words is beneficial. These are the words that would not be considered high-frequency words, but are still high-utility general vocabulary, and are often the words that contribute to an author's craft.

Tier One words are the words of everyday speech that may require instruction for automatic word recognition, but generally do not require conceptual development. A word wizard chart would not be useful as a form of assessment for Tier One words. *Tier Three* words are associated with specific disciplinary domains (e.g., *isotope, minuend, legislature*), or they are rare general vocabulary words (e.g., *anodyne, bumptious, jaundiced*). In either case, they require conceptual development. Tier Three domain words are used frequently throughout a unit of study, so they would not typically be appropriate for placement on a word wizard chart. They require instruction that is embedded within a content unit and that occurs over the course of the entire unit as conceptual knowledge of the topic expands.

The word wizard chart is an informal means of monitoring who is using the words expressively. It has high positive consequential validity. The chart serves as a personal reminder for teachers to use the words more frequently, thereby increasing the number of times that children receive exposure to the words. Figure 7.6 offers an example of a word wizard chart targeting Tier Two words.

We encourage you to make this formative metric your own. There are some common and equally valuable adaptations. One adaptation is a blank chart that only contains the children's names. Words that have been taught can be placed on a word wall or some other kind of display. Then as children use the words in their writing or conversation, the teacher places a sticky note with the date and word (or the date, word, and type of expression) on the chart next to each child's name.

Be a Word Wizard!

	wary	scowl	ridiculous	fortunate
Tom	√		√	
Sue		√	√	
Ed	√			√
Juan	√	√ √		
Maria				√
Lakesha	√		√	
Paul	√	√	√	√
Jack		√		√ √

FIGURE 7.6. Word wizard chart.

A high school English teacher we've worked with has modified the word wizard chart for the five periods of English she teaches every day. Instead of listing students' names on the left side of the chart, she lists each period (Period 1, Period 2, etc.). A few times a week, for the first 5–10 minutes of class, she asks the students to give her *examples* of the words they've found in their own lives, or out "in the world," during the past week or so. For example, for the word *martinet,* a student said, "My wrestling coach is a martinet—he made us do 100 'burpies' at the end of practice on Monday." Her different class periods compete to see which one can find the most examples of vocabulary words outside the classroom walls over a 2-week period. She is thrilled that this activity actually motivates her students to apply the vocabulary outside the classroom walls, in ways she has never seen before.

Teacher Check Sheets for Disciplinary Words

You can also make check sheets to monitor your students' acquisition of high-priority words in a disciplinary unit. Check sheets work particularly well for words in math and science units. Start by listing the students' names along one axis of the chart and the selected words along the other. Make the chart at the beginning of the unit. Throughout the unit, document the students' utilization of the target words in speech, writing, and application in disciplinary practices. In math and science, students often apply words operationally in experiments or hands-on activities. By using an abbreviated notation system on the chart, you can efficiently indicate the ways that the students demonstrate ownership of the words. Figure 7.7 is an example of a check sheet that was used to gauge the utilization of target vocabulary in a science unit on machines.

Vocabulary for Simple/Complex Machine Unit					
	Jenna	Joaquim	Khanh	Alexa	Dino
friction	T	AT		AT	T
force	DT	DT	DWT	AT	DWAT
effort	DAT	DAT	DAT	DAT	DAT
resistance	DWAT	DWAT	DWAT	DWAT	DWAT
lever	WAT	WAT	WAT	AT	WAT
pulley	DAT	A	DAT	DAT	AT
inclined plane	DAT	A	DAT	DAT	AT
screw	AT	AT	AT	AT	AT
wheel and axle	AT	AT	AT	AT	AT
wedge	AT	AT	DWAT	AT	DWAT

FIGURE 7.7. Teacher check sheet of machine terms. All students' names are pseudonyms. D, used in discussion; W, used in writing; A, applied; T, tested.

ACADEMIC LANGUAGE

Academic language has received increased attention as an essential aspect of the CCSS and other new educational standards. The melding of disciplinary content and literacy instruction has brought academic language to the forefront. Rather than simply having students read more informational texts, the Standards call for students to engage in the discourse of the disciplinary community. Nagy and Townsend (2012, p. 92) define *academic language* as "the specialized language, both oral and written, of academic settings that facilitates communication and thinking about disciplinary content." This definition makes clear that academic language is more than a list of words in a content unit to be taught and tested in a matching or multiple-choice format. Academic language is the particular way that insiders within a disciplinary community communicate their thinking and values. It is essential to the construction of conceptual knowledge within the discipline.

Teachers have become much more mindful of integrating informational texts into their literacy instruction. However, simply incorporating informational text and a list of discipline-specific vocabulary words into an ELA block does not constitute academic language. The ultimate goal is to teach students to use the texts and academic language as a means of mediating thought and conceptual development in the ways that experts within each discipline do. In order to accomplish this goal, the academic words must be nested within academic language that is written and spoken. Students have to read, write, and speak the discourse of the discipline. The implications for assessment are that measures will need to assess receptive and expressive ownership of the words, and the tasks will need to be nested within the disciplinary content. Research has not yet demonstrated whether the best measures of academic vocabulary can be separated from measures of disciplinary knowledge (Nagy & Townsend, 2012). Consequently, the best course of action is to conduct some tests of isolated word knowledge for target vocabulary, and to assess more general disciplinary knowledge that allows you to gauge your students' usage of vocabulary in written and spoken formats.

Categories of Academic Vocabulary

Academic vocabulary falls into two categories: general and discipline-specific. General academic words tend to be multiple-meaning words that are used across disciplines. Discipline-specific words are those Tier Three words that are conceptually associated with particular fields of study. Students need various opportunities to work with both categories of words in authentic contexts (Wright & Cervetti, 2016).

General Academic Vocabulary

Coxhead's (2000) Academic Word List (AWL) is a popular list of 570 general academic words (*www.victoria.ac.nz/lals/resources/academicwordlist/sublists*). Knowledge of these words will help students in their academic activities and in their comprehension of academic texts. The list includes some words (e.g., *similar, respond, draft*) that are likely to have a common meaning across disciplines. However, a few cautions are required. First, the AWL includes only words that are not on the General Service List (West, 1953), the 2,000 most frequently occurring words from the corpus of written English. Although many words on the General Service List are common everyday words, there are many that elementary students do not know and that contribute to general academic success. The AWL is drawn from college texts and intended for use with secondary students, although we see it introduced in some of the elementary schools where we work. Second, although labeled as a list of general vocabulary words, the meanings of many AWL words are discipline-specific. For example, *culture* is defined differently in science and social studies. *Volume* has three very different meanings in literature, science, and math. Finally, some administrators are encouraging teachers to teach and test these as isolated lists of words and definitions, rather than embedding them when relevant within disciplinary instruction. Contextualizing the study of these words is imperative (Wright & Cervetti, 2016).

Discipline-Specific Vocabulary

Within each unit of disciplinary study, particular words form the conceptual networks that are integral to understanding the content of the unit. The students' ability to apply these words in speech and writing provides a window into their understanding of the content.

Bravo, Cervetti, Hiebert, and Pearson (2008) designed integrated science literacy units to teach students to think, read, write, speak, and analyze like scientists. The unit test consisted of two parts. The first part provided brief passages related to the unit, followed by open-ended questions that prompted students to apply comprehension strategies and text features associated with scientific texts. The second part of the test required the children to display scientific knowledge. For example, the students might label diagrams and write sentences about them, or use scientific knowledge acquired in the unit to solve a novel problem or to write an argument using scientific evidence. Bravo et al. (2008) incidentally found that second- and third-grade students used more discipline-specific vocabulary words in constructed-response disciplinary unit posttests than in the unit pretests. The results were statistically significant for both English learners and native English speakers on the frequency of usage of academic words and discipline-specific words.

These assessments looked very similar to the kinds of common formative assessments that many school districts are currently creating as intermittent measures of the Standards. School personnel who are designing common formative assessments related to disciplinary units of study may want to deliberately include items or scoring mechanisms for measuring the acquisition of target vocabulary.

Assessing Academic Vocabulary

The first step in planning academic vocabulary assessments is to acquire or create a list of discipline-specific target words that you have decided are important for your students to know. We continue to be surprised when we visit schools and discover that many grade-level teams of teachers have not explicitly identified a set of 15–25 words within each unit that they will teach and test. Of course, the teachers are working hard to teach the words that are often listed in the textbook or curriculum materials. However, often those materials list 40–50 words that are associated with the units. The first step is for a grade-level team of teachers to prioritize the 15–25 target words that are essential for understanding the concepts of the unit. Students are likely to encounter these words throughout the unit. We want to be certain that students understand and can use these target words. We recommend posting the target words in the classroom throughout the unit, and providing special education teachers and teachers of English learners (EL) with a copy of this word list.

This planning process presents a good opportunity to cross-check the AWL to select general academic words that are likely to be useful in each disciplinary unit. Nagy and Townsend (2012) caution that academic words often possess one or more traits that can cause them to be difficult for students to learn. They may be:

- Conceptually dense
- Abstract
- Latin or Greek derivatives
- Morphologically complex
- Grammatical metaphors (everyday terms used in a different ways)

When you are assessing academic vocabulary, it is necessary to employ multiple instruments that will enable you to gauge Cronbach's (1942) dimensions of word knowledge.

Testing Breadth of Word Knowledge

We want an assessment that includes the entire list of target words in isolation. This assessment gauges the breadth of word knowledge that our students have acquired across the unit. Typically, this assessment tests our students' receptive facility with the words, and it may take the shape of a traditional vocabulary test such as a matching test, a fill-in-the-blank test, or the Vocabulary Recognition Task (VRT; Stahl & Bravo, 2010).

The VRT is a formative, yes–no test designed to assess recognition of discipline-specific vocabulary within a content unit. Anderson and Freebody (1983) determined that the yes–no task is a valid, reliable measure of vocabulary assessment. This task eliminates the psychometric and semantic complexities of choosing foils for each item on a multiple-choice test, of particular concern on teacher-made tests. Anderson and Freebody found that the yes–no task serves as a better measure of student knowledge than a multiple-choice test, particularly with younger students. The VRT was originally used and validated as a vocabulary assessment with second graders, but it can be adapted for use in other elementary grades (Stahl, 2008; Stahl & Bravo, 2010).

To construct a VRT, identify between 15 and 25 target vocabulary words that you intend to hold your students accountable for learning throughout the unit. By the end of the unit, you expect your students to be able to read these words and know their meanings. Then select between four and seven foils—that is, words that are unrelated to your unit. Create a test that looks something like Figure 7.8. During the pretest, students are directed to circle each word that meets two criteria: (1) A student can read the word, and (2) the word is related to the upcoming unit of study. Figure 7.8 is the VRT for a second-grade unit on insects. As a posttest, simply readminister the yes–no task. Additionally, students can be asked to categorize the selected words on a graphic organizer (see Figure 7.9).

There are three alternative ways to score the VRT. The simplest is to tally "hits" (H; correct word choices) and "false alarms" (FA; mistakenly circled foils). Deduct the number of false alarms from the hits to arrive at a raw score. Alternatively, you can calculate

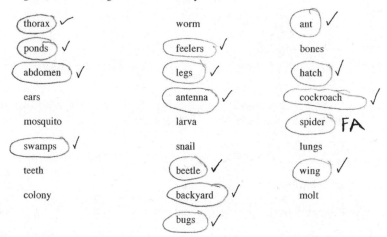

FIGURE 7.8. Vocabulary Recognition Task (VRT) pretest and posttest. From Stahl and Bravo (2010). Copyright © 2010 the International Literacy Association/John Wiley & Sons, Inc. Reprinted by permission.

a total percentage of correct choices. Stahl (2008) applied a more complicated formula that employed Anderson and Freebody's (1983) correction formula to account for guessing. The proportion of words truly known, P(K), was determined by using the following formula:

$$P(K) = \frac{P(H) - P(FA)}{100 - P(FA)}$$

If this process seems complex, remember that it is only one alternative, and it can be easily built into an Excel spreadsheet so that all you'll ever need are the raw numbers.

The students received two scores for the web: (1) the total number of words correctly sorted by category, and (2) the percentage of words correctly selected on the VRT that were correctly sorted by category. (See Figure 7.9.)

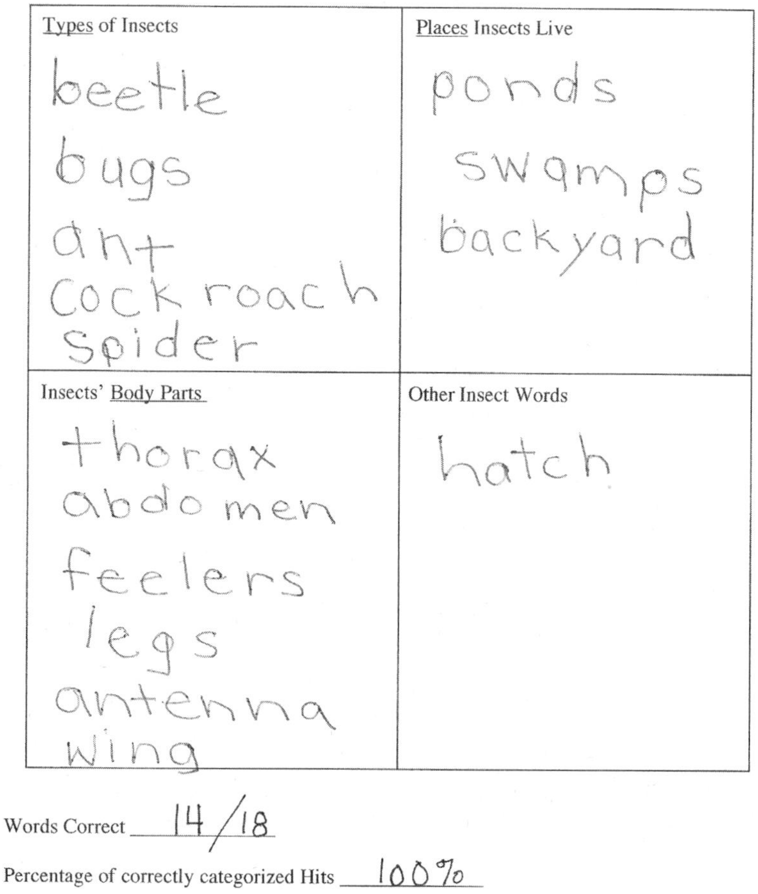

VRT Web (Posttest Only)

Types of Insects	Places Insects Live
beetle bugs ant cockroach spider	ponds swamps backyard
Insects' Body Parts	Other Insect Words
thorax abdomen feelers legs antenna wing	hatch

Words Correct __14/18__

Percentage of correctly categorized Hits __100%__

FIGURE 7.9. VRT web posttest. From Stahl and Bravo (2010). Copyright © 2010 the International Literacy Association/John Wiley & Sons, Inc. Reprinted by permission.

Testing Depth of Word Knowledge

Because the disciplinary unit is likely to result in repeated opportunities to teach, learn, and apply the target words, it includes opportunities for teachers to assess the students' usage of the words expressively in projects, conversation/discovery/inquiry groups, compositions, and constructed-response tests. The use of teacher checklists, like the one we have discussed in the previous section, is one way to document students' ownership of the words in their writing, speaking, and other forms of disciplinary application.

Vocabulary Assessment Magazine. Common formative assessments are a useful way to test complex skill sets and knowledge acquisition. According to Nagy and Townsend (2012), it may not be desirable, or even possible, to separate the assessment of academic vocabulary from the assessment of knowledge acquisition within a disciplinary unit of study. Therefore, it makes sense to embed vocabulary assessment within broader assessments of disciplinary knowledge, similar to the Vocabulary Assessment Magazine (VAM) used by Bravo et al. (2008; see also Stahl & Bravo, 2010).

To construct a VAM, grade-level teams of teachers create an assessment that calls for students to read a few short passages related to the unit of study, and then to answer both short and extended constructed-response questions about the passages that reflect important conceptual knowledge associated with the unit. This type of assessment enables teachers to measure students' expressive writing abilities with the target vocabulary, and it provides a lens for viewing students' ability to situate the vocabulary appropriately in relationship to other semantically related words. There are likely to be multiple items that call for the students to apply some of the most important words. Multiple items are essential for determining depth of knowledge. The students' ability to use the target vocabulary in multiple contexts documents the depth of their receptive and expressive knowledge.

This test would be likely to serve as an end-of-unit test. For science units, students could be required to complete tables, interpret figures and tables, and label diagrams in keeping with interpreting the evidence valued by scientists. For social studies units, students would be expected to construct arguments reflecting evidence valued by historians and create flowcharts or procedural descriptions that apply vocabulary from the unit. Figure 7.10 illustrates a task by McKenna and Robinson (2014), requiring students

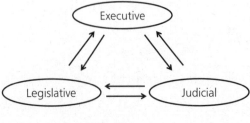

Word Bank

impeachment, veto, judicial review, confirmation, appointment

FIGURE 7.10. Government vocabulary task.

to place words representing the checks and balances among the three branches of government on the arrow.

In addition to a holistic score for the overall test, a vocabulary subscore can be calculated. To calculate a vocabulary subscore, count the times that students use target vocabulary appropriately in their constructed responses. Partial credit might be applied for imprecise use of the vocabulary as a means of recognizing the incremental nature of vocabulary development. Grade-level teams might also provide a subscore for disciplinary writing, based on the writing rubric that is valued (Partnership for Assessment of Readiness for College and Careers [PARCC], Smarter Balanced, Six Traits, or some other state-selected rubric). Using metrics such as this common formative assessment will contribute to creating a "lean and mean" assessment system that carries predictive indicators for the new generation of high-stakes tests—those related directly to the CCSS and those being developed along parallel lines in nonadopting states. Providing experience with this test format also eliminates the need for commercial test prep materials.

A few key considerations will contribute to the success of using a VAM as a vocabulary measure at the end of a unit (Stahl & Bravo, 2010). First, throughout the unit, students should be encouraged to use the target vocabulary in ways that clearly articulate the disciplinary concepts. We urge teachers to provide students with a reminder to show off their sophisticated vocabulary on the test. Other test considerations include (1) monitoring student access to any texts that students are asked to read and respond to, (2) documenting target vocabulary that incorporates general academic and discipline-specific vocabulary, (3) ensuring sufficient opportunities for students to apply the vocabulary in their responses, and (4) focusing on a manageable number of target words that can be taught extensively and to the point where native English students and English learners alike feel confident using them.

Focus Questions with Vocabulary Banks. The use of focus questions with vocabulary banks (Templeton et al., 2015) is one of our favorite, easy-to-implement vocabulary assessment strategies for older learners; it can also do double duty as a powerful instructional strategy. This strategy assesses students' ability to actually use the target academic vocabulary words in the context of thinking about and wrestling with the key questions and big ideas in a unit of study. Figure 7.11 is an example of three focus questions with a supporting vocabulary bank that could be used before and after reading a chapter on immigration from an American history textbook.

To use this strategy, first identify one or more focus questions that get at the big ideas and key concepts in a unit. Next, preselect key academic vocabulary terms that you want students to use when answering these questions. Place these words in a "vocabulary bank" for students to draw from when answering the focus questions. Notice how the vocabulary bank in Figure 7.11 includes both discipline-specific (e.g., *push factors, Industrial Revolution*) and general academic (e.g., *resulted in, for example*) vocabulary words and terms that represent key concepts or are signal words. After students have attempted to answer these questions individually in writing, they can share with the class to spark a class discussion, or you can collect them as informal assessments.

Focus questions with vocabulary banks can also serve as engaging, effective instructional activities before, during, and/or after reading or interspersed during a lesson. It's

Focus Questions

1. What factors do you think "pushed" emigrants out of their native lands to want to move elsewhere?

2. What factors do you think "pulled" immigrants to the United States in the mid-1800s?

3. What hardships do you think immigrants faced on their journeys? And when they arrived? How do you think they attempted to overcome these obstacles and hardships?

Use the words and phrases below to help you answer the three focus questions.

Population boom caused	Pull factors
Cheap and abundant land	Crop failures and famine
Industrial Revolution	Freedom
Push factors	Hardships
Prejudice	For example,
This led to	resulted in

FIGURE 7.11. Focus questions with vocabulary bank for a unit on immigration.

become a "go-to" strategy for many middle-grades teachers we work with, because (1) it is so easily adaptable to any topic/content area; (2) it requires little planning time or teaching time (a teacher can create focus questions on the spot, and it only takes a few minutes for students to write an answer to such a question); and (3) it serves as both a quick assessment and a way to reengage learners who are beginning to "wilt." We've seen this strategy used (1) before class as an entrance ticket to assess prior learning, activate background knowledge, and set a purpose for learning; (2) during class as a small-group discussion activity; and (3) at the end of class as an exit ticket.

NORMED, STANDARDIZED TESTS

A very different approach to vocabulary assessment is to determine the extent of a student's conceptual vocabulary relative to age peers. The aim is not to test the knowledge of specific target words. Rather, the goal is to select words representative of a large pool of words. This means that the items do not reflect a particular curriculum, and they do not represent the content of a unit. The point is to compare a student's standing with respect to the U.S. population. Let's consider two important examples of such tests and how they are used.

The Peabody Picture Vocabulary Test—Fifth Edition (PPVT-5; Dunn, 2019) is a norm-referenced, individually administered test that focuses solely on receptive vocabulary. It is co-normed with the Expressive Vocabulary Test—Third Edition (EVT-3; Williams, 2019), a norm-referenced, individually administered test that focuses on expressive vocabulary. In administering the PPVT-5, the examiner says a word, and the examinee selects one of four pictures that best describes the word. In the EVT-3, the examiner asks a question about a picture, and the examinee must respond with a label, synonym, or phrase to describe the picture. Students are not required to do any reading on either test. In addition to the age and grade-level norms, growth-scale value scores are now available that increase the tests' sensitivity to smaller changes over time. Using both tests allows the examiner to compare an individual's abilities in receptive and expressive vocabularies in ways that are not confounded by reading and writing abilities. These tests require 15–20 minutes for each administration, and the examiner must also possess expertise in test administration, because baselines and ceilings are used.

The primary function of these tests is psychometrically differentiating students, not informing instruction (Pearson et al., 2007). As a result, classroom teachers and general education interventionists do not usually administer them. School psychologists often include these tests as part of a battery to determine eligibility for special education.

ASSESSMENT DIMENSIONS

Whether you are constructing your own vocabulary assessments or evaluating commercially produced assessments, three dimensions of vocabulary assessment should be considered (Read, 2000). Although Read defined these dimensions on the basis of his work with assessments for English learners, they can be applied to all vocabulary assessments.

Comprehensive to Selective

The continuum from *comprehensive* to *selective* addresses the corpus of words that were used to select a sample of representative words. Many commercial tests like the PPVT-5 and EVT-3 select their words from the entire corpus of words in the English language. Pearson et al. (2007) suggest that words on large-scale, normed vocabulary tests are chosen for their psychometric properties, not for linguistic reasons. Consequently, these tests are at the comprehensive end of this continuum. It is very difficult for children to show gains on tests that are at the comprehensive end.

When teachers develop an assessment based on a small set of words that were explicitly taught as part of a unit, the test is selective. These tests are strongly influenced by instruction. When you assess the words derived from a single storybook, you are constructing an assessment that falls at the extremely selective end of the continuum. When you construct a test based on words that you taught in a disciplinary unit, you are constructing a test that is less selective than a vocabulary test derived from a storybook. A state science test that assesses science vocabulary that should be acquired across one or two grade levels is more comprehensive than the unit test but more selective than the PPVT-5.

Discrete to Embedded

The continuum from *discrete* to *embedded* defines the degree to which vocabulary is treated as a separate construct or is holistically embedded within a broader context. A test that requires students to match definitions to words is at the discrete end of this continuum. Teacher check sheets and VAMs, on the other hand, are clearly embedded measures: One has to mine the text or discussion for the vocabulary. Some standardized tests, such as the NAEP (National Assessment Governing Board, 2013), ask vocabulary questions about words that are embedded in a larger comprehension measure, but they report a vocabulary subtest score. This approach is embedded.

Context-Independent to Context-Dependent

The continuum from *context-independent* to *context-dependent* represents the need to engage with a context to derive the correct meaning of a word. Certainly, an isolated test that calls for students to match a word to a picture would be at the extreme end of the context-independent continuum. However, if a student can define the words in text passages without reading the passages, those items are also context-independent. For example, a child would not have to read the passage to define the word *pebble*, which only has a single definition. Many of today's tests, such as the NAEP (National Assessment Governing Board, 2013), only ask vocabulary questions about polysemous words. Students need to discriminate among several definitions and choose the one that describes how the word was used in the passage. These vocabulary items are context-dependent.

Teacher Self-Study of Vocabulary Assessment

When we work with teachers who are beginning to think about new alternatives for assessing vocabulary, we like to engage them in a brief self-study or inventory of their current practices. They often discover that they are already doing a lot to assess their students' vocabulary knowledge. However, this process also illuminates the voids in their current battery of assessment tools. As a result, teachers begin to let go of some of the tasks they have been using, and to integrate some new techniques from this chapter and other resources to develop a more comprehensive toolkit for tapping multiple dimensions of their students' vocabulary knowledge. Form 7.1 (p. 193) can be used by teachers who wish to inventory their existing assessment practices.

GUIDELINES FOR ASSESSING AND TEACHING CONCEPTUAL VOCABULARY

Academic vocabulary, conceptual knowledge, and background knowledge play an important role in reading comprehension and general academic success, especially as students progress throughout their school career (see Chapter 11 for a more complete description). Thus teachers must assess their students' vocabulary growth to plan for instruction and monitor content learning. While these considerations apply to all learners, they are particularly important with older learners.

   1. *Assess and teach academic vocabulary in context.* We cannot assess or teach academic vocabulary divorced from the related conceptual knowledge of a discipline or unit of study (Wright & Cervetti, 2016). For example, can you truly understand a vocabulary

word such as *immigration* without also understanding key related concepts like *push factors* and *pull factors*? In their meta-analysis of vocabulary instruction, Wright and Cervetti determined that simply teaching large numbers of words that were not associated with particular texts or units of study did little to improve general comprehension. For this reason, the richest and most authentic vocabulary instruction and assessments are the ones embedded in the context of reading, writing, and talking about the key concepts and big ideas in a unit of study. The VRT, vocabulary concept webs, and word wizard charts work very well for students in the primary grades. Vocabulary magazines, focus questions with vocabulary banks, and word wizard charts are excellent vehicles for assessing older learners' ability to use academic vocabulary in context.

2. *Assess and teach vocabulary and conceptual knowledge "before."* Vocabulary knowledge is the single best predictor of reading comprehension (Anderson & Freebody, 1981; Davis, 1944). A student who doesn't know the meanings of key vocabulary words and related concepts before reading will struggle to comprehend during reading. In the upper grades, students are increasingly likely to read texts for which they have limited background and vocabulary knowledge. Therefore, it's critical to (1) identify key vocabulary terms and related concepts that students need to have some knowledge of in order to grasp a passage, concept, or unit of study; and (2) assess your students' knowledge of this vocabulary before reading. Many of the assessment methods we've discussed will work well for this purpose, including simply asking students prior knowledge questions about key words/concepts (e.g., "What do you know about atoms? What's in an atom?"), vocabulary rating scales, the VRT, and focus questions with vocabulary banks. If students lack key vocabulary/conceptual knowledge that's assumed by the author, you will have to preteach it.

3. *Use cognitively engaging activities to assess and teach learners.* Students need to know the definitions of words, but having them learn dictionary definitions is less impactful than activities that call for cognitive engagement, manipulation, and building networks of word relationships. All evidence suggests that students require multiple exposures to the target vocabulary words throughout the units. We just aren't sure exactly how many exposures are needed, and it varies by word (Wright & Cervetti, 2016).

4. *Not all words are created, or assessed, equally.* Decide which terms are your "heavy hitters." These critical concepts will be few in number and represent the most important ideas in your unit of study. Assess these with in-depth activities like an elaborated knowledge rating scale, which calls for students to demonstrate their knowledge by providing definitions, sentences, illustrations, or other relevant information. The remaining vocabulary words might be assessed for a more basic level of knowledge with a traditional matching or fill-in-the-blank quiz.

5. *Assess learners' ability to semantically "chunk" vocabulary, and teach them to do so.* A hallmark of the upper-grades curriculum is the sheer number of new vocabulary terms students are expected to learn. To make sense of this vast array of new concepts, learners must *chunk* them—that is, store them in manageable, logical categories. We know that chunking helps significantly with long-term memory of concepts. For example, a high school history teacher we worked with couldn't believe how much it helped his

students when he chunked the 30-plus vocabulary terms from a World War II unit into three simple categories: (1) "Before the War," (2) "During the War," and (3) "After the War." As part of your vocabulary assessment at the end of a unit, ask students to sort the vocabulary terms into the categories that make sense in that particular unit. Most teachers we work with use one "big picture" graphic organizer that ties together all of the vocabulary terms in the unit or chapter. For the end-of-unit assessment, students must write the vocabulary terms in the appropriate place in this "big picture," to show that they understand how all the concepts fit together (as opposed to thinking of vocabulary as a long, unrelated list of names, dates, and battles).

6. *Test vocabulary the way you teach vocabulary.* If you are going to assess your students' vocabulary knowledge at the end of a unit by using focus questions with vocabulary banks, then provide your students throughout the unit of study with multiple opportunities to use this strategy in both spoken and written formats, applying the target vocabulary words multiple times in varied configurations.

FUTURE DIRECTIONS IN VOCABULARY ASSESSMENT

Researchers still have a long way to go in developing easy-to-use, sensitive, informative vocabulary assessments. Until research-validated, commercially produced assessments are available, the best option is the creation of common formative assessments. The National Reading Panel (2000) supported the use of teacher-generated assessments. In regard to vocabulary assessment, the National Reading Panel determined that "the more closely assessment matches the instructional context, the more appropriate the conclusions about the instruction will be" (p. 4.26). Recognizing that there is no single "silver bullet" that can be used to assess vocabulary is the first step in addressing vocabulary within our larger assessment system.

FORM 7.1

Vocabulary Assessment Measures: Teacher Self-Study

Common formats used: Check as many as apply.

Test format	Check formats you use	Which of your units of study include this kind of vocabulary assessment?
Match word to definition		
Write definition		
Fill appropriate vocabulary word in blank		
Write a sentence		
Multiple-choice: Definitions–words		
Multiple-choice: Which definition is applied to word in a passage?		
Illustrate a word		
Make new words with affixes and roots		

(continued)

Vocabulary Assessment Measures: Teacher Self-Study *(page 2 of 2)*

Vocabulary assessment inventory for a single unit of study

Assessment	Breadth (volume of words)	Depth of knowledge (dimensions)	Reading the words	Hearing the words	Speaking/oral usage of the words	Writing (sentences/ passages using the words)

EIGHT

Comprehension

There has always been an intense interest in the assessment of reading comprehension. After all, comprehension could be called the "bottom line" of reading. Measuring it provides an indicator of how well all the subprocesses of reading are working together. Comprehension assessment is a somewhat controversial topic, however, in that no general agreement exists on how best to do it. Most reading experts would certainly acknowledge that comprehension assessment is more ambiguous than assessing constrained skills such as alphabet knowledge, phonics patterns, and even fluency. However, most experts would also agree that useful estimates can be reached of (1) how well a child can comprehend overall, and (2) how well a child has comprehended a particular selection.

TWO REASONS TO ASSESS COMPREHENSION

There are two principal reasons for assessing reading comprehension. The first reason is to gauge the degree to which a student has comprehended a particular selection. Chapter tests and other postreading assessments often serve this function. The second reason is to estimate general level of reading proficiency. The result of this kind of assessment might be an estimate of the instructional reading level by means of an IRI, or a normative judgment by means of an achievement test. Mastery tests of specific comprehension skills also correspond to this purpose.

WHAT MAKES COMPREHENSION ASSESSMENT TRICKY?

Several aspects of comprehension make it tricky to assess. First, it is an "in-the-head" process. Therefore, we can only use artifacts that represent comprehension to see what is inside the reader's mind. Comprehension can only be measured via written or oral expression. A reader's writing and speaking abilities will thus influence our assessment of how well he or she has understood a text.

Second, comprehension is never all or nothing. Rather, comprehension is multidimensional, with a variety of factors working together to yield understanding that ranges from a minimal recognition of the key ideas to a thoughtful, critical evaluation of the text or the generation of deductive inferences that go beyond the text. Contextual factors that influence the degree of comprehension are instructional supports, purpose for reading, genre, and text structure. Individual factors include decoding ability, fluency, prior knowledge, interest, vocabulary, working memory, and self-regulation. The way that these "pressure points" work together creates a reading threshold (Paris & Hamilton, 2009; Perfetti & Adlof, 2012). We have all encountered a child who knows a lot about trains or dinosaurs and successfully reads and comprehends a related passage that is well beyond his or her identified instructional reading level. Acknowledging the dynamic of multiple pressure points means that we cannot count on a single comprehension assessment measure to provide anything more than an estimate of comprehension. It also forces us to recognize that it is necessary to use multiple assessment measures that employ a range of texts and various response formats in order to gauge a reader's comprehension strengths and weaknesses.

ASSESSING THE READABILITY OF MATERIALS

Whenever we assess comprehension, it is essential to know and report the text genre and readability level. If we know the difficulty of the materials we ask our students to read, we are in a better position to ensure the likelihood of success and to identify specific challenges. The term *readability* refers to the difficulty level of prose, expressed as a grade level. It can be estimated by several means. You might:

- Use your subjective judgment of qualitative text features.
- Apply a readability formula.
- Submit a passage to the Lexile Analyzer.

Today there are several qualitative systems for use in estimating the difficulty level of early reading materials. The Fountas and Pinnell (2006) criteria for leveling text constitute one of the more popular qualitative leveling systems, and many publishers of early reading texts are currently using similar systems. Qualitative leveling systems typically consider a text's predictability, content density, content familiarity, page layout, length, text structure, language characteristics, and decodability in determining the readability level. Subjective, qualitative estimates of readability provide useful approximations when teachers are considering texts for young children who are still acquiring the foundational reading skills en route to fluency. However, the game changes as children become fluent, capable readers (typically around middle to late second grade). Then, as texts become more complex conceptually and there are more areas of individual difference (pressure points), the utilization of a quantitative readability band tends to be a more accurate gauge of whether or not a student will be able to make sense of a text.

Readability formulas are quantitative procedures that yield an estimated grade level based on surface features of text that make a book easy or difficult to understand. These features are typically limited to the length of sentences, length of words, or frequency of word use in standard English text. Some computerized formulas are much more sophisticated and tap other characteristics, such as cohesiveness. In years gone by, teachers had to calculate the readability of a text by spending time counting combinations of letters, words, sentences, and syllables in multiple passages within a text, and then comparing those figures to complex grids that would provide a readability estimate. Due to technological advances, future readability scales are likely to become more inclusive of text cohesion and linguistic relationships among the words in the text (Graesser, McNamara, Louwerse, & Cai, 2004).

Today the most popular approach to readability is the Lexile framework. A *Lexile* is a metric based on word frequency and sentence length, and it is computed only through software, thus bypassing the need to apply formulas. There are two ways to use Lexiles, and both are free, although you must register at the Lexile website (*www.lexile.com*). The first is to locate a book title in the vast database. The odds are good that it has already been analyzed. The second is to upload a file in plain text format (i.e., with the extension *.txt*). You can easily change a Word file to plain text simply by saving it in this format. To interpret the Lexile score, you must use a table that converts it to an approximate grade level. Table 3.2 in this book may serve as a guide to grade-level Lexile conversions that are aligned with the CCSS.

Remember that even quantitative approaches to readability can lead to results that are at odds with one another. Although we believe that they can give useful guidance, numerical approaches provide estimates only. If a student's instructional level is determined by using passages or tests that have been assigned Lexiles (abbreviated as L when combined with a number), the long-standing guideline has been to add 50L to arrive at the top of the reader's reading range and subtract 100L to determine books at the easy end of the continuum for the student.

APPROACHES TO COMPREHENSION ASSESSMENT

Let's consider the major approaches to assessing comprehension and examine the strengths and limitations of each.

Questions

The most traditional method of testing reading comprehension is asking questions. The use of questions offers great administrative flexibility, ranging from formal testing situations to class discussions. Questions allow teachers to focus on particular facts, conclusions, and judgments in which the teachers have an interest. By posing questions at various levels of thinking, a teacher can get a glimpse of how the child has processed a reading selection.

Types of Questions

There are many ways of categorizing questions. Bloom's (1969) taxonomy is sometimes used, for example. A far simpler approach is to think of questions in terms of levels of comprehension. We conventionally speak of three levels.

1. *Literal questions* require a student to recall a specific fact that has been explicitly stated in the reading selection. Such questions are easy to ask and answer, but they may reflect a very superficial understanding of content. Edgar Dale (1946), an eminent reading authority during the first half of the 20th century, once referred to literal comprehension as "reading the lines" (p. 1).

2. *Inferential questions*, like literal questions, have factual answers. However, the answers cannot be located in the selection. Instead, the reader must make logical connections among facts in order to arrive at an answer. The answer to a question calling for a prediction, for example, is always inferential in nature even though we are uncertain of the answer, for the reader must nevertheless use available facts in an effort to arrive at a fact that is not stated.

Answers to inferential questions are sometimes beyond dispute and sometimes quite speculative. Let's say that a class has just read a selection on New Zealand. They have read that New Zealand is south of the equator and was colonized by Great Britain. If a teacher were to ask whether Auckland, New Zealand's capital, is south of the equator, the answer would require inferential thinking. There is no dispute about the answer, but the selection does not specifically mention Auckland, and the students must infer its location in relation to the equator.

On the other hand, were the teacher to ask the students if English is spoken in New Zealand, the answer would be inferential as well as speculative. The mere fact that Britain colonized New Zealand does not guarantee that English is spoken there today. For all inferential questions, the reader must use facts that are stated to reach a conclusion about a fact that is not stated. For this reason, Dale (1946) described inferential comprehension as "reading between the lines" (p. 1).

3. *Critical questions* call upon students to form value judgments about the selection. Such judgments can never be characterized as right or wrong, because these types of answers are not facts. They are evaluations arrived at on the basis of an individual's value system. Critical questions might target whether the selection is well written, whether certain topics should have been included, whether the arguments an author makes are valid, and whether the writing is biased or objective. Understandably, Dale (1946) equated critical comprehension with "reading beyond the lines" (p. 1). (Hint: A shortcut to asking a critical-level question is to insert the word *should*. For example, "Should the author have included the part about . . . ?" Doing so always elevates the question to the critical level. Of course, there are other ways to pose critical questions, but this method is surefire.)

A teacher's judgment of how well a child comprehends may depend in part on the types of questions asked. Thus the choice of question type can affect a child's performance during a postreading assessment. A student may well do better if asked questions that are entirely literal than if asked questions at a variety of levels. The issue of which type(s) of question(s) to include in any postreading assessment is therefore an important one. Therefore, if you are using assessment to determine an instructional level, it is best to use a standardized list of questions that have been field-tested. These should be provided with any commercial product. During instruction or formative assessment, it is important to ask a variety of question types, so that students get experience with each type of question in a setting that leads to instructional feedback.

A final issue concerning types of comprehension questions is whether to subdivide each of the three levels into specific skills. For example, the literal level is often seen as composed of skills involving the identification of key ideas, sequences of events, cause-and-effect relationships, comparisons, and the like. Does it make sense to ask questions corresponding to each of these skills? Yes, as long as very little is made of the results. Skill-related questions can assure us that a range of comprehension skills is being developed, but when we attempt to compute scores for each subskill, we often run into trouble. First, there are seldom enough questions for reliable measurement. Second, scores on specific skill tests tend to be almost perfectly correlated, suggesting that the skills are difficult to separate for assessment. In other words, a student who scores high on a test of literal sequences almost always scores high on a test of literal cause-and-effect relationships. Finally, a student's ability to answer a question is often more reliant on text factors and background knowledge than on subskill question type. It's hardly worth the effort to splinter comprehension to this extent.

Questions Based on Reading Dependency

Reading dependency (also called *passage dependency*) is the need to have read a selection in order to answer a particular comprehension question. Consider the following example. The children have just read a story about a girl who brings a green frog to school for Show and Tell. The frog jumps out of her hands and causes merry havoc in the classroom. The teacher then asks two comprehension questions:

1. "What did the girl bring to Show and Tell?"
2. "What color was the frog?"

These two questions are both literal. That is, they both require the students to respond with facts explicitly stated in the story. They differ considerably, however, in terms of their reading dependency. Even children with extensive experience of participating in Show and Tell would be unlikely to predict the answer to the first question simply on the basis of experience. In short, it is necessary to have read the story in order to answer the question. The second question is another matter. Most children know that nearly all North American frogs are green, and the children would not need to have read the passage in order to respond correctly. On the other hand, if the girl had brought some rare South American species that was, say, red and yellow, the same question would have been reading-dependent.

Which of these two questions tells the teacher more about whether the students comprehended the text? Clearly, questions that can be answered without having adequately comprehended a selection fail to assess reading comprehension. They may well be justified in the interest of conducting a worthwhile discussion, but teachers should not be misled into assuming that such questions will help them monitor their students' comprehension.

We have noted that even the questions in commercial test instruments tend to have problems regarding reading dependency. Many studies (e.g., Sparfeldt, Kimmel, Löwen-kamp, Steingräber, & Rost, 2012) have shown that when given only the questions and *not* the selections on which they are based, students do far better than chance would have predicted. This outcome implies that they are using prior knowledge to answer some of the questions correctly. The challenge in devising assessment instruments, or even informal approaches, is that it is difficult to determine what children are likely to know before they read a selection. This problem is especially troublesome with nonfiction text because of its factual content. Children already familiar with the content may find themselves with an unintended advantage in responding to postreading questions.

To better understand the concept of reading dependency, read the simple nonfiction example, "Crows," in Figure 8.1. The four comprehension questions that follow the passage represent four basic possibilities in regard to the degree of reading dependency reflected in the question. For most adults, the answer to question 1 lies not only in the passage, but also in their prior knowledge. This means that the question is not reading-dependent and is not a good indicator of reading comprehension. The answer to question 2, on the other hand, lies entirely within the adult's prior knowledge (in this case, prior experience), but not within the passage. The answer to question 3 lies in the passage, but not in a typical adult's prior knowledge. This makes question 3 a reading-dependent one—and a much better indicator of comprehension. Finally, the answer to question 4 lies neither in prior knowledge (typically) nor in the passage. The issue of reading dependency boils down to a single guideline: If your intent is to assess reading comprehension, then your comprehension questions should target information that lies within the passage, but that is not likely to lie within the student's prior knowledge. The Venn diagram in Figure 8.1 may help conceptualize the four types of questions in relation to effective comprehension assessment.

Keep in mind that reading dependency is related to how much the reader knows in advance. What if question 3 were addressed to an ornithologist? Because an expert on birds could probably answer the question without needing to read the passage, the

Crows

Crows are large black birds that pose a threat to farmers. They belong to the genus *Corvus*.

1.   What color are crows?
2.   Have you ever had a pet crow?
3.   To what genus do crows belong?
4.   How long do crows usually live?

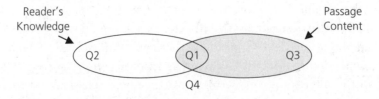

FIGURE 8.1. Examples of reading dependency.

very same question is no longer a reading-dependent one. It all depends on the person you're asking. This is why the problem of reading dependency sometimes gets the better of commercial test developers. It's hard to predict what students, in general, may or may not know!

Readability of Questions

A third aspect of reading comprehension questions involves their readability. It is possible for the question itself to be harder to comprehend than the selection on which it is based. Written questions should be kept as simple as possible. Their difficulty level should certainly be no higher than that of the selections on which they are based, and ideally should be simpler. Consider, in particular, the vocabulary you use in framing a question, and also the complexity of your sentence structures. The KISS method (Keep It Simple, Sweetheart!) has much to recommend it when you are formulating comprehension questions.

Cloze Assessment

Cloze testing involves deleting words from a prose selection and asking students to replace them on the basis of the remaining context. The ability to provide logical replacement words is thought to indicate the extent to which a student is able to comprehend the material. Cloze testing has several important advantages. First, it can be administered in a group setting, once students have been introduced to its rather unusual format. Second, it does not require comprehension questions. This means that issues such as reading dependency and question readability do not arise. Third, cloze scores correlate highly with more conventional methods of assessing comprehension, such as asking questions. Finally, cloze and modifications of cloze tests have been successfully used as forms of EL and bilingual assessment. The cloze method allows an EL reader to devote processing resources to comprehension (Francis, 1999).

On the other hand, cloze testing has significant limitations. Its strange format can confuse some students. Spelling and fine-motor limitations can prevent students from displaying what they have actually comprehended. (In fact, cloze testing is rarely administered below fourth grade for this reason.) Finally, research indicates that cloze assessments, as unusual as the format may appear, tend to assess comprehension at only a very low level. A student's ability to integrate information across sentences and paragraphs is not readily tapped by cloze items.

Figure 8.2 provides streamlined suggestions for constructing, administering, and scoring a cloze test. The sample cloze test in Form 8.1 (p. 218) serves as a model of what a cloze test should look like in its conventional format. You might try your hand at taking this test and then scoring it, using the answer key in Figure 8.3. In scoring the test, make sure to give yourself credit only for verbatim responses—that is, for the exact word that was deleted in each case. You may be tempted to award credit for synonyms and other reasonable responses, but this temptation must be resisted. There are three reasons for accepting only verbatim replacements:

Construction

- Start with a passage of about 300 words. Shorter passages may be used, but reliability could be jeopardized.
- Choose any word as the first to be deleted, but leave a sentence or so intact at the beginning of the test.
- Thereafter, mark every fifth word, until there are 50 in all.
- Word-process the test so that the words you've marked are replaced by blanks.
- The blanks must be of equal length.
- For younger students, leave blanks of around 15 spaces to give them room to write.
- For older students, you may wish to number the blanks so that students can write their answers on a separate sheet.

Administration

- It is generally unwise to administer cloze tests prior to grade 4.
- Make certain students know that each blank represents only one word.
- Explain that this is more like a guessing game than a test. Even the best readers will not be able to guess many of the words.
- Encourage them to try to guess the word that was actually there—the word the author used.
- There is no time limit.

Scoring and Interpretation

- Give credit for verbatim answers only. Synonyms and other semantically acceptable responses are considered incorrect.
- Minor misspellings are counted as correct. However, spellings that indicate that the child might have been thinking of another word are counted as incorrect. Examples:

Original word	Child's answer	Scoring
Mississippi	Missisippi	Correct
scarlet	crimson	Incorrect

- Compute the percentage of correct answers and use the following scoring guide:

  Independent level: above 60%
  Instructional level: 40–60%
  Frustration level: below 40%

FIGURE 8.2. Guidelines for cloze testing.

1. Verbatim scoring is more objective than the policy of awarding credit for synonyms. Otherwise, different scorers would tend to produce different scores.
2. Verbatim scoring leads to tests that are far easier to grade. Imagine how long it would take if you had to stop and carefully consider the semantic acceptability of every wrong answer.
3. Scoring criteria are based on verbatim scoring. If you give credit for synonyms and other logical responses, it will be nearly impossible to interpret the results. This reason alone is sufficient to justify giving credit for verbatim replacements only. The numerous studies establishing the scoring criteria have assessed a variety of populations, including elementary students, middle and secondary students, college students, vocational–technical students, and even various special education categories. If your score on the sample cloze test was 60% or higher, it is reasonable to conclude that the passage is at your independent reading level. Instructional level ranges from 40 to 60%. A score below 40% indicates frustration level.

> **From *The Tell-Tale Heart***
> **Edgar Allan Poe**
>
> True!—nervous—very, very dreadfully nervous I had been and am; but why *will* you say that I am mad? The disease had sharpened my senses—not destroyed, not dulled them. Above __all__ was the sense of __hearing__ acute. I heard all __things__ in the heaven and __in__ the earth. I heard __many__ things in hell. How, __then__, am I mad? Hearken! __and__ observe how healthily, how __calmly__ I can tell you __the__ whole story.
>
> It is __impossible__ to say how first __the__ idea entered my brain; __but__ once conceived, it haunted __me__ day and night. Object __there__ was none. Passion there __was__ none. I loved the __old__ man. He had never __wronged__ me. He had never __given__ me insult. For his __gold__ I had no desire. __I__ think it was his __eye__! Yes, it was this! __He__ had the eye of __a__ vulture—a pale blue __eye__, with a film over __it__. Whenever it fell upon __me__, my blood ran cold; __and__ so by degrees—very __gradually__—I made up my __mind__ to take the life __of__ the old man, and __thus__ rid myself of the __eye__ forever.
>
> Now this is __the__ point. You fancy me __mad__. Madmen know nothing. But __you__ should have seen *me*. __You__ should have seen how __wisely__ I proceeded—with what __caution__, with what foresight, with __what__ dissimulation I went to __work__! I was never kinder __to__ the old man than __during__ the whole week before __I__ killed him. And every __night__, about midnight, I turned __the__ latch of his door __and__ opened it—oh, so __gently__! And then, when I __had__ made an opening sufficient __for__ my head, I put __in__ a dark lantern, all closed, closed, so that no light shone out, and then I thrust in my head. Oh, you would have laughed to see how cunningly I thrust it in! I moved it slowly—very, very slowly, so that I might not disturb the old man's sleep. It took me an hour to place my whole head within the opening so far that I could see him as he lay upon his bed. Ha!—would a madman have been so wise as this?

FIGURE 8.3. Answers to sample cloze test.

Maze Task

The maze task, introduced by Guthrie, Seifert, Burnham, and Caplan (1974), is a multiple-choice variation of the cloze task. The maze task is appealing because of its ease of administration and scoring: It can be administered in an individual or group setting, manually or through a computer program. The multiple-choice format makes it easy to score. Maze items can be presented in various ways. For example, the options can be stacked vertically or arranged horizontally:

The boy climbed the { tree / pole / ladder / vine } in his backyard.

The boy climbed the [tree, pole, ladder, vine] in his backyard.

The student circles or underlines the correct choice while reading.

In recent years, timed maze tasks have been adopted as another form of CBM. The passages in a timed maze should be between 100 and 400 words long to allow for internal coherence (Parker & Hasbrouck, 1992). Since CBM progress is reflected in gains, passages should have approximately the same readability. The greatest source of psychometric concern is the selection of distractors (Parker & Hasbrouck, 1992). The number, quality, and lexical characteristics of distractors can vary greatly. Parker and Hasbrouck (1992, p. 216) recommend that test designers choose four distractors that are (1) the same part of speech as the deleted word; (2) meaningful and plausible within one sentence; (3) related in content to the passage (when possible); (4) as familiar to the reader as the deleted word; and (5) either clearly wrong or less appropriate, given broader passage content.

Evidence indicates that maze tests are sensitive to the reading comprehension development of novice readers (Francis, 1999; Shin, Deno, & Espin, 2000). The minimal demands placed on working memory, spelling, and fine-motor development are advantageous for younger students.

Oral Retellings

Comprehension is sometimes assessed by asking a student to retell orally the content of the reading selection. The degree of detail provided and the general coherence of the retelling are used to gauge comprehension. A checklist of text elements is used as a scoresheet to record which points the student includes in the retelling. The best scoresheets are text-specific. However, Form 8.2 (p. 219) and Form 8.3 (p. 220) can be used as models for basic scoresheets for simple narrative and informational texts. They should be adapted to reflect the increasing episodes and sections as texts become more complex. Facts that go unmentioned in a student's retelling can be assessed by using probe questions that are posed following the retelling. Retellings have the advantage of (1) being naturalistic, (2) gauging how well the child internalized the content of a selection, (3) identifying the student's conceptual organization of the passage, and (4) avoiding many of the pitfalls of questioning. The openness of the retelling task allows for observation of the child's thought processes, what the child values as important, and cultural influences in story interpretation. Story retellings have been used successfully with children as early as kindergarten and first grade.

Retellings demonstrate consequential validity, which means that the examinee experiences positive consequences as a result of the retelling. Studies have demonstrated that just the practice of retelling narrative and expository texts results in improvements in adherence to story grammar, selection of high-level propositions, and cued recall. In other words, we use retellings for assessment purposes, but they have an instructional benefit as by-products.

But retellings have major limitations as well. They rely very heavily on a student's oral expressive ability, and a deficiency in this area could lead to an inaccurate judgment about how well the student has understood the selection. Variations in administration and scoring often yield unreliable data collection. Before reading begins, all students should be reminded that they will be asked to retell when they finish. Additionally, one should always prompt students to retell the story (or informational text) as though they were telling it to a classmate who had not read it. We find that requiring teachers to use a laminated card copy of the script in Figure 8.4 yields more reliable and valid retelling results. Because orchestrating the retelling task is cognitively demanding for students, one must always supplement a retelling task with questions about the story to ensure a comprehensive measure of the student's text comprehension.

Before the child reads the text, listens to the text, or views the video, tell the child, "Be sure to pay close attention to the meaning of the [*story/informational text/video*], because at the end I am going to ask you to tell me everything that you remember and ask you some questions about the [*story/informational text/video*]."

After the child reads, listens, or views the video, tell the child, "Now I want you to tell me everything you remember about the [*story, informational text or video*]. I want you to tell it to me as though you were telling it to your [*brother/sister/friend*] who has never [*heard/seen*] it."

Use prompts as needed to encourage a comprehensive retelling. Allow the child to tell as much as he or she can recall unprompted. Then conclude with "Do you remember anything else?"

For children who say they don't recall anything or only recall one or two ideas, you may want to choose some of the prompts below. Indicate the level of prompting on your record-keeping sheet. Also, be sure that the prompts you provide match the structure of the text or video.

Narrative	Informational
How did the story begin?	What was the book/video about?
What was the problem?	What were the big ideas? What was the most important information that you remember? Is there anything else that you remember?
What happened next?	What did the author want us to know about the topic?
How did *character* solve the problem? How did the book end?	Was there anything that you read/saw that was interesting to you or that was new to you?

FIGURE 8.4. Procedures for administering a retelling assessment. From Stahl and Garcia (2015, p. 151). Copyright © The Guilford Press. Reprinted by permission.

Written Responses to Text

In learning and assessment settings beyond second grade, students are most often called on to demonstrate their comprehension or new knowledge acquisition through writing, Therefore, it is important for children to have many classroom opportunities to write in response to what they have read or what has been read aloud to them. The writing should take a variety of forms. Prompting students to compose short responses to inferential questions should be a frequent class activity. Teaching writing through extended writing projects that are related to themed units provides the opportunity for showing models of good writing, and allows the sustained time for explicit instruction in the composition process.

In Chapter 2, we have discussed the development of common formative assessments, one of the most popular outgrowths of the CCSS. These assessments can address a range of proficiencies, including comprehension. They are created by grade-level teams of teachers, who present them to their students at the conclusion of a disciplinary unit. As in the construction of the VAM, discussed in Chapter 7, teachers work together to create reading and writing activities that call for children to demonstrate comprehension of passages related to a topic of study. These tests require children to answer some short constructed-response questions about each passage and to compose one or two extended responses. Afterward, the grade-level team of teachers meets to score the tests, using a rubric that they have agreed upon and have used instructionally to help students evaluate their own writing.

We recommend that teachers use the same writing rubric that will be used to evaluate their students on their state ELA assessment. Both PARCC and Smarter Balanced have created rubrics to evaluate students according to the criteria established in the CCSS. By using these rubrics throughout the school year, teachers can get a sense of what skills need to be taught to move their students closer to the learning targets on high-stakes tests. See the PARCC (*https://parcc-assessment.org*) and Smarter Balanced (*www.smarterbalanced.org*) websites to access the most up-to-date versions of the rubrics.

Other Assessment Formats

Questions, cloze tests, and retellings are the three most popular approaches to comprehension assessments. These three by no means exhaust the possibilities, however. Other comprehension assessment formats include the following:

- Oral miscue analysis.
- Sentence verification.
- Student-generated questions.
- Performance tasks based on the selection.
- Evaluations of student participation in high-level discussions or book clubs.

The last three are particularly well suited to assessing older students' content-area reading comprehension in complex texts and tasks (e.g., a performance assessment asking an eighth grader to compare and contrast the leadership characteristics of Nelson Mandela and Mahatma Gandhi). You may have used still other formats for assessing your students' comprehension of a text. The relative merits of the various formats used to assess reading comprehension vary considerably in their advantages and drawbacks. The debate over which is best is not likely to be resolved in the near future.

WORD LISTS FOR GENERAL COMPREHENSION ASSESSMENT

A shortcut to assessing general comprehension ability is to examine a student's ability to pronounce words, presented in the form of graded lists. Scoring criteria are then used to estimate a student's instructional level, based on how far the student can progress through these lists of increasing difficulty. Offsetting the obvious efficiency of this approach to comprehension assessment lies an important challenge to validity: It seems dubious to estimate a child's instructional reading level through an assessment that involves no actual reading and no measure of comprehension. On the other hand, research indicates that the correlation between word-list performance and more conventional approaches to reading comprehension assessment is high. A graded word list is probably best thought of as a shortcut to estimating a child's overall proficiency as a reader. It can be used to determine a text-level starting point for a more elaborated measure of reading comprehension. Such lists are, however, no substitute for the "real thing."

One of the most popular graded word lists in the public domain is the San Diego Quick Assessment (SDQA; LaPray & Ross, 1969). We offer the SDQA in its entirety, including the student version of the word cards, as Form 8.4 (p. 221). The scoring protocol will help you organize all the results of a single testing. The protocol may be included in a student's portfolio and updated through subsequent testing from time to time.

COMPUTER-BASED COMPREHENSION ASSESSMENTS

In the last few years, advances in technology have resulted in increases in the number and types of computer-based comprehension assessments. The most long-standing tests are those that simply translate a paper-and-pencil multiple-choice test into a computer format. However, the newest tests take advantage of technology's affordances to test comprehension in new ways.

Tests such as multiple-choice comprehension checkups administered after a student completes a single book or a reading selection have been used to transfer tasks that once were completed with paper and pencil to the computer. This makes differentiation and data management easier. In programs such as Accelerated Reader and LightSail, students read different books, take different comprehension tests, and move to new levels based on results recorded within the product data management system.

Many states, Smarter Balanced, and PARCC are continuing to develop the use of online formats for summative end-of-the year performance tests. These tests differ from the previous tests in that the use of technology enhancements alter the format of the test. For example, Smarter Balanced requires students to respond to questions after viewing informational videos. Sometimes enhancements influence item response formats, such as reorganizing a series of events much as one would do on a pocket chart, or creating a graphic organizer that reflects a text's structure.

Computer-Adaptive Tests

Computer-adaptive tests (CATs) are tests that adjust the difficulty of the questions and/or passages, contingent upon the accuracy of student responses. This enables each child to take a test tailored to his or her ability level. Students who are performing below grade level read easier passages than the ones read by children who are performing at grade level. "High fliers" receive more challenging texts and questions than other students in their grade-level cohort.

We recommend using CATs rather than benchmark kits above second grade as screening tools to estimate instructional reading levels. For those students whose estimated CAT reading level is well below grade level, or for those you suspect have other reading issues not picked up by a CAT, we still recommend an IRI and possibly a spelling inventory to gain a full picture of the students' reading strengths and areas of need—in particular, measures of word knowledge and fluency, which a CAT does not measure directly. Certainly for children reading below third grade level, a benchmark kit is still needed to determine a text level. However, in third grade and beyond, a CAT has several advantages.

Purchasing a CAT requires an investment in time and money. Therefore, we recommend that school personnel carefully investigate several products before choosing the one that most closely matches their needs. It is a good idea to compare three or four products, using the Computer-Adaptive Test (CAT) Comparison Worksheet (Form 8.5, p. 227), to dig deeply into the characteristics described in each of the following sections.

Advantages of CATs

Theoretical Construct of Comprehension. Unlike the decoding constraints of reading in the primary grades, the pressure points of comprehension cause more variation in comprehension scores for individual older students. Once students have accumulated a bank of high-frequency words, mastered the most common orthographic patterns, and acquired strategies for attacking multisyllabic words, the likelihood of reading accuracy increases. At this developmental juncture, particularly as an older student gains greater control over his or her reading fluency, reading comprehension tends to become more malleable and dependent on the student's interest in the topic, prior knowledge, knowledge of conceptual vocabulary, purpose for reading, and self-regulation. Therefore, any single estimate of the intermediate or advanced reader's comprehension is going to serve similarly to one line on a meteorologist's so-called "spaghetti plot" for predicting a hurricane. So, instead of identifying a single instructional level (e.g., grade 5) for a student, it is often more accurate and instructionally useful to estimate a possible instructional reading *range* (e.g., grades 4–6). Just as a meteorological spaghetti plot forecasts a *range* of possible hurricane pathways contingent upon dynamic weather conditions, multiple measures of comprehension are necessary to indicate an ability range contingent upon dynamic circumstances.

Time Allocation for Administration. Due to the variation in and malleability of a postnovice reader's ability to comprehend a text, it is unreasonable to lose days of instructional time trying to ascertain a single letter or number to represent a reading level for every student. To return to the spaghetti plot metaphor, a bandwidth indicator that varies depending on the pressure points of each reading experience is more valuable than any single score. Most CATs can be administered on the computer in 30–45 minutes.

Reading Levels. Most CATS use Lexiles to gauge the difficulty of the passages and to report student reading levels. This is consistent with the CCSS and with reading material resources such as ReadWorks, Newsela, and Lexile.com.

Test Reliability. One of the disadvantages of IRIs and benchmark kits is the lack of teacher-to-teacher reliability. CATs are easier to administer uniformly, and scoring is standardized. Technical reports provided by a CAT's commercial producer include evidence of the reliability and validity of the test. Most even provide prediction guides for performance on your state test. Be sure to ask for the technical guides and research based on pilot testing before purchasing any commercial product. See the CAT Comparison Worksheet (Form 8.5).

Additionally, when students are reading passages at their level, they remain cognitively engaged. However, when students read well below the passage level (e.g., students with disabilities), their scores typically fall in the lower tail of proficiency distribution, with scores around the chance level (Minnema, Thurlow, Bielinski, & Scott, 2000).

Data Management. The reports provided by a CAT's commercial producer make it easy to trace student progress and school performance over time. Particularly in middle schools, having a common data management program that is easily accessible and comprehensible to all teachers is an important consideration.

Cautions Regarding CATs

As with any test, CATs have some disadvantages that must be weighed in a school's consideration regarding adoption and utilization. When considering which commercial CAT to purchase, we strongly suggest using the CAT Comparison Worksheet (Form 8.5).

Technology Factors. In order to use a CAT, a school must have the appropriate technology resources. There must be enough updated computers to administer the tests to the school's population, either on carts or in the students' possession. Teachers and students alike need to have baseline comfort and proficiency levels for working on computers. The school needs to have a technology expert on site who can do basic troubleshooting in the event of a problem.

Assessment System Component. CATs make excellent screeners, but they are not intended to replace a school assessment system, even at the middle school level. Occasionally students who are performing poorly in classes score surprisingly well on a CAT. In that case, common formative assessments from each content area need to be brought to grade-level data meetings to plan a course of action, including instructional adjustments and possibly some form of diagnostic assessment based on the cognitive model (see Figure 8.5, below). For students whose proficiency is below grade level, we recommend that (1) an ORF test be administered and triangulated with the data from (2) an upper elementary developmental spelling inventory to determine the role that automatic word recognition may be playing in overall reading performance. Additionally, a listening capacity test using IRI materials or 300- to 400-word passages from grade-level instructional materials can be administered. Students who are identified as needing supplementary support will need to undergo the process described in the next sections.

PATHWAYS TO COMPREHENSION ASSESSMENT

Before considering instructional strategies designed to improve comprehension, let's return to the cognitive model. The assessments we discuss in Chapters 7–9 go well beyond foundational skills and provide data that can help determine which pressure points should guide instructional planning. It is important to remember, of course, that a particular child may have instructional needs in *both* foundational *and* higher-order proficiencies. Figure 6.1 can guide you in planning for the former. Figure 8.5 offers pathways for the remainder of the cognitive model and links each step to key assessments.

ADDRESSING COMPREHENSION DIFFICULTIES

It is not enough to determine that a child has a problem with comprehension. It is essential to ask *why*. The answer to this question will help us sharpen our instructional response. We suggest three questions that can help clarify the issue.

Cognitive Pathway 1: Is Comprehension Hindered by Poor Decoding?

Students who spend too much time and mental energy figuring out words have little of either to devote to comprehension. If comprehension improves when a child listens as a selection is read aloud (i.e., the child's listening comprehension level), this improvement would be evidence of inadequate decoding ability as the fundamental problem. However, it is easy to be deceived into believing that if we improve decoding, comprehension will automatically improve. Often such a child may need instruction in both decoding *and* comprehension strategies. Automatic word recognition is necessary but not sufficient for comprehension. All intervention sessions should include attention to comprehension. Students who have strong listening comprehension but poor word knowledge (including decoding and/or spelling) are going to need extensive support in composing written responses to text. In addition, as part of classroom instruction, they should be read aloud to and participate in shared reading at the upper edge of their listening comprehension level. This will ensure that, despite their poor decoding skills, they still have access to their grade-level texts and the associated curriculum, content, and academic vocabulary.

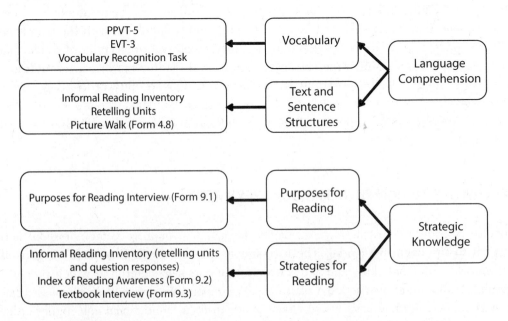

FIGURE 8.5. Diagnostic paths for identifying comprehension difficulties.

Cognitive Pathway 2: Is Comprehension Hindered by Limited Prior Knowledge and Vocabulary?

We have mentioned the strong relationship between one's knowledge base, including knowledge of word meanings, and one's ability to comprehend. Building knowledge and vocabulary are long-term school goals, of course, and their effects on comprehension ability will be gradual and cumulative. Teachers can facilitate comprehension of particular selections, however, by providing thorough background information in advance, including preteaching key vocabulary.

The best way to ensure that students have the prerequisite conceptual knowledge and vocabulary is to embed literacy instruction within disciplinary units (Cervetti, Barber, Dorph, Pearson, & Goldschmidt, 2012; Stahl, 2014; Wright & Cervetti, 2016). In a meta-analysis of vocabulary studies conducted over the last 40 years, Wright and Cervetti found that explicitly teaching word meanings supported comprehension of text containing those target words in all cases! Situating reading comprehension within knowledge building, inquiry, writing, and discussion takes away the mystery attached to a student's prior experiences with a topic. Instruction that focuses on this kind of interactive processing is more impactful than simply providing a definition or dictionary activities (Wright & Cervetti, 2016).

A conventional way of imparting this sort of instruction is the directed reading activity, which begins with background-building activities. This lesson format is useful for students whose prior knowledge is not greatly deficient, but what about children who need more help before they can begin to comprehend what they read? A promising alternative is the *listen–read–discuss* technique.

Listen–Read–Discuss

Manzo and Casale (1985) introduced a technique for improving comprehension that assumes little or no background knowledge for a nonfiction reading selection. Rather than creating a foundation of knowledge that will be useful for comprehending the additional knowledge presented in the selection, the teacher actually *covers* the content of the selection. That is, the teacher presents, in advance, everything the students will read about, almost as if there were no reading to be done. There is no guesswork or preassessment about what information the students may already know. The teacher assumes that they know little or nothing.

The question many teachers raise when they learn about the listen–read–discuss method is this: Why bother to have the students read, then? If the teacher presents—via lecture, discussion, demonstration, and the like—the entire contents of the selection, then what is the point of asking students to read it? The answer is that their reading will be greatly facilitated. Listen–read–discuss may not be the most exciting technique ever devised, but it permits children who have limited prior knowledge to experience proficient comprehension—often for the first time. The studies conducted by Manzo and Casale (1985) and later by Watkins, McKenna, Manzo, and Manzo (1994) have established the listen–read–discuss procedure as a viable approach to the problem of limited prior knowledge and vocabulary. Consider using this technique when students are reading the most difficult texts in your curriculum, or when the students with the lowest instructional reading levels are reading complex texts. Requiring the students to read the same content that was covered orally serves as a scaffold for future shared or independent reading on the same topic.

Reading Guides

A *reading guide* is "a document containing questions to be answered, charts and diagrams to be completed, and other tasks that students are to undertake while reading. A reading guide may also contain page numbers and subheadings to help students keep their place as they read" (Walpole, McKenna, & Philippakos, 2011, pp. 122–123). Reading guides focus a child's attention on the key ideas of the reading selection, and in so doing model the process of strategic reading. Reading guides are not the same as postreading questions, because students complete the guides *while* they read, not afterward.

Each guide is unique in that a teacher must first decide what is important for students to grasp and then construct tasks for helping them do so. These tasks might include the following (McKenna & Robinson, 2014):

- Questions to be answered.
- Charts to be completed.
- Diagrams to be constructed.
- Pictures to be drawn.
- Responses to be written.

There is really no limit to the ways such tasks can be created and interwoven, and there is certainly an element of creativity in constructing a good reading guide! The following steps may be helpful:

- Read the selection carefully.
- Decide which ideas and facts are important to know.
- Create tasks that help students attain this knowledge.
- Include a variety of tasks, not just questions.
- Aim for simple wording.
- Leave plenty of space for children to write.
- Arrange the tasks sequentially.
- Include page numbers and/or subheads.
- Where appropriate, include comprehension aids.

Using reading guides can be effective, but only with adequate preparation. Teachers sometimes balk at the work involved in developing a good guide, but because they are to be completed in class, as a teacher circulates and assists, there is no need to create a conventional lesson. If you teach students at grade 3 or higher, we urge you to try reading guides.

Cognitive Pathway 3: Is Comprehension Hindered by Poorly Developed Strategies?

We use the word *strategies* to refer to methods proficient readers deliberately employ to facilitate their own comprehension. *Skills,* on the other hand, enable a reader to employ strategies, but are used automatically. Afflerbach, Pearson, and Paris (2008) have offered a distinction that may help clarify the confusion that has long surrounded these terms:

> Reading strategies are deliberate, goal-directed attempts to control and modify the reader's efforts to decode text, understand words, and construct meanings of text. Reading skills are automatic actions that result in decoding and comprehension with speed, efficiency, and fluency and usually occur without awareness of the components or control involved. The reader's deliberate control, goal-directedness, and awareness define a strategic action. (p. 368)

The National Reading Panel (2000) has determined that instructing students to monitor their reading, answer high-level comprehension questions, generate questions about the text, identify and organize ideas based on the text's structure, and summarize the text increases reading comprehension. There is also some support for teaching students to apply their prior knowledge and to create mental images during text reading. Our experience and research support indicate that struggling readers almost invariably profit from strategy instruction. Although the National Reading Panel's findings were primarily based on studies of strategy instruction that were conducted in the intermediate grades, Shanahan et al. (2010) determined that there is a strong evidence base for providing strategy instruction in grades K–3. Stahl and Garcia (2015) provide a user-friendly guidebook for putting this research into action with young children. Not surprisingly, a number of evidence-based approaches can be integrated with the existing curricula being used in most classrooms and intervention settings. We summarize a few of these in the following pages.

Explicit Strategy Instruction

Explicit strategy instruction incorporates instruction provided in three types of knowledge: *declarative, procedural,* and *conditional* (Paris, Lipson, & Wixson, 1983). Declarative knowledge involves teaching the children what the strategy is. Instruction in how to use the strategy develops procedural knowledge, and the instruction in when and why the strategy is most useful (or not applicable) constitutes conditional knowledge.

Effective strategy instruction also utilizes a gradual-release-of-responsibility instructional model (Pearson & Gallagher, 1983). Teachers begin instruction with explicit teaching, model the application of the strategy (perhaps with a think-aloud), and provide guided practice before asking the students to apply the strategy independently. Over time, the responsibility for cognitive decision making and putting strategies into practice is released to the students.

Many of the evidence-based approaches described in the following pages can be used during these phases of instruction.

Think-Alouds

In a think-aloud, the teacher models how to flexibly use cognitive strategies or handle a comprehension problem that may arise during reading. Proficient readers continually find themselves in minor comprehension predicaments. What distinguishes them from struggling readers, however, is the fact that good readers can apply strategies for "fixing" such problems. These "fix-up" strategies (McKenna, 2002) include the following:

1. Reading ahead to see whether the problem can be resolved.
2. Rereading to see whether something has been misunderstood.
3. Reflecting on what has been read to see whether some alternative explanation can be inferred.
4. Seeking information beyond the text (from an individual or a second print source) in order to resolve the dilemma.

In a think-aloud, a teacher models this fix-up process or strategy use by articulating it. In the words of Scott Paris (1985), the teacher should "make thinking public," so that students are privy to how a proficient reader contends with problem situations. For example, suppose a teacher is reading the following sentence aloud in science class:

Of the more than 26,000 types of spiders in the world, all are poisonous.

The teacher pauses at this point and says aloud to the students, "Wait a minute. How can there be so many poisonous spiders? Did I read that wrong? I'd better go back and check." The teacher then rereads the sentence. "Yeah, that's what it says. I thought there were only a few poisonous spiders. Maybe it'll explain if we keep reading." Sure enough, the passage continues:

However, very few spiders are dangerous to humans.

"I think I get it now," the teacher observes. "The dangerous ones are the ones I was thinking of. I didn't think the others were poisonous at all, but I guess they are."

Student-Generated Questions

Self-questioning helps students appraise their understanding of the important ideas in a text. Students may find that self-questioning helps them clarify and resolve challenging text. In a review of 26 intervention studies investigating student-generated questions, Rosenshine, Meister, and Chapman (1996) determined that the most effective heuristics seem to be those that are most concrete and easy to use. Studies that taught students the use of signal words (*who, where, when, why,* and *how*) or of generic question stems ("How are _____ and _____ alike? What is the main idea of _____? How is _____ related to _____? Why is it important that _____?") yielded the most success, especially with the youngest students. Using a story grammar model to develop questions was also fairly effective.

Reciprocal Questioning (ReQuest)

Manzo's (1969) technique of *reciprocal questioning* (ReQuest) has been effectively used for five decades. It involves students actively in asking questions of the teacher (or one another) during a discussion. The basic idea is that in order to ask good questions, a reader must understand the content reasonably well. If a student reads with the aim of asking questions, then comprehension is apt to be good. In the years following its introduction, research has continually validated ReQuest, and many variations of the technique have been developed. This approach works well after some preliminary explicit instruction on how to ask a good question. It can be used to provide guided practice incorporating the stems that have been taught and posted on a chart or provided to students as a bookmark.

In one approach, the teacher introduces the reading selection and asks the students to begin reading. At a predetermined point, the students stop reading, and one student is called on to ask questions of the teacher. When the student has completed asking his or her set of questions, the teacher may ask the student additional questions. Another student is called on for the next segment of the reading selection.

An alternative technique is for the teacher to call on a student at random after the selection has been completed. The student asks the teacher one question, and the teacher asks the student a question. The teacher then calls on another student, and so forth.

In still another variation, the teacher begins the postreading discussion by calling on a student. The student asks a question, but instead of answering it, the teacher passes it to another student, who must try to answer. This second student may then ask a question, which the teacher passes to a third student, and so forth. The teacher may use his or her knowledge of students' abilities to decide which questions to pass to which students.

Summary Writing

Studies have clearly shown that having students write summaries improves their comprehension of the material that has been read and enhances their comprehension ability generally (see Pressley & Woloshyn, 1995). These are impressive claims! One reason summary writing is so effective is that it compels students to transform content into their own words and expressions; doing so requires active thought. Another reason is that students must make repeated judgments about the relative importance of ideas. Instruction in summarization teaches students to select important ideas, eliminate details, eliminate redundancies, and integrate the ideas in a synthesized and organized manner. We briefly describe three evidence-based, step-by-step approaches to summary writing.

Barbara Taylor (1986) developed a five-step method of assisting middle schoolers in writing coherent hierarchical summaries:

1. Read only the subheadings of a chapter.
2. List the subheadings on paper.
3. Read the material.
4. Convert each subheading into a main-idea sentence.
5. For each main-idea sentence, add one to three sentences containing supporting details.

Contrast her approach with that of David (Jack) Hayes (1989), who developed an effective group strategy for teaching summary writing. He called it the *guided reading and summarizing procedure* (GRASP). GRASP also has five steps:

1. After the students have read a section of text, ask them to turn their books face down. Ask them to recall whatever they can from the material. Record their input in a list on a SMART Board or on chart paper.
2. Allow the students to return to the text to locate more information and to make corrections.
3. With student participation, rearrange the information into categories.
4. Help the students write a topic sentence for each category and detail sentences that support it.
5. Engage the students in revising the summary to make it more coherent.

A strategy that has been used successfully with older students and might be useful with younger students is a procedure called *generating interactions between schemata and text* (GIST) (Cunningham, 1982; Frey, Fisher, & Hernandez, 2003). In GIST, students begin creating summaries for sentences, using 15 spaces. The teacher gradually increases the amount of text being summarized in the 15 spaces. GIST is conducted as a whole-class procedure first, then in small groups, and finally individually.

Graphic Organizers

A large body of evidence supports the use of graphic organizers to help students organize their ideas. The use of graphic organizers, including story maps, can help students recall the most important story elements. Graphic organizers that reflect the text structures of expository text can help students recall and organize the ideas in informational texts.

Strategy Repertoires

Proficient readers apply multiple strategies flexibly, as needed, to make sense of text. An overarching teaching approach that encompasses several effective strategies is that of *reciprocal teaching*. Modeled after ReQuest, this approach was introduced by Palincsar and Brown (1984). Reciprocal teaching is among the most thoroughly validated of comprehension strategy repertoires, and it deserves careful consideration.

Students work in small groups, applying comprehension strategies to a new selection during reading. The teacher and students engage in a discussion about a segment of text structured by four strategies: summarizing, questioning, clarifying, and predicting (Palincsar & Brown, 1984). Initially, the teacher explicitly teaches and models each of these strategies for the students. After the strategies have been modeled, the students take turns leading the discussion about each segment of text.

The students begin by examining the reading selection and *predicting* the topic it seems likely to cover. To do so, they consider subtitles, pictures, boldface terminology, and graphic aids. Then the students read a segment of text. A student leader facilitates a dialogue that focuses on the four strategies. The student leader generates a group discussion to clarify any impediments to comprehension. New content may well contain concepts and ideas that are not entirely clear while students are reading. In *clarifying,* they focus on words, ideas, and even pronunciations that may require further explanation. Others in the group may be able to help, as can the teacher. The important point is that they realize where their problems lie.

Students are asked to engage in *questioning* once they have read each portion of a selection. The student discussion leader asks a question about the important information in the text; the other students answer the question and may suggest others. They are encouraged to ask questions at a variety of comprehension levels. Then the student leader *summarizes* the text and predicts what is likely to come next, including a justification for the prediction. The process continues with the students reading the next section of text, followed by a discussion led by a different student.

A proficient reader applies all of these strategies internally and independently. The strategies form a kind of dialogue through which good readers attempt to monitor their own comprehension in order to ensure understanding. Struggling readers frequently lack this internal "conversation," and their comprehension suffers as a result. Reciprocal teaching is a means of fostering these healthy mental habits.

Reciprocal teaching can be employed effectively in both the primary and upper grades and across a variety of texts. Evidence indicates that with modifications, it also works with students in primary grades. A related approach, *collaborative strategic reading* (CSR), has been particularly beneficial for students with learning disabilities and for EL, as well as for low- and average-achieving students in grades 4–8 (Klingner, Vaughn, Dimino, Schumm, & Bryant, 2001). CSR is designed to be used with expository texts. Small groups of students *preview* the text before reading to activate prior knowledge and make purposeful predictions. During reading they self-monitor *clicks and clunks,* using fix-it strategies as needed, and *get the gist* for each section of text. After reading all assigned sections, the students *wrap up* with questioning each other about the text and creating a summary of the text.

Both reciprocal teaching and CSR have long histories of demonstrated effectiveness. The purpose of these and other strategy repertoires is to scaffold and habituate the utilization of multiple strategies flexibly as needed to overcome the meaning-making hurdles of text.

Sample Cloze Test

From *The Tell-Tale Heart*
by Edgar Allan Poe

True!—nervous—very, very dreadfully nervous I had been and am; but why *will* you say that I am mad? The disease had sharpened my senses—not destroyed, not dulled them. Above _____ was the sense of _____ acute. I heard all _____ in the heaven and _____ the earth. I heard _____ things in hell. How, _____, am I mad? Hearken! _____ observe how healthily, how _____ I can tell you _____ whole story.

It is _____ to say how first _____ idea entered my brain; _____ once conceived, it haunted _____ day and night. Object _____ was none. Passion there _____ none. I loved the _____ man. He had never _____ me. He had never _____ me insult. For his _____ I had no desire. _____ think it was his _____! Yes, it was this! _____ had the eye of _____ vulture—a pale blue _____, with a film over _____. Whenever it fell upon _____, my blood ran cold; _____ so by degrees— very _____—I made up my _____ to take the life _____ the old man, and _____ rid myself of the _____ forever.

Now this is _____ point. You fancy me _____. Madmen know nothing. But _____ should have seen *me*. _____ should have seen how _____ I proceeded—with what _____, with what foresight, with _____ dissimulation I went to _____! I was never kinder _____ the old man than _____ the whole week before _____ killed him. And every _____, about midnight, I turned _____ latch of his door _____ opened it—oh, so _____! And then, when I _____ made an opening sufficient _____ my head, I put _____ a dark lantern, all closed, closed, so that no light shone out, and then I thrust in my head. Oh, you would have laughed to see how cunningly I thrust it in! I moved it slowly—very, very slowly, so that I might not disturb the old man's sleep. It took me an hour to place my whole head within the opening so far that I could see him as he lay upon his bed. Ha!—would a madman have been so wise as this?

Narrative Retelling Record

Reading _____   Listening _____   Video _____

Name _____   Date _____

Title _____   Level _____

Teacher _____

Script: "Tell me everything you remember about the story. Tell it to me as though you were telling it to your [*friend/brother/sister/parent*] who has never [*read/heard/seen*] it." When the student concludes, ask, "Do you remember anything else?"

Spontaneous (S) or prompted (P)	Does the student include . . .	Student quotes and other notes
	Setting and its role?	
	Characters?	
	A goal, problem to be solved, or initiating event?	
	Episode 1 or attempt to solve problem?	
	Episode 2 or attempt to solve problem?*	
	Episode 3 or attempt to solve problem?*	
	Solution to problem?	
	Clear ending or resolution?	

*Use as needed for each story; add more if necessary.

For students who say they do not recall anything or only recall one or two ideas, choose appropriate prompts, such as these:

"How did the story begin? What happened next?"

"What was the problem? How did the character solve the problem/achieve the goal? How did the book end?"

"What do you think [*character*] learned? What does the author want us to learn from the story?"

Informational Retelling Record

Reading _____ Listening _____ Video _____

Name _____ Date _____

Title _____ Level _____

Teacher _____

Script: "Tell me everything you remember about the [*text/video*]. Tell it to me as though you were telling it to your [*friend/brother/sister/parent*] who has never [*read/heard/seen*] it." When the student concludes, ask, "Do you remember anything else?"

Spontaneous (S) or prompted (P)	Does the student include . . .		Student quotes and other notes
	Main idea?		
	*Key ideas? 1. 2. 3.	*Supporting details? a. b. c. a. b. c. a. b. c.	
	Application of text structure to organize the retelling?		
	Importations and inferences?		
	Erroneous information?		
	Utilization of conceptual vocabulary?		
	Clear ending or resolution?		

*Use as applicable to the text; add more if necessary or adapt to the expository structure.

For students who say they do not recall anything or only recall one or two ideas, choose appropriate prompts, such as these:

"What was the book/passage/video about? What were the big ideas? What was the most important information that you remember? Is there anything else you remember?"

"What did the author want us to know about the topic?"

"Was there anything that you read/saw that was interesting to you or that was new to you?"

From Stahl and Garcia (2015). Copyright © The Guilford Press. Adapted by permission.

San Diego Quick Assessment, Form I

Description: Beginning with the three readiness levels (RR[1], RR[2], RR[3]) of recognizing letters as similar, saying letter names, and matching sounds to letters, this test proceeds to recognition of words. Level 1 is representative of PP, Level 2—Primer, Level 3—Grade 1, and to Level 13, which is representative of Grade 11.

Appropriate for: Students at the end of summer vacation or new students entering the classroom without recent or detailed records.

Ages: 5–16, or older students with learning disabilities.

Testing Time: 2 minutes.

Directions for Use: *Preparation:* For this test you will need copies of the 13 SDQA assessment cards. Sequence the cards in ascending order of difficulty.
    You will also need copies of the attached SDQA record sheet.

Administration: Administer each form of the SDQA individually, as follows:

1. Begin with a card that is at least 2 years below the student's grade-level assignment.
2. Ask the student to read the words aloud to you. If he or she misreads any on the list, drop to easier lists until the student makes no errors. This indicates the base level.
3. Place a checkmark (✔) at the appropriate entry on the record sheet for each correct response. This indicates the base level.
4. Direct the child as follows:

    RR[1]:   "Which letters are alike?"
    RR[2]:   "Name these letters."
    RR[3]:   "Circle the letter you think this word begins with."
    1–13:   "Read as many of the words on this list as you can."
             "Try to sound out words that are new to you."
             "Don't be afraid to tell me ANY part of a word that you recognize."
    1–13:   "Each list gets harder. You won't be able to recognize all of the words,
             but do the best you can."

5. Encourage the student to read words he or she does not know so that you can identify the techniques the student uses for word identification.

Scoring: The list in which a student misses no more than one of the 10 words is the level at which he or she can read independently. Two errors indicate his or her instructional level. Three or more errors identify the level at which reading material will be too difficult for the student.
The type of errors noted in the word substitutions dictates the remediation to be used. For example, students who consistently miss words by starting the word incorrectly:

> *toad* for *road*
> *give* for *live*
> *digger* for *bigger*
> *right* for *night*

need exercises stressing initial consonants. This is equally true of medial and final errors.

(continued)

From LaPray and Ross (1969). Copyright © John Wiley & Sons, Inc. Reprinted by permission.

B	B		
A	C		
M	M		
C	C		
S	Q		
J	J		
T	T		
H	H		
D	L		
W	M		I–RR[1]

B	
A	
M	
C	
S	
J	
T	
H	
D	
W	I–RR[2]

D	B	A	
A	E	K	
L	F	M	
B	C	G	
O	S	P	
A	B	J	
D	G	T	
A	H	B	
D	I	M	
W	G	J	I–RR[3]

see	
play	
me	
at	
run	
go	
and	
look	
can	
here	I–1

(continued)

you		road	
come		live	
not		thank	
with		when	
jump		bigger	
help		how	
is		always	
work		night	
are		spring	
this	I–2	today	I–3
our		city	
please		middle	
myself		moment	
town		frightened	
early		exclaimed	
send		several	
wide		lonely	
believe		drew	
quietly		since	
carefully	I–4	straight	I–5

(continued)

decided		scanty	
served		business	
amazed		develop	
silent		considered	
wrecked		discussed	
improve		behaved	
certainly		splendid	
entered		acquainted	
realized		escape	
interrupted	I–6	grim	I–7
bridge		amber	
commercial		dominion	
abolish		sundry	
trucker		capillary	
apparatus		impetuous	
elementary		blight	
comment		wrest	
necessity		enumerate	
gallery		daunted	
relativity	I–8	condescend	I–9

(continued)

capacious		conscientious	
limitations		isolation	
pretext		molecule	
intrigue		ritual	
delusions		momentous	
immaculate		vulnerable	
ascent		kinship	
acrid		conservatism	
binoculars		jaunty	
embankment	I–10	inventive	I–11
zany		galore	
jerkin		rotunda	
nausea		capitalism	
gratuitous		prevaricate	
linear		risible	
inept		exonerate	
legality		superannuate	
aspen		luxuriate	
amnesty		piebald	
barometer	I–12	crunch	I–13

(continued)

SAN DIEGO QUICK ASSESSMENT   Student _____

I–1 (Preprimer)

_____ see
_____ play
_____ me
_____ at
_____ run
_____ go
_____ and
_____ look
_____ can
_____ here

I–2 (Primer)

_____ you
_____ come
_____ not
_____ with
_____ jump
_____ help
_____ is
_____ work
_____ are
_____ this

I–3 (1st reader)

_____ road
_____ live
_____ thank
_____ when
_____ bigger
_____ how
_____ always
_____ night
_____ spring
_____ today

I–4 (Grade 2)

_____ our
_____ please
_____ myself
_____ town
_____ early
_____ send
_____ wide
_____ believe
_____ quietly
_____ carefully

I–5 (Grade 3)

_____ city
_____ middle
_____ moment
_____ frightened
_____ exclaimed
_____ several
_____ lonely
_____ drew
_____ since
_____ straight

I–6 (Grade 4)

_____ decided
_____ served
_____ amazed
_____ silent
_____ wrecked
_____ improve
_____ certainly
_____ entered
_____ realized
_____ interrupted

I–7 (Grade 5)

_____ scanty
_____ business
_____ develop
_____ considered
_____ discussed
_____ behaved
_____ splendid
_____ acquainted
_____ escape
_____ grim

I–8 (Grade 6)

_____ bridge
_____ commercial
_____ abolish
_____ trucker
_____ apparatus
_____ elementary
_____ comment
_____ necessity
_____ gallery
_____ relativity

I–9 (Grade 7)

_____ amber
_____ dominion
_____ sundry
_____ capillary
_____ impetuous
_____ blight
_____ wrest
_____ enumerate
_____ daunted
_____ condescend

I–10 (Grade 8)

_____ capacious
_____ limitations
_____ pretext
_____ intrigue
_____ delusions
_____ immaculate
_____ ascent
_____ acrid
_____ binoculars
_____ embankment

I–11 (Grade 9)

_____ conscientious
_____ isolation
_____ molecule
_____ ritual
_____ momentous
_____ vulnerable
_____ kinship
_____ conservatism
_____ jaunty
_____ inventive

I–12 (Grade 10)

_____ zany
_____ jerkin
_____ nausea
_____ gratuitous
_____ linear
_____ inept
_____ legality
_____ aspen
_____ amnesty
_____ barometer

I–13 (Grade 11)

_____ galore
_____ rotunda
_____ capitalism
_____ prevaricate
_____ risible
_____ exonerate
_____ superannuate
_____ luxuriate
_____ piebald
_____ crunch

DATE: _____

ESTIMATED READING LEVELS:

INDEPENDENT _____

INSTRUCTIONAL _____

FRUSTRATION _____

Computer-Adaptive Test (CAT) Comparison Worksheet

	Test 1 (Example)	Test 2
Cost	$12.00/student	
Grade levels/subjects	ELA/math	
Administration logistics (time allocations, frequency, test window restraints)	45–60 minutes 3×/year 21-day window	
Test format	ELA: Adaptive, mult. choice Math: Mult. choice, object manipulation	
Technology information	iPad Chromebook Laptop Requires clicking, dragging, and dropping	
Score reporting	Lexiles, percentiles Subgroup filters Class breakdown by goal report Excellent visuals	
Management system utility	Includes excellent school reports for this test. However, it requires manual entry of any other external data.	
Site design	Tabs provide clean design, easy access to levels of data.	
Reliability and other technical information	Renormed every 3 years. 10 million students in sample. .70 correlation with our state ELA test. .74 correlation with our state math test.	
RTI adaptability, cutoff scores	Goal-setting worksheet that includes projected growth.	
Progress-monitoring materials	Not available.	
Accommodations for English learners and special-needs learners	Not available in Spanish. Text to speech available for a fee.	
Professional development	Online training is included. Fidelity checks available. On-site training available for $3,000.00/day.	
Freebies	Pilot video training accessibility.	
Advantages	Data remain accessible for 3 years.	
Other miscellaneous info	PowerPoint provided at the end of each year to display trends in testing.	
Next steps		

Worksheet and data are from Queensbury Middle School, Queensbury, New York. Adapted by permission.

NINE

Strategic Knowledge

When you first picked this book up, you had a purpose. You knew what you wanted to get out of it and had some tentative strategies that you intended to use to achieve your purpose. If you intended to use this book to find measures that you might use for an individual assessment of a child with reading difficulties, then you have probably skipped over the introductory chapters, since they did not match your purpose. If you are reading this book for a college course, then you might have spent a little more time, possibly taking notes. Odds are good that you have been reading the book in a place that you ordinarily use for studying. Some people like quiet when they study; others like music. You are probably in an environment of your choice. You might be using a highlighter or note cards. Again, different people prefer to use different study techniques. Chances are that you will flip through the material to find out how long it is and how difficult you think it will be. You will estimate the amount of time you will need and compare it with the amount of time that you have before dinner or bed or some other point in the future. You are also likely to be asking yourself what information your instructor will think is important, as well as what information you feel you need to get out of the reading. If you are reading this book for a course, you will want to earn as good a grade as possible, which requires figuring out what the instructor will want you to know and making sure you know it.

A second situation is reading a book for pleasure. Here you are likely to be sitting in a comfortable chair or on a couch, or even lying in bed. You might read before you go to sleep or outdoors on a sunny weekend. You will not be concerned with how much you remember or what an instructor would ask; nor would you plan to use cards, a highlighter, or any study aids.

These two situations differ in terms of the text used and the purpose for reading— and these differences lead to the use of different strategies while reading. As an accomplished reader, you have a broad range of strategies that you can apply to a number of different purposes and texts. In addition, if you are not achieving your purpose during reading, because the text is more difficult than you thought or for some other reason, you can adjust your strategies so that you do achieve those purposes. You will probably also allocate different amounts of time for different purposes. For example, you will allot more time for reading a text in detail if you know that you might be tested on it.

In the work we have done with students who have reading problems, we find that they often have no idea how to deploy different strategies to achieve different purposes. Often they are even unaware of their purpose for reading. Students with reading problems tend to focus on the basic decoding of a text, rather than on what they need to get out of it—a habit that persists even after they become competent at decoding and word recognition.

Consider a particular child from one of our clinics. When he was asked how he would study a textbook, he said that he would "start at the beginning and read through to the end." Since he had previously said that he read very slowly, he was asked whether he often made it to the end. He said that he didn't. When asked whether he paid any special notice to boldface words or any features of the text, such as a summary or headings, he said that he did not. Finally, when asked what kind of grades he received while reading in this way, he replied, "D's and F's." It was unclear from this interview whether he knew that his system of studying was not working, or, if he did, whether he felt there was any other way of doing it.

Given the paucity of strategy instruction in schools, it is likely that no one taught you to be as flexible in your strategy use as we are assuming that you are. Instead, you developed these abilities through trial and error, probably in high school and college. Research has found that teaching children strategies can improve their reading and studying abilities (Afflerbach & Cho, 2009; Pressley & Woloshyn, 1995). This instruction can help diminish some of the differences between proficient and struggling readers.

We have found that interviews or self-reports are the best ways of ascertaining how strategically children approach their reading. An alternative is to have children think aloud during reading or studying. If children are comfortable with thinking aloud, this approach can supply a very valuable form of data. But most children are not comfortable thinking aloud, so if you do not get useful information, it could be either because a child is not able to think about reading strategies or because the child does not know how to handle thinking aloud. The Textbook Interview is a structured way in which children can demonstrate their thinking during reading, which might suffice for this purpose.

GENERAL PURPOSES FOR READING

Proficient and struggling readers differ in their knowledge of general reading purposes. If you asked a proficient reader in fifth grade or above a question such as "What makes someone a good reader?" or "If I gave you something to read, how would you know you were reading it well?", the answer would probably focus on comprehension. For example, the student might reply that good readers understand what they read, or that people are reading well if they understand what they read, if they get the main ideas from their reading, and so on. Struggling readers, even into middle school, tend to focus on decoding. To a struggling reader, good readers are those who say the words correctly, and people who are reading well pronounce all the words correctly in a story. For a question such as "What makes something difficult to read?", proficient readers tend to focus on the ideas or the difficult vocabulary, whereas struggling readers cite "big words."

These differences are likely to be significant; after all, if one does not know the desired end of reading instruction, it is difficult to get there. Differences in the instruction given to children of different reading abilities certainly affect the way they view reading. Allington (1983), reviewing a number of observational studies, identified the following differences:

- Proficient readers tend to have a greater focus on comprehension in their lessons; struggling readers focus more on word recognition.
- When they miss a word during reading, proficient readers are more likely to be given meaning cues than are struggling readers, who tend to receive more decoding cues.
- Proficient readers are interrupted fewer times during their lessons than struggling readers are.
- Proficient readers are more likely to read a whole story during a reading period; struggling readers are more likely to read a portion of a story.
- Proficient readers are more likely to read silently; struggling readers are more likely to read aloud.
- Proficient readers cover more material in the course of the school year than struggling readers do (Allington, 1984). Moreover, because practice in reading is related to progress, the gap between struggling and proficient readers appears to widen as children move through school (Stanovich, 1986).

The different cues that readers receive, the different areas of instructional focus, whether students read a story as a whole or not, and how much they are interrupted during reading all seem to lead to different orientations toward reading. These orientations can be turned around relatively easily through comprehension-oriented reading instruction. Even if the immediate instructional goals are decoding and fluency, a teacher should make sure that the child understands that the purpose of reading is comprehension.

SPECIFIC PURPOSES AND STRATEGY KNOWLEDGE

As we have noted earlier, proficient readers can differentiate among different purposes for reading and can adapt their strategies to accomplish those purposes. We have provided three assessments that can help you ascertain how children adapt their reading for different purposes. The first is the Purposes for Reading Interview (Form 9.1, p. 232). This protocol is short and easy to administer. The second is the Index of Reading Awareness (Jacobs & Paris, 1987; Form 9.2, p. 233). This instrument has a multiple-choice format and can be group-administered. Finally, the Textbook Interview (Form 9.3, p. 239) can be used to obtain a more detailed look at how a particular child approaches a reading task.

Two points are central to conducting interviews. The first is that the questions are intended only as guides. The idea is to participate in an informal conversation about reading. This means that you must "think on your feet" and modify your approach whenever a student's responses warrant a change in direction. The second is that the question of how a student reads, though basically a cognitive matter, is associated with the student's self-concept as a reader and the value he or she places on reading.

Finally, the Internet has created the need for its users to be strategic in navigating hypermedia environments. Its use requires readers to apply additional strategies that have few or no counterparts in print settings (Coiro & Dobler, 2011). Unless we are merely "surfing" with no particular goal in mind, it is important to choose from among the many available pathways those that are most likely to get us the results we desire. How well can children pursue purposes when the information they encounter is not arranged as linear text, but is presented as an assortment of text segments, graphics, videos, and other features? The interviews we have discussed so far are intended for print environments. They do not get at strategic questions associated with hypermedia settings that children encounter online. To fill this gap, Donald Leu and his colleagues (2013, 2015) have created online tasks that require students to use strategic skills to navigate purposefully and comprehend successfully in the complex digital environments of the Internet. A student's performance on an Online Research and Comprehension Assessment (ORCA) can reveal much about how the student is developing as a digital reader. A website for the ORCA Project (*www.orca.uconn.edu/orca-project/project-overview*) provides teachers with a variety of resources. The simulated Internet environments of the ORCAs have been crafted to align with the CCSS and are appropriate for students in grades 5–9. The ORCAs are now available free of charge for use with your students; you can obtain them by contacting the research team at *AccessORCA@gmail.com.*

Purposes for Reading Interview

1. What makes someone a good reader?

2. When you're reading something for class, how do you know when you're done?

3. Should a person read everything at about the same speed?

4. What do you do when something doesn't make sense when you're reading?

5. What would make you a better reader?

6. What do you think about while you're reading a story?

7. What do you think about while you're reading a book with lots of information?

Index of Reading Awareness

Administration and Scoring

Because of its multiple-choice format, the Index of Reading Awareness can be administered in a group setting. If significant decoding deficits are suspected, it may be wise to read each item aloud to the students (both stem and choices).

The instrument comprises four subtests of five items each. These are Evaluation, Planning, Regulation, and Conditional Knowledge. Each student earns a score for each of these subtests. No composite score is computed. The subtest scores are computed by using the following key. The response to each item receives 0, 1, or 2 points. The subtest score is simply the sum of these points for the five items of that subtest.

Once the subtest scores are determined, the following scale can be used to interpret them:

Subtest score	Interpretation
8–10	No significant weakness.
6–7	Some instructional support needed.
0–5	Serious need for instruction in this area.

Name _____

1. What is the hardest part about reading for you?
   a. Sounding out the hard words.
   b. When you don't understand the story.
   c. Nothing is hard about reading for you.

2. What would help you become a better reader?
   a. If more people would help you when you read.
   b. Reading easier books with shorter words.
   c. Checking to make sure you understand what you read.

3. What is special about the first sentence or two in a story?
   a. They always begin with "Once upon a time . . . "
   b. The first sentences are the most interesting.
   c. They often tell what the story is about.

4. How are the last sentences of a story special?
   a. They are the exciting action sentences.
   b. They tell you what happened.
   c. They are harder to read.

(continued)

5. How can you tell which sentences are the most important ones in a story?

  a. They're the ones that tell the most about the characters and what happens.

  b. They're the most interesting ones.

  c. All of them are important.

6. If you could only read some of the sentences in the story because you were in a hurry, which ones would you read?

  a. Read the sentences in the middle of the story.

  b. Read the sentences that tell you the most about the story.

  c. Read the interesting, exciting sentences.

7. When you tell other people about what you read, what do you tell them?

  a. What happened in the story.

  b. The number of pages in the book.

  c. Who the characters are.

8. If the teacher told you to read a story to remember the general meaning, what would you do?

  a. Skim through the story to find the main parts.

  b. Read all of the story and try to remember everything.

  c. Read the story and remember all of the words.

9. Before you start to read, what kind of plans do you make to help you read better?

  a. You don't make any plans. You just start reading.

  b. You choose a comfortable place.

  c. You think about why you are reading.

10. If you had to read very fast and could only read some words, which ones would you try to read?

  a. Read the new vocabulary words because they are important.

  b. Read the words that you could pronounce.

  c. Read the words that tell the most about the story.

11. What things do you read faster than others?

  a. Books that are easy to read.

  b. When you've read the story before.

  c. Books that have a lot of pictures.

12. Why do you go back and read things over again?

  a. Because it is good practice.

  b. Because you didn't understand it.

  c. Because you forgot some words.

(continued)

13. What do you do if you come to a word and you don't know what it means?
    a. Use the words around it to figure it out.
    b. Ask someone else.
    c. Go on to the next word.

14. What do you do if you don't know what a whole sentence means?
    a. Read it again.
    b. Sound out all the words.
    c. Think about the other sentences in the paragraph.

15. What parts of the story do you skip as you read?
    a. The hard words and parts you don't understand.
    b. The unimportant parts that don't mean anything for the story.
    c. You never skip anything.

16. If you are reading a story for fun, what would you do?
    a. Look at the pictures to get the meaning.
    b. Read the story as fast as you can.
    c. Imagine the story like a movie in your mind.

17. If you are reading for science or social studies, what would you do to remember the information?
    a. Ask yourself questions about the important ideas.
    b. Skip the parts you don't understand.
    c. Concentrate and try hard to remember it.

18. If you are reading for a test, which would help the most?
    a. Read the story as many times as possible.
    b. Talk about it with somebody to make sure you understand it.
    c. Say the sentences over and over.

19. If you are reading a library book to write a report, which would help you the most?
    a. Sound out words you don't know.
    b. Write it down in your own words.
    c. Skip the parts you don't understand.

20. Which of these is the best way to remember a story?
    a. Say every word over and over.
    b. Think about remembering it.
    c. Write it down in your own words.

(continued)

SCORING GUIDE

Evaluation

1. What is the hardest part about reading for you?

1 a. Sounding out the hard words.

2 b. When you don't understand the story.

0 c. Nothing is hard about reading for you.

2. What would help you become a better reader?

1 a. If more people would help you when you read.

0 b. Reading easier books with shorter words.

2 c. Checking to make sure you understand what you read.

3. What is special about the first sentence or two in a story?

1 a. They always begin with "Once upon a time . . . "

0 b. The first sentences are the most interesting.

2 c. They often tell what the story is about.

4. How are the last sentences of a story special?

1 a. They are the exciting action sentences.

2 b. They tell you what happened.

0 c. They are harder to read.

5. How can you tell which sentences are the most important ones in a story?

2 a. They're the ones that tell the most about the characters and what happens.

1 b. They're the most interesting ones.

0 c. All of them are important.

Planning

6. If you could only read some of the sentences in the story because you were in a hurry, which ones would you read?

0 a. Read the sentences in the middle of the story.

2 b. Read the sentences that tell you the most about the story.

1 c. Read the interesting, exciting sentences.

(continued)

7. When you tell other people about what you read, what do you tell them?

2   a.   What happened in the story.

0   b.   The number of pages in the book.

1   c.   Who the characters are.

8. If the teacher told you to read a story to remember the general meaning, what would you do?

2   a.   Skim through the story to find the main parts.

1   b.   Read all of the story and try to remember everything.

0   c.   Read the story and remember all of the words.

9. Before you start to read, what kind of plans do you make to help you read better?

0   a.   You don't make any plans. You just start reading.

1   b.   You choose a comfortable place.

2   c.   You think about why you are reading.

10. If you had to read very fast and could only read some words, which ones would you try to read?

1   a.   Read the new vocabulary words because they are important.

0   b.   Read the words that you could pronounce.

2   c.   Read the words that tell the most about the story.

Regulation

11. What things do you read faster than others?

1   a.   Books that are easy to read.

2   b.   When you've read the story before.

0   c.   Books that have a lot of pictures.

12. Why do you go back and read things over again?

1   a.   Because it is good practice.

2   b.   Because you didn't understand it.

0   c.   Because you forgot some words.

13. What do you do if you come to a word and you don't know what it means?

2   a.   Use the words around it to figure it out.

1   b.   Ask someone else.

0   c.   Go on to the next word.

(continued)

14. What do you do if you don't know what a whole sentence means?

1   a. Read it again.

0   b. Sound out all the words.

2   c. Think about the other sentences in the paragraph.

15. What parts of the story do you skip as you read?

1   a. The hard words and parts you don't understand.

2   b. The unimportant parts that don't mean anything for the story.

0   c. You never skip anything.

Conditional Knowledge

16. If you are reading a story for fun, what would you do?

1   a. Look at the pictures to get the meaning.

0   b. Read the story as fast as you can.

2   c. Imagine the story like a movie in your mind.

17. If you are reading for science or social studies, what would you do to remember the information?

2   a. Ask yourself questions about the important ideas.

0   b. Skip the parts you don't understand.

1   c. Concentrate and try hard to remember it.

18. If you are reading for a test, which would help the most?

1   a. Read the story as many times as possible.

2   b. Talk about it with somebody to make sure you understand it.

0   c. Say the sentences over and over.

19. If you are reading a library book to write a report, which would help you the most?

1   a. Sound out words you don't know.

2   b. Write it down in your own words.

0   c. Skip the parts you don't understand.

20. Which of these is the best way to remember a story?

0   a. Say every word over and over.

1   b. Think about remembering it.

2   c. Write it down in your own words.

Textbook Interview

Name _____ Date _____

Grade _____

Directions: For this section, select a piece of literature that is representative of classroom reading materials. Place the text in front of the student. As each question is asked, open the appropriate text in front of the student to help provide a point of reference for the question.

Fiction

Open to a story that the student has not yet read.

1. Why do we read this kind of book? [*Note*: Possible answers might be "to learn to read" or "enjoyment."]

2. Why do you think your teacher wants you to read this book?

3. Describe how you might read this story in class.

4. Do you enjoy reading this type of material? [Probe for a fuller answer than "yes" or "no."]

5. What do you need to do to get a good grade in reading?

(continued)

Information Text

Directions: For this section, use an informational text (textbook or passage), preferably something the student uses in the classroom. Choose a text that has a great many features, such as boldface words, headings, a summary, etc. Place the text in front of the student. As each question is asked, open the appropriate text in front of the student to help provide a point of reference for the question. This is an informal interview. You can integrate questions 8–12 into a natural conversation.

6. Why do we read this kind of text? [*Note*: Possible answers might be "to learn from" or "to learn to read from."]

7. Why do you think your teacher wants you to read this text?

8. [Open to a chapter or section somewhat beyond where the child has already reached.] Suppose you were to be given a test on this chapter [or text]. How would you read it? [Have the child model his or her reading, showing you the things that he or she would do.]

9. Would you pay attention to any particular parts of the text? [Possible answers: boldface words, chapter summary, headings, etc.]

10. [If not included in the answer to #9] Would you pay attention to these? [Point to bold-face words.] What are these for?

11. [If not included in the answer to #9] Would you pay attention to these? [Point to headings.] What are these for?

12. [If not included in the answer to #9] Would you pay attention to this? [Point to summary at the end of the chapter.] What is this for?

(continued)

13. [If not included in the answer to #9] Would you pay attention to these? [Point to questions at the end of the chapter.] What are these for?

14. Does the teacher do anything additional to help you study? [Probe for study guides, prequestioning, and so on.]

15. How well do you do on tests of this type of reading?

16. What do you have to do to get a good grade in _____?

17. What do you think you need to do in order to do better?

18. Have you ever tried skimming before you read a chapter to get an idea of what it's about?

19. Have you ever tried summarizing or making notes to remember what you've read?

20. Have you ever tried asking yourself questions to remember what you've read?

TEN

Affective Factors

If you hope to have a truly substantial influence on students' motivation to read, you must first know how they feel about reading. How positive are their attitudes? What are their likes and dislikes? How do their friends and family feel about reading? How much do they value the ability to read? Do they view themselves as readers? A good starting point is to familiarize yourself with a few of the basic forces that influence whether an individual is intrinsically motivated to read. In this chapter, we focus on four of the most important of these forces: attitudes, interests, value, and self-concept. We begin with the consensus definition of each one, recently drawn from the research literature by Conradi, Jang, and McKenna (2014):

> *Attitude:* A set of acquired feelings about reading that consistently predispose an individual to engage in or avoid reading.
>
> *Interest:* A positive orientation toward reading about a particular topic. An *individual* interest is a relatively stable and enduring positive orientation toward reading about a particular topic; a *situational* interest is a context-specific, often momentary, positive orientation toward reading about a particular topic.
>
> *Value:* An individual's beliefs about the extent to which reading is generally useful, enjoyable, or otherwise important.
>
> *Self-concept:* An individual's overall self-perception as a reader, including one's sense of competence and the role ascribed to reading as a part of one's personal identity.

READING ATTITUDES

Attitudes are learned. They are not innate, but develop over time as the result of cultural forces and our own day-to-day experiences with reading and books. The more positive these forces are, the more likely it is that a child will become a lifelong reader. We can summarize these forces quite simply. Our attitudes toward reading are shaped by:

1. Each and every reading experience.
2. Our beliefs about what will happen when we open a book.
3. Our beliefs about how those we hold in high regard feel about reading.

All three of these forces are subject to teacher intervention—even the last! Effective attitude-building strategies, such as those described here, target one or more of the factors.

Studies have led to several important conclusions that are useful in understanding what we as teachers can expect (McKenna, 2001; McKenna, Conradi, Lawrence, Jang, & Meyer, 2012; McKenna, Kear, & Ellsworth, 1995). Here, in brief, are the major findings of reading attitude research:

1. Reading attitudes tend to worsen over time.
2. Reading attitudes worsen more rapidly for poor readers.
3. Girls tend to possess more positive reading attitudes than boys do.
4. Ethnic group membership is not, in itself, strongly related to reading attitudes.
5. Instructional methods can have a positive influence on attitudes.

READING INTERESTS

An interest area is really an attitude toward reading about a particular topic. In other words, we have not only a general attitude toward reading, but specific attitudes toward reading about certain subjects. For instance, you may love to read, but hate the thought of reading science fiction books. Knowing about children's interest areas arms teachers with the knowledge they need to recommend books that match existing enthusiasms. Through these positive experiences, children come to realize that books afford a means of satisfying and furthering the interests they already have. Teachers possess power in influencing their students' situational reading interests. Teaching literacy through sustained disciplinary units and inquiry-based learning gives students the opportunity to expand their current interests and develop new interests.

READING VALUE

We suspect that any teacher reading this book shares an abiding belief in the value of reading. We know the economic potential of reading well and the consequences of reading poorly. We also know that reading can help to ensure a more fulfilled life—one in which reading edifies, informs, and entertains. Motivated students acknowledge its value as well, and it is important that we instill in the less motivated an appreciation of that value.

Your first impression may be that *value* is equivalent to *attitude*, and it's true that the two are closely connected. However, there are subtle differences. Think back to a college course that you didn't find particularly engaging, but that you nevertheless needed to pass. The required readings may have held little interest for you. Your attitude toward reading them may have been extremely negative. You probably told yourself there were better ways of spending your time! But the value you ascribed to comprehending the assigned texts was high, despite your negative feelings. This example shows how value is a distinct force influencing motivation. It is a proper target of assessment and subsequent planning.

READING SELF-CONCEPT

A colleague of ours once remarked that when she died, a proper epitaph might be "Here Lies a Reader." Can you say this about yourself? The answer involves the place reading occupies in your life—and it necessarily involves your perception of how proficient you are as a reader. If we acknowledge the importance of our students' becoming lifelong readers, it makes sense to learn where they stand in relation to that goal and to take steps to help them attain it. When we use what we know about a child's attitudes, interests, value, and self-concept, we are poised to take these steps.

ASSESSING ATTITUDES AND INTERESTS

It is vital to keep in mind that conclusions based on research are simply generalizations. Although they adequately describe large populations of children and can guide our thinking as we plan instruction and form broad expectations, the attitudes and interests of an individual child may differ sharply from the norm. This is why it is always important to assess children and not merely assume that they conform to stereotypical patterns. Some useful ways of gathering information about your students include the following:

- Conducting focused classroom observations.
- Tracking entries in students' reading journals.
- Administering open-ended questionnaires.
- Administering interest inventories.
- Administering attitude surveys.

These activities complement each other nicely. The information offered by each is unique and contributes to a complete picture of the child as a developing reader. Let's look briefly at each.

Classroom Observations

Observing children as they take part in classroom activities can provide you with valuable information about their likes and dislikes. One way to systematize these observations is to jot them briefly into a log, which can be kept in a child's portfolio. Entries might include notations such as these:

9/25   Beth told me she really liked the Critter books.

10/14   Beth's mom said she wants to be a scientist.

11/2   Beth checked out two books about snakes.

Reading Logs and Journals

Another means of gathering data about students' attitudes and interests is reading the entries in their reading logs and journals. Many schools require that students maintain a simple log to document their daily reading. The simplest logs with a date, title, and time or pages can be useful in analyzing a student's habits and interests. The logs provide information on the genres and topics that students are selecting on their own. They also provide a window into the difficulty levels of self-selected texts and reading sustenance.

Some teachers require students to make regular entries in more elaborate journals. These typically include the title of each book they complete, the completion date, and a brief response to the material. Journals may also contain general commentaries about reading. An advantage of reading journals is that they compel students to reflect upon their feelings toward reading and about their emerging identities as readers. Journaling also encourages students to form critical judgments about what they've read and conveys the message that their opinions count. This significance becomes especially evident to students when teachers add written responses to their entries. Reading journals also offer a good opportunity for writing development and provide a meaningful context in which to apply writing skills.

An important cautionary note about reading journals: Do not allow them to turn into a series of book reports. You do not want to create the expectation that every book your students read for "pleasure" will inevitably be followed by a laborious writing exercise. Setting some guidelines at the beginning regarding your expectations—and making sure those expectations are modest—can prevent this undesirable shift from occurring.

Open-Ended Questionnaires

A good get-acquainted activity involves asking students to respond to incomplete sentences designed to elicit personal beliefs about reading as well as existing interests. These need not be long and involved; a few statements can go a long way. Completing these statements can be used as a written activity in a group setting (in which case they also reveal information about writing development), or the statements can be used individually as an interview guide, in which you provide each sentence starter orally and jot down the student's response. Try using the questionnaire in Form 10.1 (p. 253) as a starting point, and modify it as appropriate.

In middle school, disciplinary content-area teachers might periodically ask students to complete a questionnaire about their engagement with content-specific reading in their classes. Neugebauer (2017) determined that the Dynamic Reading Motivation Measure was sensitive to content-area-specific reading motivation and the social aspects of reading activities, reading performance, and knowledge building. Form 10.2 (p. 254) is a questionnaire that middle school teachers can use or modify as an exit ticket for a particular class reading activity.

Interest Inventories

An interest inventory is a list of topics used to identify those that individual students find most appealing. Such inventories are easy to create and simple to give, and the results can be very helpful in recommending books that are likely to engage students' interest. In other words, interest inventories can make you a better book broker! They can be given to your class as a group as long as you read the choices aloud, so that poor decoding does not prevent children from making informed choices.

Form 10.3 (p. 255) is a sample interest inventory that you are free to duplicate or modify. Or you can start from scratch. Whichever route you take, here are some guidelines that might help:

- Save your inventory as a Microsoft Word document, so that you can add or delete topics after you've used it a few times.
- Make sure you can deliver the goods; don't include topics for which you have no materials.
- Provide a wide range of topics, including those typically of interest to boys and to girls.
- Include topics that might suggest nonfiction titles as well as fiction.
- Add a few blank lines at the end. An interest inventory is like a ballot, and a place for write-ins should be provided! (Trying to anticipate all of kids' interests can be frustrating.)
- Don't mention reading when you give the directions. A negative attitude may lead to negative responses even for genuine interests.
- Make it easy to respond. Try asking kids to "grade" each topic, just as a teacher might, using whatever grading system they know (e.g., A, B, C, D, F). This method provides more detailed information than a checklist, because it indicates the *strength* of the interest.
- Keep completed inventories where you can find them, perhaps in portfolios.
- Use the topics that receive the highest "grades" to recommend books to individual students.

Attitude Surveys

Rating scales are available for assessing the general reading attitudes of your students. The results can be easily quantified and will provide an accurate barometer of how positive (or negative) attitudes may be. They also can be used on a pre–post basis to document progress over the course of a year.

Elementary Reading Attitude Survey

The Elementary Reading Attitude Survey (ERAS; McKenna & Kear, 1990) is based on the cartoon character Garfield. Cartoonist Jim Davis, creator of Garfield and codeveloper of the ERAS, has granted teachers permission to duplicate the survey for classroom use. Directions for administering, scoring, and interpreting the survey, and the ERAS in one-page format is provided as Form 10.4 (pp. 256–259). You'll also find a table of percentile ranks, so you can see how your students compare to a national sample of more than 17,000 children. A downloadable version of the survey using a larger font and with pictures is available on this book's companion website (see the box at the end of the table of contents).

Survey of Adolescent Reading Attitudes

The Survey of Adolescent Reading Attitudes (SARA), designed by McKenna et al. (2012), is intended to complement the ERAS by targeting students in middle and secondary grades. It contains four subscales, incorporating (1) recreational reading in print settings, (2) academic reading in print settings, (3) recreational reading in digital settings, and (4) academic reading in digital settings. Administering this survey will provide evidence that not all students prefer recreational reading and working in digital formats. Student responses enable teachers to tease out important attitude profiles that might offer clues about how best to reach older students. The SARA appears in Form 10.5 (p. 260).

ADDRESSING NEGATIVE ATTITUDES

To make progress with children who are not predisposed to read, it is important to ask why they do not enjoy this crucial activity. The answers are not always clear, but a few basic questions can help clarify the situation.

Is the Attitude Problem the Result of Poor Decoding?

No one voluntarily engages in an activity that is frustrating. Dysfluent reading, with all of its natural frustrations, can be a barrier to positive attitudes. Apart from fostering proficiency, teachers can initiate the following actions:

• *Read aloud to children.* Doing so relieves students of the burden of decoding, while acquainting them with interesting books and giving them a clearer vision of the benefits of proficient reading.

• *Make materials of appropriate difficulty available.* Sometimes called "hi–lo" books, these materials aim to interest older children, but place few demands on their limited decoding and vocabulary. An excellent annotated list of such books is provided by Phelan (1996). Additionally, Newsela (*https://newsela.com*) provides free reading materials in all content areas that correspond to national literacy and disciplinary standards, and that are available in multiple versions to match students' reading levels.

• *Use electronic supports.* E-books with pronunciation supports can make it possible for students to read independently, because they remove the decoding barrier without the need for constant teacher presence. Text-to-speech applications allow students to scan printed materials that are not available in digital formats (e.g., some class novels or textbooks). The application "reads aloud" the scanned text (more recent versions of these applications sound more natural than earlier ones). Most supportive are audio-books. Although these can bring literature to life and provide access to texts for students with the lowest reading levels, they do little to further word-recognition development. This is why, in addition to listening to audiobooks for these readers, we recommend direct instruction in word recognition and extensive practice with reading in appropri-ate, engaging material.

Is the Attitude Problem the Result of Uninteresting Materials?

As we have hinted above, teachers must become "brokers"—using their knowledge of books on the one hand, and of children's interests on the other, to recommend appropri-ate matches. This is why interest inventories can be so important. Teachers must still "deliver the goods," however. Specifically, we recommend the following possibilities:

- *Establish an extensive classroom library.* Don't worry about the condition of the materials; aim for quality and variety. Include back copies of magazines that you can get from the media specialist. Visit garage sales and flea markets. Don't forget the free books you can earn by having your children participate in book clubs. House the books in plastic tubs or baskets.

- *Don't forget nonfiction.* Teachers often forget that nonfiction can be just as appeal-ing to students of all ages and genders as fiction. In fact, many find it more engaging. Moreover, the ability to read nonfiction is vital to eventual success in the workplace, so there is a powerful educational rationale for including nonfiction titles in your classroom library. Strive for an effective balance.

- *Note the winners of Children's and Teen Choice Book Awards.* In our experience, award-winning books are not always popular with children, at least when the awards are decided by adults. Awards are frequently given to the authors of the kinds of books we, as teachers, would like to see our students reading, rather than the kinds of books chil-dren might prefer to read. The fact that a particular book attains critical appeal should not be regarded as unerring testimony about how well kids will like it. One means of contending with this dilemma is to consider polls conducted among children and teens themselves. Each year the Children's Book Council and the International Literacy Asso-ciation conduct two such polls: one among children ages 5–13, and the other among students in grades 7–12. The books evaluated in these polls are submitted by publish-ers and must meet certain criteria before they are distributed to classrooms around the country for rating. For example, each book submitted for consideration as a Teen Choice must have received two positive published reviews. In reality, then, adults do have a say about which books qualify, but students render the final ratings—a vital difference. Lists of past winners are available online (*http://everychildareader.net/choice/past-winners*).

- *Include series books.* These can be sequential books (e.g., the Laura Ingalls Wilder series, *The Hunger Games*) or books that simply reuse characters (e.g., *Curious George, Clifford*). One advantage of series books is that if a reader becomes interested in one, then an entire line of additional books suddenly attains high appeal. A second advantage is that such books are easier to comprehend, because so much of the prior knowledge needed to understand them (information about characters, setting, and typical plot structures) is already present as a result of having read other books in the series. Moreover, binge-reading high volumes of words increases reading skills. Finally, many series (e.g., *Harry Potter, The Mortal Instruments*) develop large social communities of readers who follow the series. Participation in such a community can be a powerful motivator for readers of all ages.

- *Include illustrated books.* Research shows that older struggling readers often lack the ability to visualize the events about which they read. Illustrated books can support them by providing visual images, and this support will likely lead to a greater willingness to read. The *Illustrated Classics,* for example, provide one drawing on every other page; they are "naturals" for coaxing reluctant readers into extended reading by providing them with the support they need.

- *Include digital resources.* Today's schools are increasingly incorporating e-books and online sources as means of extending the limits of their classroom libraries. It's important to remind students that the reading they do on devices is in fact "real" reading. This statement may seem odd, but students tend not to equate such reading with the reading they do in print (Conradi, 2014). By reminding them that it is simply a different kind of reading, we can make it possible for their enthusiasm to affect their attitudes and self-concepts.

What Instructional Techniques Are Effective in Fostering Positive Attitudes?

Although there is no magic bullet for fostering positive attitudes toward reading, some techniques and activities have yielded good results.

- *Employ social settings.* Whether learners are reading informational texts or literary texts, research suggests that student discussion groups can lead to improved attitudes toward reading (e.g., Guthrie & McCann, 1996; Leal, 1993; Neugebauer, 2017). Literature groups offer one way to model the sort of behavior that teachers should seek to foster in children if they are to participate in a literate culture. Typically, literature circles or book clubs bring students together to discuss the *fiction* book(s) they have all read. Exposure to peers with positive reading attitudes may improve a struggling reader's perception of reading. Moreover, discussion among readers has the potential to broaden children's critical perspectives on what reading is.

- *Try idea circles.* Guthrie and McCann (1996) discovered that using *nonfiction* as the basis of these discussions can be highly motivating as well. Best of all, kids need not have read the same selection. Rather, the common element is the topic. Guthrie and McCann define an *idea circle* as a "peer-led, small-group discussion of concepts fueled by multiple text sources" (p. 88). In an idea circle, everyone has something unique to contribute to the discussion by virtue of having read a different source. You can differentiate these assignments deftly, to ensure that abler readers undertake more challenging materials. You may need to take precautions, however, to guard against one or two students' taking over the discussion and eclipsing others. Spelling out some simple ground rules in advance can increase the quality of the discussions.

• *Don't forget technology.* Tech applications, like literature and idea circles, are another way to take advantage of the social dynamics that are important in motivating students. Internet projects, for example, afford opportunities for students to collaborate in ways that simultaneously build proficiency and motivate. "By asking students to collaborate on a Google doc or blog or VoiceThread," Conradi (2014) has observed, "we are in fact providing opportunities for deeper meaning making. These experiences help to ensure that reading occupies an important part of their self-concept and that their attitudes become more positive" (p. 56).

• *Provide time for independent-choice reading.* This protected block of time has been called Drop Everything and Read (DEAR), Uninterrupted Sustained Silent Reading (USSR), and Self-Selected Reading (SSR). Regardless of the name, it is a method of scheduling time during the school day for purposeful, independently chosen reading. This reading can serve multiple purposes: building a literacy community around a theme or genre; providing opportunities for discussing such reading with peers; and reflecting and responding to texts in a variety of ways, including on social media or as inspiration to read the next text. Finally, it also affords students another means of becoming more proficient by reading in pleasant, authentic contexts.

Additionally, do not discount the independent-choice reading of informational texts that students may be selecting to work on an inquiry project or research. Curiosity is an important element of motivation, and reading to deeply investigate a self-selected question is engaging. Becoming an expert in a topic is a powerful means of building self-esteem for struggling readers of all ages.

• *Bring in adult models.* Try inviting a variety of adults over the course of a year to speak to your class about their own reading. Individuals such as the principal, the custodian, or the school nurse can convey the message that *everybody* reads; of course, outside visitors can bring the same message. Consider extending invitations to those who reflect the cultural backgrounds of your class.

• *Be a good model yourself.* If reading is worth doing, you must be seen doing it yourself. Children must observe that you, in fact, practice what you preach. Bring and talk about what you've read, whether it's a bestseller, a teacher resource book, or an article from a magazine or newspaper. You will be modeling not only the value of reading as a part of life outside school, but the social process of sharing what we read with one another.

• *Consider cross-age tutoring.* Placing older and younger children together for tutoring can bolster the attitudes of the older students, particularly if they themselves are experiencing problems. The logistics of coordinating your efforts with another teacher are worth the effort. The tutoring need not be technical and is perhaps best when limited to the sharing of books chosen by the older partner.

• *Be cautious about incentive programs.* Outside incentive programs designed to encourage children's reading are a matter of ongoing debate. The Accelerated Reader, Pizza Hut's Book-It program, Scholastic's Reading Counts, and various schoolwide goals (e.g., the principal's or library media specialist's kissing a pig or jumping into a tub of Jell-O) are now commonplace in elementary and middle schools. There is no debate about the fact that these programs can increase the amount of reading children do. Whether they lead to lifelong reading habits is far less certain, although two facts argue that some children may indeed come to value reading more highly. First, the increased amount of reading undoubtedly makes some children more proficient, and having to contend with poor proficiency is a sure way *not* to become an avid reader. Second, by reading in quantity, children are inadvertently exposed to a variety of books, and their perspectives on what is available are broadened. One clever modification is to use *books* as an incentive!

ADDRESSING VALUE AND SELF-CONCEPT

Jackie Malloy and her colleagues have recently revised an excellent assessment of value and self-concept. The Motivation to Read Fiction (MRF) and Motivation to Read Nonfiction (MRNF) profiles can be used in classrooms for grades 3–6 (Malloy et al., 2017). Originally developed at the National Reading Research Center and used with students across the country, the newest iterations of these surveys offer valid and reliable means of assessing these important two components of motivation regarding reading. Both of these 20-item multiple-choice profiles can be administered in a whole-class or small-group context. However, it is best to administer them a week apart.

These areas are cause for concern in students who exhibit problems. Interpreting the results of the MRF and MRNF is a good first step toward making an instructional plan. Keep in mind, however, that changes in the affective dimensions of reading tend to be incremental. They rarely occur overnight or as the result of an "Aha!" moment.

Value of Reading

Value may be the most often ignored of the factors influencing motivation (Jang, Conradi, McKenna, & Jones, 2015). A good way to address the value of reading is to recognize that there are two kinds of value students might ascribe to reading. *Attainment value* lies in doing well on a task. When a student aims to achieve an award for reading, the value lies in attaining the award rather than in engaging in text to learn or to be entertained. In contrast, the *utility value* of reading lies in how important or useful a student perceives it to be. Schunk, Meece, and Pintrich (2014) define *utility value* as "the usefulness of the task for individuals in terms of their future goals" (p. 64). Jang et al. (2015, p. 243) encourage teachers to regularly take the time to "explicitly discuss the value of reading, both as an attainment and for its utility." They offer the following vignette of how one teacher makes this happen:

> In the third-grade classroom of Mrs. Layton, the students' love of reading is evident. Students are scattered across the room with reading material in hand. Some are discussing their thoughts about books with their peers. They use notebooks to record new vocabulary words and to enter codes that communicate their thinking to peers and Mrs. Layton. The classroom has a poster with student-recommended books as well as those recommended by teachers. These third graders recognize that reading is a way of building their knowledge and of being included in the social interaction of the classroom.

In addition, Mrs. Layton always gives a reason for each reading task to her students based on the weekly unit theme and the entire semester curriculum. She often asks her students to write exit slips expressing how meaningful the text was to them and how they can use the contents for other tasks. This strategy allows Mrs. Layton and her students to discuss the many ways that reading is important.

Reading Self-Concept

Naturally, instilling proficiency is a prerequisite to the development of a positive reading self-concept. Before proficiency is achieved, however, there are simple steps teachers can take along the way that can help directly. Jang et al. (2015) point to the work of Carol Dweck for its implications about building self-concept. Dweck (2007) discusses *growth* versus *fixed* mindsets as they relate to an individual's self-perception. An individual with a growth mindset is open to the possibility of improving. Such an individual might say:

"Although some of the words are hard, I can still make sense of a lot of what I am reading."
"Every year I get better as a reader."

A fixed mindset, in contrast, is defeatist and dismissive. It is a stance that teachers must work to change when they hear comments like the following:

"That text level is too hard for me."
"I'm just not good at reading, so I'd rather do something else."

Dweck (2007) suggests that teachers always provide *specific* feedback. For example, instead of saying, "You're a good reader," a teacher could say. "You've learned so many new words this month." The latter comment stresses growth. And Dweck warns that praising good readers with comments like the first can have unintended consequences. Telling children that they are good readers helps create a fixed mindset that can actually make them hesitant to try new things and risk not doing well—because if that happens, they would no longer be "good readers." The takeaway lessons here are simple: *Always be specific and stress growth, not status.* This is especially true for students whose self-concepts need to be reinforced. Your assessments can tell you who they are.

Here's How I Feel about Reading

Name _____

1. I like to read about _____.

2. My friends think reading is _____.

3. My favorite book is _____.

4. I like books about _____.

5. When I read on the phone, computer, or iPad, I am reading _____.

6. When I am in a library, I choose _____.

7. At home, I choose to read _____.

8. On weekends, my favorite thing to do is _____.

9. The best thing about reading is _____.

10. The worst thing about reading is _____.

Things I Read

Books	Computer/Internet
Magazines	iPad or Kindle
Newspapers	Phone
Graphic novels	Social tools: Facebook, Twitter, e-mail, texts

Content-Area Exit Ticket Menu

	Not true for me	A little bit true for me	Mostly true for me	Completely true for me
I wanted to learn about the topic that I read about today.				
My full attention was on the information in the text.				
I wanted to understand the concepts that I read about today.				
I enjoyed making connections between what I read and my own ideas.				
After we discussed the text in class, I wanted to read more about it.				
Working with others in my group helped me understand more about the topic.				
Working with others in my group helped me enjoy the activity.				
I read because I was curious about the topic.				
I did not want to stop reading.				

From Neugebauer (2017). Copyright © Sage Publications, Inc. Reprinted by permission.

FORM 10.3
Tell Me What You Like!

Name _____

Which topics do you like the most? Pretend you're a teacher and give each one of these a grade. Give it an A if you really like it, a B if you like it pretty well, a C if it's just OK, a D if you don't like it, and an F if you can't stand it! If I've missed some topics you really like, please write them on the lines at the bottom of the page.

_____ sports		_____ monsters
_____ animals		_____ horses
_____ magic		_____ detectives
_____ jokes and riddles		_____ love
_____ exploring the unknown		_____ famous people
_____ sharks		_____ ghosts
_____ camping		_____ other countries
_____ superheroes		_____ dogs
_____ spiders		_____ cooking
_____ science		_____ the ocean
_____ drawing, painting, art		_____ music
_____ history		_____ science fiction
_____ friendship		_____ cats
_____ snakes		_____ families
_____ the wilderness		_____ nature
_____ fishing		_____ technology

What other topics do you really like? Write them here:

_____

_____

_____

Elementary Reading Attitude Survey (ERAS)

Directions for Use

The Elementary Reading Attitude Survey provides a quick indication of student attitudes toward reading. It consists of 20 items and can be administered to an entire classroom in about 10 minutes. Each item presents a brief, simply-worded statement about reading, followed by four pictures of Garfield. Each pose is designed to depict a different emotional state, ranging from very positive to very negative.

Administration

Begin by telling students that you wish to find out how they feel about reading. Emphasize that this is not a test and that there are no "right" answers. Encourage sincerity.

Distribute the survey forms and, if you wish to monitor the attitudes of specific students, ask them to write their names in the space at the top. Hold up a copy of the survey so that the students can see the first page. Point to the picture of Garfield at the far left of the first item. Ask the students to look at this same picture on their own survey form. Discuss with them the mood Garfield seems to be in (very happy). Then move to the next picture and again discuss Garfield's mood (this time, a little happy). In the same way, move to the third and fourth pictures and talk about Garfield's moods—a little upset and very upset. It is helpful to point out the position of Garfield's mouth, especially in the middle two figures.

Explain that together you will read some statements about reading and that the students should think about how they feel about each statement. They should then circle the picture of Garfield that is closest to their own feelings. (Emphasize that the students should respond according to their own feelings, not as Garfield might respond!) Read each item aloud slowly and distinctly; then read it a second time while students are thinking. Be sure to read the item number and to remind students of page numbers when new pages are reached.

Scoring

To score the survey, count 4 points for each leftmost (happiest) Garfield circled, 3 for each slightly smiling Garfield, 2 for each mildly upset Garfield, and 1 point for each very upset (rightmost) Garfield. Three scores for each student can be obtained: the total for the first 10 items, the total for the second 10, and a composite total. The first half of the survey relates to attitude toward recreational reading; the second half relates to attitude toward academic aspects of reading.

Interpretation

You can interpret scores in two ways. One is to note informally where the score falls in regard to the four nodes of the scale. A total score of 50, for example, would fall about midway on the scale, between the slightly happy and slightly upset figures, therefore indicating a relatively indifferent overall attitude toward reading. The other approach is more formal. It involves converting the raw scores into percentile ranks by means of the table on the next page. Be sure to use the norms for the right grade level and to note the column headings (Rec = recreational reading, Aca = academic reading, Tot = total score). If you wish to determine the average percentile rank for your class, average the raw scores first; then use the table to locate the percentile rank corresponding to the raw score mean. Percentile ranks cannot be averaged directly.

(continued)

Midyear percentile ranks by grade and scale

Raw Scr	Grade 1			Grade 2			Grade 3			Grade 4			Grade 5			Grade 6		
	Rec	Aca	Tot	Rec	Aca	Tot	Rec	Aca	Tot	Rec	Aca	Tot	Rec	Aca	Tot	Rec	Aca	Tot
80			99			99			99			99			99			99
79			95			96			98			99			99			99
78			93			95			97			98			99			99
77			92			94			97			98			99			99
76			90			93			96			97			98			99
75			88			92			95			96			98			99
74			86			90			94			95			97			99
73			84			88			92			94			97			98
72			82			86			91			93			96			98
71			80			84			89			91			95			97
70			78			82			86			89			94			96
69			75			79			84			88			92			95
68			72			77			81			86			91			93
67			69			74			79			83			89			92
66			66			71			76			80			87			90
65			62			69			73			78			84			88
64			59			66			70			75			82			86
63			55			63			67			72			79			84
62			52			60			64			69			76			82
61			49			57			61			66			73			79
60			46			54			58			62			70			76
59			43			51			55			59			67			73
58			40			47			51			56			64			69
57			37			45			48			53			61			66
56			34			41			44			48			57			62
55			31			38			41			45			53			58
54			28			35			38			41			50			55
53			25			32			34			38			46			52
52			22			29			31			35			42			48
51			20			26			28			32			39			44
50			18			23			25			28			36			40
49			15			20			23			26			33			37
48			13			18			20			23			29			33
47			12			15			17			20			26			30
46			10			13			15			18			23			27
45			8			11			13			16			20			25
44			7			9			11			13			17			22
43			6			8			9			12			15			20
42			5			7			8			10			13			17
41			5			6			7			9			12			15
40	99	99	4	99	99	5	99	99	6	99	99	7	99	99	10	99	99	13
39	92	91	3	94	94	4	96	97	5	97	98	6	98	99	9	98	99	12
38	89	88	3	92	92	3	94	95	4	95	97	5	96	98	8	97	99	10
37	86	85	2	88	89	2	90	93	3	92	95	4	94	98	7	95	99	8
36	81	79	2	84	85	2	87	91	2	88	93	3	91	96	6	92	98	7
35	77	75	1	79	81	1	81	88	2	84	90	3	87	95	4	88	97	6
34	72	69	1	74	78	1	75	83	2	78	87	2	82	93	4	83	95	5
33	65	63	1	68	73	1	69	79	1	72	83	2	77	90	3	79	93	4
32	58	58	1	62	67	1	63	74	1	66	79	1	71	86	3	74	91	3
31	52	53	1	56	62	1	57	69	0	60	75	1	65	82	2	69	87	2
30	44	49	1	50	57	0	51	63	0	54	70	1	59	77	1	63	82	2
29	38	44	0	44	51	0	45	58	0	47	64	1	53	71	1	58	78	1
28	32	39	0	37	46	0	38	52	0	41	58	1	48	66	1	51	73	1
27	26	34	0	31	41	0	33	47	0	35	52	1	42	60	1	46	67	1
26	21	30	0	25	37	0	26	41	0	29	46	0	36	54	0	39	60	1
25	17	25	0	20	32	0	21	36	0	23	40	0	30	49	0	34	54	0
24	12	21	0	15	27	0	17	31	0	19	35	0	25	42	0	29	49	0
23	9	18	0	11	23	0	13	26	0	14	29	0	20	37	0	24	42	0
22	7	14	0	8	18	0	9	22	0	11	25	0	16	31	0	19	36	0
21	5	11	0	6	15	0	6	18	0	9	20	0	13	26	0	15	30	0
20	4	9	0	4	11	0	5	14	0	6	16	0	10	21	0	12	24	0
19	2	7		2	8		3	11		5	13		7	17		10	20	
18	2	5		2	6		2	8		3	9		6	13		8	15	
17	1	4		1	5		1	5		2	7		4	9		6	11	
16	1	3		1	3		1	4		2	5		3	6		4	8	
15	0	2		0	2		0	3		1	3		2	4		3	6	
14	0	2		0	1		0	1		1	2		1	2		1	3	
13	0	1		0	1		0	1		0	1		1	2		1	2	
12	0	1		0	0		0	0		0	1		0	1		0	1	
11	0	0		0	0		0	0		0	0		0	0		0	0	
10	0	0		0	0		0	0		0	0		0	0		0	0	

(continued)

Student Name _____   Grade _____

Teacher _____   Administration Date _____

Scoring guide

4 points   Happiest Garfield

3 points   Slightly smiling Garfield

2 points   Mildly upset Garfield

1 point   Very upset Garfield

Recreational reading   Academic reading

1. _____   11. _____

2. _____   12. _____

3. _____   13. _____

4. _____   14. _____

5. _____   15. _____

6. _____   16. _____

7. _____   17. _____

8. _____   18. _____

9. _____   19. _____

10. _____   20. _____

Raw score: _____   Raw score: _____

Full-scale raw score (Recreational + Academic): _____

Percentile ranks   Recreational

                          Academic

                          Full scale

(continued)

Elementary Reading Attitude Survey

School _____   Grade _____   Name _____

1. How do you feel when you read a book on a rainy Saturday?

2. How do you feel when you read a book in school during free time?

3. How do you feel about reading for fun at home?

4. How do you feel about getting a book for a present?

5. How do you feel about spending free time reading?

6. How do you feel about starting a new book?

7. How do you feel about reading on summer vacation?

8. How do you feel about reading instead of playing?

9. How do you feel about going to a bookstore?

10. How do you feel about reading different kinds of books?

11. How do you feel when the teacher asks you questions about what you read?

12. How do you feel about doing reading workbook pages and worksheets?

13. How do you feel about reading in school?

14. How do you feel about reading your school books?

15. How do you feel about learning from a book?

16. How do you feel when it's time for reading class?

17. How do you feel about the stories you read in reading class?

18. How do you feel when you read out loud in class?

19. How do you feel about using a dictionary?

20. How do you feel about taking a reading test?

Survey of Adolescent Reading Attitudes (SARA)

The Survey of Adolescent Reading Attitudes (SARA; McKenna et al., 2012) is a group assessment that is easy to administer and score. A student responds to 18 questions on a scale from 1 to 6, with 6 being the most positive. The items are classified by purpose and medium. The purpose for reading is either recreational or academic, and the medium is either print or digital. By pairing purpose and medium, four categories are created:

1. Recreational reading in print settings (e.g., reading a novel in print form).
2. Recreational reading in digital settings (e.g., reading the same novel on a tablet).
3. Academic reading in print settings (e.g., reading an article in print form).
4. Academic reading in digital settings (e.g., reading an informational website).

A score is produced for each of these categories, and the teacher can compare the scores to make judgments. The idea is that each of us has not a single attitude toward reading but several, and two of the most important factors are the reason we're reading and the setting in which we read.

Administering SARA

SARA can be administered either to gather data concerning a particular student or to gauge the attitudes of a group. If a single student is to be evaluated, it is vital to garner honest responses. To encourage sincerity, the teacher should lower the stakes of the assessment by explaining that the results will not be used in grading. If the goal is to assess an entire class, sincerity can be largely ensured by not asking students to identify themselves by name.

Scoring SARA

Although we have explained elsewhere how the survey can be hand-scored (Conradi et al., 2013), it is far easier to use a simple Excel spreadsheet. We have already created this resource, and you may download it at no cost. After a teacher keys in a student's response to all of the items, Excel automatically computes the four subscale scores and looks up the percentile rank corresponding to each. (Because there are separate norms for males and females, students must specify their gender even if the survey is otherwise anonymous.) You may download the Excel scoring spreadsheet here: *https://ila.onlinelibrary.wiley.com/doi/full/10.1002/JAAL.183#support-information-section*.

Interpreting the Results of SARA

There are two ways to interpret each of the four subscale scores. One is to think of the score on a scale from 1 to 6, where 6 corresponds to feeling "very good" about one of the four areas listed above and 1 corresponds to feeling "very bad" about the area. Think of a student's score in relation to 3.5, the midpoint of the scale. The higher a score is relative to 3.5, the more positive the attitude.

A second way to interpret the results is to compare the score on each subscale with the national norms computed from the nationwide survey (McKenna et al., 2012). These norms allow a teacher to compare the attitudes of a given student with students of the same grade level and gender. Norms are available for grades 6–8; if SARA is given in high school, only the first method of interpreting scores can be used—that is, thinking of them along a scale from 1 to 6.

Each of these approaches to interpreting SARA subscale scores is useful in understanding the predispositions of a class or individual student. They are equivalent to the criterion- and norm-referenced approaches to the interpretation of test scores.

Conradi and her colleagues (2013, pp. 570–572) have suggested a step-by-step strategy for interpreting the results of SARA and using them to plan. They have included both of these approaches and have suggested how to compare the subscales.

(continued)

1. *Note the norms.* The percentile rank corresponding to each of the four subscale scores can give you a frame of reference. How far above or below average (the 50th percentile rank) is each score? Are there pockets of strength? Areas of real concern?

2. *Take other information into account.* View the results of SARA as part of a larger profile. Considering a student's reading achievement, areas of interest, and peer relationships can shed light on the pattern of SARA scores.

3. *Look for differences in scores.* If a student's scores are all negative to about the same extent, then they suggest no clear target for building attitude. This is not necessarily bad news, however, because such a profile indicates that a wide variety of approaches may be appropriate. On the other hand, if one or two scores are substantially below the others, it will help you narrow the focus of the approaches you select.

4. *Determine whether medium matters.* Compare each of the digital scores with the corresponding print score. If one medium is preferred over the other for both academic and recreational purposes, then medium may be an important key to motivating the student.

5. *Determine whether purpose matters.* Make a similar comparison to see if the student favors one purpose over the other regardless of medium. If so, then purpose for reading is another clue. Although it is likely that a struggling student will prefer recreational to academic reading, this fact should not be taken for granted.

6. *Remember that your role is that of broker.* Interpreting a profile of scores is an empty exercise unless you can respond in a way that is likely to improve a student's attitudes. You must be able to recommend a broad range of print and digital resources. A library media specialist can help. You must also be aware of activities and assignments that are likely to target the medium and purpose you have chosen.

7. *Remember that the student's role is that of client.* In a customer relationship, a salesperson does whatever it takes to make the customer happy. But in a client relationship, the service provider recommends what the client needs. For teachers, this means exercising caution about recommending a particular source or activity simply because it is likely to make a student happy. Is it acceptable for a student to browse through magazines simply because there is text here and there? (A principal we know calls this "grazing.") Is playing video games a productive use of time simply because there are occasionally directions and messages to be read? We believe there is common ground between activities and sources that are likely to motivate a particular student and that, at the same time, are rich (and enriching) reading experiences. With a little thought, an activity or source can have both qualities.

8. *Mount a two-pronged attack.* Two very different strategies are possible. One is to target the most negative of the four attitudes (most likely, academic print) and attempt to make that attitude more positive by means of carefully chosen activities and sources. For example, if a student harbors an especially negative attitude toward reading print for academic purposes, a teacher might suggest a book that is aligned with the curricular goal but that also reflects an interest area of the student. The other strategy is to exploit a strength among the attitudes. A struggling student whose attitude toward recreational digital reading is a relative strength (also likely) might be given opportunities to engage in activities of this nature that are connected with curricular goals.

(continued)

Percentile Ranks by Grade and Gender

Percentile Ranks
for the Recreational Print Subscale

Grade	Gender	Percentile rank				
		10	25	50	75	90
6	Girls	14	17	22	26	29
	Boys	9	13	18	22	26
7	Girls	13	16	21	25	29
	Boys	9	13	17	22	26
8	Girls	13	17	21	25	29
	Boys	8	12	17	21	25

Percentile Ranks
for the Recreational Digital Subscale

Grade	Gender	Percentile rank				
		10	25	50	75	90
6	Girls	11	15	*a*	17	18
	Boys	9	13	16	17	18
7	Girls	10	14	17	—	18
	Boys	8	12	16	17	18
8	Girls	13	15	*b*	*c*	18
	Boys	10	13	16	17	18

[a]A score of 16 corresponds to the 38th percentile rank.
[b]A score of 16 corresponds to the 26th percentile rank.
[c]A score of 17 corresponds to the 33rd percentile rank.

Percentile Ranks
for the Academic Print Subscale

Grade	Gender	Percentile rank				
		10	25	50	75	90
6	Girls	10	14	17	21	25
	Boys	8	12	16	20	23
7	Girls	10	13	17	21	24
	Boys	8	12	15	19	23
8	Girls	10	13	17	21	24
	Boys	8	12	16	19	23

Percentile Ranks
for the Academic Digital Subscale

Grade	Gender	Percentile rank				
		90	25	50	75	90
6	Girls	14	18	21	25	28
	Boys	11	15	20	23	27
7	Girls	14	17	20	24	27
	Boys	12	15	19	23	27
8	Girls	13	16	20	23	26
	Boys	11	15	19	22	26

(continued)

Survey of Adolescent Reading Attitudes (SARA) Scoresheet

Student Name _____ Grade _____

Teacher _____ Administration Date _____

	Print	Digital
	2.	4.
	8.	10.
Recreational raw score: ____	9.	15.
	11.	
	13.	
	Raw score/Avg: ____/____ ____%ile	Raw score/Avg: ____/____ ____%ile
	Print	Digital
	3.	1.
	6.	5.
Academic raw score: ____	14.	7.
	17.	12.
	18.	16.
	Raw score/Avg: ____/____ ____%ile	Raw score/Avg: ____/____ ____%ile
	Print full raw score/Avg: ____/____	Digital full raw score/Avg: ____/____

(continued)

Survey of Adolescent Reading Attitudes

1. How do you feel about reading news online for class?

   Very Good   Very Bad

   6   5   4   3   2   1

2. How do you feel about reading a book in your free time?

   Very Good   Very Bad

   6   5   4   3   2   1

3. How do you feel about doing research using encyclopedias (or other books) for a class?

   Very Good   Very Bad

   6   5   4   3   2   1

4. How do you feel about texting or e-mailing friends in your free time?

   Very Good   Very Bad

   6   5   4   3   2   1

5. How do you feel about reading online for a class?

   Very Good   Very Bad

   6   5   4   3   2   1

6. How do you feel about reading a textbook?

   Very Good   Very Bad

   6   5   4   3   2   1

7. How do you feel about reading a book online for a class?

   Very Good   Very Bad

   6   5   4   3   2   1

8. How do you feel about talking with friends about something you've been reading in your free time?

   Very Good   Very Bad

   6   5   4   3   2   1

9. How do you feel about getting a book or a magazine for a present?

   Very Good   Very Bad

   6   5   4   3   2   1

10. How do you feel about texting friends in your free time?

    Very Good   Very Bad

    6   5   4   3   2   1

11. How do you feel about reading a book for fun on a rainy Saturday?

    Very Good   Very Bad

    6   5   4   3   2   1

12. How do you feel about working on an Internet project with classmates?

    Very Good   Very Bad

    6   5   4   3   2   1

13. How do you feel about reading anything printed (book, magazine, comic books, etc.) in your free time?

    Very Good   Very Bad

    6   5   4   3   2   1

14. How do you feel about using a dictionary for class?

    Very Good   Very Bad

    6   5   4   3   2   1

15. How do you feel about being on social media like Facebook, Instagram, or Twitter in your free time?

    Very Good   Very Bad

    6   5   4   3   2   1

16. How do you feel about looking up information online for a class?

    Very Good   Very Bad

    6   5   4   3   2   1

17. How do you feel about reading a newspaper or a magazine for a class?

    Very Good   Very Bad

    6   5   4   3   2   1

18. How do you feel about reading a novel for class?

    Very Good   Very Bad

    6   5   4   3   2   1

ELEVEN

Assessing Readers in Grades 4–8

Guiding Concepts

THREE STRUGGLING OLDER READERS: A PREFACE

Consider these three adolescent readers:

Maya is an eighth grader who possesses rich background knowledge on a variety of topics, has a strong oral vocabulary, and regularly offers insightful comments in her world history and earth science classes. Furthermore, she can understand most texts read aloud to her when she listens to her audiobooks. When she reads herself, she can recognize many short, high-frequency words automatically (e.g., *the, for, can*); however, she struggles to decode the longer, polysyllabic words (e.g., pronouncing HOPPING for *hoping*) and content-area vocabulary words containing multiple word parts (e.g., *transcontinental railroad, calibrate*) found in her textbooks. She says that her decoding difficulty "slows my reading way down," and "makes it hard to understand what I read," particularly in texts higher than her fifth-grade instructional reading level.

Zach is a sixth grader who can fluently read nearly any material he is given. While reading narrative texts, he is able to make sensible predictions and inferences, particularly when he has some background knowledge related to a topic. However, in informational texts, he often struggles to identify the main ideas and summarize key points, and his difficulties are impairing his comprehension in his classes. His history and science textbooks, in particular, contain an overwhelming number of unfamiliar vocabulary terms and concepts (e.g., *isolationism, osmosis, synapse*) and difficult varied text structures (e.g., compare–contrast, cause–effect, problem–solution). When asked what he does when his reading comprehension breaks down, he admits that he doesn't have any "go-to" strategies to use, so he just "kind of struggles through it."

Michael is a fifth grader who says he "can't stand having to read the kinds of books we get in school." When he is engaged, he can fluently read and comprehend some grade-level texts. However, he often appears disengaged, looking out the window, sighing, and putting his head down on his desk—anything to avoid reading. Michael's teachers note that his lack of reading practice is beginning to have negative effects on his content knowledge, vocabulary, and general comprehension in more complex texts. If they cannot find a way to engage him in successfully reading more complex texts, they are concerned that he will fall farther behind his peers as he moves into middle school and beyond.

Like the three children described at the beginning of Chapter 1, these three older children were each categorized as *Not Proficient* on their high-stakes state assessments. However, they each struggled with the test for different reasons, and they each need different instructional interventions. The children described above are composites of real cases, as the ones in Chapter 1 are—and, like the Chapter 1 children, they represent important profiles of reading difficulties that teachers must be prepared to identify and address.

OLDER READERS WHO STRUGGLE: THE STATISTICS

Unfortunately, older readers who struggle—like Maya, Zach, and Michael—are not alone. In fact, on the 2017 NAEP Reading Report Card, more than 60% of students in grades 4 and 8 did not achieve at the Proficient or Advanced levels (National Center for Education Statistics, 2017), the levels usually associated with successfully reading at or above grade level. In view of this alarming statistic, it's not surprising that adolescent literacy experts estimate that nearly 70% of adolescents across the United States struggle to read on grade level. The result is a national adolescent literacy crisis (Biancarosa & Snow, 2006).

Time is ticking for millions of older students who struggle to read. If reading is the gateway to learning in the content areas, many of these students feel as if their gate has been shut. Too many have already given up on school. An astonishing 7,000 high school students drop out of school *every single day* in the United States (Alliance for Excellent Education, 2006); experts cite the lack of adequate academic literacy skills necessary for success in the middle and secondary curricula as a primary reason (Kamil, 2003).

OLDER READERS' DEVELOPMENTAL STAGES: START WITH WHAT THEY KNOW

Behind these alarming and staggering numbers lie individual students like Maya, Zach, and Michael with their own strengths, hopes, and dreams. For their entire academic lives, many of these older students have too often been told—directly or indirectly— what they *can't* do. To get to know these students and address their individual needs, we first need to find out what they *can* do as readers, writers, and learners. Skilled and thoughtful use of authentic reading assessments, in conjunction with a developmental approach, is a powerful way to do this.

Most of the older readers in grades 4–8 that we work with find themselves in one of the following three developmental reading stages: *transitional, intermediate,* or *advanced.* Table 11.1 illustrates important characteristics of these three advanced stages. (See Table 1.2 in Chapter 1 for an overview of all five developmental stages.)

These three developmental stages serve as an organizing framework for the rest of

TABLE 11.1. The Development of Reading, Writing, and Spelling across Transitional, Intermediate, and Advanced Stages

Reading/ spelling stage (from Bear et al., 2020)	Reading levels	Reading strategy: How readers process and store words	Reading and writing characteristics and focus	Word-study focus (spelling, decoding, and vocabulary)
Transitional readers/ within word pattern spellers	Late first to late third grades	• Consolidated alphabetic phase (Ehri, 1998) • Processes words in letter "chunks" or patterns as single units (*-ake* in *cake*)	• Approaching reading and writing fluency • Beginning to read silently, with expression and in phrasal units • Increases reading rates, nearing 100 WPM by end of stage	Word-study features: • Common long-vowel patterns (*cake, rain*) • *r*-Influenced vowels (*care, store*) • Less common vowel patterns (*eight*) • Complex consonant patterns (*judge, patch*) • Ambiguous vowels (*brown, soil*) • Homographs and homophones (*bear* vs. *bare*)
Intermediate readers/ syllables and affixes spellers	Late third to sixth grades	• Processes multisyllabic words by syllable (*autocracy* as *au-toc-ra-cy*) • Processes and stores words by across-syllable patterns (VCCV, *hopping,* vs. VCV, *hoping*)	• Solid reading fluency by end of stage • Reading challenges stem increasingly from conceptual load, vocabulary, and background knowledge • Increased focus on strategic reading, content-area learning, and writer's craft	Word-study features: • Compound words (*pancake*) • Inflectional endings and doubling (*hopping* vs. *hoping*) • Open and closed syllables (VCCV, *button,* vs. VCV, *bacon*) • High-frequency prefixes and suffixes with base words (*reuse, redo*)
Advanced readers/ derivational relations spellers	Sixth grade and up	• Processes words by morphemes, including Greek and Latin affixes/roots (*autocracy* as *auto-cracy*)	• Exploring and developing expertise in specific topics, genres, styles, texts, and academic vocabulary • Learning discipline-specific reading/ writing/thinking approaches (e.g., reading like a historian)	• Word-study features: • Prefixes and suffixes (*inter-*, "between"— *intercontinental*) • Consonant and vowel alternations (*sign/signal/ signature*) • Greek and Latin word elements (*-crat/-cracy,* "rule" —*democracy*)

Note. Based on Bear, Invernizzi, Templeton, and Johnston (2020) and Ehri (1998).

this chapter as we discuss assessing reading with older students in grades 4–8. Consider the following points regarding these stages:

- Students at each stage possess certain strengths and skills. As you assess and work with these students, make sure you let the students know what they can already do well. A good place to start is to remind them that they've "mastered" everything at the previous stage. In this way, you begin with a focus on assets rather than deficits—a critical point for older students who may have struggled for much of their time in school.

- When assessing or working with older students, pay close attention to their reading, writing, and spelling characteristics—both what they can do (the skills they have mastered) and what they are ready to work on next (their ZPD; see Chapter 3). This will help you determine which stage of development most closely matches their knowledge and skills, and what their instruction should focus on. For example, Maya (the eighth grader described at the start of the chapter) is an intermediate reader who demonstrates strong listening comprehension and background knowledge, but still needs to work on (1) her decoding and spelling of multisyllabic words and (2) her reading fluency. Parents and teachers often tell us that this type of developmental information—explaining the reading, writing, and spelling characteristics of a student at a particular stage—is much more informative than simply saying, "Maya is an eighth grader reading at the fifth-grade level."

- These stages are not rigidly sequential, so don't be surprised if a student who is moving from one stage to the next exhibits some characteristics from each stage; however, this developmental framework is a powerful general tool for identifying where a student is, and thus what to work on next.

- Older students who struggle with reading may have many different needs. We have found that progress is sometimes held back by well-intentioned instruction that tries to do too much at once. It is imperative for teachers to analyze the assessment in order to identify and prioritize a few target areas for sustained instruction and practice.

READING AND READING ASSESSMENT IN THE MIDDLE GRADES: WHAT'S THE SAME AND WHAT'S DIFFERENT?

While the statistics on struggling readers are certainly alarming, there is hope. We know that excellent, knowledgeable teachers can make a real difference with older readers who struggle. And, as with younger students, assessment is the first step in addressing their needs. Many of the core principles of assessment described earlier in this book apply to older readers, with modifications regarding how they are implemented. However, there are some important differences, too.

In the remainder of this chapter, we introduce these similarities and differences in terms of eight critical concepts we believe are essential for assessing and working with older readers (see Figure 11.1). We finish our discussion of each assessment concept with a subsection titled "Assessment Application," in which we highlight how you can apply that concept in your classroom and school with older readers. We discuss Assessment

---

Assessment Concepts for Older Readers

Concepts for Getting Started

1. Older students who struggle to read are not all the same.
2. Identify and target developmental-level needs.

Cognitive Pathway 1

3. Word-recognition struggles continue, but may look different, for older readers.
4. Fluency still requires attention for many older readers.

Cognitive Pathway 2

5. Reading challenges stem increasingly from the "what"—conceptual load, background knowledge, and academic vocabulary.
6. Listening comprehension level (vs. instructional reading level) is a critical concept for older readers who struggle.

Cognitive Pathway 3

7. Assess target strategies and ways of thinking (the "how") in authentic content-area texts and tasks.
8. Engagement is the engine that drives reading growth.

FIGURE 11.1. Reading and reading assessment in the middle grades: What's the same and what's different?

Concepts 3–8 below in terms of the three cognitive pathways we have introduced in Chapter 1. Assessment Concepts 1 and 2 are important for getting started.

CONCEPTS FOR GETTING STARTED

Assessment Concept 1: Older Students Who Struggle to Read Are Not All the Same

As noted at the beginning of this chapter, Maya, Zach, and Michael were each identified as *Not Proficient* on their high-stakes state assessments. However, as is true of younger readers who struggle, *older struggling readers are not all the same*. Although they all struggled on the test, each struggled for different reasons and in different components of literacy:

- Maya demonstrates strong listening comprehension, but struggles to decode multisyllabic words and read grade-level texts fluently.
- Zach can read most school texts fluently, but experiences difficulty with unfamiliar vocabulary terms and concepts and comprehension of informational texts.
- Michael has become disengaged from reading and doesn't see how "school reading" can be connected to his own life. Because he avoids reading, he's falling farther and farther behind his peers.

Each of these three readers represents a common profile of older readers we have actually worked with. Because they are all different, a "one size fits all" program or single approach won't work for them. While this may seem obvious, we are continually surprised at the overreliance on "this program" or "that approach" as the cure-all to teach our neediest students. We strongly believe that programs don't teach students, teachers do.

Assessment Application: Use Assessments, Not Programs, to Plan Instruction

1. Find the "where" for each student. Assess your students to find their developmental levels (e.g., fourth-grade reading level, spelling at the within word pattern stage). Use Table 11.1 to help determine their literacy stage. This will let you know where to start instruction.
2. Find the "what." Assess your students to find their specific reading profiles, including strengths and areas of need (e.g., strong in fluency, struggles with comprehension). Our cognitive model (again, see Chapter 1) will help you determine what components of reading to target for instruction.
3. *Do not* blindly use a "one size fits all" program with your students. Programs are tools; they are never the complete answer.
4. *Do* use approaches, instructional strategies, and programs (or parts of programs) thoughtfully, basing your instructional decisions on each student's assessment information, including their individual patterns of strengths and needs.
5. Use progress-monitoring tools to assess incremental growth. This ensures fidelity to each student, not to the program.

Programs, in the hands of expert literacy teachers, can be extremely useful tools. However, rather than putting all of our educational eggs in the basket of a single cure-all program, we believe it is much more effective to prepare high-quality, expert, thoughtful teachers to identify (1) our older students' reading strengths and (2) their areas of need, in order to develop (3) intervention plans that are individually designed to meet them *where they are*. The use of a simple diagnostic report template is demonstrated in the Appendix (Case Study 1: Moe), and such a template can be helpful in documenting this process.

Assessment Concept 2: Identify and Target Developmental-Level Needs

When assessing an older student who reads below grade level, we are often confronted with a dilemma that's all too common in the upper grades: What if the student's developmental-level needs do not match his or her grade-level expectations? What if no time in the day or no place in the grade-level curriculum is set aside to work on what they actually need?

Take the example of the eighth grader, Maya, introduced at the start of the chapter. Based on Maya's IRI and spelling inventory, we start with what she already knows, which includes the ability to read and spell most short- and long-vowel, ambiguous-vowel, and *r*-influenced vowel patterns (see the characteristics of transitional readers/within word pattern spellers in Table 11.1). However, we also find that she struggles to spell and decode many multisyllabic words (e.g., she decodes HOPING for the word *hopping* and spells *pilot* as PILLOT—miscues characteristic of intermediate readers in the syllables and affixes spelling stage). Now we know exactly where we need to start her decoding and spelling instruction.

Grade-Level Expectations versus Developmental-Level Needs

Thus, from a developmental perspective, it makes perfect sense to start Maya's word-study work at the syllable and affixes stage with multisyllabic words. This is Maya's ZPD (again, see Chapter 3). However, as illustrated in Table 11.2, there is a mismatch between Maya's developmental-level needs and her eighth-grade-level curricular expectations.

As highlighted in Table 11.2, Maya's eighth-grade state standards say *nothing* about accurately reading multisyllabic words in context. This is because the "average" eighth grader is assumed to have already mastered many of these skills by approximately fifth grade. Put simply, what Maya needs is not provided in her eighth-grade curriculum. (Her grade-level curriculum does focus on vocabulary, which is a strength for Maya and which she, like all eighth graders, also needs.)

Assessment Application: Find Mismatches between a Student's Developmental-Level Needs and the Grade-Level Expectations

If we only follow the grade-level curriculum, we may never address the very areas that students like Maya need to work on. Unfortunately, for many older readers who struggle like Maya, the middle school curriculum and classroom schedules are often not set up to differentiate instruction as easily as they are in a typical elementary school classroom. We need to take a step back and address Maya's needs, so that she can eventually catch up to her grade-level peers in decoding and spelling. In Maya's case, as with many struggling readers, *a step back is a step forward* (Bear et al., 2020).

Therefore, we recommend the following after assessing older students and identifying their developmental needs:

1. Review the grade-level curriculum and create a needs–expectations chart like Maya's in Table 11.2. Charts like this can be created at the classroom level or grade level to group students who have common needs.
2. If there is a mismatch between what a student needs and what the normal cur-

TABLE 11.2. The Mismatch: Maya's Developmental-Level Needs versus Eighth-Grade-Level Expectations

Maya's areas of instructional need	Maya's developmental-level needs[a]	Eighth-grade-level expectations
Word study	Syllables and affixes work (spelling and decoding multisyllabic words)	Main focus is vocabulary

[a]These are *not* part of the typical eighth-grade curriculum.

riculum provides, create an *intervention plan* that fills in the instructional gap in the day and the curriculum.

3. For this intervention plan, identify (a) *what* each student needs (e.g., word study with multisyllabic words); (b) *when* the student will receive this instruction (e.g., during ELA and during reading support class); and (c) *who* will provide the instruction (e.g., Mr. Halpin and Ms. Jeffries).

While identifying an older reader's needs and then providing targeted instruction in those areas may seem ridiculously obvious, it is startling how often, for older students in particular, the grade-level expectations and curriculum become the default instruction. This default then takes valuable time, energy, and resources away from a student's specific literacy needs.

COGNITIVE PATHWAY 1: AUTOMATIC WORD RECOGNITION

Assessment Concepts 3 and 4 fall under Pathway 1 in our cognitive model (see Chapter 1).

Assessment Concept 3: Word-Recognition Struggles Continue, but May Look Different, for Many Older Readers

There is a common misconception that only a tiny percentage of older students who struggle to read still have word-recognition and decoding problems once they reach the upper elementary and middle school grades. This flawed logic often goes something like this: Once students learn a core set of 100–300 high-frequency words and some basic phonics and decoding skills in the primary grades, they've got all the decoding and spelling knowledge they really need to move forward as readers and writers. From this point on, they really only need to work on their comprehension and vocabulary. This is a myth. In fact, among older students who struggle to read, *a significant percentage still struggle to recognize words accurately and automatically and to read grade-level text fluently*. While this percentage may vary from school to school, a few studies can give us an estimate of the size of this group.

In one classic study of fifth graders who failed a fourth-grade state reading assessment, Valencia and Buly (2004) identified six different profiles of struggling readers. Students exhibiting one profile ("struggling word callers") struggled with both word recognition and comprehension when reading connected text. Others ("slow comprehenders") did not read fluently, but still managed to comprehend. Importantly, *at least 41% of the struggling fifth-grade readers in this study had word-identification problems*. If we add "slow word callers" (those students who could decode words accurately, but not automatically, which we argue is a word-recognition issue), this percentage of struggling readers with word-recognition issues rises to 58%. Other studies estimate that one-third or more of older readers who struggle experience decoding issues, along with other literacy skills (Catts, Hogan, & Adolf, 2005; Deshler, Palinscar, Biancarosa, & Nair, 2007; Hock et al., 2006; Leach, Scarborough, & Rescorla, 2003).

In sum, while the specific percentages may vary from school to school, it's likely that one-third or more of older struggling readers will have decoding and word-recognition issues that still need to be addressed. And if they have word-recognition issues, it's likely that they will have struggles in other areas of literacy, too, like fluency and comprehension (see our cognitive model in Chapter 1). Clearly, it's critical to have a battery of reading assessments and related interventions that address decoding and word knowledge with those older readers who need it.

Many Older Struggling Readers Need Work with Multisyllabic Words

Maya is an example of an "older struggling word caller." While she can decode most high-frequency and single-syllable words, she struggles to decode and spell the more complex types of multisyllabic words that so frequently appear in middle and high school reading material. Importantly, she does *not* need phonemic awareness instruction, basic phonics instruction, or the simpler letter-by-letter decoding strategies we use with beginning readers in the primary grades or with students who have poor phonological processing problems. Rather, she needs the more sophisticated work on word knowledge and decoding that will equip her with the knowledge and skills to break down, store, and recognize more difficult words by pattern, syllable, and morpheme (e.g., *com-plain, hop-ping, retro-spect, un-govern-able*).

Assessment Application:
Assess and Teach Word Knowledge by Pattern, Syllable, and Morpheme

Use a developmental spelling inventory and the Multisyllabic Words subtest of the Informal Decoding Inventory (Walpole & McKenna, 2017; see Form 5.3) to assess transitional, intermediate, or advanced readers' word knowledge. What's most important when you are analyzing these assessments with older students is to identify which stage each student is in. Doing so will let you know where to start and focus your word-study instruction. So, instead of focusing on phonemes, single letters, short vowels, and blends and digraphs, you'll most likely be focusing on the following more sophisticated aspects of word knowledge with older readers who need word-knowledge work:

- *Pattern.* Transitional readers in the within word pattern stage should focus on common long- and abstract-vowel patterns (e.g., *ai* in *rain*, *oa* in *soap*, *ou* in *cloud*).
- *Syllable.* Intermediate readers in the syllable and affixes stage should focus on multisyllabic words, including the critical across-syllable patterns (e.g., the VCCV pattern in *hopping*, the VCV pattern in *pilot*).
- *Morpheme.* Advanced readers in the derivational relations stage should focus on high-utility prefixes, suffixes, and Latin and Greek roots (e.g., *trans-*, "across"—*transfer, transatlantic, transcontinental*).

Two important caveats are in order for word study with older readers:

1. Remember that word-study instruction alone won't "fix" older readers' word-recognition or decoding issues. They also need to practice and apply what they learn

in context. This means a lot of engaging reading in instructional-level texts (in addition to more supported reading in "stretch" texts) and writing for meaning across their day, week, month, and year. Too often, we work with older students who are taught with an explicit decoding program, but who don't read enough to internalize and apply these skills in context. This would be like learning to do a jump shot in a basketball drill, but never being given time to practice it in a scrimmage or game. Remember, the goal of word-study instruction is to create better readers and writers.

2. It's not uncommon for some older students to be good readers and poor spellers (Frith, 1980). In fact, we can all read words that we can't spell; Bear et al. (2020) call this phenomenon the *reading–spelling slant*. What this means for instruction is that we can often teach older students some decoding skills and vocabulary at a slighter higher level than their developmental spelling stage (where we teach spelling). So, for a student like Maya, we can teach her decoding and spelling at the syllables and affixes stage and still work with her on some high-utility Latin and Greek roots (the focus of the next stage, derivational relations) for her vocabulary work. This is an excellent way to meet her developmental-level needs while still working on her grade-level expectations.

Assessment Concept 4:
Fluency Still Requires Attention for Many Older Readers

As discussed in Chapter 6, *fluency* means being able to read a text (1) accurately, (2) automatically, and (3) with appropriate prosody. As they do with word knowledge, a significant percentage of older readers who struggle experience issues with fluency. In fact, word-recognition and fluency issues often occur together; a reader who has difficulty accurately and automatically recognizing individual words is also likely to have difficulty reading words effortlessly and fluently in context.

This is a critical point, because we've worked with a number of older students who have fluency issues and are only working on fluency. Fluency work alone won't solve a reader's problems if weak word knowledge is a root cause of fluency issues (see our cognitive model as depicted in Figure 6.1). If this is the case, the intervention needs to address both word knowledge and fluency.

Many older readers who still need to work in fluency are caught in the stage of transitional reading and within word pattern spelling (see Table 11.1). Because of this, our colleague Regina Smith calls the transitional stage the "black hole" of reading for older readers. If you don't put an intervention plan in place, the default instruction too often becomes the grade-level curriculum. And because the typical curricula in the middle and secondary grades assume that older readers have already "mastered" fluent reading, these dysfluent readers won't get what they need. However, with proper instruction and support, they can escape this black hole and continue to grow as readers and writers. Once you have assessed an older reader who has fluency issues, identify the component(s) of fluency that the reader is struggling with the most: prosody, reading rate, or accuracy. Next, match the student's fluency need(s) with a few of the appropriate strategies found in Chapter 6.

Assessment Application: Miscue Analysis with Older Students—Analyzing Bigger Word Parts, Including Patterns, Syllables, and Morphemes

When we analyze miscues with intermediate and advanced readers, we are looking at how they process "bigger word parts" than they did in the primary grades. This is important and can change how you interpret a reader's miscue. To see how this might play out in your analysis, consider Figures 11.2 and 11.3, which show the "Graphically similar?" section of the Miscue Analysis Chart (Form 3.2) for two readers: Mika, a first-grade beginning reader, and KJ, a seventh-grade intermediate reader.

Mika, when attempting to read the word *cat,* instead read the word *can.* If this same pattern held for the majority of her miscues, we might conclude that Mika is strong at decoding the beginning and middles of words; however, we need to draw her attention to the ends of words during word-study instruction and contextual reading. Importantly, for Mika, by "ends of words" we mean words ending in single letters (the *-t* in *cat*) and possibly ending blends and digraphs (the *-sh* in *wish*), because single letters, blends, and digraphs are the word parts that beginning readers can recognize, store, and process.

Contrast this with KJ, who attempted to read the word *constriction* as con-strict-TYE-ON. We would definitely give KJ credit for processing the beginning (the prefix *con-*) and middle (the root *-strict-*) parts of the word. This is because prefixes and roots like *con-* and *-strict-* are morphemes, the "bigger word parts" we want older readers to be able to store and process.

However, should we give KJ credit for pronouncing the suffix ending the word, *-tion,* letter by letter—that is, as TYE-ON rather than /shun/? We would argue no. As an intermediate reader, we expect KJ to be able to process bigger word parts (e.g., syllables and morphemes) than Mika can handle. So, while analyzing KJ's miscues, we are holding him to a higher standard, because he is an intermediate reader and knows more about words and word parts than Mika. This is where our knowledge of reading development helps us to analyze his reading more insightfully and precisely.

Additional Fluency Considerations with Older Readers

• The vast majority of reading that most middle and high school students do each day will probably be silent. Older students' silent reading rates should be faster than their oral reading rates. If students are experiencing difficulty moving into silent reading (most likely at the transitional reader stage), a powerful strategy we've used in our clinics to move them gradually from oral to silent reading is the so-called "1 + 1 + 1" strategy (Morris, 2014), in which (1) the teacher models a chunk of text orally, (2) the student reads a second chunk orally, and (3) the student reads a third chunk silently. The teacher

Text says	Student says	Graphically similar?		
		B	M	E
cat	can	+	+	

FIGURE 11.2. Miscue analysis for Mika, a first-grade beginning reader.

Text says	Student says	Graphically similar?		
		B	M	E
constriction	con-strict-TYE-ON	+	+	

FIGURE 11.3. Miscue analysis for KJ, a seventh-grade intermediate reader.

gradually increases the silent chunk of reading as the student improves his or her reading stamina.

• As much as possible, incorporate fluency work with content-area learning. Famous speeches (history) and poetry (ELA) are excellent possibilities.

• Some older students have strong accuracy and rate, but struggle with prosody. This is often due to the difficult language patterns (e.g., complex sentence structures with multiple clauses) found in more complex texts. Tell older readers that each phrase is an "idea unit." Help students visually highlight phrases and clauses in complex sentences, and model how to break them down into these "idea units." Model what each idea unit contributes to the entire sentence. This is a powerful way to connect prosody and comprehension for older students.

COGNITIVE PATHWAY 2: ORAL LANGUAGE COMPREHENSION

Assessment Concepts 5 and 6 fall under Pathway 2 in our cognitive model (see Chapter 1).

Assessment Concept 5: Reading Challenges Stem Increasingly from the "What"—Conceptual Load, Background Knowledge, and Academic Vocabulary

To get a sense of just how overwhelming the "what" of the upper-grades curriculum can be to an older learner, consider Figure 11.4, which presents 24 terms and related con-

Hawaiian Annexation	Bayonet Constitution	McKinley Tariff
Spanish-American War	Platt Amendment	Treaty of Paris
Boxer Rebellion	Open Door Policy	Queen Lili'uokalani
Grover Cleveland	Emilio Aguinaldo	Theodore Roosevelt
Rough Riders	William Randolph Hearst	yellow journalism
imperialism	Expansionism	jingoism
Manifest Destiny	Roosevelt Corollary	dollar diplomacy
protectorate	sphere of influence	Social Darwinism

FIGURE 11.4. American imperialism: 24 domain-specific vocabulary terms and concepts.

cepts a middle or high school American history student might be expected to learn from just one typical history textbook chapter titled "American Imperialism."

Now imagine that you are Zach, the sixth grader introduced at the beginning of this chapter. Zach can read nearly anything fluently but struggles with comprehension, largely due to lack of background knowledge in content-area topics and academic vocabulary issues. For Zach and many other older students, these 24 *domain-specific* terms and concepts—sophisticated academic vocabulary items that are usually only encountered in a history class—represent an overwhelming deluge of unfamiliar ideas that they will have to learn from the ground up. As addressed in Chapter 7, these Tier Three vocabulary terms require in-depth knowledge of the new concepts surrounding them, not just synonyms for familiar concepts.

Not only are these 24 history-specific terms and concepts overwhelming to Zach, but as he begins to read the chapter, he also encounters *general academic language* he's seen used across science, social studies, and math—terms that also contribute to his confusion, such as *moreover, preceding, ultimately, notwithstanding, the former,* and *as a result of.*

The history example above highlights a number of important challenges posed by the textbooks and other reading materials typically encountered in the upper elementary grades, middle school, and high school:

1. The sheer number and depth of *domain-specific* terms and related concepts.
2. The use of an unfamiliar *general academic vocabulary,* which serves to tie the domain-specific terms and concepts together (e.g., *moreover, notwithstanding*).
3. The fact that, in contrast to the primary grades, students often possess limited relevant background knowledge related to many unfamiliar vocabulary terms and major concepts (e.g., *Social Darwinism, yellow journalism, isotope, polynomial*).
4. The utilization of unfamiliar academic language that includes discourse styles unique to each discipline.

Assessment Application: Identify an Instructional-Level <u>Range</u>, as Opposed to a Single Instructional Reading Level

As you can see from the history example given above (and as discussed in Chapter 3), the interaction of multiple pressure points—prior knowledge, academic vocabulary, genre, text structure, working memory, self-regulation, and motivation—plays an increasingly greater role in reading success for older students. And because of the dynamic interaction among these multiple factors, it becomes increasingly difficult to identify reading levels as you move up the grades. Therefore, with fluent intermediate and advanced readers, it's not uncommon—and instructionally very useful—to identify an instructional-level *range* for many older readers (e.g., sixth to eighth grades), as opposed to a single instructional level (e.g., seventh grade).

For example, Zach, a sixth grader, is able to read sixth-grade-level narrative stories with strong comprehension. However, on informational IRI passages, he is only able to read up to a fourth-grade level with solid comprehension. Thus it appears that Zach has two different reading levels: fourth grade for informational texts and sixth grade for narrative texts.

However, suppose we work with Zach and find that that simply preteaching him a few key concepts and vocabulary terms before reading a science text significantly improves his comprehension of that text. In this case, we might identify Zach as having an instructional reading range of fourth to sixth grades, depending on the following factors: (1) the type of text (narrative vs. informational); (2) his level of background knowledge related to that text; and (3) the types of comprehension supports we put in place, such as "front-loading" key vocabulary terms and concepts.

We find that identifying an instructional reading range (rather than a single level) not only provides a more accurate, complete picture of a reader; it can also be instructionally more useful with older students, because it allows us to determine precisely what types of supports these students need in order to comprehend increasingly rigorous texts. In this way, we can "push" Zach, with appropriate supports and within reason, to read more difficult reading material successfully.

Assessment Application: Use Questions before, during, and after Reading to Assess Prior Knowledge and Comprehension

Prior-Knowledge Questions (before Reading). Research has made it clear that readers with richer prior knowledge of a text comprehend better than readers with less prior knowledge (Alvermann, Smith, & Readance, 1985; Lipson, 1983). Furthermore, older readers are more likely to encounter texts in school for which they don't possess a lot of background knowledge (think of your high school physics textbook!). With this in mind:

- If readers *do* have prior knowledge of a text, it's important to find out how well they can/cannot use it to help them comprehend the text.
- If readers *do not* possess much prior knowledge (a common scenario in many upper-grades content classes), it's also important to find out to what degree they can successfully make sense of the text.

Some IRIs include questions you can ask before a student reads a passage that tap a student's prior knowledge of the concepts in the upcoming passage. Or, if you are asking a student to read an IRI or a textbook passage that does not include prior-knowledge questions, you can develop your own. Three to four of these questions are usually sufficient. We rate prior knowledge holistically, based on the overall sum of a student's answers to all of our prior-knowledge questions, using a 3-point scale: (3) strong relevant prior knowledge; (2) adequate/mixed/some relevant prior knowledge; (1) little to no relevant prior knowledge.

Think of the following when you are developing prior-knowledge questions:

- What are the key concepts or critical ideas for which a reader needs to have some background knowledge to get the gist of a passage of text? Examples: "What are amphibians? What's a black hole? Why do immigrants move to new countries?"

- What are important vocabulary words, terms, or phrases that represent critical concepts and/or are necessary to understand the passage? Examples: "What does it mean to be *oppressed*? Can you give an example? What does a *mediator* do? Why might we need *mediators*?"
- What are the important people, things, or events that are central to the passage? Examples: "Who was Sojourner Truth? Have you heard of the Domesday Book? What is it? What happened on D-Day?"

Embedded Questions (during Reading). As with prior-knowledge questions, you can either use the embedded questions included in an IRI, or develop your own. Embedded questions allow you to tap into a reader's comprehension *during* the reading process. Pick one to three stopping points at natural places in the next (for narrative stories, points of anticipation for an upcoming event; for informational texts, ends of sections or concept explanations). All the guidelines for question types discussed in Chapter 8 apply here. To dig deeper into a reader's thinking (both during reading and at any other time), ask questions such as these: "Why? Why do you think that? How do you know that? Where in the text does it support this? Was your initial predication/hypothesis right? Did you modify or change it? How do you know? Why/why not?" For instruction that requires students to read complex or lengthier texts, consider providing a reading guide that prompts students to answer questions at intermittent points in the reading task.

"Look-Back" Questions (after Reading). "Look-back" questions provide optimal comprehension levels with older readers. Imagine that Zach, the fluent sixth-grade reader with comprehension difficulties, has just finished reading a section of the history textbook chapter on American imperialism. Just as he's about to answer the comprehension questions at the end of the section—questions about many unfamiliar, difficult concepts—his teacher tells him that he's not allowed to look back in the chapter to answer the question. How would Zach feel? If you were in Zach's shoes, how would you feel? Is this a good, useful, accurate measure of Zach's comprehension?

Allowing students to look back in the text to answer questions is a more accurate, more ecologically valid measure of our older readers' comprehension ability. Here's why:

- Texts in the upper grades are usually more concept-dense, unfamiliar, and longer, placing considerably greater demands on memory than most primary-grade texts do.
- When you do not allow a student to look back in a text to address a question he or she did not immediately know the answer for, you may be assessing memory and recall, not comprehension.
- Effective readers can look back in a text and locate pertinent information. So when you allow readers to look back, you're also assessing a characteristic that skilled readers exhibit.
- For the large majority of classroom reading experiences (and lifetime reading experiences), we look back in a text to jog our memories, clarify a point, or answer a question. Look-backs mirror how we actually read in school and in life.

Thus comprehension question scores that do *not* allow look-backs may actually *underestimate* an older reader's actual comprehension level. This is why we place more weight on comprehension scores that include look-backs. In sum, for any comprehension question students do not correctly answer after reading an IRI passage or text, do the following:

1. Allow them to look back in the text to find the answer.
2. Note whether they start rereading from the beginning, or whether they are able to locate the relevant information in the appropriate place in the text quickly. This may indicate the extent of their text structure knowledge.
3. For older readers, the look-back comprehension score is probably a better indicator than a comprehension score without a look-back of their optimal comprehension ability. This is why we use the look-back comprehension score as the primary comprehension score.

Assessment Concept 6: Listening Comprehension Level (vs. Instructional Reading Level) Is a Critical Concept for Older Readers Who Struggle

Does Maya, the bright and knowledgeable eighth grader who reads instructionally at the fifth-grade level, struggle with comprehension? At first glance, one might say yes, because she struggles to comprehend her content-area textbooks when she reads them independently. However, when we dig deeper, we find that it's not actually Maya's ability to comprehend grade-level concepts, vocabulary, and ideas that is the issue; rather, the root cause of her reading difficulty is actually her lack of decoding skills, which has become a major roadblock to her comprehension.

How do we know this? When Maya uses audiobooks that are *read aloud to her* (thus bypassing her decoding struggles), her comprehension is quite strong. On the other hand, when she attempts to read these very same texts on her own, her inability to decode the more difficulty vocabulary terms (e.g., *Social Darwinism, antebellum*) understandably gets in the way of her comprehension.

Listening Comprehension Level Is Often Higher Than Instructional Reading Level

We have found that for many older readers who struggle as Maya does, their listening comprehension is higher (sometimes much higher) than their instructional reading level. This is incredibly important information, because we've found that listening comprehension level provides a general indication of a student's ability to comprehend grade-level texts; grasp content, concepts, academic vocabulary, and written language structures; and follow along during class discussions. Listening comprehension is the student's "reading potential."

To find an older student's listening comprehension level, we recommend reading aloud IRI passages (that the student has not already read) and scoring the comprehension questions as you normally would. Suppose we find that Maya has solid listening comprehension ability in eighth-grade-level narrative and expository texts. This information can be a game-changer for her, because it means that comprehension is not her issue; she *can* grasp grade-level texts, concepts, academic language, and essential vocabulary. Knowing this strength, we have to capitalize on it during our instruction.

Just imagine the potential payoff in learning if Maya were to receive regular, easy access to *all* of her required textbooks and class novels as audiobooks. This listening work could be done as homework, in class, or with a partner reading along. With the ubiquity of individual technology devices in today's schools, we've found that there is little stigma for students to have earbuds in as they listen to an audiobook while following along during classroom work time. Our goal is to stretch Maya's comprehension through her ears, at the cutting edge of her listening comprehension level, while simultaneously providing word-study and fluency intervention that continues to bridge the gap between her listening comprehension and reading comprehension levels.

Assessment Application: Conduct Individual and Whole-Class Listening Comprehension Assessments

We strongly recommend identifying listening comprehension levels for older readers who struggle. For individual students, simply *read aloud* passages to the students (instead of the students' reading the passages themselves) from an IRI, and ask the comprehension questions as you normally would. You can start at a student's grade level and move up or down as appropriate. Use passages from the Adolescent Literacy Inventory (Brozo & Afflerbach, 2011) if you want grade-level passages that are specific to each content area (e.g., ELA, social studies, science, and math). These will give you a better feel for a student's discipline-specific knowledge and comprehension ability, and thus may be more "ecologically valid" than the more general narrative or informational text passages found in most other IRIs.

We have worked with classroom content-area teachers who understandably don't feel they have the time to assess each of their students individually. They simply want a quick, efficient way to check their entire class's ability to comprehend the key ideas and concepts as presented in the content-area textbook. So, at the beginning of the year, they simply read aloud a representative section of the content-area textbook to the whole class, allowing students to follow along if they want in their own copies of the textbook. Afterward, they ask their students to answer, in writing, five to eight questions that get at the key concepts and main ideas from the reading. Some teachers also ask their students to write a one-paragraph summary of what was read aloud. Just as with other comprehension assessment options we've discussed, teachers can (1) calculate a basic comprehension score (e.g., 80%) from the questions, and/or (2) analyze the students' summaries on a 3-point scale (target = 3, developing = 2, emerging or not present = 1). This procedure can serve as an efficient whole-class screening for students who may struggle with content-area reading and writing.

COGNITIVE PATHWAY 3: STRATEGIC KNOWLEDGE

Assessment Concepts 7 and 8 fall under Pathway 3 in our cognitive model (see Chapter 1).

Assessment Concept 7: Assess Target Strategies and Ways of Thinking (the "How") in Authentic Content-Area Texts and Tasks

Older readers are expected to think critically and creatively in increasingly sophisticated ways while reading—the "how" of middle and secondary reading. This includes the ability to independently apply target strategies and ways of thinking such as *summarizing, hypothesizing,* and *sourcing evidence* in support of arguments. Often these ways of reading and thinking are specific to each discipline (e.g., applying the scientific process). In other words, it's not just *what* students are reading that's changing in the upper grades; *how* they are expected to read the texts is also changing. It's not just the *texts* that pose increasing demands; it's also the *tasks*.

Again, let's take the example of Zach from the chapter introduction. In early elementary school, Zach's teachers assessed his comprehension by using the typical retelling and comprehension questions at the end of an IRI. These general comprehension measures worked quite well as an assessment of Zach's overall understanding of a text through the primary grades.

However, these general comprehension assessments by themselves were not specific enough as Zach progressed through the middle grades. Zach's teachers needed comprehension assessments that were more "ecologically valid" in a middle-grades classroom. They needed authentic assessments that more precisely targeted and mirrored the types of tasks, activities, strategies, assignments, and thinking he was asked to perform on a daily basis in his sixth-grade content-area classes. These included (1) summarizing the main idea in a current events article; (2) evaluating primary sources (e.g., speeches and letters) in social studies; and (3) applying the scientific process (e.g., make an observation, form a question, make a hypothesis) while writing his lab reports.

Assessment Application: Assess Target Strategies and Ways of Thinking in Authentic Content-Area Texts and Tasks

The following steps and guidelines can help you develop, administer, and interpret informal comprehension assessments that target older readers' ability to apply important target strategies and ways of thinking in their content-area reading. Some refer to these as *performance assessments,* since we are assessing how students "perform" a target strategy while reading. You can use performance assessments (1) with content-area reading material (textbook sections, articles, novels) to see to what extent students can apply a target strategy in their usual school reading materials; and/or (2) with IRI passages when we want to determine to what extent an older reader is able to apply a target strategy while reading an instructional-level passage.

Steps for Assessing Target Strategies and Ways of Thinking

1. *What exactly do you want your students to be able to do with this content?* How do you want them to be able to read and think about the text? What target strategy do you want them to be able to apply while reading? Do you want them to be able to identify the main ideas and summarize a social studies textbook section? Compare and contrast two viewpoints presented in speeches by Frederick Douglass and Abraham Lincoln? Identify

and provide evidence for the symbolism of Santiago as a Christ-like figure in Hemingway's *The Old Man and the Sea*? This question forces you to clarify precisely which aspect of comprehension, target strategy, or way of thinking you want your students to learn and apply while reading.

2. *What type of text will they be reading?* A textbook section? A poem? A speech by Sojourner Truth? A science article? Choose the types of texts that are commonly read in your classroom and important for your students to negotiate in your content area.

3. *What will the students produce as evidence of their learning and comprehension?* A one-sentence summary? A completed compare–contrast graphic organizer? The students' products should match your target strategy or way of thinking. You will analyze these products to assess your students' reading comprehension.

4. Choose either a whole text (provided it's not too long), a shorter passage from the text (more common), or an IRI passage. Make sure the passage is long enough that it coheres, but not so long that it can't be read in 5–10 minutes or so.

5. Ask the student to read the text (usually silently, unless you are also checking for fluency) and apply the target strategy before, during, and/or after the reading, as appropriate: "Zach, I want you to read this text, using the three-step summarizing strategy we've been working on in class. You'll hand in your one-paragraph summary at the end. I'll also ask some follow-up questions about what you learned."

6. Evaluate a reader's ability to apply the target strategy or way of thinking as your more specific content-area comprehension performance measure. We find that a 3-point scale is usable and helpful: (3) target (reader applies the target strategy successfully and consistently while reading); (2) developing (reader partially or inconsistently applies the target strategy); or (1) absent (student does not apply the target strategy).

Table 11.3 illustrates how Zach's teachers might use these steps to assess his ability to apply target strategies and ways of thinking—the "how" of reading—in discipline-specific ways in his actual content-area reading texts and tasks.

Assessment Concept 8:
Engagement Is the Engine That Drives Reading Growth

Many middle-grades teachers consistently tell us that engaging older readers who struggle is the most difficult challenge they face every day. Asking a disengaged reader to read is like trying to drive a car without a working engine: You won't get very far.

Michael, the fifth grader introduced at the beginning of this chapter, is a disengaged reader. Because he doesn't enjoy reading, he rarely reads unless required to in school. Although he's been explicitly taught reading comprehension strategies, he doesn't use them while reading, and he rarely attempts to connect the new knowledge in the text to what he already knows. For Michael, reading is something to get through, not something to dive into, relish, or learn from.

With the increasingly difficult reading challenges awaiting Michael in middle school and beyond, his lack of engagement is troubling. Disengaged readers, like Michael,

TABLE 11.3. Assessing the "How" for Zach: Target Strategies, Ways of Thinking, and Tasks

Content area	Assessment goal	Text	Target strategy	Product
—	What exactly do I want my students to be able to do with the content/reading?	What type of text will they be reading?	What strategy or way of thinking is critical in my content area/for this task?	What product will the student produce (instead of or in addition to the general comprehension questions or a retelling to assess comprehension)?
Social studies	I want my students to be able to summarize a social studies textbook section.	Social studies textbook	Summarizing (using the three-step summarizing strategy)	A completed one-paragraph summary, using a summary frame and showing the three summarizing steps.
Science	I want each of my students to be able to read his or her partner's lab report and explain the experiment, including all components of the scientific process.	Lab partner's lab report	Scientific process	A completed "scientific process" graphic organizer, correctly identifying and explaining all components of the scientific process.

read *500% less* than engaged readers do (Guthrie, 2004). Less reading practice leads to diminished reading skills, which lead to negative reading experiences and further decreases in motivation and engagement. If left unchecked, this negative downward-spiraling cycle—termed the *Matthew effect* by Keith Stanovich (Stanovich, 1986; Cunningham & Stanovich, 1991)—can result in long-term, ever-increasing deficits in reading achievement.

Michael's reading profile is all too common in the middle and secondary grades. However, there is good news:

1. Instructional methods can have a positive influence on attitudes and reading engagement (McKenna, 2001).
2. We know that there is a very strong correlation between engaged reading and reading comprehension achievement (Guthrie, 2004).

What can we do with a reader like Michael to improve his engagement? The assessments and instructional strategies we discuss in Chapter 10 apply to older students like Michael, and are perhaps even more important with older readers. In fact, we know that reading attitude and engagement tend to become worse over time for our students as they move into the upper grades, particularly for older struggling readers. We believe that one of the major reasons for this is that, in contrast to the way elementary schools are usually set up, traditional middle and secondary schedules and curricula are too often directly at odds with what we know fosters engaged readers.

When Michael enters middle school, he is placed in a reading support class with a reading specialist, Mr. Jenkins. Mr. Jenkins sits down with Michael to get to know him as a reader and a person. Using an interest inventory and the SARA (McKenna et al., 2012; see Form 10.5), Mr. Jenkins finds out that Michael:

- Enjoys and is skilled at drawing, particularly cartoons (he is signed up for art class in middle school).
- Enjoys science fiction and fantasy movies, anime, cartoons, and graphic novels.
- Skateboards with his friends.
- Dislikes textbooks and being told what to read.
- Enjoys some online reading, particularly shorter articles he chooses, and uses Instagram.

Table 11.4 illustrates a possible plan to reengage Michael and give him more ownership and control of his reading as he begins sixth grade. The first column identifies research-based instructional practices that foster engagement, including (1) choice (limited choice of five texts from genre study), social collaboration (idea circles), and relevance (creating a hypermedia "Skateboarding How-To Manual" for nonskateboarders) (Guthrie, 2004). The middle column lists "traditional" middle and secondary classroom instructional practices. For those of us working with older students, note how many of these traditional practices are at odds with proven practices for engaging readers like Michael. This means that for many older students, we need to do things differently if we

TABLE 11.4. Instructional Plan to Reengage Michael with Reading

Instructional practices that promote engagement	Aspects of traditional middle and secondary instruction as possible obstacles	Michael's plan
Choice in reading texts, tasks, and topics (including limited choice)	• Little to no choice. Required reading in most classes at most times. • Single classroom textbook or novel.	• Limited choice in English class. Let Michael choose novels from a set offered by teacher (e.g., choose a historical fiction novel from a set of five choices during genre study of history fiction). • Give Michael opportunities to choose reading in digital or print formats.
Texts and tasks: An abundance and variety of engaging texts at both Michael's instructional reading level and his listening level; task choices	• Single class textbook or novel. • Worksheets. • Answering questions at end of each section/chapter.	• Teachers work with the school librarian/media specialist to supply a variety of engaging instructional-level and stretch books for Michael, including graphic novels, anime, and online reading resources (e.g., Newsela.com). • Michael's goal is to create a hypermedia "Skateboarding How-To Manual" for nonskateboarders in his class.
Time to read texts at his instructional reading level (at least 30 minutes/day)	• Most reading is to be done at home. • Classroom time is devoted to lectures and discussion.	• 20 minutes/day reading in reading support class. • 20 minutes/day reading in ELA class.
Social collaboration: Opportunities for sharing and discourse around texts	• Reading is done independently. • Students are held accountable through quizzes, worksheets, and tests.	• Whole-class discussions. • Small-group text discussions (literature circles, idea circles centering on anime and skateboarding) • Idea circles creating digital movies for the class on their chosen texts and topics.

want to bring about dramatic changes in their reading engagement and achievement. The right column identifies a possible workable plan for Michael to reengage him as a reader, writer, and student.

Note that the changes listed in the right column of Table 11.4 are not radical in terms of cost. However, in relation to traditional literacy instruction in the upper grades, they *are* radical in terms of:

1. *What* the students are reading. The textbook is no longer the only instructional material. Students are given increased choices in a large variety of engaging texts and media formats that span not only readability, but also complexity of multimedia learning resources (textbooks, novels, graphic novels, digital texts, news articles, informational texts, speeches, and poems). The choices also begin at the students' instructional reading level and "stretch" texts up to their listening level.
2. *How* they are reading. There is increased social collaboration—thinking, talking, debating, and sharing—over texts. with an emphasis on engaging activities that require students to process texts deeply in small and whole groups.
3. *How much* they are reading. Students dramatically increase the time they spend reading every day, week, month, and year. This means at least 30 (with a target of 90) minutes per day in school reading—the equivalent of at least a chapter a day and/or a book per week.

TWELVE

Preparing a Diagnostic Reading Report

Reports can serve a number of different functions. They can be nothing more than short notes to summarize an assessment for a staff meeting, or they can be more elaborate, formal documents. Because all aspects of the literacy performance are addressed as much as possible, reports are also useful for communicating with parents, teachers, principals, and others. When you are composing such a report, it is always best to assume that you do not know who will be reading it, and so you must spell out exactly what actions you took in the assessment process. In the Appendix, you will find examples of three reports that range from simple to elaborate, to fulfill three different functions that are described more fully at the end of the chapter.

The reports discussed in this chapter are the more formal kind: reports written about a comprehensive assessment. Although most teachers will never write such a report, we address the topic for several reasons. To begin with, classroom teachers are sometimes asked to interpret reports written by reading specialists or special educators. Understanding the logic and structure of report writing can be useful for this purpose. Second, we have written this book with a broad readership in mind, and we recognize that the classroom teachers who read this book today may become the reading specialists of tomorrow. Finally, we include this topic as an exercise in systematic thinking. Both preservice and inservice teachers benefit from learning how to analyze a student's reading strengths and challenges. Writing a formal report requires thinking about the child and your procedures in a comprehensive and analytic manner, rather than simply declaring that a child is a successful or a striving reader. To write a thorough report, you must ask yourself questions about the child's overall performance and about how the different pieces of the assessment puzzle fit together. Then, on the basis of those findings, you must determine what instructional interventions will support the child. You must also think about how to communicate this information to a parent or another teacher, explaining clearly what you did and what you found. This process, or portions of this process, are particularly important today as part of the RTI or MTSS framework that many districts require as a prerequisite for identifying eligibility for special education (Stahl & McKenna, 2013). Following are some suggestions for writing a formal report.

PREPARATION

1. Spread out all the material from your testing—protocols, notes, and so on—on a table. Ask yourself mentally the questions listed in Table 12.1 about the child's perfor-

TABLE 12.1. Guiding Questions for Interpreting a Reading Profile

Question	Source of information
Is the student able to read texts at his or her grade placement with automatic word recognition and adequate expression?	
• Does the student make use of context to monitor his or her reading?	Informal reading inventory (IRI); running records (Chapter 3)
• Is the student fluent?	Timed oral reading; fluency scale (Chapter 6)
• Is the student able to recognize high-frequency words automatically?	High-frequency word list such as the Dolch or Fry list (Chapter 5); IRI
• Does the student apply knowledge of decoding strategies?	Decoding inventories (Chapter 5)
• Does the student have adequate phonological awareness (PA)?	Comprehensive Test of Phonological Processing—Second Edition; informal PA tests (Chapter 4)
Is the student able to comprehend the language of the text?	
• Does the student have an adequate vocabulary:	
○ for his or her age and grade?	Formal measures such as the Peabody Picture Vocabulary Test—Fifth Edition
○ to comprehend a specific text?	Formative measures (Chapter 7)
• Does the student have the background knowledge necessary to understand the particular passage that he or she is reading?	Prereading questions (Chapter 8)
Is the student able to use common text structures to aid in comprehension?	Retelling; answers to questions; written responses (Chapter 8)
• Does the student have adequate knowledge of the purposes for reading and strategies available to achieve those purposes?	
• Does the student have a set of strategies that can be used to achieve different purposes in reading?	Textbook Interview; Index of Reading Awareness (Chapter 9)
• What does the student view as the goal of reading in general?	Purposes for Reading Interview (Chapter 9)
• What concepts of print does the student have?	Observations and concepts of print tasks (Chapter 4)
What is the student's attitude toward reading?	Attitude and interest inventories (Chapter 10)

mance. Think about both the level of his or her performance on the various tasks and the quality of that performance (i.e., the processes used to produce the performance). You should have an answer to each of these questions before you begin to write your report. These questions will guide you in understanding the assessment materials in front of you.

BACKGROUND INFORMATION

2. Begin by describing the reason for referral. Couch the comments made by the teacher or parent in terms such as "The teacher reports . . . " and so on. Be careful about "dangerous" or "loaded" statements, such as saying that a child is reported to be "hyperactive" or "behaviorally disordered." Unless you are a qualified clinical psychologist who has conducted an appropriate assessment and rendered the diagnosis, you cannot classify children in these ways. Similarly, you cannot classify someone as having a "speech impairment" or "intellectual disabilities" unless you have appropriate training and have conducted appropriate assessments. Furthermore, do not report intimate family details (e.g., difficulties experienced by siblings or incarceration) that might prejudice a person meeting the child for the first time. *Remember that your report may be the first impression someone gets about this child.* Do not prejudice the reader by making statements that go beyond what you yourself have observed about the child. The statements in the background section should describe behaviors you have seen or reports that you have read. Use professional language to create a portrait of the child, and be careful to distinguish fact from interpretation.

3. Describe the setting in which the assessment was conducted. Was the child cooperative? Were any factors present that might invalidate some of the results? Were there interruptions that made it difficult for the student to focus? Was the child too shy or anxious to respond in an informative manner?

TESTS ADMINISTERED

4. List the tests administered, with the results. If the tests do not lend themselves to numerical results, just list the tests. Table 12.2 indicates the assessment tasks that are likely to be administered at each grade level, together with the tools we have presented in this book.

OBSERVATIONS DURING TESTING

5. This section, in which you detail your observations, should be the longest of the report. For each reading construct (Oral Reading, Silent Reading, Word Recognition, Decoding, Language, etc.), report *all* of the measures that have an impact on that area. If you administered two oral reading measures, list them both under "Oral Reading." You may use any set of categories or any order that makes sense in presenting your data.

TABLE 12.2. Basic Assessment Tools

	K–Grade 1	Grades 2–4	Grades 5–8
Concepts about print	• Concepts about print and book-handling tasks (Forms 4.1, 4.2, 4.3) • Hearing and Recording Sounds in Words (Form 4.6)		
Alphabet identification and phonological awareness	• Alphabet Recognition Chart (Form 4.4) • Tests of Phonological Awareness (Form 4.5) • Hearing and Recording Sounds in Words (Form 4.6)		
Development of word recognition	In isolation • High-frequency words (Form 5.4 or 5.5) • Informal Phonics Inventory (Form 5.2) • Informal Decoding Inventory (Form 5.3) In context • Running records and IRIs	In isolation • High-frequency words (Form 5.4 or 5.5) • Informal Decoding Inventory (Form 5.3) or Z-Test (Form 5.1) In context • Running records and IRIs	*Optional* • In isolation: Test of Word Reading Efficiency—Second Edition • In context: Running records and IRIs
Spelling development	• Developmental Spelling Analysis (DSA) Screening Inventory (Form 5.6)	• DSA Screening Inventory (Form 5.6) • In context: Analyze spelling errors in a writing sample	• DSA Screening Inventory (Form 5.6) • In context: Analyze spelling errors in a writing sample
Reading fluency	• Prosody rating (Tables 6.1, 6.2) • Beginning mid-grade 1, rate (WCPM) (Table 6.4)	• Rate (WCPM) (Table 6.4) • Prosody rating (Tables 6.1, 6.2)	• Rate (WPM/WCPM) (Table 6.4)

Comprehension	• Running record or IRI
	  Error analysis
	  Retelling
	  Prompted recall
	• Narrative Wordless Picture Book Task (Chapter 4, Form 4.8, and Form 4.9)
		• IRI
		  Retelling
		  Prompted recall
			• IRI
			  Retelling
			  Prompted recall

Strategic reading			• Interview (selections from Chapter 9)
Motivation/ attitudes	• Elementary Reading Attitude Survey (ERAS) (Form 10.4)	• ERAS (Form 10.4)	• Survey of Adolescent Reading Attitudes (Form 10.5)

Note. This table describes the basic assessment tasks that are typically administered at each grade level. The need to administer additional or different tasks may be indicated by a child's performance on a few preliminary assessments.

Table 12.2 can help you organize your data by reading construct. If you give a test (e.g., a phonemic awareness measure) because you noticed a weakness in another area (e.g., decoding), you might want to order your list so that the reader can follow the progression of your thinking. The goal is to organize the results in the best possible manner to present a clear, insightful picture of the student as a reader.

6. For each area, do the following:

   a. Describe the tests given. Write descriptions in a few sentences that are clear and understandable to parents.

   b. Present the quantitative results. At what level is the child performing? How well did the child score numerically? Remember, this portion of the report is an informational text. Use graphs and charts to make the information that you are presenting as clear, succinct, and sensible as possible to the reader. For example, if you are trying to make the point that the child's reading rate decreased as the texts became more difficult, a graph makes the point more clearly than four sentences describing the decrease.

   c. Present the qualitative analysis of these results—perhaps, for example, a mis-cue analysis of oral reading, an analysis of a word-recognition list describing patterns that you have seen, an analysis of spelling, and so on. What process was the child using during this activity? Make interpretations. When mak-ing interpretative statements, consider using language such as "These results indicate/suggest . . . " For each interpretive statement, give examples, such as miscues, spellings, word readings, and so forth.

   d. When possible, compare the test results to those of other tests that measure different aspects of the same construct. For example, if you are discussing a child's skill with high-frequency words, it is important to look at the child's ability to read the words in isolation (using the Dolch or Fry list) and to com-pare that performance with the child's recognition of the words in context. Next, compare the child's ability to read the high-frequency words with his or her mastery and precision of writing those high-frequency words in isolation and in context. A good rule of thumb is to think about each skill in the follow-ing ways:

      o Reading
      o Writing
      o In isolation
      o In context/in running text

SUMMARY AND RECOMMENDATIONS

7. Within the first three sentences of the first paragraph, the summary should always explicitly state the student's age, grade level, and instructional reading level. The first paragraph of the summary should also recap the information in the previous sections of

the report. *In a report, do not be afraid to be redundant.* Make sure this first paragraph contains a brief summary of the student's performance in the significant areas assessed.

8. Compare the student's performance across the different areas. Begin with a description of the student's major literacy strengths (always remember to start with what a student knows and can do), and follow with a description of his or her reading challenges. Interpret those strengths and weaknesses, if appropriate. This is a place to focus on target skill areas without repeating the broader continuum of mastery and deficit that may have been addressed within the thorough descriptions of performance on each specific test. Be succinct. Do not include so many details or test scores that the student's key strengths and weaknesses get buried in the verbiage.

9. Finally, list and describe the major goals for tutoring or intervention. We recommend that you set between three and five goals. We've found that setting more goals than this often leads to well-intentioned plans that don't lead to significant growth in any area. Describe each goal briefly, and explain why it is important. Then describe sample activities that you plan to use to achieve each goal. You also may append longer descriptions of the activities to the report. These can be your own descriptions or photocopies of activity descriptions. Good sources for such descriptions include the following:

Bear, D. R., Invernizzi, M., Templeton, S., & Johnston, F. (2016). *Words their way: Word study for phonics, vocabulary, and spelling instruction* (6th ed.). Boston: Pearson.

Blevins, W. (2017a). *Phonics from A to Z: A practical guide* (3rd ed.). New York: Scholastic.

Blevins, W. (2017b). *Teaching phonics and word study in the intermediate grades* (2nd ed.). New York: Scholastic.

Fisher, D., Brozo, W. G., Frey, N., & Ivey, G. (2014). *50 content area strategies for adolescent literacy* (3rd ed.). Upper Saddle River, NJ: Merrill/Prentice Hall.

Harris, K., Graham, S., Mason, L., & Friedlander, B. (2008). *Powerful writing strategies for all students*. Baltimore: Brookes.

Harvey, S., & Goudvis, A. (2017). *Strategies that work: Teaching comprehension for understanding, engagement, and building knowledge* (3rd ed.). York, ME: Stenhouse.

Hayes, L., & Flanigan, K. (2014). *Developing word recognition*. New York: Guilford Press.

Klingner, J. K., Vaughn, S., & Boardman, A. (2015). *Teaching reading comprehension to students with reading disabilities* (2nd ed.). New York: Guilford Press.

Kuhn, M. R., & Levy, L. (2015). *Developing fluent readers: Teaching fluency as a foundational skill*. New York: Guilford Press.

O'Connor, R. E. (2014). *Teaching word recognition: Effective strategies for students with learning difficulties* (2nd ed.). New York: Guilford Press.

Rasinski, T. V., & Smith, M. C. (2018). *The megabook of fluency*. New York: Scholastic.

Silverman, R., & Meyer, A. G. (2015). *Developing vocabulary and oral language in young children*. New York: Guilford Press.

Stahl, K. A. D., & Garcia, G. E. (2015). *Developing reading comprehension: Effective instruction for all students in PreK–2*. New York: Guilford Press.

Templeton, S., Bear, D. R., Invernizzi, M., Johnston, F., Flanigan, K., Townsend, D. R., et al. (2015). *Words their way: Vocabulary for middle and secondary students* (2nd ed.). Boston: Pearson.

Tierney, R. J., & Readence, J. (2005). *Reading strategies and practices: A compendium* (6th ed.). Boston: Allyn & Bacon.

OTHER POINTS

Be clear and concise, and avoid jargon. If you use a technical term, explain it. The audience is an intelligent layperson (a parent, teacher, etc.), not a specialist. A good exercise to see if you are striking the right tone is to share the report with your mother/father, your spouse/partner, or your roommate. If this person does not understand what you have written, it is unlikely that a parent or teacher who is not a reading specialist will comprehend it.

Make sure you explain yourself clearly, professionally, and unambiguously. Read through the report after it is drafted, and try to misinterpret it; if something you have said can be misinterpreted, it will be. Be honest and professional in your descriptions. Struggling readers often have difficulty staying on task and sustaining their focus; they may avoid taking risks, instead engaging in avoidance behaviors. It's important not to characterize those readers as "lazy" or simply "needing to try harder."

Redundancy is fine in a report, as we've noted, because many people do not read the report from beginning to end, but instead look for parts that answer their particular questions or concerns. Indeed, positioning information in several places (e.g., a list or chart, the body of the report, a summary) increases the chance that a reader will come across that information.

SAMPLE REPORTS

Three sample student case studies are included in the Appendix. They have slightly different formats, but each contains the essential elements of a diagnostic report. They progress from basic to elaborated and from least sophisticated to most sophisticated.

Basic Template

Case Study 1: Moe (see Appendix) applies a basic template for reporting the results from a school screening test, a complete IRI results summary, a developmental word study inventory, and a writing sample. It provides places to note the student's reading, writing, and word-study levels; to identify strengths and weaknesses; and to make instructional recommendations. Schools can easily modify this template to include the screening and diagnostic tests that they use to identify and support students with literacy needs as part of their RTI/MTSS documentation. There is not a place for a detailed qualitative analysis of the results. This template also lays the groundwork for writing up a more complete report, like the ones found in the two more detailed two case studies that follow.

This template should work well in a school setting to help interventionists and special education teachers prepare for a meeting with classroom teachers or parents, or to evaluate the status of students who either need or have been receiving some form of intervention. In secondary schools, it should be a useful tool for identifying specific intervention targets and the appropriate instructional interventions for students who have many needs. It should also be suitable for a tutor who has only been hired to provide homework help and to provide moderate levels of reading support. We have known tutors who offer this alternative to families without the financial resources required to pay for the time needed to write the more elaborate reports. Most teachers with an initial teaching degree should have the knowledge required to complete the template.

Test-by-Test Report

Case Study 2: Quetzal (see Appendix) applies a straightforward diagnostic report format that works well for teachers who are in the beginning stages of writing reports. Kay uses the test-by-test format for students in her literacy methods classes who will graduate with the qualifications for an initial dual certificate in Elementary–Special Education. They are novices at administering tests and analyzing results, but as prospective special educators they require diagnostic skills and knowledge of research-validated instructional practices. It is also imperative for them to learn the discourse of report writing. The test-by-test format provides an overview of the student, a description of each test, the results of each test (quantitative and qualitative), a summary of results, and instructional recommendations.

Formal Diagnostic Report

Case Study 3: Lee (see Appendix) is a comprehensive report that will probably be used to create a diagnostic intervention plan for a student, complete with follow-up posttesting after a period of intervention. The synthesis of diagnostic information requires a more experienced teacher and is suited to the needs of a reading interventionist or special educator. It provides the best and most complete picture of the student's needs because of the detailed analysis. The analysis and thought processes required to write the elaborated diagnostic report result in the creation of an intervention plan that is precisely matched with the student's needs. Table 12.2 can support the process of synthesizing information from multiple tests into a logical diagnostic evaluation. This level of precision increases the likelihood of the student making accelerated progress. The Case Study 3 format is best suited to clinical settings, tutoring models designed to yield reading growth, and special education.

The sample reports in the Appendix contain boilerplate descriptions of the tests used. If you use the same assessments, do not worry about trying to rewrite these descriptions; use them "as is." Copying the generic test descriptions with a citation is not plagiarism, but simply a way to avoid wasting time that is better spent analyzing the assessment data and creating an effective intervention plan that will lead to accelerated student achievement.

Case Studies

Case Study 1: Moe

Name: Moe	**Date of report:** Oct. 10, 20XX
Grade: 6	**Dates of testing:** Sept. 30 and Oct. 2, 20XX
School: Champion Highway Middle School	**Date of birth:** Aug. 27, 20XX
Homeroom teacher: Vanessa White	**Age at testing:** 11.1
Examiner: Alexa Trebeck	

BACKGROUND INFORMATION

Moe, a sixth grader at Champion Highway Middle School (CHMS), was born on August 27, 20XX. He attended Fortune Lane Elementary School. Both his fifth-grade teachers and current sixth-grade teachers report that Moe is a hard-working, compliant student who gets along well with other students in his classes. He has a rich social life and is actively involved in school and community sports teams. He lives with his mother, his stepfather, and his younger half-sister. He spends every other weekend with his father, his stepmother, and an older stepsister, who is in eighth grade in CHMS.

Because of his below-grade-level score on the STAR screening assessment, the results of the grade-level spelling screener, and recommendations from his fifth-grade teachers, the CHMS Response to Intervention Team selected Moe to undergo additional diagnostic literacy tests. Additionally, Moe had received supplementary Tier 2 intervention in grades 4 and 5. I selected a battery of tests that would enable me both to determine the severity of his needs and to target Moe's strengths and weaknesses in literacy.

I administered the assessments in our school's quiet intervention suite, immediately after Moe's lunch period. Despite his lack of familiarity with me, Moe was outgoing and friendly during the test sessions and became increasingly verbose as the testing process progressed. At two points during the passage reading, he began a spontaneous discussion, and I redirected him to finish reading the story before discussing it. At points of difficulty, Moe exerted effort without showing outward signs of frustration. He never asked for help.

DIAGNOSTIC REPORT

The following tables present a summary of Moe's test results.

STAR Screener	Goal: 1070L	Score: 935L (835–985L)									

IRI	Word Recognition in Isolation (WRI)		Oral Reading in Context					Silent Reading in Context			
Levels	Flashed	Untimed	Accuracy (% WRC)	NAEP Prosody	Rate in WCPM / %ile	Comp. %age	Rate in WPM	Comp. %age	Overall Reading Judgment	Listening Comp.
Primer	100^I	—									
First	100^I	—									
Second	90^I	100									
Third (Expository)	90^I	100	99^I	4	138^S / 50–75	87^S			Ins.		
Fourth (Expository)	85^S	100	96^S	3	122^S / 25–50	63^G			Ins.		
Fourth (Narrative)							140^S	63^G	Ins.		
Fifth	75^S	100	97^S	2	110^F / <25	38^F			Frus.	50^F	
Sixth	65^G	95									
Upper Middle School	45^F	80									

	Number of Words			Ideas	Organi-zation		Voice	Word Choice	Conven-tions	Overall Writing Judgment
Writing Sample	36	Summary of Gr. 3 passage (10 minutes); District Middle School 5-Point Rubric		2	2		1	1	2	Emerging

	Points	Words Correct	Mastered	Review	Teach Explicitly	Stage
Spelling	48/68	16/27	Vowels, complex consonants	Inflected endings	Unaccented final syllables; affixes	Late syllables and affixes

Note. I, Independent (Ind.); S, Instructional (Ins.); F, Frustration (Frus.); G, Gray. WCPM %ile is based on Hasbrouck and Tindal's (2017) norms (see Table 6.4 of this book).

Estimated Independent Level: Grade 3 or 750L–885L	Estimated Instructional Level: Grade 4 or 835L–985L	Estimated Frustration Level: Grade 5 or >990L
Justification: Accuracy: 99% (Ind.) Prosody: 4/4 Rate: 138 WCPM/ >50th %ile Comprehension: 87% (Ins.) Moe read the grade 3 IRI passage accurately and fluently at an independent level. He got one question incorrect, resulting in an overall judgment of instructional. Additionally, his verbal and written summaries of the expository passage identified the key ideas, but there was little spontaneous elaboration on the details of the passage. Based on STAR data, Moe is likely to be able to read and understand texts that are rated at 750L–885L with minimum support. Combining all sources of information makes it appear likely that Moe could read most grade 3 materials independently.	*Justification:* Accuracy: 96% (Ins.) Prosody: 3/4 Rate: 122 WCPM (25th–50th %ile) 140 WPM (silent) Comprehension: Narrative, 63% (Gray); Expository, 50% (Gray) Accuracy and fluency are at instructional levels. Narrative and expository comprehension are in the gray range. Due to strength of word recognition, we have determined this to be the instructional level. STAR results were consistent in determining a reading level that approximates grade 4 materials. Moe is likely to be able to read most grade 4 materials or texts rated at 835L–985L with instructional support for comprehension and writing in response to text.	*Justification:* Accuracy: 97% (Ins.) Prosody: 2 Rate: 110 WCPM (<25th %ile) Comprehension: 38% (Frus.) Although accuracy remained high, Moe's fluency and comprehension dropped considerably when he was reading the grade 5 text. Therefore, many grade 5 materials are likely to be challenging and frustrating for Moe. There was no discrepancy between Moe's reading and listening comprehension. This provides substantiation that Moe's challenges with comprehension are rooted in comprehension; they are not caused by challenges with decoding or fluency.

SUMMARY AND RECOMMENDATIONS

Strengths and Areas of Need by Literacy Area

Literacy Area	Strengths	Areas of Need
Word Knowledge	Moe is strong in word recognition, both in isolation and in context. Moe can decode many multisyllabic words in context, when given time. He uses chunks and meaning (context) to refine his approximations of unknown words.	

Literacy Area	Strengths	Areas of Need
Fluency	When reading texts that are well below grade level, Moe reads expressively and at an appropriate rate.	Moe needs to improve his reading fluency (both his reading rate and prosody). He reads carefully, often repeating words and phrases. His careful analysis of unknown words often causes him to lose his place and train of thought. This tends to disrupt his comprehension and results in reading with uneven prosody.
Word Study–Spelling	Moe has mastered the foundational word-recognition skills.	Moe needs additional instruction and practice with the most common word parts, including roots and affixes. He also needs instruction and practice in spelling common unaccented syllables.
Comprehension	Moe monitors for meaning as he reads and often attempts to self-correct when the texts do not make sense.	Although Moe reads accurately, he has difficulty recalling details, retelling, and summarizing both verbally and in writing. He also has difficulty making inferences.
Writing		Although Moe says that he likes to write, he has difficulty knowing what to write. He needs to work on formulating ideas and using strategies to organize his thoughts in the prewriting stage so that he can write productively.

Instructional Recommendations

The following recommendations are ranked in order of literacy-area priority from 1 to 4. Specific instructional recommendations include activities, strategies, and materials.

Word Recognition 4	Fluency 3	Comprehension 1	Writing 2
Instruction is needed in manipulating and reading the most common word parts. Have Moe practice spelling and reading unaccented syllable patterns (distributed practice must continue, using large word lists, after preliminary instruction).	Have Moe do charted repeated readings. Continue drills of ongoing lists of Fry high-frequency words. Have partners (Read for America volunteers, parents?) do paired reading with Moe, to improve his reading rate, prosody, and comprehension.	Use the Directed Reading–Thinking Activity to improve Moe's ability to recall details (primarily using informational text). Teach text structures as tools for organizing and remembering information in texts. Have Moe use sticky notes.	Improve Moe's ability to formulate and organize ideas, using text structures. Improve his ability to write clearly developed paragraphs/compositions. Use Self-Regulated Strategy Development (Graham & Harris).

Case Study 2: Quetzal

Name: Quetzal	**Date of report:**
Grade: 1	**Dates of testing:**
School: Park Elementary	**Date of birth:** June 20, 20XX
Parents:	**Age at testing:** 6.4
Address:	**Examiner:** Natalie Levy[1]
Telephone:	

BACKGROUND INFORMATION

Quetzal, a first grader at Park Elementary School, was born on June 30, 20XX, in Mexico. She is a bilingual student who speaks Spanish at home, though she seems to prefer to use English for both academics and socializing. She currently lives within walking distance of Park Elementary School, with her mother, father, and 2-year-old brother. Quetzal has mentioned on more than one occasion that her mother reads with her every night in Spanish, and that she herself enjoys reading out loud to her younger brother in English and Spanish. Her hobbies include watching television, playing video games, and cooking with her mother.

Quetzal has an individualized education program (IEP), which stipulates that she be placed in a collaborative team teaching classroom. She is classified as having a speech or language impairment, and she is accordingly mandated to attend speech and language therapy sessions three times a week. The meetings are conducted in English and primarily target Quetzal's articulation and pronunciation; these target areas seem to be the most palpable demonstrations of her disability, as it is sometimes difficult to decipher her oral language.

Quetzal is a sweet and confident child who seems to genuinely enjoy school. Her teacher, Mrs. Goldman, requested the evaluation of Quetzal's literacy performance because she struggles socially during literacy lessons. Mrs. Goldman also wanted to learn more about the influence that Quetzal's speech and language background may be having on her literacy development. When given a choice, Quetzal prefers to sit by herself, whether on the carpet or at the table. During communications with both her peers and her teachers, she rarely maintains eye contact; instead, she has a tendency to rotate her body in an effort to look elsewhere. She is consistently eager to participate in classroom activities, though she does sometimes become overexcited; she may demonstrate this feeling by shouting out an answer, getting up out of her chair, or crying in response to not being called on by a teacher. During whole-group literacy instruction, Quetzal often raises her hand and is easily frustrated when not called upon. In these situations, Quetzal must be explicitly reminded of appropriate behavioral expectations. A verbal warning, independent of a punitive consequence, usually incites her to correct her behavior and put a smile on her face within a span of 2–3 minutes.

During one-on-one work or small-group work in literacy, she does seem to become more outgoing and participatory than in whole-group settings or in other subjects. During our conversations, she proudly calls herself an author as she shows me various stories that she has written independently.

---

[1]Thanks to Natalie Levy, a graduate of New York University's Childhood Education Master's Certification Program. Natalie's case study has been used as a foundation, but Quetzal is a pseudonym, and all student information has been extensively revised to create a composite student.

TESTS ADMINISTERED

Letter ID/Alphabet Recognition

The purpose of this test is to assess a student's knowledge of letter names. In order to administer the test, the teacher presents a single sheet of printed letters, both uppercase and lowercase, that are randomly ordered. A total of 54 symbols are included: each uppercase letter and each lowercase letter, including the varying formats of letters a (a) and g (g). The student must say the name of each letter. The score is the number of correctly pronounced letter names out of a total of 54.

Concepts about Print

The purpose of this test is to evaluate a student's knowledge of the basic conventions that surround how books are formatted and how we read them. These include, but are not limited to, the left-to-right directionality of English, the fact that spaces are word boundaries, the fact that we read from the top of the page to the bottom, the fact that the words on the page (apart from the illustrations) convey meaning, and so forth. These concepts are not only fundamental to an appreciation of how print works, but also provide the foundation on which decoding skills develop; they can and should be developed long before formal reading instruction. In order to administer the test, a teacher reads the student a book that has both pictures and a written story. During the read-aloud, the teacher asks the student to perform certain tasks that prove mastery of the previously listed concepts. The results of the assessment are useful for demonstrating what a student already knows about print, as well as identifying what concepts may need further review or instruction.

Hearing Sounds in Words Assessment

The purpose of this test is to evaluate a student's phonological awareness—that is, the understanding that words are made up of abstract sounds. This awareness is not only critical to future reading success, but it also stimulates growth in spelling (Bear et al., 2020). In order to administer the test, a child is asked to record a dictated story; the score represents the number of correctly represented phonemes. Points are scored for writing a possible correct letter representation for each sound, not necessarily the precise spelling of the word. In examining the invented spelling that results from this assessment, a teacher can learn about that child's grasp of alphabetic knowledge, known whole-word units, print concepts, and phonemic awareness.

Writing Vocabulary Assessment (Clay, 2013)

The purpose of this test is to investigate which words a child can spell correctly in 10 minutes. This test may reveal which high-frequency words teachers have taught, but children also display words learned in experiences outside of school or through exposure to books in the classroom. To administer the test, the teacher simply provides the student with a piece of paper and a writing utensil, then encourages him or her to write down all of the words that he or she knows.

Words Their Way Spelling Inventory (Bear et al., 2020)

The spelling inventory is an assessment that helps the teacher determine the child's stage of spelling development. The words become increasingly difficult and contain spelling features that can be analyzed to determine what a child already understands about spelling words and what is still difficult for the child.

Sight-Word Inventory (Fry List)

The purpose of this test is to survey a student's ability to pronounce various high-frequency words at sight. Recognizing a word "at sight" means doing so in 1 second or less. To administer it, a teacher shows the child a word (on a flash card, in list form, or on a device) and asks for a pronunciation.

Running Record

The purpose of this test is to record and analyze a "snapshot" of a student's oral reading. In order to administer the running record, a teacher asks the student to read aloud a selection of 100–200 words, and then uses a specific coding system to record the reading on paper. The level of this selection is pertinent, as it should roughly correspond to the student's reading abilities. The student's *quantitative rate of accuracy* (i.e., the number of words read correctly out of the total number of words) is used to determine whether the given passage is at the student's frustration, instructional, or independent level. Clay defines these levels, respectively, as less than 90% accuracy, 90–95% accuracy, and 96–100% accuracy in a cold read. The specific miscues that a student makes can be analyzed to determine his or her mastery of meaning, structure, and visual cues. Additionally, the fluency and phrasing with which a student has read the passage can be evaluated using the NAEP Oral Reading Fluency Scale (divided in four levels, with one being the lowest and four being the highest). Overall, the data provided by the running record should be utilized to inform a teacher about what a student has control over, and what areas require additional review or instruction.

TEST RESULTS

Letter ID/Alphabet Recognition Assessment: 54/54

Quantitative Data

Uppercase: 26 out of 26
Lowercase: 28 out of 28

Qualitative Data

Quetzal independently noticed the basis of the division between the letters, exclaiming that the top part of the page has "big" letters and the bottom part of the page has "lowercase" letters. After recognizing the categories, Quetzal recited the names of all of the letters in a quick and confident manner. She pointed to each letter as she said the name. Additionally, she demonstrated directionality as she moved her finger from left to right, then from top to bottom. Capital *A*, in other words, was her starting point; she moved across each line, followed by a return sweep, until she finished with lowercase *g*. Quetzal initially read lowercase *q* as lowercase *g*. Quetzal's self-corrected error was, most likely, based on the similar configuration between lowercase *q* and lowercase *g*. She recited two more letters (lowercase *w* and lowercase *n*) before going back and correcting her mistake.

Concepts about Print

Quetzal seems very comfortable and experienced when handling a book. Quetzal mastered the following concepts:

- ✓ Orientation of book
- ✓ Print carries message
- ✓ Directional understanding
- ✓ Speech-to-print match
- ✓ Concept of first and last (letter/part of story)
- ✓ Letter concept/word concept
- ✓ Concept of capital letter

Quetzal was less capable with basic punctuation marks. She initially struggled to answer the question "What is this for?" When I repeated the question two or three times, she was able to supply answers regarding the function of all the marks except for periods, commas, and question marks.

Period: "Use a normal voice." [She did not note that it indicates the end of a sentence, however.]
Exclamation point: "Something is really exciting!"
Comma: "I don't know why people use that one."
Question mark: "Yeah, I don't know that one either."

Additionally, Quetzal struggled to identify the lowercase match for an uppercase letter *F* that I had pointed out. Initially, she pointed to the lowercase letter *b*. She immediately self-corrected herself, though, and pointed to a lowercase *f*.

Hearing Sounds in Words Assessment: 35/39

Quantitative Data

Quetzal correctly represented 35 out of 39 possible phonemes.

Qualitative Data

I read Quetzal the following story and asked her to write it: "Dad went to his job at the mill. He is working late today." Her writing reveals a wealth of information about her grasp of alphabetic knowledge, phonemic awareness, print concepts, and spelling skills. Quetzal clearly sees words as units; her words are separated by distinct spaces. She has a bank of high-frequency words that she can spell: *Dad, to, her, at, the, she, is,* and *today.* She seems to have mastered the alphabetic principle, as she understands that certain letters represent certain sounds in a systematic way. Quetzal is aware of and acknowledges vowels, rather than simply building a consonant framework.

She knows how to form her letters in a decipherable and consistent way, though she does not yet discriminate between upper- and lowercase letters. Uppercase letters begin the initial word of each sentence, but they also appear in various word endings or at the onset of words that are not the first of a sentence (**DaD, weNt, Job**).

Quetzal has not fully mastered the concept of a sentence, indicated by the fact that she did not put appropriate punctuation at the end of the second sentence. She has not yet mastered the use of silent *e* as a long-vowel marker, indicated by her spelling of the word *late* as *layt*. Though she understands that the word has the long-*a* sound, she does not know how to represent the sound appropriately. The absence of several phonemes from the word *working* may indicate a struggle that Quetzal has with the representation of longer words.

Writing Vocabulary Assessment: Test Score: 30; Stanine: 4

Quantitative Data

Writing vocabulary: 6.01–6.50 years

Test score: 30 correctly spelled words

Stanine group: 4 (slightly below average)

Qualitative Data

After I outlined the instructions and goals of this exercise, Quetzal was excited to complete it and showed me lots of words that she knew how to write. She never exhibited any signs of anxiety, and she wrote words for the entire 10 minutes, pausing briefly from time to time but never requiring prompting to continue.

Quetzal arranged the words on the pages as though she was writing a paragraph, not in a list format. She moved from left to right with a return sweep from top to bottom. Uppercase letters and lowercase letters were used indiscriminately at the beginning of words, but with few exceptions she used lowercase letters in the middle and end of words.

Though many of her words were seemingly written at random, she did write certain conceptual word families such as body parts (*eye, Nos, moth, chin, Fingr*) and rime families (*Ball, Wall, Small, Hall*). She correctly spelled many high-frequency words: *our, the, on, off, not, but*.

Quetzal's writing vocabulary seems to be between the late letter name–alphabetic stage and the within word pattern spelling stage. She consistently and correctly uses short vowels (*sun, big, chin, bed*), though she continues to confuse long-vowel markers (*cheas* for *cheese*, *nos* for *nose*, *tayval* for *table*). She correctly represents consonant digraphs: *moth, chair*. She includes preconsonantal nasals (*fingr* for *finger*).

SPELLING INVENTORY: <u>7/26</u>

Developmental Stage: Early Within Word Pattern

Quantitative Data:

- Power score, or the number of words that Quetzal spelled correctly in every detail: 7 out of 26.
- According to Bear et al. (2020), children who get a power score of 7 on a primary spelling inventory are likely to be in the late letter name–alphabetic/early within word pattern stage.
- Feature points: 35 out of 56
  - Consonants (initial): 7 out of 7
  - Consonants (final): 7 out of 7
  - Short vowels: 7 out of 7
  - Digraphs: 6 out of 7
  - Blends: 6 out of 7
  - Common long vowels: 0 out of 7

- o Other vowels: 1 out of 7
- o Inflected endings: 1 out of 7
- Based on the feature guide analysis, Quetzal's current developmental stage is the *late letter name/early within word pattern*.

Qualitative Data

Quetzal's performance on this assessment provided information on her spelling habits. She explicitly sounds out phonemes as she is writing. She often uses a capital letter to initiate words.

Quetzal has control over initial consonants, final consonants, and short vowels. She seems to have knowledge of both digraphs (e.g., *th* in *thorn*; *sh* in *shouted*) and blends (e.g., *sl* in *sled*; *cr* in *crawl*), but because she missed one item in each category, we will do a brief review. She is using, but confusing, common long vowels, other vowels, and inflected endings. When spelling the word *fright*, Quetzal exclaimed, "Silent *e*!" She is clearly using and confusing the long-vowel marker; she has realized that long-vowel sounds need some sort of marker, and is ready to learn the orthographic representation. Direct and explicit instruction should begin with common long vowels, at a moderate instructional pace.

Sight-Word Inventory (Fry List)

Quantitative Data

First 100 Words	*Second 100 Words*
89/100 sight words	66/100 sight words
1/100 word attack	9/100 word attack
9/100 mispronounced	25/100 mispronounced
1/100 self-correct	0/100 self-correct
0/100 skip	0/100 skip

Qualitative Data

Quetzal seems to prioritize speed over accuracy in her word list reading. Quetzal did not skip unfamiliar words. She generally tried to sound out an unknown word using a few of the letters without strategically puzzling out the word from beginning to end or chunking the word.

Running Record (RR)

Quantitative Data

- Previous RR administration by classroom teacher: Text level F—96% accuracy
- Current book: *Fancy Dance*, text level G
- Rate of accuracy: 17 errors out of 150 words is 89% accuracy. (Although Clay states that the instructional level requires 90–95% accuracy, I used teacher judgment to determine that level G is Quetzal's current instructional level.)

Qualitative Data

After looking at the cover of the book and briefly skimming the pictures, Quetzal was eager to read aloud for me. Before reading, I did prompt her to calm down and focus. "Do your best job reading the story," I told her. "I will only help if you really need it. Be sure to think about the story as you are reading, because when you finish reading, I am going to ask you to tell me about the story and I will ask you a few questions about what happened."

Quetzal's overall decoding and comprehension of *Fancy Dance* demonstrated that the book was at her instructional level. In other words, it will be the reading level at which her instructional activities, such as guided reading, take place. Quetzal's reading errors were consistent with the errors that she made when reading words in isolation, such as those on the Fry list, and when spelling words. Quetzal tends to attend to the first consonant or consonant cluster when decoding; she often doesn't pay close attention to what follows the beginning of a word. For example, during the running record, she read *silver* as *silly*, *bright* as *beautiful*, *begins* as *bing*, and *whirls* as *whines*. She attended to initial visual cues, but she did not monitor for visual precision in the middle or end of the word and did not cross-check meaning or structure to monitor that what she was reading looked right, made sense, and sounded right. The attention to the vowel onward requires knowledge about more than short-vowel sounds. As Quetzal increases her knowledge of long vowels, irregular vowels, and chunking multisyllabic words, we can expect her reading precision to increase.

When I asked Quetzal to retell the story, I did have to prompt her by asking her, "What happened first?" and "What happened after that?" Afterward, she was able to tell me the name of the main character, as well as the big ideas of the plot: "Joe was going to dance the Fancy Dance. At the beginning, he felt shy because he didn't want to dance, but then he felt happy when it was done." Quetzal was also able to recall several details from the storyline, such as the feathers and bells that adorned Joe's dancing costume.

On the basis of the NAEP Oral Reading Fluency Scale, Quetzal read the passage at a Level 3; the majority of her phrasing was appropriate, and she preserved the syntax of the author. She read primarily in phrase groups of three or four words. That being said, much of the story was read without expressive interpretation.

SUMMARY AND RECOMMENDATIONS

Quetzal, a first-grade student, is at the G instructional reading level and the early within word pattern developmental spelling stage. Her first language is Spanish, which is spoken in her home. However, she speaks English fluently and is not classified as an English language learner.

Quetzal is a skilled reader and writer. She has achieved an instructional reading level of text level G, the benchmark goal for first graders at this point in the school year. Throughout the assessments of this case study, she demonstrated her numerous literacy strengths and strategies. She is unfalteringly comfortable when handling reading materials. She is familiar with the English language's left-to-right directionality and top-to-bottom progression.

Quetzal has acquired mastery of letter recognition and formation. During the Letter ID/ Alphabet Recognition Assessment, she quickly identified the uppercase and lowercase letters. She forms her letters in a decipherable and consistent manner. Although there is some variance in the size of her handwriting between various words, the size remains fairly uniform within each word. Quetzal also demonstrated ease when using writing materials; she held pencils and pens with an appropriate grip.

Quetzal consistently proved her ability to recognize and use words as individual units that contain meaning. During both reading and writing tasks, Quetzal skillfully called upon a bank of high-frequency words that she has at her disposal.

Quetzal has reached a developmental stage in which she readily recognizes and uses short vowels. She also has relatively stable control over initial and final sounds, including consonant digraphs and blends. She demonstrated this knowledge in reading and writing, both in isolation of words and in connected text.

In addition to the literacy strengths that Quetzal exhibited, there are several concepts that she seems to find tough or confusing. For example, her writing shows that she is unsure about the correct placement of uppercase and lowercase letters; she tends to overuse uppercase letters, primarily for initial and final consonants.

Quetzal's biggest struggle when reading is her tendency to make approximations for unknown words based predominantly on the initial consonant letters and a random selection of the remaining letters; she also fails to cross-check whether her guess makes sense or matches the precise letter sequence. Quetzal needs instruction that teaches her to self-monitor her own reading to confirm that what she is reading looks right, sounds right, and makes sense.

The most pertinent difficulty that Quetzal encounters during her writing is the use of long-vowel markers. She realizes that long-vowel sounds warrant some sort of indicator, but has not yet mastered its orthographic representation. When writing the story during the Hearing Sounds in Words assessment, she spelled *late* as *layt*. Similarly, her Writing Vocabulary list included spellings of *cheese* as *cheas*, *nose* as *nos,* and *table* as *tayval*. This difficulty with long vowels is also contributing to her inability to arrive at a precise reading of unfamiliar words and to her resorting to guessing at an unknown word based on a few letters.

Although Quetzal is reading successfully compared to the expectations for first graders at this point in time, both her reading achievement and social success in classroom settings will be enhanced by providing her with instruction that is geared to her learning needs. It should certainly include a brief, explicit review of the rules that guide the placement of uppercase and lowercase letters. One possible activity might present her with a series of sentences that have misplaced uppercase or lowercase letters, and then guiding her toward correcting the sentences based on the corresponding rules. Additionally, providing a model of the uppercase and lowercase letters for easy retrieval and a proofreading checklist that reminds her to self-monitor her writing will help her begin the proofreading habit.

Quetzal is ready to receive explicit instruction that addresses long-vowel patterns. *Words Their Way* (Bear et al., 2020) recommends beginning this instruction with a comparison of short-vowel words and words with the corresponding long-vowel sounds that end with the silent *e*. During this introduction to long vowels, Quetzal can review blends and digraphs in her new spelling lists or in quick review games that include short-vowel words. As a means of rectifying Quetzal's confusion with encoding long-vowel markers, instruction might also incorporate various word sorts: picture sorts that contrast short- and long-vowel sounds and word sorts that emphasize long-vowel patterns. Assessment can be informal and ongoing; the teacher should monitor Quetzal's use of long-vowel markers in her day-to-day writing.

In order to ensure that Quetzal attends to each letter of a word before reading it, instruction should home in on the skill of pausing at an unknown word, examining its letters, and then making an approximation; she should learn to confirm or adjust this approximation in accordance with the visual, meaning, and structure cueing systems. This instruction could be delivered in small-group reading lessons of instructional-level texts (level G, in this case), which should take place between three and five times a week. The effectiveness of instruction should continue to be measured by Quetzal's performance during oral reading, by using tools such as running record assessments.

Finally, Quetzal demonstrated reading skills that place her slightly above the level of the typically developing first grader. Quetzal's teachers must provide instruction that offers her an adequate challenge, including rich texts and high-level discussions. To increase her interactions with other children, Quetzal will benefit from sharing leadership positions in classroom book clubs and collaborative research projects with her peers.

Case Study 3: Lee

Name: Lee	**Date of report:**
Grade: 3	**Dates of pretesting:** January 20XX
School: P.S. 555	**Date of posttesting:** April 20XX
Parents:	**Date of birth:**
Address:	**Age at testing:** 8.4
Telephone:	**Examiner:** Megan Monaghan[2]

BACKGROUND INFORMATION

Lee is an 8-year-old boy in third grade. Lee's teacher, Lindsey, recommended that I work with Lee because he is struggling in literacy and is currently lagging behind his peers. She hopes that one-on-one targeted instruction based on individual assessments will help him improve in reading and writing.

Lee lives with his grandmother. Over the last few years he has switched schools several times, but always seems to return to his current school. Because Lee has transferred schools so many times, a comprehensive record has not been available to Lindsey. Based on running records and conferences with Lee, she determined that level K was his instructional reading level. Fountas and Pinnell (1996) identify level K as approximately mid-second-grade level. Lindsey indicated that Lee has a hard time retaining directions given to him orally. Directions typically need to be repeated, and he requires frequent reminders to stay on task. She said he sometimes has a hard time staying focused on a single task, and that this is more apparent during ELA than during other times of the day.

Lindsey showed me Lee's reading response journal. His entries are typically one paragraph long, focusing on what he did not understand in the text, compared to the other students in class, who write about a page per entry and reflect upon what was read. Lee is not currently receiving any extra services.

The assessments took place during the third-grade literacy block, which is in the morning. Lee and I sat together in the hallway outside his classroom. He seemed very shy at first, but warmed up to me after we worked together a couple times. When there is a lot of activity going on in the hallway, Lee gets distracted, but responds well to gentle redirection.

PRETESTS ADMINISTERED (JANUARY XX, 20XX)

Elementary Reading Attitude Survey

	Raw score	Midyear percentile rank
Recreational reading	31	57
Academic reading	32	74
Reading attitude total	63	67

---

[2]Thanks to Megan Monaghan, a graduate student in the New York University Clinical Practicum at the time of first publication, for her contribution. Megan's case study has been used as a foundation, but Lee is a pseudonym, and all student information has been extensively revised to create a composite student.

Qualitative Reading Inventory

Graded Word Lists[3]

	One	Two	Three
Automatic	80%	80%	40%
Total correct	90%	90%	40%
Level[2]	IND	IND	FR

Reading Passages

Title	*Who Lives Near Lakes?*	*Mouse in a House*
Readability level	Primer	Grade 1
Total accuracy	100%	98%
Total acceptability	100%	100%
Rate	106 WCPM > 50th %ile	117 WCPM > 50th %ile
Retelling	44%	36%
Comprehension		
Explicit	4 correct	3 correct
Implicit	2 correct	2 correct
Total	6/6 (100%)	5/6 (83%)
Passage level	IND	INS

Title	*The Brain and the Five Senses*	*Father's New Game*
Readability level	Grade 1	Grade 2
Total accuracy	98%	91%
Total acceptability	100%	93%
Rate	109 WCPM > 50th %ile	89 WCPM 25th–50th %ile
Retelling	21%	31%
Comprehension		
Explicit	4 correct	3 correct
Implicit	2 correct	2 correct
Total	6/6 (100%)	5/8 (63%)
Passage level	IND	FR

Title	*Whales and Fish*
Readability level	Grade 2
Total accuracy	89%
Total acceptability	93%
Rate	80 WCPM 25th %ile

---

[3]IND, independent (Lee can read successfully without assistance); INS, instructional (Lee can read with assistance from a teacher); FR, frustration (Lee is unable to read the material with adequate word identification or comprehension).

Title	*Whales and Fish (continued)*
Retelling	47%

Comprehension
Explicit	3 correct
Implicit	2 correct
Total	5/8 (63%)

Passage level	FR

Fry Sight-Word Inventory

First 100 Words
Recognized immediately	96
Recognized with hesitation	2
Incorrect response	2
No response	0

Second 100 Words
Recognized immediately	90
Recognized with hesitation	3
Incorrect response	6
No response	1

Third 100 Words
Recognized immediately	84
Recognized with hesitation	5
Incorrect response	11
No response	0

Elementary Spelling Inventory

Consonants (beginning)	2/2	100%
Consonants (final)	5/5	100%
Short vowels	3/4	75%
Digraphs and blends	6/8	75%
Long-vowel patterns	5/6	83%
Other vowel patterns	0/4	0%
Syllable junctures and easy prefixes and suffixes	1/4	25%
Feature points	22/53	42%
Words attempted	15/25	60%
No. of correct words attempted	6/15	40%

Spelling stage: late within word pattern

Writing Sample

Qualitative Spelling Checklist: Within Word Pattern Stage

Dynamic Indicators of Basic Early Literacy Skills:
Oral Reading Fluency and Retell Fluency (Third Grade)

Benchmark 2.1:   78 WCPM
                    49 words in retell

Benchmark 2.2:   39 WCPM
                    8 words in retell

Benchmark 2.3:   72 WCPM
                    25 words in retell

OBSERVATIONS DURING PRETESTING

Development of Word Recognition

Qualitative Reading Inventory

The Qualitative Reading Inventory (QRI) is an informal assessment that helps teachers determine a child's independent, instructional, and frustration reading levels. The teacher can also assess the child's background knowledge in an area, keep track of reading miscues, learn about the child's fluency, and evaluate the child.

First, the child reads a graded word list. The child's ability to read each graded word list helps the teacher determine the appropriate grade-level passage of connected text. Some of the passages in the QRI are narrative and some are expository. In addition to using the word list, the teacher asks the child a few questions to determine whether the child has some prior knowledge about the content of the text. Then the child reads a story aloud. After the child reads, the teacher asks the student to retell what he or she remembers from the story. Next, the teacher asks the child a series of comprehension questions about the given passage. Older students have an option of looking back in the story to find the answers to questions they answered incorrectly.

I started the word list at Lee's grade level (grade 3) and then went down to an easier level. Lee read the third-grade reading list at 40% accuracy. This is definitely a frustration level for him. He had a tendency to use initial letters to guess at the words and did not attempt to read five of them. For example, Lee read the word *lion* as *long*, the word *rough* as *round*, and the word *worried* as *wouldn't*. At the second- and first-grade levels, Lee read 80% of the words automatically and 90% with some hesitation. This would be Lee's instructional/independent level for these words.

Fry Sight-Word Inventory

The Fry Sight-Word Inventory assesses a child's ability to recognize 300 words that occur often in text. Lee's incorrect responses indicate that he relies heavily on initial letters of each word. This was consistent with his word-attack pattern in the QRI graded word list. Examples are included below:

Word	Lee's reading
along	alone
example	explain
life	lift

always	away
while	white
turn	true
Indian	indent

Spelling Development

Elementary Spelling Inventory

The Elementary Spelling Inventory (Bear et al., 2020) is an assessment that helps the teacher determine the child's stage of spelling development. Each word on the test is more difficult than the previous word and contains features that the teacher can analyze to determine what the child understands about spelling and what is difficult for the child.

According to the feature guide and error guide that accompany the spelling inventory, Lee is currently in the late within word pattern stage of spelling. Lee demonstrated mastery of beginning and final consonant sounds and short-vowel sounds. He would benefit from a review of consonant blends, consonant digraphs, and long-vowel patterns. Lee requires explicit instruction of "other vowel patterns," which include *oi, er, ew,* and *ar.*

Qualitative Spelling Checklist

The Qualitative Spelling Checklist is an informal assessment that a teacher can use to help determine a child's stage of spelling. It can be used in conjunction with the spelling inventory or it can be used with other writing the student has done. For this assessment, I looked at an expository essay that Lee wrote about his friend Javon. The results of the analysis of Lee's spelling in the writing sample were consistent with the spelling test of words in isolation. Lee demonstrated mastery of patterns within the letter name stage of spelling. All short-vowel words were spelled correctly in his essay. In the category of within word pattern, Lee often uses, but confuses, long-vowel spelling representations. Lee spells blends and digraphs inconsistently. These features confirm that Lee is currently in the within word pattern stage of spelling. Examples of Lee's spelling errors are shown below.

Word	Lee's spelling
meet	mete
guys	gais
people	popel
reason	reuisn
fight	fitgt
great	grat

Reading Fluency

Dynamic Indicators of Basic Early Literacy Skills: Oral Reading Fluency and Retell Fluency

The Dynamic Indicators of Basic Early Literacy Skills (DIBELS) Oral Reading Fluency and Retell Fluency are assessments of accuracy and reading rate of connected text, as well as a check of comprehension. The child reads a graded passage for 1 minute, then has a minute to retell the events in the passage. The teacher keeps track of any errors the child makes when reading, provides pronunciation of words that are not read within 3 seconds, and keeps track of how many words are included in the child's retelling of the passage.

In the middle of the year at grade 3, students who are reading below 67 words correct per minute (WCPM) are considered at risk; students who are reading between 67 and 92 WCPM are considered at some risk; and students who are reading above 92 WCPM are considered at low risk. Using his median score of 72 correct, as advised on the DIBELS website, Lee is categorized as a student at some risk. If a student is not reading fluently, comprehension will be affected. This effect can be seen in Lee's retelling. When he read 78 WCPM, his retell consisted of 49 words. However, when Lee read at 39 WCPM, his retell was only 8 words long; he did not comprehend this text as well as the previous one.

Qualitative Reading Inventory

During the administration of the QRI, the child reads a passage aloud while the teacher listens and marks down any of the child's miscues. Lee's rate was higher on the QRI passages than on the DIBELS passages. He read 109 and 117 WCPM on the first-grade passages of the QRI. His rate dropped to 89 and 80 WCPM on the second-grade passages. These scores place him between the 25th and 50th percentile on a below-grade-level passage compared to other children in third grade reading a grade-level passage. The DIBELS passages were third-grade level, so it makes sense that he would be able to read easier passages of the QRI more fluently. On both the DIBELS assessment and the QRI, Lee's reading was monotone and lacked expression. His inattention to punctuation and meaning often resulted in awkward word grouping or phrasing.

Comprehension

The QRI graded passages are vehicles that teachers can use to assess many different aspects of reading. The teacher ascertains the student's prior knowledge by asking a few questions and rating the given answers. The child then reads a passage aloud while the teacher listens and records the child's miscues. After the passage is read, the child provides a retelling of it and answers comprehension questions.

According to the QRI results, Lee is reading independently at the preprimer and primer grade levels. Although Lee's reading accuracy ranged from an independent to an instructional level on the second-grade passages, and his reading rate was closer to the expected range for a third-grade student, his comprehension was at the frustration level. Lee had the most difficulty with the inferential questions. In addition, his retellings consisted of a few explicit story details and lacked themes or important story elements. Overall, it seemed as though Lee was making efforts to call words without making sense of the text along the way. First-grade material is likely to be at Lee's independent level. Lee's instructional reading level is early second grade. Although he is able to recognize the words in second-grade texts, he will need strong instructional support to comprehend texts at this level.

MOTIVATION/ATTITUDES

The Elementary Reading Attitude Survey is a quick survey that indicates the student's attitudes toward reading. I read each statement aloud and had Lee choose a Garfield picture that displays the emotion he feels about the statement. Overall, Lee has a positive attitude about both academic and recreational reading when compared with other children in third grade (67th percentile). In general, he has extremely positive feelings about academic reading (74th percentile). Lee does not like reading aloud during class, and he also prefers not to read over summer break. Lee enjoys reading during free time at school and at home.

SUMMARY OF PRETEST RESULTS (JANUARY XX, 20XX)

Lee is a third-grade boy in New York City with an early-second-grade instructional reading level. He is likely to be able to read and understand first-grade texts independently. He has a wonderful attitude about reading. This enjoyment of reading will be a valuable strength as we work together to strengthen some of Lee's reading challenges.

Lee is currently in the late within word pattern spelling stage. He has mastered the short vowels. He needs to refine his knowledge of long-vowel patterns and word endings, especially blends and digraphs. After refining this knowledge, Lee will need to be introduced to other more complex vowel patterns.

Lee has trouble reading many words that occur frequently in texts to which he is exposed. When approaching unknown words, he overrelies on initial letters. Lee needs practice identifying high-frequency words automatically. He also needs coaching in utilizing his knowledge about both short and long vowels when he comes to an unfamiliar word.

Lee needs to strengthen his reading fluency. The DIBELS Oral Reading Fluency suggests that Lee is at some risk because of his rate of reading. In addition, Lee has trouble reading with prosody; his reading sounds choppy and expressionless. Lee's lack of expression is associated with his comprehension difficulties.

Reading comprehension is an area that requires attention and explicit instruction. Lee's perception of comprehension seems to focus on the repetition of key words and isolated details from the text. He needs practice in identifying themes and the big ideas in texts. Currently, Lee has difficulty extending explicit information in text to generate inferences and personal connections.

RECOMMENDATIONS

There are many areas of literacy that Lee needs to strengthen. I have established a few goals for us to work on in the coming months. If Lee is able to become stronger in these areas, he will begin to catch up to his classmates and, in time, he will be reading at grade level.

Primary Goals

Increase rate, accuracy, and prosodic features of oral reading.
Improve reading comprehension: theme identification, story elements, inferences.

Secondary Goals

Increase automatic recognition of high-frequency words.
Increase accuracy in reading and spelling words with long-vowel patterns, diphthongs, and
   consonant blends.

Fluency and Prosody

Fluency and prosody are extremely important in reading. A fluent reader is able to read text so automatically that word recognition is not distracting him or her from making sense of the text. Prosody is also an important component of fluency. The term *prosody* means reading with expression. If a child is reading with prosody, he or she will sound conversational. Instead of the reading sounding choppy or robotic, the child's phrasing and inflection will reflect the meaning.

Echo Reading

Echo reading builds reading fluency. During the lesson, the teacher reads first and the student repeats what was read. This can be done with paragraphs or even full pages. The reader will echo not only the actual words, but also the prosody used by the teacher. Echo reading will provide Lee with an explicit model of fluent reading and provide the support he needs when encountering difficult vocabulary.

Partner Reading

During partner reading, two persons work together as a team to read a given text. Typically, the partners take turns reading. While one partner reads a portion of the story aloud, the other partner monitors and provides any necessary support. In working with Lee, the use of partner reading will enable us to read lengthier, more sophisticated texts in a reasonable time frame. The use of sophisticated texts will provide the substance needed for comprehension instruction and maintain Lee's good attitude about reading.

Repeated Reading

Repeated reading is an approach in which a child reads a piece of text multiple times. Through this repetition, Lee's increasing familiarity with the text will result in increasing fluency. Evidence seems to indicate that with each repetition, the child recognizes the words more quickly and can spend more energy reading with expression and gaining meaning from the text. I plan to use repeated reading of passages and poetry. Additionally, I will introduce Lee to some books from series to increase the likelihood that other texts in the series contain similar language and patterns to support his independent reading of the texts beyond our tutoring setting.

Reading Comprehension

The main goal of reading is to understand what is being read. Lee has difficulty comprehending text, and he retells a story by listing details or exact text phrases. Answering questions about a text is difficult for Lee. He needs instruction that will help him focus on the most important parts of text, and he needs to work on generating and answering comprehension questions.

Story Maps/Five-Finger Retelling

Lee's retellings tend to include every detail he remembers, rather than focusing on the most important aspects of the story. Story maps are graphic representations that focus on the most important features, including the characters, setting, problem, resolution, and lesson, thereby helping students to see how information from the story is organized. Instruction and modeling the use of a story map will help Lee identify the key elements in most stories. Once Lee is comfortable with the story map elements, he can use the five-finger retelling to summarize what he read by including only important elements: characters, setting, problem, resolution, and plot points that are essential to describing these aspects of the text. Lee will better understand what he is reading once he learns to focus on these parts, rather than trying to remember every detail in a story.

Teacher-Generated Questions

Lee needs practice answering both explicit questions (questions that can be answered directly through the text) and inference questions (questions that do not have a concrete answer in the text). Questions should help him focus on important parts of a story. It would be helpful for him to understand the different question types and how to go about answering them.

Development of Word Recognition

According to the QRI graded word lists and the Fry Sight-Word Inventory, Lee is not automatically recognizing as many words as he should for a child in third grade. Both his recognition of high-frequency words and his ability to use word-attack strategies to unlock an unknown word are preventing Lee from being able to read fluently.

Word Bank

This activity will help Lee master high-frequency words and other words that cause trouble during oral reading. The words are placed on index cards and practiced during each work session. Upon reading the word correctly three times, the word is placed in a separate word bank. These words are revisited periodically to confirm mastery.

Word Sorts

Word sorting is a way to engage students in constructing and owning their knowledge about how words work. Children are given lists of words to divide into categories based on features in the words. This type of activity will allow Lee to see many different words and compare how they are similar and different. Lee can apply these patterns to unfamiliar words when he is reading connected text or creating a written composition during writer's workshop. We will begin with a focus on long-vowel words that contain blends and digraphs. As Lee progresses, we will move into the exploration of complex vowel patterns.

SUMMARY OF THE TUTORING

Lee and I worked together twice a week from January 16 until May 1. We had 22 sessions together. I spent the first session observing Lee in his classroom and two sessions administering pretutoring assessments. During most of our time together, we focused on fluency and comprehension. During our last two sessions, I administered postassessments.

It was a pleasure for me to work with Lee. He was always eager to meet with me in the hallway and take part in our activities. He was never absent or late for school. We normally worked in the hallway, and the traffic could be distracting. Over time, he seemed to become more focused and less distracted by other students in the hallway.

Based on the results of initial assessments, my primary goals were to increase Lee's fluency and comprehension. As you can see from the descriptions of the activities below, prosody and text comprehension were always involved in fluency work. Simply reading faster was never an instructional objective.

Echo Reading

Echo reading was a common activity. First we would look at the text selection together and talk about the title and what the selection might be about. If we were reading part of a chapter book, Lee would summarize what had been previously read and make a purposeful prediction about what might be in the next section of text. Typically, I would begin reading a few lines of text or a paragraph. This procedure worked well with a few *Nate the Great* books by Marjorie Sharmat. We often followed this procedure with poetry. For more difficult poems, I would echo-read the poem line by line and then repeat by stanza. The repetition helped Lee with unfamiliar words, inflection, and stress as he tried to copy my model. Echo reading also helped Lee increase his rate of reading and confidence level. During our time together, Lee became a fan of poetry by Jack Prelutsky and Shel Silverstein.

Assisted Reading: Partner Reading and Paired Reading

In order to engage Lee with easy chapter books, we participated in partner reading and paired reading (Topping, 1987). I wanted Lee to read chapter books so that he would be exposed to a greater volume of words, to provide a scaffolded experience for take-home reading, and to engage in reading fun stories with fairly predictable story structures. Because I only worked with Lee twice a week, the use of easy chapter book series (*Nate the Great, Horrible Harry*) provided a way to sustain Lee's reading when I wasn't present. During the tutoring sessions, assisted reading provided a way to get through a significant amount of text in a short period, while modeling prosodic reading. When Lee and I worked together, we might partner-read the text by taking turns reading alternate pages, or we might do paired reading. During paired reading, we started out reading simultaneously (duet), and Lee later had the option of signaling that he wished to read solo. If he had trouble, I told him the word, and we continued in duet until he tapped to indicate his desire to return to solo reading. Assisted reading helped Lee gain confidence in reading aloud and helped him sustain fluent and prosodic reading with engaging chapter books. We would stop reading intermittently to discuss the characters and events in the book.

Fluency Development Lesson

After working with Lee for a few weeks, I began using a combination of the approaches above in a more intense routine. This approach is an adaptation of the fluency development lesson (Rasinski, Padak, Linek, & Sturtevant, 1994). First, we would read a chapter together using paired reading. Sometimes we would read three or four poems. We discussed the meaning of the chapter or each poem. Then Lee selected his favorite story part or individual poem and read it into a tape recorder. Next, I read it aloud and emphasized inflection, stress, and phrasing. At this point we discussed the relationship of relevant print functions (punctuation, paragraph, or stanza structure), fluency, and meaning. Then we echo-read Lee's selection. After echo reading, Lee and I divided up the lines and took turns reading them. We often did several different arrangements, resulting in multiple repeated readings. Finally, Lee read the poem aloud independently, and I recorded him again. At the end of the activity, I played back both recordings, and we talked about the differences between them. Hearing the improvement increased Lee's prosodic awareness and his motivation.

Listening Comprehension

For a portion of each lesson, I read aloud to Lee. This was an opportunity to remind Lee that the purpose of reading is to make sense of the text. During this reading, I asked questions and discussed the vocabulary and characters in the text. This was also the portion of the lesson that included instruction in story elements. Over time, Lee used the five-finger retelling to summarize the important elements: characters, setting, problem, attempts to solve the problem, and resolution.

Word Study

Word-study activities were fast-paced and fun for Lee. During each session, we did a quick activity to review and increase Lee's automatic recognition of high-frequency words. Lee enjoyed the Three Strikes activity. Fry words and some miscues from his daily reading were incorporated in this game. Each session also included a word sort or game that addressed consonant blends, long-vowel patterns, and diphthongs.

Writing

Although writing was not the main focus of our time together, Lee's teacher asked me to work with him on several occasions in the classroom setting. Lee seemed to have a difficult time getting started on his writing assignments, but he was able to do well with scaffolding and encouragement.

One of Lee's biggest difficulties was staying focused and organized. The writing workshop model in his class was designed to give children time to write every day after mini-lessons. Revising took place after multiple days of writing. Lee had paragraphs on different pages in a seemingly random order. To help Lee, I used small sticky notes to number his pages in the correct sequence. This system seemed to help him focus and aided his ability to revise.

Staying on task during the writing period was difficult for Lee. After the teacher's mini-lesson, I worked with Lee individually to discuss different ways to approach that day's writing task. If I stayed with Lee, he sat and wrote, sometimes asking questions about what he should do next, but usually writing independently. However, if I left his side to assist other students, he often got distracted and stopped writing. In order to motivate Lee, I began using a timer between my drop-ins with him. Explicitly stating expectations for his writing combined with the time limit worked well. Each time I returned to Lee's seat, he had achieved his writing goal!

POSTTEST RESULTS (APRIL XX, 20XX)

Qualitative Reading Inventory

Graded Words Lists

	One	Two	Three
January			
Automatic	80%	80%	40%
Total correct	90%	90%	40%
Level	IND	IND	FR
April			
Automatic	90%	90%	55%
Total correct	100%	95%	55%
Level	IND	INS	FR

Reading Passages

Passage level	Acc	WCPM	Comp	Level
January				
PP	100	126	100%	IND
Primer N	100	97	100%	IND
Primer E	100	106	100%	IND
1 N	100	117	83%	INS
1 E	100	109	100%	IND
2 N	93	89	63%	FR
2 E	93	80	63%	FR
April				
1 N	100	121 >50th	100	IND
1 E	100	140 >75th	100	IND
2 N	100	120 >50th	100	IND
2 E	96	89 25th–50th	75	INS
3 N	98	122 >50th	75	INS
4 N	94	75 <25th	50	FRUS

Fry Sight-Word Inventory

	January	April
First 100 Words		
Recognized immediately	96	99
Recognized with hesitation	2	1
Incorrect response	2	0
No response	0	0
Total recognized	98	100
Second 100 Words		
Recognized immediately	90	92
Recognized with hesitation	3	6
Incorrect response	6	1
No response	1	1
Total recognized	93	98
Third 100 Words		
Recognized immediately	84	93
Recognized with hesitation	5	5
Incorrect response	11	2
No response	0	0
Total recognized	89	98

Elementary Spelling Inventory

	January		April	
Consonants (beginning)	2/2	100%	2/2	100%
Consonants (final)	5/5	100%	5/5	100%
Short vowels	3/4	75%	3/4	75%
Digraphs and blends	6/8	75%	8/8	100%
Long-vowel patterns	5/6	83%	5/6	83%
Other vowel patterns	0/4	0%	3/6	50%
Syllable junctures and easy prefixes and suffixes	1/9	11%	3/9	33%
Feature points	22/53	42%	29/53	55%
Words attempted	5/25	60%	17/25	68%
No. of correct words attempted	6/15	40%	10/17	59%

DIBELS: Oral Reading Fluency and Retell Fluency

January Midyear Benchmarks

Benchmark 2.1:   78 WCPM
                 49 words in retell

Benchmark 2.2:   39 WCPM
                 8 words in retell

Benchmark 2.3:   72 WCPM
                 25 words in retell

April Third-Grade Progress Monitoring

Progress monitoring 1:   126 WCPM
                         77 words in retell

Progress monitoring 2:   106 WCPM
                         67 words in retell

Progress monitoring 3:   82 WCPM
                         43 words in retell

Progress monitoring 4:   79 WCPM
                         55 words in retell

Progress monitoring 5:   100 WCPM
                         42 words in retell

Progress monitoring 6:   128 WCPM
                         87 words in retell

Summary of Results

Lee's assessment scores on measures of comprehension, fluency, and retelling have all increased. According to the QRI results, Lee is reading independently at second-grade level. Test results indicate that he is likely to be able to successfully read third-grade materials if provided with instructional support. This indicates reading improvement from his January levels of frustration when reading narrative and expository second-grade materials.

Lee's overall progress in reading may be attributed to improvements in specific reading behaviors. He increased his automatic recognition of high-frequency words. Increased knowledge of particular vowel sounds and spelling patterns was indicated on the Elementary Spelling Inventory (Bear et al., 2020). Lee's choppy reading gave way to fluent reading with natural phrasing. He pays more attention to punctuation and is able to gain and retain more meaning from text.

During the pretest, comprehension questions often had to be rephrased before he was able to frame a response. He no longer needs this scaffolding. Although not every question was answered correctly, he no longer needed to clarify the meaning of the questions. The explicit instruction in reading purposefully has also helped his overall comprehension. Lee has shown great success over the last few months. According to his teacher, Lee's success has transferred to his literacy performance in the classroom, and she has observed increased engagement and motivation.

FURTHER RECOMMENDATIONS

In the future, Lee should continue many of the same activities in which he participated throughout his tutoring sessions. Continuing with a program that includes rereading texts, reading new texts, and developmentally based word study will address many of the reading difficulties that Lee continues to experience.

In addition to the recommendations already given, it is important to note three other suggestions that could not be covered in the short tutoring sessions that I had with Lee but would aid in his development as a reader. These include the application of fluency-oriented approaches with content-area materials, comprehension strategy instruction, and the use of concrete means to define a task and demonstrate expectations and progress. These are explained in the following material.

Fluency-Oriented Approaches in Content Areas

One activity that greatly benefits Lee and is a lot of fun for him is my modification of the fluency development lesson (Rasinski et al., 1994). This activity helps Lee in several areas, including fluency, prosody, word recognition, vocabulary, and comprehension. The technique worked very well with Lee during our time together, and it may continue to support Lee's efforts with increasingly difficult text. Continuing this activity will provide a fluency maintenance program and provide the close reading that Lee still needs to support comprehension and vocabulary development. In addition, this technique might incorporate famous speeches and other documents related to content-area instruction. The radio reading (see Rasinski, 2010) technique would also be a good approach for Lee. During radio reading, each student in a small group is assigned to rehearse one section of a larger informational text. Each student assumes responsibility for reading that section of text to the small group and asking one or two comprehension questions based on that segment of text.

Comprehension Strategy Instruction

Lee would benefit from explicit instruction of comprehension strategies such as activating prior knowledge, summarization, questioning, self-monitoring, generating inferences, and text structures. I initiated instruction in narrative text structure and in how to answer teacher-generated questions. These two strategies gave Lee greater self-regulation in being able to provide a retelling of a narrative and to answer comprehension questions. However, this was a meager beginning. For Lee to make sense of the complex texts that he will encounter in the intermediate grades, he will need far more instruction in the cognitive strategies used by proficient readers to derive meaning and evaluate texts. Tools such as graphic organizers, utilization of short hypertext selections, and conversational application of the strategies might be motivational and effective with Lee. The use of graphic organizers and conversation are also likely to support Lee in translating his comprehension of text to his own written products that reflect his understanding.

Defining a Task

Lee responded well when expectations and markers of progress were clearly defined. He was able to use a structure defined by common story elements to improve the quantity and quality of his retellings. Using charts to analyze his errors and prosodic reading improved his fluency in dramatic ways. Even in the classroom, assigning a small, specific composition task within a time frame was met with success. Lee's learning seems to be enhanced when he can have a visual target, graphic representation, or clearly stated goal set before him. These elements might be kept in mind when planning a wide range of instruction for Lee.

References

Adams, M. J. (1990). *Beginning to read: Thinking and learning about print.* Cambridge, MA: MIT Press.

Adams, M. J. (1998). The three-cuing system. In J. Osborn & F. Lehr (Eds.), *Literacy for all: Issues in teaching and learning* (pp. 73–99). New York: Guilford Press.

Afflerbach, P., & Cho, B. (2009). Identifying and describing constructively responsive comprehension strategies in new and traditional forms of reading. In S. E. Israel & G. G. Duffy (Eds.), *Handbook of research on reading comprehension* (pp. 69–90). New York: Routledge.

Afflerbach, P., Pearson, P. D., & Paris, S. G. (2008). Clarifying differences between reading skills and reading strategies. *The Reading Teacher, 61,* 364–373.

Alliance for Excellent Education. (2006). *Who's counted? Who's counting?: Understating high school graduation rates.* Washington, DC: Author.

Allington, R. L. (1983). Fluency: The neglected reading goal. *The Reading Teacher, 37,* 556–561.

Allington, R. L. (1984). Content coverage and contextual reading in reading groups. *Journal of Reading Behavior, 16,* 85–96.

Alvermann, D. E., Smith, L. C., & Readance, J. E. (1985). Prior knowledge activation and the comprehension of compatible and incompatible text. *Reading Research Quarterly, 20,* 420–426.

Anderson, R. C., & Freebody, P. (1981). Vocabulary knowledge. In J. Guthrie (Ed.), *Comprehension and teaching: Research reviews* (pp. 77–117). Newark, DE: International Reading Association.

Anderson, R. C., & Freebody, P. (1983). Reading comprehension and the assessment and acquisition of word knowledge. *Advances in Reading/Language Research, 2,* 231–256.

Anderson, R. C., & Freebody, P. (1985). Vocabulary knowledge. In H. Singer & R. B. Ruddell (Eds.), *Theoretical models and processes of reading* (3rd ed., pp. 343–371). Newark, DE: International Reading Association.

Anderson, R. C., & Pearson, P. D. (1984). A schema-theoretic view of basic processes in reading. In P. D. Pearson (Ed.), *Handbook of reading research* (pp. 255–292). White Plains, NY: Longman.

Beach, S. A. (1992). *Toward a model of the development of reader resources in the emergence and acquisition of literacy skill.* Unpublished doctoral dissertation, University of California, Riverside.

Bear, D. R., Invernizzi, M., Templeton, S., & Johnston, F. (2020). *Words their way: Word study for phonics, vocabulary, and spelling instruction* (7th ed.). Boston: Pearson.

Beck, I. L., & McKeown, M. G. (2001). Text talk: Capturing the benefits of read-aloud experiences for young children. *The Reading Teacher, 55,* 10–35.

Beck, I. L., Perfetti, C., & McKeown, M. G. (1982). Effects of long-term vocabulary instruction on lexical access and reading comprehension. *Journal of Educational Psychology, 74*(4), 506–521.

Betts, E. A. (1946). *Foundations of reading instruction.* New York: American Books.

Biancarosa, G., & Snow, C. E. (2006). *Reading next: A vision for action and research in middle and high school literacy. A report to Carnegie Corporation of New York* (2nd ed.). Washington, DC: Alliance for Excellent Education.

Biemiller, A. (1970). The development of the use of graphic and contextual information as children learn to read. *Reading Research Quarterly, 6,* 75–96.

Bloom, B. S. (1969). *Taxonomy of educational objectives: The classification of educational goals.* New York: Longman.

Bradley, B. A., & Jones, J. (2007). Sharing alphabet books in early childhood classrooms. *The Reading Teacher, 60,* 452–463.

Bravo, M. A., Cervetti, G. N., Hiebert, E. H., & Pearson, P. D. (2008). From passive to active control of science vocabulary. In D. W. Rowe et al. (Eds.), *Fifty-sixth yearbook of the National Reading Conference* (pp. 122–135). Chicago: National Reading Conference.

Brown, L. T., Mohr, K. A. J., Wilcox, B. R., & Barrett, T. S. (2018). The effect of dyad reading and text difficulty on third graders' reading achievement. *Journal of Educational Research, 111*(5), 541–553.

Brozo, W. G., & Afflerbach, P. P. (2011). *Adolescent Literacy Inventory: Grades 6–12.* Boston: Pearson.

Byrne, B. (1998). *The foundation of literacy: The child's acquisition of the alphabetic principle.* Brighton, UK: Psychology Press.

Carbo, M., Dunn, R., & Dunn, K. (1986). *Teaching students to read through their individual learning styles.* Englewood Cliffs, NJ: Prentice-Hall.

Carroll, J. B., Davies, P., & Richman, B. (1971). *Word frequency book.* Boston: Houghton Mifflin.

Catts, H. W., Hogan, T. P., & Adolf, S. M. (2005). Developmental changes in reading and reading disabilities. In H. W. Catts & A. G. Kahmi (Eds.), *The connections between language and reading disabilities* (pp. 25–40). Mahwah, NJ: Erlbaum.

Cervetti, G. N., Barber, J., Dorph, R., Pearson, P. D., & Goldschmidt, P. G. (2012). The impact of an integrated approach to science and literacy in elementary school classrooms. *Journal of Research in Science Teaching, 49,* 631–658.

Chall, J. S. (1996). *Stages of reading development* (2nd ed.). Fort Worth, TX: Harcourt Brace College.

Chomsky, C. (1979). Approaching reading through invented spelling. In L. B. Resnick & P. A. Weaver (Eds.), *Theory and practice of early reading* (Vol. 2, pp. 43–65). Hillsdale, NJ: Erlbaum.

Clay, M. M. (1993). *Reading Recovery: A guidebook for teachers in training.* Portsmouth, NH: Heinemann.

Clay, M. M. (2000). *Running records for classroom teachers.* Portsmouth, NH: Heinemann.

Clay, M. M. (2013). *An observation survey of early literacy achievement* (3rd ed.). Portsmouth, NH: Heinemann.

Clymer, T. (1963). The utility of phonic generalizations in the primary grades. *The Reading Teacher, 16,* 252–258.

Coiro, J., & Dobler, E. (2011). Exploring the online reading comprehension strategies used by sixth-grade skilled readers to search for and locate information on the Internet. *Reading Research Quarterly, 42,* 214–257.

Conant, L. L., Liebenthal, E., Desai, A., & Binder, J. R. (2014). fMRI of phonemic perception and its relationship to reading development in elementary-to-middle-school-age children. *NeuroImage, 89,* 192–202.

Conradi, K. (2014). Tapping technology's potential to motivate readers. *Phi Delta Kappan, 96*(3), 54–57.

Conradi, K., Jang, B. G., Lawrence, C., Craft, A., & McKenna, M. C. (2013). Measuring adolescents' attitudes toward reading: A classroom survey. *Journal of Adolescent and Adult Literacy, 56,* 565–576.

Conradi, K., Jang, B. G., & McKenna, M. C. (2014). Motivation terminology in reading research: A conceptual review. *Educational Psychology Review, 26,* 127–164.

Coxhead, A. (2000). A new academic word list. *TESOL Quarterly, 34*(2), 213–238.

Cronbach, L. J. (1942). Measuring knowledge of precise word meaning. *Journal of Educational Research, 36,* 528–534.

Cunningham, A. E., & Stanovich, K. E. (1991). Tracking the unique effects of print exposure in children: Associations with vocabulary general knowledge, and spelling. *Journal of Educational Psychology, 83,* 264–274.

Cunningham, J. W. (1982). Generating interactions between schemata and text. In J. A. Niles & L. A. Harris (Eds.), *New inquiries in reading research and instruction: Thirty-first yearbook of the National Reading Conference* (pp. 42–47). Rochester, NY: National Reading Conference.

Cunningham, J. W., Erickson, K. A., Spadorcia, S. A., Koppenhaver, D. A., Cunningham, P. M., Yoder, D. E., et al. (1999). Assessing decoding from an onset–rime perspective. *Journal of Literacy Research, 31,* 391–414.

Cunningham, P. M. (2001). *Phonics they use.* New York: HarperCollins.

Cunningham, P. M. (2012). *Phonics they use: Words for reading and writing* (6th ed.). New York: Pearson.

Cunningham, P. M., & Hall, D. P. (2001). *Making big words: Multilevel, hands-on spelling and phonics activities.* Greensboro, NC: Good Apple.

Cunningham, P. M., & Hall, D. P. (2008). *Making words: First grade: 100 hands-on lessons for phonemic awareness, phonics, and spelling.* Greensboro, NC: Good Apple.

Dale, E. (1946). The art of reading. *Ohio State University News Letter, 9,* 1.

Dale, E. (1965). Vocabulary measurement: Techniques and major findings. *Elementary English, 42,* 895–901.

Davis, F. B. (1944). Fundamental factors of comprehension in reading. *Psychometrika, 9,* 185–197.

Davis, A. P., & McDaniel, T. R. (1998). An essential vocabulary: An update. *The Reading Teacher, 52,* 308–309.

Deshler, D. D., Palinscar, A.S., Biancarosa, G., & Nair, M. (2007). *Informed choices for struggling adolescent readers: A research-based guide to instructional programs and practices.* New York: Guilford Press.

Dolch, E. W. (1936). A basic sight vocabulary. *The Elementary School Journal, 36,* 456–460.

Donahue, P. L., Voelkl, K. E., Campbell, J. R., & Mazzeo, J. (1999). *NAEP 1998 reading report card for the nation* (prepublication ed.). Washington, DC: U.S. Department of Education, Office of Educational Research and Improvement.

Dunn, D. M. (2019). *Peabody Picture Vocabulary Test* (5th ed.). Bloomington, MN: NCS Pearson.

Dweck, C. S. (2007). *Mindset: The new psychology of success.* New York: Random House.

Ehri, L. C. (1998). Grapheme–phoneme knowledge is essential for learning to read words in English. In J. L. Metsala & L. C. Ehri (Eds.), *Word recognition in beginning literacy* (pp. 3–40). Mahwah, NJ: Erlbaum.

Ehri, L. C., & Robbins, C. (1992). Beginners need some decoding skill to read words by analogy. *Reading Research Quarterly, 27,* 12–26.

Ehri, L. C., & Sweet, J. (1991). Fingerpoint-reading of memorized text: What enables beginners to process the print. *Reading Research Quarterly, 26,* 442–462.

Elkonin, D. B. (1973). U.S.S.R. In J. Downing (Ed.), *Comparative reading* (pp. 551–579). New York: Macmillan.

English, F. W., & Frase, L. B. (1999). *Deciding what to teach and test: Developing, aligning, and auditing the curriculum.* Thousand Oaks, CA: Corwin Press.

Evans, M., Bell, M., Shaw, D., Moretti, S., & Page, J. (2006). Letter names, letter sounds, and phonological awareness: An examination of kindergarten children across letters and of letters across children. *Reading and Writing, 19,* 959–989.

Farr, R. (1992). Putting it all together: Solving the reading assessment puzzle. *The Reading Teacher, 46,* 26–37.

Flanigan, K. (2006). "Daddy, where did the words go?": How teachers can help emergent readers develop a concept of word in text. *Reading Improvement, 43*(1), 37–49.

Flanigan, K. (2007). A concept of word in text: A pivotal event in early reading acquisition. *Journal of Literacy Research, 39*(1), 37–70.

Fountas, I. C., & Pinnell, G. S. (1996). *Guided reading: Good first teaching for all children.* Portsmouth, NH: Heinemann.

Fountas, I. C., & Pinnell, G. S. (2006). *Leveled book list K–8.* Portsmouth, NH: Heinemann.

Fountas, I. C., & Pinnell, G. S. (2010). *Benchmark Assessment System* (2nd ed.). Portsmouth, NH: Heinemann.

Fountas, I. C., & Pinnell, G. S. (2017). Progress monitoring by instructional text reading level. Retrieved from *www.fountasandpinnell.com/Authenticated/ResourceDocuments/Progress-Monitor-10mos%20-%20by%20level_OCT2017.pdf.*

Francis, N. (1999). Applications of cloze procedure to reading assessment in special circumstances of literacy development. *Reading Horizons, 40,* 23–44.

Frey, N., Fisher, D., & Hernandez, T. (2003). "What's the gist?": Summary writing for struggling adolescent readers. *Voices from the Middle, 11*(2), 43–49.

Frith, U. (1980). Unexpected spelling problems. In U. Frith (Ed.), *Cognitive processes in spelling* (pp. 495–515). London: Academic Press.

Fry, E. B. (1980). The new Instant Word List. *The Reading Teacher, 34,* 284–289.

Fuchs, D., & Fuchs, L. (2005). Peer-Assisted Learning Strategies: Promoting word recognition, fluency, and reading comprehension in young children. *Journal of Special Education, 39*(1), 34–44.

Fuchs, D., Fuchs, L. S., Mathes, P. G., & Simmons, D. C. (1997). Peer-Assisted Learning Strategies: Making classrooms more responsive to diversity. *American Educational Research Journal, 34*(1), 174–206.

Ganske, K. (2014). *Word journeys: Assessment-guided phonics, spelling, and vocabulary instruction* (2nd ed.). New York: Guilford Press.

Garner, R., & Kraus, C. (1981). Good and poor comprehender differences in knowing and regulating reading behaviors. *Educational Research Quarterly, 6,* 5–12.

Gaskins, I. W., Downer, M. A., Anderson, R. C., Cunningham, P. M., Gaskins, R. W., Schommer, M., et al. (1988). A metacognitive approach to phonics: Using what you know to decode what you don't know. *Remedial and Special Education, 9,* 36–41.

Gaskins, I. W., Ehri, L. C., Cress, C., O'Hara, C., & Donnelly, K. (1996). Procedures for word learning: Making discoveries about words. *The Reading Teacher, 50,* 312–328.

Gill, J. T. (2019). *Concept of Word Scale.* Unpublished manuscript.

Good, R. H., & Kaminski. R. A. (2011). *DIBELS Next assessment manual.* Eugene, OR: Dynamic Measurement Group.

Goodman, K. S. (1993). *Phonics phacts.* Portsmouth, NH: Heinemann.

Gough, P. B., Juel, C., & Griffith, P. L. (1992). Reading, spelling, and the orthographic cipher. In P. B. Gough, L. C. Ehri, & R. Treiman (Eds.), *Reading acquisition* (pp. 35–48). Hillsdale, NJ: Erlbaum.

Graesser, A. C., McNamara, D. S., Louwerse, M. M., & Cai, Z. (2004). Coh-Metrix: Analysis of text on cohesion and language. *Behavior Research Methods, Instruments, and Computers, 36,* 193–202.

Green, T. M. (2008). *The Greek and Latin roots of English* (4th ed.). Lanham, MD: Rowman & Littlefield.

Guthrie, J. T. (2004). Teaching for literacy engagement. *Journal of Literacy Research, 36,* 1–30.

Guthrie, J. T., & McCann, A. D. (1996). Idea circles: Peer collaborations for conceptual learning. In L. B. Gambrell & J. F. Almasi (Eds.), *Lively discussions!: Fostering engaged reading* (pp. 87–105). Newark, DE: International Reading Association.

Guthrie, J. T., Seifert, M., Burnham, N., & Caplan, R. (1974). The maze technique to assess, monitor reading comprehension. *The Reading Teacher, 28,* 161–168.

Harste, J. C., Burke, C. L., & Woodward, V. A. (1982). Children's language and world: Initial encounters with print. In J. A. Langer & M. T. Smith-Burke (Eds.), *Reader meets author: Bridging the gap* (pp. 105–131). Newark, DE: International Reading Association.

Hasbrouck, J. E., & Tindal, G. (2006). Oral reading fluency norms: A valuable assessment tool for reading teachers. *The Reading Teacher, 59,* 636–644.

Hasbrouck, J., & Tindal, G. (2017). *An update to compiled ORF norms* (Technical Report No. 1702). Eugene: Behavioral Research and Teaching, University of Oregon. Retrieved from *www.brtprojects.org/wp-content/uploads/2019/05/TechRpt_1702ORFNorms.pdf.*

Hayes, D. A. (1989). Helping students grasp the knack of writing summaries. *Journal of Reading, 33,* 96–101.

Hayes, L., & Flanigan, K. (2014). *Developing word recognition.* New York: Guilford Press.

Henderson, E. H. (1981). *Learning to read and spell: The child's knowledge of words.* DeKalb: Northern Illinois University Press.

Hock, M. F., Brasseur, I. F., Deshler, D. D., Catts, H. W., Marquis, J. G., Mark, C. A., et al. (2009). What is the reading component profile of adolescent struggling readers in urban schools? *Learning Disabilities Quarterly, 32,* 21–38.

Hoffman, J. (1987). Rethinking the role of oral reading. *The Elementary School Journal, 87,* 367–373.

Huang, F. L., Tortorelli, L. S., & Invernizzi, M. A. (2014). An investigation of factors associated with letter-sound knowledge at kindergarten entry. *Early Childhood Research Quarterly, 29,* 182–192.

Hutchins, P. (1968). *Rosie's walk.* New York: Simon & Schuster.

Invernizzi, M., Meier, J., & Juel, C. (2007). *PALS 1–3: Phonological Awareness Literacy Screening 1–3* (6th ed.). Charlottesville: University of Virginia.

Invernizzi, M., Sullivan, A., Swank, L., & Meier, J. (2004). *PALS-PreK: Phonological Awareness Literacy Screening for Preschoolers* (6th ed.). Charlottesville: University of Virginia.

Invernizzi, M., Swank, L., & Juel, C. (2007). *PALS-K: Phonological Awareness Literacy Screening—Kindergarten* (6th ed.). Charlottesville: University of Virginia.

Jacobs, J. E., & Paris, S. G. (1987). Children's metacognition about reading: Issues in definition, measurement, and instruction. *Educational Psychologist, 22,* 255–278.

Jang, B. G., Conradi, K., McKenna, M. C., & Jones, J. S. (2015). Motivation: Approaching an elusive concept through the factors that shape it. *The Reading Teacher, 69*(2), 239–247.

Johns, J. L. (2017). *Basic Reading Inventory: Kindergarten through grade twelve and early literacy assessments* (12th ed.). Dubuque, IA: Kendall–Hunt.

Johnston, P. H. (2000). *Running records: A self-tutoring guide* [Book and audiocassette]. Portland, ME: Stenhouse.

Jones, C. D., & Reutzel, D. R. (2012). Enhanced alphabet knowledge instruction: Exploring a change of frequency, focus and distributed cycles of review. *Reading Psychology, 33,* 448–464.

Kamil, M. L. (2003). *Adolescents and literacy: Reading for the 21st century.* Washington, DC: Alliance for Excellent Education.

Kendeou, P., Bohn-Gettler, C., White, M. J., & van den Broek, P. (2008). Children's inference generation across different media. *Journal of Research in Reading, 31,* 259–272.

Kibby, M. (1979). Passage readability affects the oral reading strategies of disabled readers. *The Reading Teacher, 32,* 390–396.

Killgallon, P. A. (1942). *A study of relationships among certain pupil adjustments in reading situations.* Unpublished doctoral dissertation, Pennsylvania State College, State College, PA.

Klingner, J. K., Vaughn, S., Dimino, J., Schumm, J. S., & Bryant, D. (2001). *From clunk to click: Collaborative strategic reading.* Longmont, CO: Sopris West.

Krahn, F. (1979). *Robot-bot-bot.* New York: Dutton.

Kuhn, M. R., & Levy, L. (2015). *Developing fluent readers: Teaching fluency as a foundational skill.* New York: Guilford Press.

Kuhn, M. R., & Stahl, S. A. (2003). Fluency: A review of developmental and remedial practices. *Journal of Educational Psychology, 95,* 3–21.

LaBerge, D., & Samuels, S. J. (1974). Toward a theory of automatic information processing in reading. *Cognitive Psychology, 6,* 293–323.

LaPray, M., & Ross, R. (1969). The graded word list: Quick gauge of reading ability. *Journal of Reading, 12,* 305–307.

Leach, J. M., Scarborough, H. S., & Rescorla, L. (2003). Late-emerging reading disabilities. *Journal of Educational Psychology, 95,* 211-224.

Lee, J., & Yoon, S. (2017). The effect of repeated reading on reading fluency for students with reading disabilities. *Journal of Learning Disabilities, 50*(2), 213–224.

Leal, D. J. (1993). The power of literary peer group discussions: How children collaboratively negotiate meaning. *The Reading Teacher, 47,* 114–120.

Leslie, L., & Caldwell, J. S. (2011). *Qualitative Reading Inventory–5.* New York: Pearson.

Leslie, L., & Caldwell, J. S. (2016). *Qualitative Reading Inventory–6.* New York: Pearson.

Leu, D. J., Forzani, E., Burlingame, C., Kulikowich, J., Sedransk, N., Coiro, J., et al. (2013). The new literacies of online research and comprehension: Assessing and preparing students for the 21st century with Common Core State Standards. In S. B. Neuman & L. B. Gambrell (Eds.), *Quality reading instruction in the age of the Common Core Standards* (pp. 219–236). Newark, DE: International Reading Association.

Leu, D. J., Forzani, E., Rhoads, C., Maykel, C., Kennedy, C., & Timbrell, N. (2015). The new literacies of online research and comprehension: Rethinking the reading achievement gap. *Reading Research Quarterly, 50,* 37–59.

Lipson, M. Y. (1983). The influence of religious affiliation on children's memory for test information. *Reading Research Quarterly, 18,* 448–457.

Malloy, J. A., Parsons, A. W., Marinak, B. A., Applegate, A. J., Applegate, M. D., Reutzel, D. R., et al. (2017). Assessing (and addressing!) motivation to read fiction and nonfiction. *The Reading Teacher, 71*(3), 309–325.

Manzo, A. V. (1969). The ReQuest procedure. *Journal of Reading, 2,* 123–126.

Manzo, A. V., & Casale, U. P. (1985). Listen–read–discuss: A content reading heuristic. *Journal of Reading, 28,* 732–734.

Marcell, B. (2011). Putting fluency on a fitness plan: Building fluency's meaning-making muscles. *The Reading Teacher, 65,* 242–249.

Martin, B., Jr. (1967). *Brown bear, brown bear, what do you see?* New York: Holt, Rinehart & Winston.

McGee, L. M., Kim, H., Nelson, K. S., & Fried, M. D. (2015). Change over time in first graders' strategic use of information at point of difficulty in reading. *Reading Research Quarterly, 50*(3), 263–291.

McKenna, M. C. (1983). Informal reading inventories: A review of the issues. *The Reading Teacher, 36,* 670–679.

McKenna, M. C. (2001). Development of reading attitudes. In L. Verhoeven & C. Snow (Eds.), *Literacy and motivation: Reading engagement in individuals and groups* (pp. 135–158). Mahwah, NJ: Erlbaum.

McKenna, M. C. (2002). *Help for struggling readers: Strategies for grades 3–8.* New York: Guilford Press.

McKenna, M. C., Conradi, K., Lawrence, C., Jang, B. G., & Meyer, J. P. (2012). Reading attitudes of middle school students: Results of a U.S. survey. *Reading Research Quarterly, 47,* 283–306.

McKenna, M. C., & Kear, D. J. (1990). Measuring attitudes toward reading: A new tool for teachers. *The Reading Teacher, 43,* 626–639.

McKenna, M. C., Kear, D. J., & Ellsworth, R. A. (1995). Children's attitudes toward reading: A national survey. *Reading Research Quarterly, 30,* 934–956.

McKenna, M. C., & Robinson, R. D. (2014). *Teaching through text: Reading and writing in the content areas* (2nd ed.). Boston: Pearson.

Messick, S. (1993). Validity. In R. L. Linn (Ed.), *Educational measurement* (3rd ed., pp. 13–103). New York: Macmillan.

Minnema, J., Thurlow, M., Bielinski, J., & Scott, J. (2000). *Past and present understandings of out-of-level testing: A research synthesis* (Out-of-Level Testing Project Report 1). Minneapolis: University of Minnesota, National Center on Educational Outcomes. Retrieved from *https://nceo.info/Resources/publications/OnlinePubs/OOLT1.html.*

Morris, D. (1993). The relationship between children's concept of word in text and phoneme awareness in learning to read: A longitudinal study. *Research in the Teaching of English, 27,* 133–154.

Morris, D. (2014). *Diagnosis and correction of reading problems* (2nd ed.). New York: Guilford Press.

Morris, D., Bloodgood, J. W., Lomax, R., & Perney, J. (2003). Developmental steps in learning to read: A longitudinal study in kindergarten and first grade. *Reading Research Quarterly, 38,* 302–328.

Morris, D., Bloodgood, J. W., Perney, J., Frye, E., Kucan, L., Trathen, W., Ward, D., & Schlagal, R. (2011). Validating craft knowledge: An empirical examination of elementary-grade students' performance on an informal reading assessment. *The Elementary School Journal, 112*(2), 205–233.

Nagy, W. E. (1988). *Teaching vocabulary to improve reading comprehension.* Newark, DE: International Reading Association.

Nagy, W. E., & Scott, J. (2000). Vocabulary processes. In M. L. Kamil, P. B. Mosenthal, P. D. Pearson, & R. Barr (Eds.), *Handbook of reading research* (Vol. 3, pp. 269–283). Mahwah, NJ: Erlbaum.

Nagy, W. E., & Townsend, D. (2012). Words as tools: Learning academic vocabulary as language acquisition. *Reading Research Quarterly, 47*(1), 91–108.

National Assessment Governing Board. (2013). *Reading framework for the 2013 National Assessment of Educational Progress.* Washington, DC: U.S. Department of Education. Retrieved from *www.nagb.org/content/nagb/assets/documents/publications/frameworks/reading-2013-framework.pdf.*

National Center for Education Statistics. (2005). *National Assessment of Educational Progress (NAEP) 2002 oral reading study.* Washington, DC: Author.

National Center for Education Statistics. (2017). *National Assessment of Educational Progress: Reading assessment.* Washington, DC: Author. Retrieved from *https://nces.ed.gov/nationsreportcard/reading.*

National Governors Association Center for Best Practices (NGACBP) & Council of Chief State School Officers (CCSSO). (2010). *Common Core State Standards for English language arts and literacy, history, social studies, science and technical subjects.* Washington, DC: Authors.

National Reading Panel. (2000). *Teaching children to read: An evidence-based assessment of the scientific research literature on reading and its implications for reading instruction. Report of the subgroups.* Washington, DC: National Institute of Child Health and Human Development.

Neugebauer, S. R. (2017). Assessing situated reading motivations across content areas: A dynamic literacy motivation instrument. *Assessment for Effective Intervention, 42*(3), 131–149.

O'Connor, R. E. (2014). *Teaching word recognition: Effective strategies for students with learning difficulties* (2nd ed.). New York: Guilford Press.

O'Connor, R. E., Bell, K. M., Harty, K. R., & Larkin, L. R. (2002). Teaching readers to poor readers in the intermediate grades: A comparison of text difficulty. *Journal of Educational Psychology, 94*(3), 474–485.

Owocki, G., & Goodman, Y. M. (2002). *Kidwatching: Documenting children's literacy development.* Portsmouth, NH: Heinemann.

Palincsar, A. S., & Brown, A. L. (1984). Reciprocal teaching of comprehension fostering and comprehension monitoring activities. *Cognition and Instruction, 1*(2), 117–175.

Paris, A. H., & Paris, S. G. (2003). Assessing narrative comprehension in young children. *Reading Research Quarterly, 38,* 36–76.

Paris, S. G. (1985). Using classroom dialogues and guided practice to teach comprehension strategies. In T. L. Harris & E. J. Cooper (Eds.), *Reading, thinking, and concept development* (pp. 105–130). New York: College Entrance Examination Board.

Paris, S. G. (2005). Reinterpreting the development of reading skills. *Reading Research Quarterly, 40,* 184–202.

Paris, S. G., & Hamilton, E. E. (2009). The development of children's reading comprehension. In S. E. Israel & G. G. Duffy (Eds.), *Handbook of research on reading comprehension* (pp. 32–53). New York: Routledge.

Paris, S. G., Lipson, M. Y., & Wixson, K. K. (1983). Becoming a strategic reader. *Contemporary Educational Psychology, 8,* 293–316.

Paris, S. G., Pearson, P. D., Cervetti, G., Carpenter, R., Paris, A. H., DeGroot, J., et al. (2004). Assessing the effectiveness of summer reading programs. In G. Borman & M. Boulay (Eds.), *Summer learning: Research, policies, and programs* (pp. 121–162). Mahwah, NJ: Erlbaum.

Parker, R. I., & Hasbrouck, J. E. (1992). The maze as a classroom-based reading measure: Construction methods, reliability, and validity. *Journal of Special Education, 26,* 195–218.

Pearson, P. D., & Gallagher, M. C. (1983). The instruction of reading comprehension. *Contemporary Educational Psychology, 8,* 317–344.

Pearson, P. D., Hiebert, E. H., & Kamil, M. L. (2007). Vocabulary assessment: What we know and what we need to learn. *Reading Research Quarterly, 42*(2), 282–296.

Perfetti, C. A., & Adlof, S. (2012). Reading comprehension: A conceptual framework from word meaning to text meaning. In J. P. Sabatini, E. R. Albro, & T. O'Reilly (Eds.), *Measuring up: Advances in how to assess reading ability* (pp. 3–20). Lanham, MD: Rowman & Littlefield Education.

Perfetti, C. A., Beck, I. L., Bell, L., & Hughes, C. (1987). Phonemic knowledge and learning to read are reciprocal: A longitudinal study of first-grade children. *Merrill–Palmer Quarterly, 33,* 283–319.

Peterson, B. (1991). Selecting books for beginning readers. In D. E. DeFord, C. A. Lyons, & G. S. Pinnell (Eds.), *Bridges to literacy: Learning from Reading Recovery* (pp. 119–147). Portsmouth, NH: Heinemann.

Peterson, J., Greenlaw, M. J., & Tierney, R. J. (1978). Assessing instructional placement with an IRI: The effectiveness of comprehension questions. *Journal of Educational Research, 71,* 247–250.

Phelan, P. (Ed.). (1996). *High interest–easy reading: An annotated booklist for middle school and senior high school* (7th ed.). Urbana, IL: National Council of Teachers of English.

Piasta, S. B., & Wagner, R. K. (2010a). Developing early literacy skills: A meta-analysis of alphabet learning and instruction. *Reading Research Quarterly, 45,* 8–38.

Piasta, S. B., & Wagner, R. K. (2010b). Learning letter names and sounds: Effects of instruction, letter type, and phonological processing skill. *Journal of Experimental Child Psychology, 105,* 324–344.

Pressley, M., & Woloshyn, V. (1995). *Cognitive strategy instruction that really improves children's academic performance.* Cambridge, MA: Brookline Press.

Rasinski, T. V. (2010). *The fluent reader: Oral and silent reading strategies for building fluency, word recognition, and comprehension* (2nd ed.). New York: Scholastic.

Rasinski, T. V., Padak, N., Linek, W., & Sturtevant, E. (1994). The effects of fluency development instruction on urban second grade readers. *Journal of Educational Research, 87,* 158–164.

Rayner, K., Pollatsek, A., Ashby, J., & Clifton, C., Jr. (2012). *The psychology of reading* (2nd ed.). New York: Psychology Press.

Read, C. (1971). Pre-school children's knowledge of English phonology. *Harvard Educational Review, 41,* 1–34.

Read, J. (2000). *Assessing vocabulary.* Cambridge, UK: Cambridge University Press.

Rhodes, L. (1981). I can read: Predictable books as resources or reading and writing instruction. *The Reading Teacher, 34,* 511–518.

Riedel, B. W. (2007). The relation between DIBELS, reading comprehension, and vocabulary in urban first-grade students. *Reading Research Quarterly, 42,* 546–567.

Riener, C., & Willingham, D. (2010). The myth of learning styles. *Change: The Magazine of Higher Learning, 42*(5), 32–35.

Rosenshine, B., Meister, C., & Chapman, S. (1996). Teaching students to generate questions: A review of the intervention studies. *Review of Educational Research, 66,* 181–221.

Rosner, J. (1975). *Helping children overcome learning difficulties.* New York: Walker.

Scarborough, H. S., & Brady, S. A. (2002). Toward a common terminology for talking about speech and reading: A glossary of "phon" words and some related terms. *Journal of Literacy Research, 34,* 299–336.

Schumaker, J. B., Deshler, D. D., Alley, G. R., Warner, M. W., & Denton, T. H. (1982). Multipass: A learning strategy for improving reading comprehension. *Learning Disability Quarterly, 5,* 295–304.

Schunk, D. H., Meece, J. R., & Pintrich, P. R. (2014). *Motivation in education: Theory, research, and applications* (4th ed.). Boston: Pearson.

Schwanenflugel, P. J., Kuhn, M. R., Morris, R. D., Morrow, L. M., Meisinger, E. B., Woo, D. G., et al. (2009). Insights into fluency instruction: Short- and long-term effects of two reading programs. *Literacy Research and Instruction, 48*(4), 318–336.

Shanahan, T., Callison, K., Carriere, C., Duke, N. K., Pearson, P. D., Schatschneider, C., et al. (2010). *Improving reading comprehension in kindergarten through 3rd grade: A practice guide* (NCEE 2010-4038). Washington, DC: National Center for Education Evaluation and Regional Assistance, Institute of Education Sciences, U.S. Department of Education. Retrieved from *https://ies.ed.gov/ncee/wwc/practiceguide/14.*

Shankweiler, D., & Liberman, I. Y. (1972). Misreading: A search for causes. In I. F. Kavanaugh & I. G. Mattingly (Eds.), *Language by eye and by ear* (pp. 293–317). Cambridge, MA: MIT Press.

Shin, J., Deno, S. L., & Espin, C. (2000). Technical adequacy of the maze task for curriculum-based measurement of reading growth. *Journal of Special Education, 34,* 164–172.

Shinn, M. R. (Ed.). (1989). *Curriculum-based measurement: Assessing special children.* New York: Guilford Press.

Silvaroli, N. J. (1977, April). *Norm-referenced tests do not diagnose.* Paper presented at the A. Sterl Artley Symposium, University of Missouri–Columbia.

Sparfeldt, J. R., Kimmel, R., Löwenkamp, L., Steingräber, A., & Rost, D. H. (2012). Not read, but nevertheless solved: Three experiments on PIRLS multiple choice reading comprehension test items. *Educational Assessment, 17,* 214–232.

Stahl, K. A. D. (2008). The effects of three instructional methods on the reading comprehension and content acquisition of novice readers. *Journal of Literacy Research, 40,* 359–393.

Stahl, K. A. D. (2014). What counts as evidence? *The Reading Teacher, 68*(2), 103–106.

Stahl, K. A. D., & Bravo, M. (2010). Contemporary classroom vocabulary assessment for content areas. *The Reading Teacher, 63,* 566–578.

Stahl, K. A. D., & Garcia, G. E. (2015). *Developing reading comprehension: Effective instruction for all students in PreK–2.* New York: Guilford Press.

Stahl, K. A. D., & McKenna, M. C. (2013). *Reading assessment in an RTI framework.* New York: Guilford Press.

Stahl, S. A. (1999). Different strokes for different folks?: A critique of learning styles. *American Educator, 23*(3), 27–31.

Stahl, S. A., Duffy-Hester, A. M., & Stahl, K. A. D. (1998). Everything you wanted to know about phonics (but were afraid to ask). *Reading Research Quarterly, 33,* 338–355.

Stahl, S. A., & Fairbanks, M. M. (1986). The effects of vocabulary instruction: A model-based meta-analysis. *Review of Educational Research, 56,* 72–110.

Stahl, S. A., & Heubach, K. M. (2005). Fluency-oriented reading instruction. *Journal of Literacy Research, 37,* 25–60.

Stahl, S. A., & McKenna, M. C. (2001). *The concurrent development of phonological awareness, word recognition, and spelling* (Technical Report No. 01-07). Ann Arbor, MI: Center for the Improvement of Early Reading Achievement. Retrieved from *www.ciera.org/librarylarchi ve/2001-07/200 lO7.htm.*

Stahl, S. A., & Murray, B. A. (1998). Issues involved in defining phonological awareness and its relation to early reading. In J. Metsala & L. C. Ehri (Eds.), *Word recognition in beginning literacy* (pp. 65–88). Mahwah, NJ: Erlbaum.

Stahl, S. A., & Nagy, W. E. (2006). *Teaching word meanings.* Mahwah, NJ: Erlbaum.

Stanovich, K. E. (1980). Toward an interactive–compensatory model of individual differences in the development of reading fluency. *Reading Research Quarterly, 16,* 32–71.

Stanovich, K. E. (1986). Matthew effects in reading: Some consequences of individual differences in the acquisition of literacy. *Reading Research Quarterly, 21,* 360–407.

Stanovich, K. E. (1991). Word recognition: Changing perspectives. In R. Barr, M. L. Kamil, P. B. Mosenthal, & P. D. Pearson (Eds.), *Handbook of reading research* (Vol. 2, pp. 418–452). New York: Longman.

Stauffer, R., Abrams, J., & Pikulski, J. (1978). *Diagnosis, correction, and prevention of reading disabilities.* New York: Harper & Row.

Sulzby, E. (1985). Children's emergent reading of favorite storybooks: A developmental study. *Reading Research Quarterly, 20,* 458–481.

Swain, K. D., Leader-Janssen, E. M., & Conley, P. (2017). Effects of repeated reading and listening passage preview on oral reading fluency. *Reading Improvement, 54*(3), 105–111.

Taylor, B. M. (1986). Teaching middle grade students to summarize content textbook material. In J. F. Baumann (Ed.), *Teaching main idea comprehension* (pp. 195–209). Newark, DE: International Reading Association.

Templeton, S., Bear, D. R., Invernizzi, M., Johnston, F., Flanigan, K., Townsend, D. R., et al. (2015). *Words their way: Vocabulary for middle and secondary students* (2nd ed.). Boston: Pearson.

Topping, K. (1987). Paired reading: A powerful technique for parent use. *The Reading Teacher, 40,* 608–614.

Torgesen, J. K., & Bryant, B. R. (2004). *TOPA-2+: Test of Phonological Awareness—Second Edition: Plus.* Austin, TX: PRO-ED.

Torgesen, J. K., Wagner, R. K., & Rashotte, C. A. (2012). *TOWRE-2: Test of Word Recognition Efficiency—Second edition.* Austin, TX: PRO-ED.

Uhry, J. K. (1999). Invented spelling in kindergarten: The relationship with finger-point reading. *Reading and Writing: An Interdisciplinary Journal, 11,* 441–464.

Valencia, S. W., & Buly, M. R. (2004). Behind test scores: What struggling readers really need. *The Reading Teacher, 57*(6), 520–531.

Vygotsky, L. (1978). *Mind in society.* Cambridge, MA: Harvard University Press.

Wagner, R. K., Torgesen, J. K., Rashotte, C. A., & Pearson, N. A. (2013). *CTOPP-2: Comprehensive Test of Phonological Awareness—Second edition.* Austin, TX: PRO-ED.

Wallach, M. A., & Wallach, L. (1979). Helping disadvantaged children learn to read by teaching them phoneme identification skills. In L. B. Resnick & P. A. Weaver (Eds.), *Theory and practice of early reading* (Vol. 3, pp. 197–216). Hillsdale, NJ: Erlbaum.

Walpole, S., & McKenna, M. C. (2006). The role of informal reading inventories in assessing word recognition. *The Reading Teacher, 59,* 592–594.

Walpole, S., & McKenna, M. C. (2017). *How to plan differentiated reading instruction: Resources for grades K–3* (2nd ed.). New York: Guilford Press.

Walpole, S., McKenna, M. C., Philippakos, Z. A., & Strong, J. Z. (in press). *Differentiated reading instruction in grades 4 and 5: Strategies and resources* (2nd ed.). New York: Guilford Press.

Watkins, J. H., McKenna, M. C., Manzo, A. V., & Manzo, U. C. (1994, April). *The effects of the listen–read–discuss procedure on the content learning of high school students.* Paper presented at the meeting of the American Educational Research Association, New Orleans, LA.

Wesche, T., & Paribakht, T. S. (1996). Assessing second language vocabulary knowledge: Depth versus breadth. *Canadian Modern Language Review, 53,* 13–40.

West, M. (1953). *A general service list of English words.* London: Longmans, Green.

Williams, K. T. (2019). *Expressive Vocabulary Test* (3rd ed.). Bloomington, MN: NCS Pearson.

Wright, T. S., & Cervetti, G. N. (2016). A systematic review of the research on vocabulary instruction that impacts comprehension. *Reading Research Quarterly, 52*(2), 203–226.

Wylie, R. E., & Durrell, D. D. (1970). Teaching vowels through phonograms. *Elementary English, 47,* 787–791.

Yussen, S. R., & Ozcan, N. M. (1996). The development of knowledge about narratives. *Issues in Education, 2,* 1–68.

Zeno, S. M., Ivens, S. H., Millard, R. T., & Duvvuri, R. (1995). *The educator's word frequency guide.* New York: Touchstone Applied Science Associates.

Zutell, J., & Rasinski, T. (1991). Training teachers to attend to their students' oral reading fluency. *Theory into Practice, 30,* 211–217.

Index

Note. *f* or *t* following a page number indicates a figure or table.